THE POLISH AUGUST

NEAL ASCHERSON

THE POLISH AUGUST

THE SELF-LIMITING REVOLUTION

THE VIKING PRESS　NEW YORK

Copyright © 1981, 1982 by Neal Ascherson
All rights reserved
Published in 1982 by The Viking Press
625 Madison Avenue, New York, N.Y. 10022

LIBRARY OF CONGRESS CATALOGING IN PUBLICATION DATA
Ascherson, Neal.
 The Polish August.
 Bibliography: p.
 Includes index.
 1. Poland—History—1945—   . I. Title.
DK4430.A83   943.8'05   81-52150
ISBN 0-670-56305-6   AACR2

Printed in the United States of America
Set in Monophoto Times Roman

Contents

To Gustaw
who ordered me to write a book about Poland

Preface

Not far from Warsaw, a little off the main road to Poznań, there is a place called Arkadia. Built for the fancy of some early nineteenth-century count, it is a sort of park where, in a wood, there stand a number of dilapidated little monuments meant to evoke one or other of the romantic emotions. There is an attempt at Stonehenge, some fragmentary temples, a rocky grotto. And there is also an elaborate fountain, now dry, decorated with the stucco relief of a naked girl offering a drinking-cup to a dragon writhing intimately alongside her. It seems to be based on a fresco in the Villa of the Mysteries at Pompeii. Underneath is written: 'L'Espérance Nourrit une Chimère, et la Vie s'Écoule.'

Since I first saw that fountain, more than twenty years ago on one of my early visits to Poland, the friends with whom I was young have grown middle-aged. Some nourished the thought that Polish Communism could, in spite of its past failures, find within itself the power to create a new synthesis of socialism and democracy which had never been seen in Europe. Others cradled the idea that the Soviet Union might one day be transformed or, less improbably, decide to withdraw behind its own frontiers. Meanwhile they raised children and, in their turn, now hear themselves explaining to sons and daughters – as their parents had explained to them – the difference between the real history of Poland and history taught at school. And life flowed away.

The events of 1980 in Poland were not, however, a chimera. The 'self-limiting revolution' which began at Gdańsk in the Lenin Shipyard was real, and whatever price Poland may eventually have to pay for it, its intangible and moral achievements are permanent. If the democratic reform of the Polish United Workers' Party and the appearance of the independent trade union Solidarity can be consolidated, this will also prove to have been the most important change in eastern Europe since the end of the Second World War. This book is an attempt to describe what took place in 1980, much of which I witnessed, to analyse some of its consequences and implications, and to ask why so many hopes had to be poured away in the preceding thirty-five years.

I have deliberately written about Poland as a European society, a member of the ancient continental family which is at present so superficially divided into alliances and 'communities', rather than as 'the problem member of the Communist bloc' – a bloodless kind of terminology. Especially in Poland, however, many people will disagree with judgements and versions of history in this book. Perhaps this is inevitable. The encounter with Poland corrodes most political assumptions, not because this is an exotic nation but because it presents a view of the squalid under-side of big concepts – the side which rests on top of human beings. Bismarck, with his grand design for European peace, becomes the man who had thousands of Polish small boys caned for speaking their own language; Churchill and Stalin lost dignity in the hour of victory in wrangles over Polish rivers and villages they could not spell. Capitalism meant that the nation's factories were owned by Germans and Frenchmen. Socialism, which in theory comes so much closer to the Polish sense of community and equality, has become a term so defiled by public squalor, private privilege and hypocrisy about the Soviet Union that it has become for the moment unrecognizable.

Ideological consistency, in Poland, is confined to leading articles in newspapers. The Poles are concerned to survive and Polish governments – however extreme they appear – are concerned not to do things to their own people that are unforgivable or irreparable. The results are often political systems whose structure mystifies the orderly mind of a foreigner, whether he is a Soviet official or an American professor. Edward Gierek's régime between 1970 and 1980, a Communist Politburo relying upon the Roman Catholic hierarchy and mortally afraid of the industrial proletariat, made all Europe stop and stare. When it fell down, there emerged a workers' revolution which walked behind the crucifix and refused to take control of the means of production. Solidarity has been infinitely distressing to many left-wingers in the West. My hope is that this book, by explaining a little, will reduce that distress.

Many people have helped me with this book; none are responsible for its contents. I would like to thank especially the *Observer*, the *Scotsman*, the *Spectator* and the *Guardian* for sending me to Poland so often in the last twenty-five years, and the Ministry of Foreign Affairs not only for so many visas but for the patience of its officials under interview. Among those who gave me assistance and encouragement in the last two years, and to whom I will always be grateful, are: Christopher Bobinski, Eric Bourne,

Michael Dobbs, Gustaw Gottesman, Krzystof Klinger, Henryk Krzecz-kowski, Oliver MacDonald, Karol and Irena Małcużyński, Wojciech Sadurski, Marek Skwarnicki, Jadwiga Staniszkis, Ambassador Artur Stare-wicz, Bolesław Sulik, Dessa Trevisan, Dr Jerzy Turowicz. I must also salute Belinda Magee for drawing the map, the British Library for Political and Economic Science for letting me work there, and especially Elisabeth Sifton of Viking for her phenomenal energy and sympathy as an editor. Finally, honour to the friends of 28 East Preston Street in Edinburgh, to Isabel Hilton, Lynda Myles, Tom Nairn and Ellen Galford, for whom what I write is written.

Chapter One

Introduction

'Our Only Guarantee Is Ourselves'

At five in the evening, on 16 December 1980, the sirens of Gdańsk began to sound. The Lenin Shipyard spoke first, and then the repair yards. From the dark city the factory whistles joined them, the voices of the docks, the locomotives in the railway yards, the buses in their depots, the boats at the yacht basin, the bass sirens of the ships alongside in the port or at their moorings in the roadstead, all combining in one interminable, groaning chord.

For minute after minute, a hundred and fifty thousand people stood outside the Lenin Shipyard gate in reverence, their hats in their hands. One after another, the sirens began to drawl down the scale into silence until the only sounds were the wail of tugs and fishing boats still lamenting somewhere in the darkness of the Bay of Hel, or at the outfall of the Dead Vistula. They too became quiet. Then for a time there was nothing at all to be heard. The sleet glittered through the floodlights and slanted past the triple spire of the new monument. At its base, where strike leaders, Catholic bishops, Communist officials, Polish generals and admirals stood shoulder to shoulder, a conductor's baton twitched. Another huge, foreboding cry burst upward, as the orchestra moved into the first bars of Krzystof Penderecki's 'Lacrimosa' chorale.

Ten years before this day, there had begun in the Lenin yard the first of the demonstrations and strikes which, within a few days, reached along the Polish coast and became a general mutiny of the working class. Those 'December Events', touched off by a reckless government decree increasing food prices just before Christmas, were met by force. In Gdańsk and Gdynia, Szczecin and Elbląg, Polish police and troops opened fire on their fellow-countrymen. But the strikers held on, and as their movement began to spread throughout Poland, threatening a total national insurrection, the authorities gave way. Władysław Gomułka, First Secretary of the Polish United Workers' Party (PUWP), was deposed with Soviet consent and replaced by Edward Gierek, the Party leader in the coal-mining country of Upper Silesia. Gierek ordered immediate pay rises and promised a new, more liberal political course, But it took a fresh round of industrial action, another occupation strike in the port of Szczecin in January 1971 and then finally a strike by female textile workers in Łódź, to get the price increases rescinded.

Perhaps nobody, not even the Polish security police, knows how many people were killed in December 1970. For Gdańsk alone, the official total – for workers and police together – was twenty-seven dead. Many will always believe that it was far higher. At this commemoration ceremony, ten years later, the actor Daniel Olbrychski read out a roll-call of the fallen; after each of twenty-seven names, a choir chanted: 'He is still with us.' At the end, Olbrychski added: '... and all the dead whose names are not known.' Then he stepped down. Up to the rostrum in his place came a small group of slightly bewildered men and women in cheap winter coats, representing the families of those who had died. They cut a cord, and a Polish flag wrapped about the legs of the monument floated free into the westerly gale.

Poles had killed Poles. For the ordinary people watching these rites, that had been the real horror of December 1970. How could a nation that had suffered so terribly at the hands of foreign enemies have added to its miseries through fratricide? This was the symbolism of the factory sirens. On the days when Poland remembers all those who perished in the national cause, the people of Warsaw go to the military cemetery at Powązki. Boys and girls in Scout uniform lay wreaths, then stand stiffly to attention before the graves which stretch away, rectangle after rectangle, under the trees – the dead of the November Rising of 1830, the dead of the January Rising of 1863, the dead of the September Campaign of 1939, the dead of the Warsaw Rising in 1944 which cost the lives of perhaps a quarter of a million men, women and children – and all over the city, as people stop in the streets and bare their heads, the sirens set up their cry. On 16 December 1980 at Gdańsk – and the next day at Gdynia and Szczecin – this sound signified that the victims of 1970 had been welcomed into the company of those who died not just for bread or higher wages, but for the nation.

For those who watched the ceremony, it was all incredible, improbable. It was a moment at which one realized how much had taken place in Poland, and how rapidly. A man in a brown anorak walked forward with a familiar, short-stepping, swaggering gait to light the eternal flame. His long ginger moustache looked black in the floodlights. It was Lech Wałęsa, leader of the ten million members of Solidarity, the new independent trade union movement born only fourteen weeks before in the Lenin Shipyard beyond the monument. Now he was one of the most powerful men in Poland, received by the First Secretary in Warsaw and soon to be the guest of the Pope in Rome, the idol of western press and television throughout the autumn of 1980. Six months earlier, his name had meant nothing. Even among the small opposition groups active in Poland before August 1980, only a few organizers operating among workers in the conurbation of Gdańsk, Gdynia and Sopot, the two port cities and the beach resort which form the so-called 'Triple City' on the south shore of the Baltic, had even heard of Wałęsa. A year before, he had sworn that in twelve months' time, on the tenth anniversary of 'the December', he and his friends would raise a monument of some kind outside the gates of the Lenin yard. For those who knew about Wałęsa's vow, it seemed little more than a gesture; the militia would be waiting for him, and have him in the back of a police wagon before he had piled so much as one stone upon another. Now he stood on the plinth. Two workers in safety helmets passed him a long oxy-acetylene torch. Twice he tried to light it, and twice the sleet bit off the spark. The third time the torch ignited. He thrust it forward, and an extravagantly huge flame gushed up past his feet. Wałęsa watched it for a moment, then waved the torch nonchalantly at the crowds.

Above him rose the monument. Three steel shafts, each ending in a cross, met 140 feet over his head. From each cross hangs a black anchor, in Poland a sign not only of the sea but of redemption and struggle. At their base, the legs of the monument have a crumpled, buckling surface to represent the fiery days of the rioting, inset with reliefs of men and women at work in the yards. The designers carved on the wall behind the monument two lines from a translation of the Psalms by Czesław Miłosz, the exiled writer who delighted Poland by winning the Nobel Prize for Literature in 1980:

> *The Lord giveth his people strength;*
> *The Lord giveth his people the blessing of peace.*

Like most Polish monuments, this one – paid for by private gifts throughout the country – is monstrously dramatic rather than beautiful. (A few miles away at the coastal fort of Westerplatte, where the first shots of the Second World War were fired on 1 September 1939, the Polish defenders are honoured by the fifty-foot-long hilt of a stone bayonet thrust into the ground.) It was designed by a local engineer with the help of technicians at the Lenin yard. A maquette some two feet high had stood on the platform of the shipyard hall where the committee of the August 1980 strike had held its sessions; even then, it seemed unlikely that the authorities could consent to the erection of anything so enormous. But the strikers were placidly confident. 'We want it big,' said one worker. 'They'll have a job knocking that down. As hard a job as they had in Paris that other time.' For a moment, I thought he was talking about some attempt to blow up the Eiffel Tower. Then I realized that he meant the destruction of the

Vendôme Column, laboriously pulled over by the revolutionaries of the Paris Commune in 1871. The Polish régime has, at least, given its working class a socialist education.

Perhaps even Wałęsa, not a man for reflection, felt a pang of incredulity as he stood there with his cutting-torch and looked upwards. He must certainly have felt such a pang when he lowered his eyes and looked at the collection of official guests in front of him. This was a monument celebrating, in fact, the triumph of common working people over a régime that had tried ten years before to hold them in their place with bullets. Before him now stood Professor Jabłoński, the head of state of the Communist republic, with a deputy member of the Politburo, a secretary of the Central Committee of the Party, a deputy premier, and the minister of culture. They, together with the local navy admiral and army general, the prefect of Gdańsk, the diplomats of many foreign countries (not the Soviet ambassador), and an assortment of strike leaders still amazed to find themselves inspecting police guards rather than the other way round, were about to hear Mass performed by the Cardinal Archbishop of Kraków as he consecrated the monument and the banners of Solidarity. It was a moment almost too strange to savour.

And yet it was not a moment for easy irony. The coming together of these disparate forces – the Party and state, the Catholic episcopate, the independent working class – was not just a show of victory by one side over another. It was an urgent political project on which the survival of Polish national independence, let alone the future of the 'independent, self-managing trade unions', seemed to depend.

For all its splendour, there was something alienating about the ceremony at Gdańsk. Andrzej Wajda, the most famous film-maker in eastern Europe, produced and directed it, with all its use of lighting, of sound, of music (the Penderecki chorale was specially composed), of the solo human voice (Olbrychski is Wajda's favourite leading actor). It was, indeed, a spectacle: the ordinary people who had brought all these things about by asserting their right to be subjects as well as objects of history now stood in darkness and watched the show as if they were watching a film. Once they intervened: when Tadeusz Fiszbach, the Gdańsk Party secretary, spoke of Poland's liberation in 1944 by the Red Army, a soft breeze of whistles ran across the crowd. But for the rest they were passive.

In a way, it had to be like that. The dead of December 1970 were now leaving their relations and friends, who had known them as they really were, and ascending from earth to a patriotic Olympus where they would dwell among the saints and heroes and martyrs of Polish nationhood. After ten years, the Polish 'establishment' – the bishops, the generals, the poli-

ticians – were taking them over and deciding what the lasting meaning of
their deaths should be. Official speeches and articles around the anniversary
left no doubt about the meaning that was intended. They did not die
simply to bring down the price of food, or to win better pay for their
families, or in the effort to burn down Party headquarters, or – as happened
here and there – because they were caught looting a shop. They were not
even allowed to have died for the right of working people to live normally,
without lies and cheating and intimidation. They died for the unity of the
nation. That was the message.

Tadeusz Fiszbach, one of the very few Party officials whom the Solidarity
leaders trusted, made this point in his own speech at the monument. 'The
memory of the December events, though it hurts, should not and must not
divide,' he said. 'It ought to unite the nation, the working class, the authorities, in a common effort to ensure that never again should we come to
such a tragedy.' Other official commentators made the point much more
coarsely, until it might have been supposed that the men who were killed
in Gdańsk and Gdynia, Szczecin and Elbląg and Słupsk, had immolated
themselves expressly to prevent a social conflict in Poland, like that Marcus
Curtius who closed the chasm which had opened in the Roman Forum by
leaping into it on his horse.

In terms of fact, it was a strange point to make in the last month of
1980. Poland was not divided. Indeed, it was more united than it had ever
been since 1944 – with the possible exception of those ecstatic months after
October 1956 when the Poles overthrew what remained of the old Stalinist
dictatorship. This sense of unity and community was the most general
effect of the summer's upheaval, of which the emergence of free trade
unions was only one consequence. It was not so much an explosion as a
geological convulsion, a long and deep tremor that finally brought down the
artificial and crumbling barriers that separated one category of Pole from
another. Before the evening ceremony that day at Gdańsk, the centre of the
city was decorated with clusters of people as workers from other parts of
Poland, who had often slept overnight on chartered coaches to arrive in
time for the dedication, met each other and the people of Gdańsk and
exchanged experiences. What was it like to be a Silesian coal miner? How
did the strike go in Lublin? Do you in Wrocław have to wait as long for
an apartment as we do in Gdańsk? These meetings, with their eager questions
and revelations, could have taken place only in a country whose press and
television had long ceased to inform.

But they were also a visible symptom of this collapse of barriers. The
nation was uniting. The division lay not vertically between one section of

society and another, as the official speeches seemed to suggest, but horizontally: between the population and the few thousand men and women who formed the leadership and the permanent bureaucracy of the Polish United Workers' Party.

And this was precisely why the Polish establishment, supported by the leaders of Solidarity, had to take over the ceremony at Gdańsk. In deciding that December 1970 was too important to be left to the people, the Party and the Church and the brand-new union leaders were implicitly declaring that August 1980 was also too important to be left to the masses. It was time to put the brakes on. The strikes of July and August had culminated in the régime's tactical surrender. Rather than use force, risking civil war and eventually Soviet intervention, Edward Gierek, the Party leader, agreed to the signing of the agreements at Gdańsk, Szczecin, Jastrzębie and elsewhere. The agreements permitted the creation of free trade unions, promised wage rises and a five-day week, and – among many other concessions – guaranteed a reduction and legal limitation of censorship.

Now, in December 1980, the question was again how to prevent a Soviet or Warsaw Pact intervention. The East German and Czechoslovak press, especially, resounded with accusations against Solidarity as an anti-socialist instrument, as the weapon of western subversion centres designed to prise Poland out of the Soviet bloc. The Soviet media also took this line on occasion. But for the Russian leaders, the real problem was not the existence of an independent trade union federation in Poland – that might be tolerated, if there was a reasonable prospect that the Party would slowly re-establish its authority and influence over the trade unions. The problem was the deadly weakness of the Party itself.

If the Polish United Workers' Party could not regain control of the situation, if it were unable to play the 'leading role' in the state that both Leninist theory and the new Polish Constitution reserved for it, if Communists meekly permitted opponents of socialism to attack the PUWP in public and go unpunished, then – the Soviet leadership would have to conclude – counter-revolution was on the move. 'Fraternal assistance', some sort of military action in Poland, would be necessary to preserve the socialist system. The Polish leadership might appeal for such armed support, or it might become so enfeebled and subverted that it was no longer able to do so. Ultimately, the decision to intervene would not be determined by whether there were Poles prepared to ask for armed assistance or not.

This seemed to be the Soviet thought. From the start, the Polish workers understood it well. To think of overthrowing the Party in Poland was madness, for it would inevitably lead to a Soviet invasion and the destruction of all the liberties gained in the past ten or even twenty-five years. The point was something else: to take much of the *substance* of power away from the Party and the state bureaucracy but to leave them with the *form*. This, it was recognized, was a delicate game, but it was the only possible game to play. Poland was like an old house living under a preservation order. The interior could be modernized, even gutted and replaced. But the façade and the roof must stay intact.

Tarnobrzeg is a long way from Gdańsk, an inland town on the Vistula which is the centre of the biggest sulphur-mining district in Europe. A few days after the Gdańsk Agreement was signed, the mines remained almost completely closed down by a strike. One of the workers told me: 'Our demands here are pretty modest. But we understand Poland's situation, and that the socialist system is tottering. It's a question of using the most cautious methods in order to prop it up so that there's no tragedy, no tanks, no bloodshed. We can solve all these problems together if the government can stabilize itself.'

But it did not stabilize. As soon as demolition work began within the house, the roof began to show signs of caving in. The Solidarity leaders had hoped that, after the agreements of August, the Party would adapt itself to the new situation. On the night of 5 September, the Central Committee replaced Edward Gierek with Stanisław Kania, a solid, shrewd personality who seemed well qualified to hold the Party together and teach it more modest ways of 'leading' Polish society. But qualifications were not enough. The Party had been devastated internally by the events of July and August, and its own cohesion and self-confidence, badly eroded over the previous few years, now began to collapse. Kania did not even manage to establish the unchallenged authority over his own colleagues that the First Secretary of a Communist Party requires – even when that authority is limited by a so-called 'collective leadership'. Within a few weeks, at least two prominent Party figures, the clever and ambitious Stefan Olszowski and Mieczysław Moczar (an ageing ex-head of security whose political style combined chauvinism and discipline in a mixture that reminded some of his opponents of Mussolini), emerged as potential rivals to Kania.

While factions stalked each other at the top, the mass membership of the PUWP began to escape the control of the Party apparatus. Some, perhaps several hundred thousand, left the Party outright. But the great majority of the working-class membership, over a million in a party totalling some three million members, stayed inside the PUWP and also joined the new Solidarity unions. An emergency congress of the Party was now expected in the early spring of 1981. In many factories and offices, the members declared that they wanted to use the congress for a total democratic transformation of the Party, through mass purges, free and open elections for Party posts, the rotation of senior Party officials and the exclusion of Party members holding state jobs from political decision-making. Worse, these new factory-floor radicals began to make contact directly with each other across the country, in defiance of the Leninist laws of Party organization which prescribe that contacts must be 'vertical' and should never short-circuit the next body up the Party hierarchy.

Instead of diminishing, the internal crisis of the Party grew steadily more alarming throughout the last months of 1980. Externally, the Party leaders, while insisting that they accepted the socialist character of the new independent, self-governing trade unions, allowed themselves to become involved in two disastrous conflicts with Solidarity, both of which they lost. An attempt, by blatant misuse of the judiciary, to force Solidarity to include an endorsement of the Party's leading role in its statutes was dropped on 11 November, as the unions threatened widespread strikes. And at the end of the month, the police seized a Solidarity supporter in Warsaw for possessing a confidential document, but were forced to back down and release him as workers throughout the Warsaw industrial region began to stop work.

The result of these confrontations, the 'Registration Crisis' and the 'Naroźniak Affair', was threefold. In the first place, the two defeats shocked the other Communist leaderships in eastern Europe, confirming fears that the Party in Poland, far from re-asserting its authority, was still in headlong and increasingly disorganized retreat before the advance of Solidarity. In early December, the whole world became aware that the possibility of armed intervention in Poland was coming rapidly closer. Secondly, the rank-and-file militants of the new trade unions, who had always regarded the Gdańsk Agreements as a mere compromise, were confirmed in their bitter mistrust of the Party; any concession, they concluded, and any offer of friendly co-operation would be exploited as a sign of weakness. Third, the Solidarity leaders, under intense pressure from Church authorities, began to revise their own strategy.

The original concept of an independent workers' movement, developed during the 1970s, had insisted that there should be no co-operation with the Party and state. The Party was terminally sick, beyond reform, and would compromise and eventually destroy any partner. An independent organization of workers, therefore, must steadfastly refuse to accept a share of responsibility either for the economy – whether at factory or national level

– or for policy, and should limit itself to defending its own members' interests, never forgetting that it existed in basically hostile territory.

This sort of thinking had been carried over into the Gdańsk Agreements. For Lech Wałęsa, and his close colleagues and advisers, the strikes did not mean any positive transformation of the governing of Poland. The victory was in a sense negative. The agreements enormously enlarged, at a stroke, the area of Polish life which the Party and the state bureaucracy did not manage. What the authorities did outside this new fence was almost a thing indifferent. Solidarity demanded and won the right to be heard when matters affecting the living standard of the working class were under discussion. But that did not mean that Solidarity would share in the power of decision. That remained the monopoly of the government. If the workers did not like the decision, they now had the ultimate right to strike. Co-existence with the régime: yes. Co-operation: no.

But for the union leaders at least, this programme soon failed to meet the new situation in Poland. The central and overwhelming danger was that of a Soviet-led invasion. Neither the Party nor the workers' representatives wanted this. Even the negotiations between the two at Gdańsk had been full of mutual references to the exigencies of the Polish *raison d'état* (in Poland, a code phrase that denotes the impossibility of breaking the Polish–Soviet alliance, whether the speaker considers the relationship a healthy one or not). The *raison d'état* warned both sides that if they did not find a peaceful solution to their argument, there would probably ensue a 'national tragedy' (another code expression, usually meaning a vain insurrection followed by the loss of national independence). Wałęsa, especially, was unwillingly impressed by the need for continuing collaboration with the Polish government. He could reject, with a clear conscience at first, any share of responsibility for the wretched national economy. But Solidarity could not morally deny that – whether its members wished it or not – it did carry, together with Kania and his colleagues, joint responsibility for the nation's independence.

As the autumn of 1980 passed, the outlines of an informal coalition began to emerge in Warsaw. It was never better than precarious, never cemented by any real mutual trust. But the leaders of Solidarity and the group around Kania began to discover that they needed each other. In the first place, their contact was a patriotic imperative, if they were to prevent the sort of civil strife that would induce the Soviet Union to intervene. Second, both leaderships were in danger from their own extremists. For Kania, it was the hard-line factions in the Party that had opposed the Gdańsk settlement and were still waiting for him to make a mistake; reckless militancy on the part of Solidarity might give them their chance. For Wałęsa, the threat came from impatient local activists in the union who suspected the authorities were preparing to cheat them of the fruits of Gdańsk; during the 'Narożniak Affair', he and others discovered that striking workers could defy Solidarity's instructions to go back to work. Kania needed Wałęsa to restrain the working class and make his task in the Party possible; Wałęsa needed Kania to regain control of the Party and commit it to a programme of democratic reform, so that his followers would no longer be inflamed by stupid Party provocations. And, as we shall see, the dominant powers in the Catholic hierarchy, even more obsessed by the danger to Poland's independence than Kania or Wałęsa, worked desperately to convince Wałęsa that the new unions must only act 'responsibly' – by which they meant: with responsibility for the entire nation.

So it came to the ceremony at Gdańsk on 16 December, with its magnificence and its inhibitions, its ambiguous symbols. The three crosses seemed to stand for many things at once: for three shipyard workers who had been killed on that spot ten years before; for the three previous post-war risings of the Polish working class in 1956, 1970 and 1976; for the Triple City; for the triple power-balance of Party, workers and Church. And one could add that the workers in August had made three broad demands: for a better life, for more freedom and for vengeance – at law – on those who were responsible for ordering men to open fire in December 1970. But that last demand remained, and remains, unsatisfied. It was not mentioned at Gdańsk on 16 December 1980, although the city's longing to see the guilty punished was in a way the shadow thrown by the new monument. (At Szczecin next day, Marian Jurczyk, the local strike leader who was now regional head of Solidarity, did bring the matter up when a memorial tablet was unveiled outside the Adolf Warski Shipyard. The words were cut out of the version of his address carried in the Warsaw papers. But Jurczyk was a man at once less agile and less suggestible than Wałęsa, and his relations to the Church were more distant.)

When it was Wałęsa's turn to speak, he seemed ill at ease. The common people of Gdańsk, his constituency, were invisible behind the glare of the lights and removed beyond security fences. This was the first speech he had ever read, he explained (it was in fact partly composed by a priest, Father Jankowski, who had become a close counsellor) and he read it haltingly. Much of it consisted of quotations: from the declaration by the monument's construction committee, from the Pope's message to Poland, from the recent communiqué of the Polish episcopate calling for restraint and order and condemning those who wished to use public unrest for their own ends. He took care to refer to Poland by the official title of the Communist régime: 'Our fatherland, Polska Rzeczpospolita Ludowa' – the Polish People's Republic.

In his peroration, he gave the crowd six commandments:

'I charge you, all who are present here and all Poles, all people of good will, to accept full responsibility for the fate of our fatherland;

'I charge you to keep peace and order, and to respect all laws and authorities;

'I charge you to show prudence and reflection in all actions for the good of our fatherland;

'I charge you to be vigilant in the protection of our fatherland's safety and sovereignty;

'I charge you never to forget that this family home, this house which is our fatherland, bears the name of Poland;

'I charge you to make sure that Poland becomes more of a home for its people, that in it there may prevail justice, liberty, peace, love and solidarity.'

With this little patriotic sermon, in substance so much the official rhetoric of the hour, in form so obviously ecclesiastical, Wałęsa reproached nobody, threatened nobody, incited nobody. Instead, he was inviting Solidarity and the working class to cool down, to accept the provisional authority of this coalition of Party, Church – and Wałęsa. A few sparkles of the old Lech survived the editing of this speech. He recalled how, a year before, he and his comrades had agreed to come on this day with stones in their briefcases, if they had to, to lay the foundations of a monument. And at the end, after his six commandments, Lech Wałęsa suddenly added a few unscripted words, a phrase thrown beyond the platform party and the official press (which did not record it) to the enormous crowd beyond. He said: 'We are the guarantee of all this!'

This was his old language. It was the language of the August strikes, when everything seemed much simpler. Then, the Polish workers were asking nothing more from the Party and the government than their signature under a list of demands. They were not asking to share power. They were not asking to govern Poland or become a party-political rival to the PUWP. They most certainly did not want to 'accept full responsibility for the fate of our fatherland', which would mean accepting some of the blame for the Party's mistakes, and endorsing policies which they detested but which could not be changed without altering Poland's *raison d'état* – in other words, without taking Poland out of the Warsaw Pact. They did not pretend that the Gdańsk Agreements were a happy end, or that the promises extorted from the authorities by strike action amounted to reliable guarantees for all time to come. When the strike committee wondered how permanent their victory was, Wałęsa and his lieutenant, Andrzej Gwiazda, would tell them: 'Our only real guarantee is ourselves!'

Less than four months later, the political priorities had changed. It was still true that the summer's agreements were guaranteed only by the workers' readiness to take strike action in defence of them and, in the longer term, by a degree of commitment by Solidarity's members which would prevent the Party slowly taking over commanding positions within the new unions. But all that seemed secondary now. Soviet armoured divisions had been moved up to all Poland's frontiers. Ten days before, on Friday, 5 December, the Polish leadership had been summoned to attend an emergency summit meeting of the Warsaw Pact in Moscow, and had been left in no doubt that the revolutionary process in Poland must be slowed down and, in some areas, stopped dead if military intervention was to be avoided. The western world, hoping to forestall a repetition of the invasion of Czechoslovakia in August 1968, was in an uproar of protests and warnings.

So there emerged this suspicious, provisional alliance of moderate leaders against more militant followers. Wałęsa was now discouraging Solidarity from taking further industrial action, and indeed there had been no strikes for two weeks. Kania was appealing for a disciplined 'renewal' of the Party and of Polish society, denouncing both his own ultra-conservatives and his ultra-radicals. Less obviously, the Church was also suffering from internal divisions. While several bishops, backed by much of the priesthood and many lay Catholic intellectuals, warned the Church to keep its critical distance from the régime, the majority of the Council of the Episcopate had begun to urge Poles to undertake nothing provocative, to restrain their demands, to suppress political dissidents who were openly hostile to the Soviet Union. By suggesting that Kania's programme of 'renewal' deserved the support of all Poles, the episcopate had gone further towards active support for a Communist government than at any moment since 1945. To the coalition of Stanisław Kania and Lech Wałęsa, there seemed to be added the figure of Stefan, Cardinal Wyszyński, Primate of Poland, now in his eightieth year but still infinitely the most powerful spiritual authority within Poland.

At the end of 1980, the 'coalition' looked not only tentative but very fragile. If Poland had subsided into obedience and order, the trinity might have had a chance of sticking together. But the dynamics of the situation were already beginning to drive the followers of Party, Church, and Solidarity remorselessly towards conflict.

The upheaval of 1980 left two main questions open. The West saw only one: whether the Soviet Union would invade Poland to reverse the summer's changes or not. The Poles, while admitting that the first question had a grimly terminal priority, found it almost boring. They had lived with this sort of problem, on and off, for generations. Much more interesting to them was the second question: was it possible to govern Poland by consent rather than coercion, to give creative expression to the nation's underlying unity, as long as a Communist Party retained the formal monopoly of political power? To find an answer to this question before it answered itself, the Poles returned to their own history and studied, with new perceptions, the story of their country since the end of the Second World War.

Chapter Two

Poland and Polish Communism:
Piłsudski to Gomułka

Repetitions of History

Polish post-war history is cyclical. Historians suspect such blatant patterns, but it is impossible to ignore the way in which contemporary history repeats itself in Poland. By 1980, the cycle had already spun twice. And the condition and mood of Poland in that year made it obvious to everyone that a third cycle was about to end.

The sequence varies little in its broad outline. It begins with the arrival of a shining new government, promising radical economic changes and liberal political reforms. Gradually this ruling group is affected by political decay until it degenerates into the same sort of stifling autocracy which it replaced, a clique out of touch with the needs and wishes of the Polish people. Correspondingly, the management of the economy – at the outset dedicated to raising living standards and filling the shops – drifts off course into grandiose and irrelevant investment projects. The burden returns with increasing weight to the shoulders of the most vulnerable section of society, the industrial working class. Economic discontent finally touches off a working-class revolt. This leads more or less directly to the fall of the political leadership and its replacement by a new team – in its turn flourishing promises of reform and responsiveness to public opinion. A cycle has ended. The next begins as this new leading clique, after a few months in which the newspapers are free and sausage is plentiful, is slowly drawn into the same process of degeneration.

The first and far the most violent of these working-class revolts took place in Poznań, the main industrial city of west-central Poland, in June 1956. At least seventy-five people died. In December 1970 came the explosion in the northern ports. Another eruption of strikes happened in Warsaw and – with rioting – in the big town of Radom, south of the capital, in June 1976. In the summer of 1980, almost the entire country joined a peaceful mutiny. This might suggest that the cycle is shortening, but the 1976 strikes, significant as they were, did not overthrow the leadership, which survived for another four years. So the length of the cycle still varies between ten and fourteen years.

To westerners, this periodicity might suggest a crude equivalent to their own way of changing governments. Where a bourgeois democracy resorts every four or five years to the ballot box in order to 'throw the rascals out' and renew its leadership, the Poles seem obliged to rampage through the streets every decade or so, risking death or imprisonment to achieve much the same result.

True, neither democratic elections nor these Polish revolts overthrow the constitutional régime itself. They could produce only a change of policy and leadership, a new government or a new Politburo. Belgium or Canada remain parliamentary capitalist democracies after a general election, and Poland after 1956 and after 1970 remained a People's Republic in which the Communist Party still kept the monopoly of political power. But in the end, this is the wrong parallel. The comparison reveals little except that the founding fathers of parliamentary democracy had a sound sociological instinct when they limited the life of elected assemblies to about half a decade. The processes at work that produce a cyclic appearance in Polish politics are not the same as those which operate in a western society. And eastern Europeans themselves, who were first struck by this pattern of repetition, offer very different explanations.

In 1968 Władysław Bieńkowski, an incurably inquisitive Marxist intellectual, had already lived through a few cycles of his own. He had fought in the Communist resistance to Nazi occupation, a close comrade of Władysław Gomułka, Poland's first post-war ruler. He shared his leader's disgrace when Stalinism was forced upon the Party in 1948, re-emerged in 1956 when Gomułka returned to power, became minister of education, and then fell into disfavour once more when the Party's tolerance of free discussion began to wither.

In March 1968, a complex and mysterious political earthquake shook Poland. Superficially, there were connections with the turbulence which was rising in the streets and universities of the West; at a deeper level, however, the motives and reactions which came into play were peculiarly Polish. Student demonstrations, personal ambitions, genuine protest at economic stagnation and the fomenting of anti-Semitism for political ends were all ingredients. Bieńkowski at once sat down and composed a short, piercing essay entitled 'Motors and Brakes of Socialism'.[1] It was never published in Poland, but it earned him expulsion from the Party.

In this book, Bieńkowski claimed to have discovered a cyclical process that was operating throughout the 'socialist bloc', more obviously in some countries than in others. The cycle was partly driven by a force that Bieńkowski engagingly named 'the dynamics of petrifaction'. But, as a Marxist, he was also able to produce a contrary force that acted against the dynamics of petrifaction in a dialectical manner. This was the sheer impetus of social change in a socialist environment, the 'rapid development of creative forces and the transformations in the structure of society which result from them'.

His petrifying force was the tendency of the bureaucracies and control bodies set up by Communist régimes to expand far beyond their original purpose and then fossilize into stony barriers which came to block all spontaneous social change. At the end of a cycle, the creative forces of change surging against these barriers would accumulate pressure until an explosion took place. There would then be a 'leap' forward, as the pent-up developments burst through the dam to find their own level. It was in Poland, Bieńkowski proudly asserted, that this process could be observed in its 'purest' form. In Hungary, it had been distorted by the Soviet invasion in 1956. In Czechoslovakia, it operated very slowly, so that the first cycle had only just completed itself (he was writing in early 1968, the months of the 'Prague Spring').

Bieńkowski refined his theory by claiming to identify a second phenomenon within each cycle. This was a qualitative change in the role of the secret police. In the first phase of the cycle, the power of 'security' would gradually build up until, although hidden, it was as extensive as the public and visible power of the Party and state. This phase Bieńkowski named 'political dictatorship'.* But during this phase the growth of police power was checked by certain political conventions that were left over from the departed 'bourgeois liberal' state. Some external excuse, some sudden threat or panic, was required to allow the secret police to break through these last restraints and establish its hegemony even over the Communist Party apparatus itself. Then the second phase of the cycle, 'police dictatorship', would begin. Bieńkowski argued that the first such police breakthrough had occurred in 1948–9, when Stalin suddenly shoved the satellite Communist Parties of eastern Europe into an artificial conflict both with the 'imperialist West' and with 'right-wing and nationalistic elements' in their own ranks. The events of March 1968, for him, were the same phenomenon repeated. The second phase had begun. The final explosion might not be far off.

---

* Bieńkowski is not using the word 'dictatorship' in its general sense. He is defining 'political' and 'police' phases in the 'dictatorship of the proletariat', the period after a revolution when, according to Leninist theory, the Communist Party exercises power on behalf of the working class. Like most 'liberal' Communists of his generation, Bieńkowski complained that the ruling Communist Parties of eastern Europe, including the USSR, had never managed to move forward from the dictatorship of the proletariat to the socialist democracy which was supposed to ensue.

Nor was it. In December 1970 Gomułka fell and Edward Gierek replaced him. The Gierek cycle ran for ten years, ending in an uncannily similar fashion. As a prophet, Bieńkowski had turned out reasonably accurate.

But the trouble about all cycle theories is the mechanical analogy. Bieńkowski invented a sort of internal combustion engine for Polish politics. The piston of social change compresses the elements of 'petrifaction' until there is an explosion and the piston flies back, violently turning the crank of history as it does so. It sounds wonderful: only make the cycles faster and the explosions more regular, and the Poles will go roaring into the twenty-first century at a speed which will leave their competitors nowhere. But this, of course, isn't what Bieńkowski meant at all. He wanted his cycles to be understood as destructive, no substitute for steady, uninterrupted progress. He was plainly right to see that the history of Poland after 1945 was repeating itself, and that it was liable to go on repeating itself in future. And most people would agree broadly with his identification of the forces producing these repetitions: social and technical progress conflicting with governments and hierarchies that were not dependent upon public opinion. But it is better to try to remove the mechanical element, the action-inevitably-breeds-reaction aspect, from his theory. There is nothing inevitable about the cycles, nothing to say either that the régime cannot adapt in such a way as to break out of the sequence or that the next explosion may not destroy the entire mechanism for good.

1939: The Collapse of Polish Independence

In 1945, it seemed that the traditional Poland had been destroyed for ever. Any independent state which was to be rebuilt after such material and political destruction could only be constructed on a quite new social basis, within new frontiers, secured in a different system of alliances.

Five years of Nazi occupation had left the country physically and psychologically shattered to a degree which westerners even then found hard to appreciate. One Pole in five had perished as a direct result of the war. Nearly 40 per cent of the national wealth had been destroyed (France, for comparison, lost 1·5 per cent). Half the public transport, a third of all industrial installations, 60 per cent of the schools and 62 per cent of all postal and telephone equipment had gone.[2]

Several million Poles were on the roads or clinging to the few surviving trains, searching for new homes. The entire Polish state had been moved bodily 200 miles to the west. In 1940, the Soviet Union had annexed Lithuania, whose capital, Wilno, had been a centre of Polish culture. At the end of the war, the Great Powers had agreed that the USSR should annex Polish-ruled tracts of Byelorussia and the Ukraine including the mainly Polish city of Lwów, an area amounting to roughly a third of the pre-war Polish republic. In the west, Poland had been granted an equivalent area of Silesia, Pomerania and East Prussia, lands which had once formed territories of the old Polish kingdom but which were now overwhelmingly German in population. Hundreds of thousands of other Poles were making their way home from captivity or forced labour in Germany. In Britain, the officers and men of the Polish armies in the West sat in their camps and debated whether to return or to choose exile.

Politically, Poland's self-confidence was also in ruins. It was true that the nation had resisted the German invaders, in September 1939 and then through the hell of the occupation, with spectacular courage. No section of Polish society as such, only a handful of individuals, had collaborated with the Nazis. An underground state had been established, complete down to its judiciary and its universities. Armed resistance had been maintained from the first day of occupation to the last, culminating in the colossal Warsaw Rising in the summer of 1944. And yet, for all the legitimate pride in this record, the Poles were also aware of a sense of crushing national failure. They had not failed in their loyalty to the cause of Polish independence. It was the whole project of independence itself which seemed to have failed.

The 'Polish Commonwealth', once a powerful, prosperous and in some ways innovative kingdom, had entered on a steady decline in the seventeenth century. At the end of the eighteenth century, the rump of the enfeebled state was finally partitioned between the Russian and Austrian Empires and the Kingdom of Prussia. As an attempt to obliterate the Polish nation, the partitions never looked like succeeding. Polish nineteenth-century history is punctuated by bloody insurrections, and the national literary culture (much of it composed in exile) rose to its heights of achievement in the generations of suppression. Religious persecution by the Orthodox and Lutheran authorities of Russian and Prussian Poland helped to bring about a fanatical identification of Polish nationality with the Catholic faith. Efforts, especially in the Prussian area, to stamp out the Polish language proved futile.

But the attack on the concept of Polish statehood was more insidious. The partitioning powers advanced a multitude of arguments to demonstrate that the Poles were by nature incapable of governing themselves, that the existence of a state without natural boundaries was no longer practical in modern conditions, that the idea of Polish independence had been transcended by the historical process itself as it created larger and more powerful empires out of the post-feudal patchwork of Europe. While rejecting all these rationalizations, Polish patriots did not remain entirely unaffected by them. After the failure of the last great national uprising in 1863, it was reluctantly accepted that the restoration of Polish statehood was extremely unlikely. The preservation of the nation itself, by economic development and cultural campaigns, became the immediate task. When war broke out in 1914 between Germany, Austria-Hungary and Russia, the Poles at once saw the opportunities presented to them by this conflict between the partitioning powers and hoped, at best, to extract some limited autonomy for a part of the Polish lands from the winning side.

It was the extremely unlikely contingency which was realized. All three powers collapsed, almost simultaneously. The Russian Empire was overthrown by the revolutions of 1917 and fell into impotence and chaos. A year later, both Germany and Austria-Hungary foundered in revolution and military defeat. Through a combination of Allied support and armed action at home, Polish patriots were able to restore their state in November 1918. But only the most mystical of patriots could reason that the Polish cause had triumphed because of its own inherent strength. The nation's leaders took power in a country which nobody at that point effectively controlled. Luck, rather than historical necessity, had given Poland back her independence.

This was not a comfortable foundation on which to erect a new state. It implied, with unpleasant logic, that Poland would have the greatest difficulty in maintaining full independence when and if her huge neighbours regained their strength. It also implied that, if Germany and Russia did recover, the worst case for Poland would be any alliance or *rapprochement* between them, and that Polish foreign policy ought to concentrate upon keeping them apart. The price of such a cautious and realistic policy might be the cultivation of a 'special relationship' with either Moscow or Berlin, perhaps involving a limited sacrifice of Poland's freedom of diplomatic manoeuvre.

But the new Polish republic was not in the mood for caution and realism. Two men, both tempestuously extreme in their views, dominated Polish politics between the wars. One was Józef Piłsudski, principal actor in the liberation of 1918, who became the nation's first military commander-in-

chief and seized full dictatorial powers in 1926. The other was Roman
Dmowski, leader of the National Democrats, a right-wing party that was
Poland's largest single political formation.

Piłsudski was an extraordinary, contradictory figure. Like all Polish politicians who were then trying to learn the practices of normal public life, his
political training had been that of a conspirator. Piłsudski had been a
dominating personality in the Socialist Party (PPS), but most of his activity
in the years before 1918 was given to organizing the cadres of an underground national army, and he emerged essentially as a military leader. At
independence, he became at once the largest man on the scene; it was
difficult to make politics with such an imperious person and yet, as one
parliamentary deadlock succeeded another, it was impossible to make politics without him. Violently irascible and autocratic, Piłsudski was also a
well-educated and highly intelligent man; his memoirs are a minor literary
masterpiece. Rather like Franz-Josef Strauss in West Germany today,
Piłsudski's sardonic understanding of the political scene was matched only
by his capacity to mishandle it.

As head of state after 1918 and commander-in-chief, his view of Poland's
potential in the world was immoderate. 'Poland will be a great power, or
she will not exist.' This greatness, he thought, could be established through
Poland's relationship to the smaller nationalities lying to the east and north-
east – the Lithuanians, the Byelorussians and the Ukrainians – who should
be drawn out of the Russian orbit and into a federal association with
Poland. Piłsudski himself came originally from near Wilno, in Lithuania;
his idea of a Polish 'empire' in the East was a revival of the wider Polish
Commonwealth as it had existed until the eighteenth century, and obviously
it could be achieved only at Russian expense. Piłsudski, who always regarded
Russia as the more dangerous threat to Polish independence and sought
a good relationship with Germany, acted rapidly to settle the eastern frontiers to his own taste. In May 1920, Polish troops invaded the Ukraine and
captured Kiev. But in the Bolshevik counter-offensive that followed, the
Red Army broke through into Poland and was already bypassing Warsaw
to the north when it was halted and driven into retreat by a well-
planned flank attack (the so-called 'Miracle on the Vistula') in August. The
subsequent Peace of Riga gave Poland only some western parts of Byelorussia and the Ukraine. But Piłsudski compensated his damaged ambitions
by organizing a *coup d'état* in Wilno; the city, which had been Lithuania's
capital, was finally annexed by Poland in 1922.

The Polish–Soviet War might have been understood as a warning that
Poland should take a more modest view of its position in Europe. The

Polish attack had ensured that the historical suspicion which Russians entertained about Poles would be inherited by the Soviet Union and its leaders. The Bolshevik counter-offensive had brought the Red Army into the centre of Europe; when they were stopped, the Red cavalry were already on the German frontier in East Prussia and apparently prepared to gallop on to Berlin. However, this was not the lesson Polish rulers chose to draw. Their cavalry had beaten the Russians. Poland had won a war. A grand complacency descended, especially upon the senior officer caste. Unfortunately, this group took its complacency into still higher positions of influence. After the 1926 coup, Piłsudski ruled through his old military cronies; they were not professional politicians, but they were not really professional officers either. These were not the veterans of long service in the Austrian or Prussian armies who had commanded the operations that stopped the Bolsheviks outside Warsaw. They were amateurs who had served only in Piłsudski's conspiratorial 'Legions' and knew little of real military training or campaigning. When Piłsudski died in 1935, this little Legionary junta succeeded him as a collective dictatorship. Their understanding of what the content of state independence could be was primitive and exaggerated. Where Piłsudski had leaned towards Germany to protect himself against the Russian threat, his successors tried to maintain a balance between the growing power of Hitler and Stalin, as if Poland were their equal. Inevitably, this failed. When the Nazi menace to Poland became acute, they refused to accept military co-operation with the Soviet Union. There followed the Nazi–Soviet Pact of August 1939 which, with its secret provision for a new partition of Poland, sealed the fate of Polish independence.

Internal politics in Poland between the wars were turbulent and indecisive. Before 1926, the parties representing national minorities – Jewish, Ukrainian and Byelorussian – helped to ensure that no stable parliamentary majority could be found. The Piłsudski camp never developed an authentic political movement of its own and ruled in effect by force. On the left, the Polish Socialist Party (PPS) and the small Communist Party (KPP) held great influence over the growing working class, but were outweighed by the Peasant Party (PSL). The largest single political formation, the National Democrats (Endecja) led by Roman Dmowski, dominated the right. Although it never held power for more than brief interludes, and then only in complex coalitions, its attitudes gained a wide influence over Polish public opinion, not only in the relatively small upper and middle classes, and the ghosts of Endecja instincts and prejudices can be encountered in Polish political conversations to this day.

The National Democrats, originating as a semi-clandestine movement in the late nineteenth century, showed many of the traits later to be associated with Fascism. They began as a radical nationalist party, crudely anti-Semitic and at the outset hostile both to the landowning upper class and to the Catholic hierarchy. Before the First World War, while Piłsudski preferred to manipulate Germany and Austria against the Russians, Roman Dmowski and his followers – originally for no better reason than the hope of currying favour with the Tsarist authorities in Poland – supported Russia. Dmowski's nationalism was fanatical and extreme. R. F. Leslie has written that he and his followers 'bequeathed to modern Polish nationalism the concept that the Nation is the pinnacle of all morality'.[3] Sympathy for the needs or interests of any other nation was traitorous, according to Dmowski, and socialism, with its instinctive solidarity with the poor of other nations, deserved 'absolute condemnation from the point of view of public morality'.

As they grew in influence, the National Democrats abandoned their plebeian radicalism. Their hostility to left-wing solutions brought them steadily closer to the landowners and industrialists whom they had once condemned, who saw the Endecja as their best protection against socialism and the revolutionary element in the poor peasantry. They were also able to mend their fences with the Church (itself a huge institutional landowner, and at that time vigorously anti-Semitic); after 1918, the Church's closest links remained with the National Democrats rather than with Piłsudski and his followers. The National Democrats were no less authoritarian in instinct than Piłsudski's men, and a great deal more given to the cult of racial and political violence. If they had taken power in the 1930s, their régime would have had little to distinguish it from those of Hitler and Mussolini. As it was, they developed great admiration for the Nazi system, especially for its treatment of Jews, tempered only by regret that the Nazis were Germans. Their legacy to Polish political instincts was a single creed in which they had cemented together ideas that might once have been held separately: nationalism as the supreme moral value, the identification of Jews and Marxists as enemies of the nation, the indissoluble link between Polish patriotism and the Catholic religion. Even today, it must be repeated, the Endecja's 'achievement' in fusing these elements together into a single article of faith has not been entirely dissolved. And the spectre of the Endecja's 'Russian orientation' also returned in political speculations during the 1970s, as Poles wondered whether a non-Communist but strongly authoritarian Poland, committed to a series of close alliances with the Soviet Union, might not come to seem more attractive to Moscow than an unpopular Communist régime that could no longer be made to function effectively.

In 1945, it was hard to conceive that Poles would one day be nostalgic for the pre-war political constellation. All that was plain was that a whole tradition of Polish national independence had been discredited. Poland had regained sovereign statehood, but had been unable to maintain it. The nineteenth-century conception of national independence as an absolute, without qualifications or limits on the nation-state's freedom of external and internal action, had proved impossible to defend in twentieth-century Europe. All through the war, the London government-in-exile had hoped that it would be able to restore full Polish independence, based on alliances with the West and with other, smaller, eastern European states. The Warsaw Rising of 1944 had been its last, desperate attempt to seize power in Poland, to expel the Germans just in time to receive the advancing Soviet armies as host in its own capital. But the Rising, whose timing depended on faulty intelligence, had been crushed by the Germans.[4] Poland had been liberated by the Red Army, assisted by a Polish army under Soviet command, and the country was ruled by a provisional government headed by the Communists.

Most Poles disliked this outcome. The soldiers and refugees still abroad disliked it so intensely that tens of thousands of them preferred the loneliness and poverty of exile rather than a return home. None the less, certain conclusions were generally drawn. The first was that a restored Poland could not stand alone between Germany and the Soviet Union even if it wished to. A close alliance binding Poland to Soviet policies was now inevitable, but it was also necessary. One did not have to love the Russians or be a fervent admirer of Stalin and the Soviet Union to accept this new Polish *raison d'état*. Independence could no longer mean what it had meant to the heroes of the nineteenth-century insurrections, or to Piłsudski and Dmowski. But the limited independence which seemed in 1945 to be on offer was still infinitely worth having, and worth defending.

The second conclusion was that not only a certain vision of Polish independence but a certain Poland had been found wanting. The sort of society which allowed the post-Piłsudski junta to misrule it and the National Democrats to fuddle its imagination between the wars had shown that, in the long run, it was incapable of governing itself and of maintaining the country's independence. Poland had now been offered another chance to survive as a separate political entity on the map of Europe. If the chance were to be taken, it was not only foreign policy but the entire political and economic structure of the nation that must change.

In the exhaustion and bewilderment which followed the liberation, few had a precise idea of what these changes should be. There was certainly no way back to the pre-war military régime, which had become intensely unpopular by 1939; the opposition, although badly divided, had almost certainly come to stand for the great majority of public opinion. At the end of the war, there was a hazy consensus that there should be a strong government to break the power of the landlords and take industry out of foreign hands. But only the Communists and, to a lesser extent, the members of the revived Polish Socialist Party were clear about the details of such a programme. Left-wing ideology, especially Marxism, was still unpopular in Poland. But in 1945, when all other political creeds seemed to have been so thoroughly discredited by events, socialism had no effective challenger.

Communism with a Polish Face

The question the Poles still debate today is the same question that divided them in 1944: is it possible to rule Poland by consent while a Communist Party holds the monopoly of political power? The chances of achieving such a compromise in a country strongly anti-Communist in its majority were at least better just after the war than they became when Stalinism was forced upon Poland in 1948–9. But the first doubt that had to be settled was whether the Polish Communists accepted the idea of an independent Poland at all or whether they believed that the country should become a mere territory of the Soviet Union.

This question had already been answered, although few Poles in 1945 knew it. The new leader of the Communist Party, Władysław Gomułka, who had emerged during the Nazi occupation, knew that there must be no doubts about the commitment of Polish Communists to the existence of a Polish state if the first barrier which divided his party from the population was to be broken down. Gomułka saw that the pre-war Polish Communist Party had also, in its own way, been part of that 'certain Poland' which had failed the test of history in 1939. He had been one of its leading members, and he knew that the Party had never shaken off the charge, originally well founded, that it was disloyal not just to the governments of the restored Polish state but to the independent state itself.

The lineal ancestor of the Communist Party had been a small Marxist formation known as the Social Democratic Party of the Kingdom of Poland and Lithuania (usually abbreviated to SDKPiL). Operating in partitioned Poland, where mass memberships were obviously not easy to accumulate, the SDKPiL had tended to be all brilliant Jewish chiefs and no Indians. Led by Rosa Luxemburg and Leo Jogiches, the party was emphatically internationalist. In her opposition to the restoration of a Polish state, which she considered a surrender to reactionary bourgeois nationalism, Rosa Luxemburg was in conflict not only with the much larger Polish Socialist Party (PPS) but with Lenin himself. The party merged with the left wing of the PPS in December 1918 to form the Communist Party of Poland (KPP). The following month Rosa Luxemburg, also a co-founder of the German Communist Party, was murdered in Berlin after the Spartacist revolution failed, but the KPP continued for several years to oppose openly the existence of an independent Poland. In 1920, it set up a short-lived provisional government behind the lines of the advancing Red Army, calling upon the Polish proletariat to oppose their own government. As the prospect of world revolution receded, the KPP strongly supported the internationalist doctrines of Trotsky against Stalin. Although the Party gradually moderated its platform, claiming to support a form of genuine socialist independence for Poland which could not be achieved under capitalism, it continued to compromise itself with the Polish masses by demanding that Poland should return its non-Polish eastern territories to the Soviet Union and, later, Danzig (Gdańsk) and parts of Silesia and Pomerania to Germany.

Those workers who were ready to march with the KPP's banners in industrial disputes, and there were many of them, were bewildered by the Party's eccentric decision to support Piłsudski's *coup d'état* in 1926. This earned the party no gratitude, and in subsequent years the KPP was so effectively repressed that its main role in politics became that of an indispensable bogey-man for extreme right-wing rhetoric. Meanwhile, the idealistic and courageous men and women who formed its leadership were obliged to defend themselves against Stalin's constant efforts to dictate their policies and manipulate their cadres. Stalin, for his part, came to regard the KPP as the most dangerous surviving centre of Trotskyism and opposition to his own authority in the international Communist movement. In the late 1930s, he summoned its leaders to Moscow, arrested them, and put several of them to death, together with hundreds of lesser members of the Party who simply disappeared. The KPP was abolished by the Comintern, on Stalin's instructions, in 1938.

This crime, whose full scale was not understood until long after the Second World War, did little to moderate anti-Communist feeling in Poland. Any Marxist revolutionary party would have faced a hard task in modern Poland, given the fervently accepted authority of the Catholic Church, the relative smallness of the industrial working class in a country where 63·8 per cent of the population earned their living from agriculture, and the violently anti-Russian feelings revived by the 1920 Polish–Soviet war. Even so, the grossly unfair distribution of wealth and, after 1929, the effect of the Great Depression generated regular outbursts of labour unrest and, in the urban working class, a readiness to take violent action and contemplate revolutionary solutions. The KPP could certainly have been much more effective than it was. But its negative attitude to Polish independence, above all, prevented it from taking the limited chances which the situation offered.

The Nazi–Soviet Pact of 1939, the non-aggression agreement through which Stalin bought time to prepare himself against a German attack, was signed in August. The secret protocol to the Pact provided that Poland would be partitioned between Germany and the USSR along the line of the River Bug. Hitler attacked Poland on 1 September; just over a fortnight later, the Red Army entered and began to occupy eastern Poland. The Polish armies retreating before the German attack from the west collapsed, and some 200,000 of them fell into Soviet hands. The Polish state now, once again, ceased to exist. In the Soviet-occupied areas, although Soviet anti-Polish policy never reached the scale of the systematic genocide practised by the Nazis, more than a million people were deported to Siberia or the Asian Soviet republics. The Soviet authorities treated members of the dissolved KPP little better.

In 1941, as relations between the USSR and Germany deteriorated, Stalin's attitude to the Polish Communists and socialists began to moderate. In December 1941, five months after the Nazi invasion of the Soviet Union, a group of leading Polish Communists was assembled in Moscow by the Soviet authorities and then parachuted into German-occupied Poland with instructions to form a new party, the Polish Workers' Party (PPR). From the outset, this new party followed a much broader line than the old KPP, hoping to construct a wide, Communist-led movement of resistance to the Nazis which would also become a formidable and united political movement of the left. But the leaders selected by Moscow were arrested or killed, and in November 1943 Władysław Gomułka – who had never been exposed to direct Soviet influence but had remained in Poland after 1939 – became the Secretary of the PPR.

At first, the PPR achieved little in occupied Poland. The main resistance, the underground state under the authority of the London government-in-exile, commanded a clandestine Home Army (Armia Krajowa, or AK) which by 1944 numbered more than 200,000. The Communist forces, the People's Army (AL), probably never exceeded 50,000. Gomułka's attempts to build a political alliance with the main resistance, a common front excluding only the extreme right and dedicated to a reformed and democratized Poland after the war, did not succeed.

There were two main reasons why the political leadership of the resistance kept the PPR at arm's length. The first was a persisting suspicion that Polish Communists were false patriots, whose activities were simply an extension of Soviet policies. The facts that the PPR did not belong to the Comintern, that the word 'Communist' had been kept out of its title and that its programme favoured radical social reform rather than the full 'Bolshevization' of Poland cut little ice. The second reason was a long and bitter dispute between Moscow and the London government over Poland's eastern frontiers. To the Poles in London (to whom, uneasily, he had extended diplomatic relations in July 1941) Stalin insisted that the territories seized by Soviet forces in 1939, which were in the main not demographically Polish, should remain with the USSR. The government-in-exile, in spite of frantic and prolonged pressure from the British and the Americans, insisted on the restoration of the original frontiers. Challenged to declare himself for the old frontiers, Gomułka refused. This was not merely a dispute about borders, but in substance the argument about what quality of independence the post-war Polish state should demand. The London and Warsaw resistance leaders, for all their disavowal of the follies of pre-war policy, still believed in an absolute form of independence, unqualified by binding alliances to any power. To accept the loss of the eastern territories was to accept that Poland would fall under some sort of Russian hegemony after the war. Unrealistically, they were still reluctant to accept that Poland would be liberated by the Red Army; in the London government and the AK high command, the inclination was to understand the war as a two-front struggle against both Hitler's Germany and the Soviet Union.

The negotiations were on the verge of breakdown when, in April 1943, the Germans announced the discovery of mass graves near Smolensk, in the Katyń woods, containing the bodies of thousands of Polish officers. They were identified as part of a total of 15,000 officers who had been captured by the Soviet Union in 1939 and who – in spite of repeated inquiries by Polish envoys in Moscow – remained unaccounted for. Stalin blamed the Germans, a version ill supported by evidence which the Soviet government still maintains. Few believed him. The Polish government-in-exile made it plain that it did not. A few weeks later, Stalin declared that the London government was hostile to the USSR and broke off diplomatic relations.

Within Poland, an open competition for power now began. In late 1943, Gomułka organized a National Council of the Homeland, intended to be the nucleus of a broad 'democratic front'. The other left parties, the socialists and the Peasants' Party, declined to join. But the National Council, after some misunderstandings, gained the backing of the Union of

Polish Patriots, a Moscow-based grouping of Communists and socialists. The Council also formed a link with the Polish forces in the USSR commanded by General Berling; originally a division, they expanded to become the First Army, numbering nearly 80,000 men, and fought their way westwards with the Soviet armies.*

In July 1944, the Red Army crossed the River Bug and liberated the first towns in what Stalin considered to be Polish territory. On 21 July, a Polish Committee of National Liberation was established at Chełm, supported by the National Council and the Union of Polish Patriots and composed of PPR members and left-wing socialists. The following day, the Committee issued its 'July Manifesto', proclaiming a policy of close alliance with the Soviet Union. As everyone realized, the Committee was in fact a provisional government, directly challenging the authority of the London government-in-exile. Relying on the Soviet armed forces as they moved across Poland, the Committee extended its administration in the wake of the front line. In January 1945, Stalin formally recognized the Committee as the legitimate Polish government.

By then, the London government was no longer a power in the land. The failure of the Warsaw Rising in August and September 1944 (in which Communists fought bravely in spite of their misgivings about the rising's political motives) had finally broken the Home Army (AK). AK efforts to liberate towns in eastern Poland before the Soviet forces arrived had ended in fiasco, as Soviet commanders forced the Polish partisans either to lay down their arms or to merge with the Polish regular troops of the First Army. The plan for an inner, anti-Communist resistance movement to carry on the struggle for Polish independence never came to much. The partisans began to emerge from the forests. For a time, some units and bands of lost men fought on; a desultory but savage civil war between such groups and the forces of the new government lasted into 1946 and was still burning, in remote corners of the country, in early 1947. Most of these groups, after 1945, were not from the AK but from small semi-fascist formations or from Ukrainian nationalist units that had fought for the Germans and could expect no mercy from the authorities.

---

*After the agreement of July 1941 between Stalin and the London government, Poles in the USSR were allowed to choose whether to remain. Most of them gathered at Buzuluk, in Siberia, and from there marched with their families to Iran under the command of General Anders. From Iran they were transported to join the Polish forces in the West, and fought throughout the campaigns in Italy and northern Europe.

The Landscape after the Battle

Poland was utterly exhausted, sick of killing. The land had been drenched in blood; the forest turf bulged with mass graves of unknown human beings. It was not only the Poles who had been slaughtered. Their country had been used as the site for the extermination of six million European Jews. At Auschwitz, the crematorium doors gaped in the rubble. At Majdanek, near Lublin, there now stood a small hill composed of human ash. Great offensives had blackened the countrysides and ruined the cities. After the rising the Germans had deliberately levelled much of Warsaw to the ground, so that this sub-human Slavic tribe, as Hitler judged the Poles, would never have a capital again. One third of the country had been cut away by Russia, and a quite new form of government had been installed by foreign bayonets. And, weary of killing as they were, the survivors could not drop the habit. Haggard Poles in different uniforms still fired their rusty weapons at one another in forest clearings. Men whose wives and children had been shot by the Nazis waited for other men whose families might have met the same fate – perhaps in the same round-up, against the same wall, their mouths crammed with plaster-of-paris to choke the screams – and murdered them. It was this Poland which, with all kinds of irony, celebrated victory on 8 May 1945.

Gomułka and the provisional government had moved to Warsaw as soon as the ruined capital was liberated in January. He was to control Poland for the next three years. It was a moment to assess his chances of establishing a Communist-led régime that could win the support, if not the enthusiasm, of the majority of the Polish nation. In Poland today, thirty-five years later, it is fashionable to assume that such a project was impossible from the outset. As a historical judgement, that is unsound. The balance of factors for and against Gomułka's enterprise was close, and only outside events – the Cold War and Stalin's change of policy in eastern Europe – tipped the balance against the new power.

Gomułka's gravest disadvantage was the association of Communism with Russian hegemony. To the old hostility to Russia, which dated back to the partitions and long before, were added the appalling experiences of recent years: the Nazi–Soviet Pact and the Soviet seizure of eastern Poland in 1939, the sufferings of Poles under Soviet occupation which were symbolized by the crime of Katyń, the crushing of the Warsaw Rising (most Poles believed that Stalin had deliberately halted his armies to allow the Germans to suppress it), the annexation of the eastern territories with the intensely

Polish city of Lwów. These were wounds that even a generation's passage would not heal. But if the PPR could make it plain that it was an independent political force, which put Poland's interests first and was capable of diverging from the model of Stalin's Soviet Union, these associations could be broken down.

Less definite, but harder to eradicate, was the complex of Polish mental resistances to all forms of Marxist socialism. These were strongest in the remnants of the small Polish middle class, affected by traditions represented most vigorously by the Endecja, and in the peasantry. Central to this resistance was the immense and undiminished influence of the Catholic Church. The Church in pre-war Poland had not only opposed all creeds of atheist materialism but, with the National Democrats and most of the political right, had been persistently anti-Semitic. To an ancient religious prejudice against Jews, who had constituted more than a tenth of the pre-war population, was added the belief, eagerly encouraged by political and some Church leaders, that the Jews were hostile to Polish independence and that the left parties, especially the Communists, were Jewish conspiracies plotting to absorb Poland into Bolshevik Russia.

It was true that the old Luxemburgist tradition had opposed Polish independence, and it was also true that the KPP leadership had been to a great extent Jewish. Talk of a 'Jewish problem' in pre-1939 Poland was understandable. The Jewish population, though itself mostly poor and backward, was concentrated in small towns and small businesses which made it an obvious target for the frustrations of the peasantry and the Polish petty middle class. As the Depression inflamed these resentments, successive governments condemned anti-Semitic outrages but did little to control them.

During the Nazi occupation, the attitude of the Polish population to the fate of the Jews was ambiguous. The resistance movement had given some help to the great Ghetto Rising in Warsaw in 1943, but it could have done more. The saying that 'any Jew who survived the Nazi occupation owes his life to a Pole' is fair, and the record of the Poles who risked or lost their lives in groups devoted to saving or hiding their Jewish fellow-citizens is to be revered. All the same, there were ultra-right armed bands who killed Jews on principle, and the response of a Polish peasant who found Jewish fugitives begging for shelter at his door could not be predicted. After the war, less than a quarter of a million Polish Jews remained alive, and more than half of these emigrated to Palestine during the next two years. But this did not prevent a brief, intense recrudescence of popular anti-Semitism. Some of the régime's opponents – not all – fastened on the presence in the post-war governments of Jewish Communists who had spent the war in Moscow: Jakub Berman, in charge of ideology and security, Hilary Minc, minister for industry, and others. On 4 July 1946 there took place the last 'classic' pogrom in European history, when – after the medieval myth that Jews were murdering Christian children and drinking their blood had been circulated in the town of Kielce – a group of Soviet and Polish Jews in transit to Palestine were attacked and massacred. Cardinal Hlond, then the Polish Primate, commented that such outrages were political rather than racial; they arose from 'the presence in the government of Jews who were trying to establish in Poland a régime to which the majority of the people are hostile'.[4]

To describe such attitudes is to suggest that they formed a mental Great Wall, which only a small band of Communists had resolved to storm. But the mood in Poland after liberation was not static but dynamic, and most radicals – not only the Communists – considered that such primitive prejudices would be swept away within a few years, or would survive only in pockets of bigoted provincial ignorance. To put it shortly, Poland was in a revolutionary condition. The fact that the sort of social revolution that Poland got was imposed from the Soviet Union and followed basically the Soviet pattern should not obscure the nation's real impatience for change. Well aware of this impetus, the PPR leaders and their socialist allies tried to spring astride a horse that was already galloping.

Professor Leslie has written that every Polish struggle for independence has also become a social struggle over who should be dominant in that independent Poland. The resistance to the German occupation, divided as it was, confirmed Leslie's law: in partisan war and urban resistance, privileges attached to age or class instantly cease to have meaning, while the possession of wealth and property merely raises doubts about the possessor's endurance in the struggle. If the chiefs of the A K were often pre-war officers, with much of the ideology of their caste still intact, the rank-and-file of the A K and the swarms of boys and girls who acted as runners and ancillaries were increasingly radical. They wanted to fight the enemy more effectively, and after the war they wanted a new democracy for Poland which would somehow express the equality and comradeship of the wartime underground movement.[5] Out in the countryside, uniformed A K partisans who encountered the peasantry realized that they would never return to the economic and mental bondage of pre-war village or estate life.

In this association of liberation with revolution, of resistance with social equality, the Poles were not of course alone but part of the huge revival of political energy that was experienced by almost every nation in Europe. We have no name for this episode of history. It lasted from roughly 1943 to 1948. In its power and universality, it was almost a repetition of the continental wave of revolutions in 1848, just a century before, and, like that 'Springtime of Nations', its power derived from the confluence of armed struggles for national independence with ideologies of social and economic change. Socialism, in the broad sense that encompasses more than Leninist or Marxist interpretations, took the place that romantic liberalism had occupied in the nineteenth century. But unlike 1848–9, this 'second springtime' was soon obliterated from historical view by the weight of political wreckage that fell upon it in the late 1940s as the Cold War began.

Without recognizing this European dimension it is impossible to assess Gomułka's chances of transplanting a form of Communism to Poland. The 'second spring' of 1943–8 brought Poland, almost for the first time in many centuries, into the common experience of western Europe. The Nazi occupation was one element; more important was the sense, as the war ended, that the peoples of the continent were marching politically in the same direction. The isolation of Poland dropped away for a moment. The same kind of 'Popular Front' government, with Communist and social-democrat participation, was supposed to be about to spring-clean France, Italy, Poland, Czechoslovakia and much of the Balkans. The insistence of Polish intellectuals that their country belonged spiritually to the west of the continent had not hitherto proved convincing outside Catholic circles. In 1945, however, and especially in France, Polish developments were at last treated as part of a common European movement towards social justice and international security.

In this situation, it was not absurd for the new government to hope that – after some rough years – the Poles and a Communist-dominated régime would reach an accommodation. The nation was already moving to the left, ready for a complete break with the pre-war structures – a movement which was part of the general European tide. Few Poles were enthusiastic about the prospect of close alliance with the Soviet Union, but all the alternatives had collapsed. The main political forces in the land apart from the PPR – the Polish Socialist Party under a new leadership and the more radical elements in the peasant movement – could probably be persuaded to join a common programme of reforms. Stalin was apparently prepared to let the Polish Communists strike out on a line of their own, while the presence of Soviet troops in Poland was – to put it mildly – an assurance that the remains of the pre-war rightist parties and their armed forces would not become a real danger to PPR hegemony.

The programme did not arouse much controversy, at least in its internal aspects. In September 1944, the Polish Committee of National Liberation had declared a land reform which broke up the large estates and set a maximum ownership of fifty hectares of arable land. The landowner class, most of whose grandest members now left the country, was obliterated, and some six million hectares of land were redistributed. This was not, in fact, so far from the post-war reforms proposed, also in 1944, by the non-Communist resistance (the Council of National Unity), which had also suggested the nationalization of banks and major industries and a welfare state aiming to provide full employment. The new régime set about its own nationalization programme before the last retreating German troops had been driven across the River Oder.

Gomułka himself, who was at once leader of the PPR and deputy prime minister in charge of the resettlement of the Western Territories acquired from Germany, was in many respects hard to fit into the popular Polish stereotype of a Communist. He was not Jewish; he was not a 'rootless intellectual' but a factory worker whose father was a small peasant; and he made it repeatedly plain that he did not wish Poland slavishly to imitate the Soviet model. He was both an ardent Communist and a Polish patriot. He denied that he intended to enforce a one-party system or to collectivize the private peasantry. Instead, he spoke of 'evolutionary social change' and drew a clear distinction between Poland and the USSR. In Poland, 'state power is based on parliamentary democracy ... The dictatorship of the working class or of a single party is not essential nor would it serve any useful purpose ... Poland can proceed and is proceeding along her own road.'[6]

This was misleading, in its suggestion that he intended indefinitely to accept genuine political pluralism in Poland. The road might be Polish, but the destination, for any loyal Communist of his generation, had ultimately to be the same as that for the Soviet Union: a collectivist society of the working class alone. The important point was that it was to be Polish conditions, not any directives or pressure from outside, which were to determine the route and the pace of this cautious advance towards Communism. These were bold views, which aroused misgivings among many of his colleagues in the PPR leadership who had passed the war in Moscow – like Bolesław Bierut, who was to become president of the republic in 1947. Stalin did not interfere at this stage, however, even when in the immediate post-war months Gomułka and the PPR leadership came into conflict with the often ham-handed activities of Soviet military authorities and intelligence in Poland.

Gomułka's remarks about parliamentary democracy proved equally misleading in the savage political struggles which ended in the final victory of the PPR at the elections of January 1947. Nicholas Bethell has observed that 'his mildness and lack of Communist dogma were in strange contrast to the hard and ruthless way he dealt with the opponents of "people's power" '.[7] Gomułka's main personal target was Stanisław Mikołajczyk, the Peasant Party leader who had been prime minister of the London government and who was persuaded by the Allied leaders to join the new provisional government in June 1945. Mikołajczyk's presence was useful only to give the new régime a better appearance of authenticity as it settled into power. But his renewed Peasant Party, one of the most powerful (and radical) forces in pre-war and wartime Poland, which represented the largest section of the population, was a dangerous rival to the PPR and its left-wing allies, and Gomułka set about breaking its power before the first elections were held. This was achieved by manoeuvring the PSL into untenable positions, by accusing Mikołajczyk of collusion with the surviving anti-Communist underground groups, and ultimately by a campaign of intimidation, mass arrests, physical violence and – almost certainly – electoral fraud. Although the Church instructed Catholics to vote against Communism, the declared results of the elections on 17 January 1947 gave the PPR-led 'democratic bloc' an overwhelming victory and left the Peasant Party with only 10·3 per cent of the vote. It was excluded from the new government, and in October 1947 Mikołajczyk left Poland for ever.

The PPR were scarcely more tender with the Polish Socialist Party. The PPS had accepted the joint 'democratic bloc' with the Communists for the elections, and much of its membership accepted also that a merger with the PPR was necessary. But there was strong opposition from other sections of the party who preferred close co-operation with the PPR to the loss of party independence, and it was not until the PPS leadership had carried out a purge of 'rightists' in the ranks that resistance was broken. The final fusion congress, at which the two parties jointly formed the Polish United Workers' Party (PUWP), did not take place until 15 December 1948.

By then Gomułka himself had already fallen, a victim of the first manifestations of Stalinist interference in Poland and, in a general sense, of the advancing glaciation of the Cold War. His version of a 'people's democracy' was denied the chance to develop beyond its founding struggles, and was brought to a sudden end before it could consolidate its compromise with public opinion in a period of relative stability.

Gomułka's methods of overcoming his opponents were often intolerant and unscrupulous, and his early assurances about broad alliances of 'democratic forces' turned out to be tactical rather than permanent. The unification of the PPR with the PPS, which he had almost achieved when he was deposed, left Poland in effect the one-party state which he had publicly forsworn a few years before. But the new régime did not, as its adversaries claimed, rest exclusively on a foundation of terror. The PPR accumulated a degree of popular support which the old KPP had never approached. In the later years of the German occupation, the London-led underground recognized that PPR influence was growing rapidly, even then, and that it would offer a formidable challenge after the war even if Poland did not pass under Soviet influence and occupation. By July 1944, the PPR had about 20,000 members, mostly old KPP veterans but strengthened by recruits from the left wing of the Peasant Party and the PPS.[8] After the liberation, membership went through violent fluctuations, rising to several hundred thousand in early 1945 and then plunging to some 65,000 later in the year as the result of both purges of unreliable new entrants and Mikołajczyk's revival of the Peasant Party. By 1946, PPR membership stood at some 235,000, still far smaller than the 600,000 which the Peasant Party could claim at its zenith in the same year.

The first task of Poland's provisional government was to reconstruct the shattered economy on a socialist basis, to rebuild the cities and to integrate the newly acquired Western Territories, also devastated by war, into the Polish state. All industries employing more than fifty workers per shift were nationalized, with compensation for the previous owners, and by late 1946 the state sector accounted for 91·2 per cent of industrial production.[9] This predominance of the state was meant to diminish as the economy recovered; the régime's policy, in plain contrast to Soviet practice, was to encourage an economy in which three sectors – state, co-operative, and private – functioned in harmony. This principle was carried on into a Three-Year Plan (1947–50) guided by gifted and undogmatic economists like Czesław Bobrowski and Oskar Lange, whose political background was socialist rather than Communist. The Plan laid emphasis on agriculture, which remained almost entirely in private hands, and on raising the individual standard of living and consumption.

In the few years before the Stalinist onslaught, this moderate, open and responsive form of socialism was thoroughly successful. Reconstruction, including the rebuilding of Warsaw, went ahead with a speed and energy which astonished the outside world. Living standards began to recover, and real wages rose above their pre-war levels. And the fundamental transformation of Polish society, which was later attributed to the vast mobilizations of the Stalinist period, took its first decisive steps as rapid industrialization began to draw people off the appallingly overcrowded countryside.[10] By 1948, the number of wage-earners was nearly double the total of ten years before. Large industrial plants, like the new steelworks of Nowa Huta near Kraków, were deliberately established in regions of the worst peasant over-population. This flexibility and effectiveness could not have been achieved if economic managers and planners at central and local levels had been recruited only from Party members or officials trained in blind obedience, as was to be the pattern in later years. In the Gomułka period, political loyalties mattered less than the qualification to do the job. It was this readiness to use non-Communist, patriotic enthusiasm and talent, to overlook political differences, which was the real promise of the Gomułka years. For a few, who had suffered wounds too grievous to forgive or whose ideology still equated co-operation with a Communist government with national and spiritual treason, this promise had no attractions. For most Poles, however, the 'Polish Road' to socialism began also to look like the path of patriotic common-sense. They did not for the most part agree with Gomułka's view of history, or relish the dominant Soviet connection. But the new régime tolerated the Church (in these years the leaders of Church and state attended each other's ceremonies), the land remained in private hands but very much more justly distributed than before, and the loss of the eastern borderlands with their non-Polish minorities meant that the nation had become ethnically homogeneous for the first time. The new Poland would, it seemed, be far stronger economically and socially than its predecessor.

Gomułka and the Cold War

The year 1947, when the suspicions and rivalry accumulating between the United States and the Soviet Union reached critical mass and became open confrontation, brought to an end the immediate post-war phase of eastern European politics. During this phase, the Soviet Union had consolidated the 'zone of influence' allotted to it in the wartime conferences between Churchill, Roosevelt and Stalin. But it had done so through coalition governments of 'democratic elements' in which the Communist Party usually acquired control without enforcing its own monopoly of politics. In Bulgaria, Communists led the Fatherland Front coalition, but an organized opposition survived until 1947. In Romania, the king managed to co-exist with Petru Groza's National Democratic Front until he was driven to abdicate in the same year. The Smallholders' Party remained the main party in the ruling Hungarian coalition until 1947, and in Czechoslovakia, where the Communists had emerged as the largest single party in fairly held elections in 1946, the non-Communist parties remained in government until twelve of their ministers resigned in February 1948. Only in Jugoslavia and Albania, which had not been liberated by Soviet forces and which Stalin was unable to influence directly, did Communist movements at once seize full power and embark on violently revolutionary programmes.

Poland obviously fitted into this pattern. The provisional government, in which the PPR shared the power with the PPS and left-wing peasant representatives, would not have come into existence if Stalin had not given it his broad approval. Stalin, it was argued, understood the Poles' complex historical attitudes and touchy independence, and recognized that to force the Soviet model, in all its repressive complexity, upon such a different society could only bring disaster. Time was needed. For the moment, he would be content with a 'progressive, democratic' government friendly to the Soviet Union. So at least people supposed. Then Stalin changed his mind.

Since then, we have come a good deal nearer to understanding what may have been in that mind. Little remains of the old western orthodoxy of the early Cold War. This held that Stalin meant from the outset to reduce the eastern European states to servile clones of the USSR, that he intended through the subversions of the western Communist parties to extend this zone of Europe to the Atlantic, and that the Cold War began because and when he launched this triple programme. Since then, and mostly during the sixties, a shelf-load of 'revisionist' histories of the early post-war period has appeared. Its effect has been to demolish or damage beyond repair all three assumptions. Stalin did not intend to 'sovietize' eastern Europe; he actually took steps to prevent the Italian and French Communist Parties using their enormous strength to control their political scenes; the Cold War was launched and declared – as a defensive measure – by the Americans.

The second and third points are well substantiated. It is the first, which greatly affects any view of future Polish–Soviet relations, which is not so clear. Poland, after all, is considerably the largest of Russia's western neighbours, and – because it both separates the USSR from and connects it to Germany – much the most important strategically. Was Stalin prepared indefinitely to live with a neighbour whose policies, though socialist, contradicted Soviet orthodoxy and whose leader, though a loyal Communist, might well defy him if he considered that the interests of Poland and the Soviet Union were in conflict?

Stalin brought the 'coalition' phase to an end after the proclamation of the Truman Doctrine for containment of Communism in 1947. What is not established is whether he would have done so in any case, sooner or later, without the stimulus of fear of an American campaign to undermine his European 'zone'. The Gomułka régime was not necessarily his final choice for Poland, for example. He had in the past played with other possibilities: an agreement with the London government, or members of it, which would have given him a 'bourgeois' Poland bound to the USSR by a pact; or a take-over by the commanders of the First Army, men like General Berling or the veteran leader of the International Brigades in Spain, General Świerczewski, which would have consigned liberated Poland to a sort of left-wing military junta. Stalin was certainly open-minded about the future constitution of the Polish state. After all, only five years before he had agreed with Hitler to abolish it altogether. Three years before that he had ordered the murder of the Polish Communist leaders and the abolition of their party. Stalin did not like or trust foreign Communists. Nationalism might provide a safer guarantee of foreign loyalty, it seemed to him, than ideological purity. This was probably a substantial motive for his acceptance of coalition régimes, and for his systematic discouragement of Communist enthusiasts who wanted an immediate dictatorship of the proletariat.

Isaac Deutscher considered that Stalin never finally made up his mind about the structure of the new régimes in eastern Europe until events dictated a new course. As early as 1949, Deutscher wrote: 'Stalin's actions show many strange and striking contradictions which do not indicate that he had any revolutionary master-plan. They suggest, on the contrary, that he had none.'[11] The intermediate condition of 'people's democracy', neither capitalist nor socialist, was a response to a variety of pressures and in particular expressed Stalin's hope that such moderation, as he saw it, would 'help him to preserve the condominium of the "Big Three"' which in the later war years had established the Soviet Union's status as a world power. The experiment in conciliation did not succeed in allaying the alarm of the West, but 'generated all the tension and friction which Stalin wished to prevent'.[12]

The 'people's democracies' of 1944–8 were hybrids, then, in more than a class sense. They were at once imposed from above ('the great party of the revolution, which remained in the background, was the Red Army'), and supported by varying proportions of the working class. Gomułka's unique achievement in the zone under Stalin's control was that his leadership began to transcend its origins and to root itself as an authentic political project. (Czechoslovakia, at this period, was not a 'people's democracy', and its post-war governments were not put together on Soviet instructions.)

The disillusion on the Polish left caused by his overthrow was correspondingly deep and corrosive.

The first symptoms of the gathering Cold War at once helped and hindered Gomułka. In September 1946, the United States revoked its approval of Poland's new western frontier on the Oder–Neisse line, although the victor powers had agreed to the frontier in principle at Teheran in 1943. In his 'Stuttgart speech', Secretary of State James Byrnes said that the United States would not ratify the Oder–Neisse border and that the question of how much German territory should have been ceded to Poland remained open. Byrnes had decided to play the German card against the Soviet Union, both by forcing Moscow to take the Polish side over the frontier dispute – thus alienating West German public opinion still further – and by implicitly giving American blessing to the grievances of the six or seven million Germans expelled from their homes beyond the Oder and Neisse rivers. Byrnes later wrote, 'Much of the support of the Communist cause in Germany began melting away ... As a result of our statement of policy, the sphere of influence the Soviets had hoped to extend into Berlin was moved back into Polish-controlled territory.'[13]

This change of American policy – which became western policy when Ernest Bevin, the British Foreign Secretary, adopted a similar attitude a month later – had profound effects on Poland. Non-Communists who still hoped for western support were undone at a stroke. The West now appeared ready to support a revived West German power in its ambition to seize back lands which all Poles considered to be historically Polish. Byrnes's speech, seized upon by the PPR and its allies in the election campaign, dealt a crippling blow to Mikołajczyk and his pro-western Peasant Party supporters. By successfully forcing the Russians to come off the fence – since the Potsdam Conference in the summer of 1945, Soviet utterances about the frontiers had tended to take one line with German audiences and another with the Poles – the speech also reinforced Gomułka's claim that the Soviet alliance was the foundation of Poland's *raison d'état* and the indispensable condition of the survival of any Polish state. The threat of 'German revanchism' had been born, the most effective – indeed, almost the only – hold on genuine popular support which was available to subsequent Polish leaders for the next twenty-four years.

But if Byrnes's Stuttgart speech strengthened Gomułka's position in the short run, it undermined the foundations of his régime in a less obvious way. This provisional government had sought good relations with the West, relying on the survival of warm feelings from the anti-Hitler coalition and Poland's prestige as a second-line victorious power in that coalition.

An economic connection with the United States was developing: Poland borrowed $40 million from America in April 1946, and at first responded gladly to the Marshall Plan in mid-1947. Polish diplomacy discreetly amassed good contacts throughout the western world, on the assumption that Poland's independence required a broad spread of relationships. The lack of inhibition in those days can be measured by a joking remark made to journalists by Oskar Lange, in 1946 the Polish Ambassador in Washington: 'If Britain, for example, came out in defence of our Oder frontier and the Soviet Union opposed it, then we would vote against the Soviet Union in the international arena.'[14] But after Byrnes's Stuttgart speech, and well before the violently anti-western mood of Stalinism possessed the Polish foreign ministry, Poland's relationship with the western world began to deteriorate. The government lost much of the international room for manoeuvre which was so important an element of its relative independence within the Soviet alliance. And the Soviet Union gained an irrefutable argument for co-ordinating Polish foreign policy more closely with its own.

For the next quarter-century, a generation of Polish diplomats laboured to re-open a distinctive 'Polish Road' in foreign policy. But the West's refusal to dismiss West German demands for the old frontiers of 1937 – in London and Washington, a cynical and in fact quite unnecessary policy designed to keep the Federal Republic safely anti-Russian – hung round the necks of those persevering men and women like a millstone. Its removal became their central purpose. Poland, alone in the Soviet bloc, never ceased entirely to have an authentic foreign policy of its own, even when its special tone was almost drowned in Soviet orchestrations at the most intense period of the Cold War.

No peace treaty was ever concluded after the Second World War. Polish policy was to fill this gap by a European security settlement which recognized its new post-war frontiers as permanent. After such a settlement, it was hoped, the confronting military blocs would begin to dissolve, and the smaller nations of Europe would rebuild their contacts across the dividing line. The United States and Russia would relax their concern for political uniformity within their blocs, and Poland would once again enjoy the right to shape both foreign and internal policy according to Polish needs and interests. None of this was possible until the Federal Republic and its NATO allies recognized the permanence of the Oder–Neisse border as Poland's western frontier.*

* That West German recognition, finally conceded in December 1970, is usually held to be the result of the Bonn government's *Ostpolitik*, the campaign led by the Social Democrats and Chancellor Willy Brandt in particular which persuaded West German opinion to accept the

The Stuttgart speech was followed in March 1947 by President Truman's message to Congress which expressed what has become known as the Truman Doctrine. Communism was to be contained, he argued, and the United States would support any nation that resisted Communism. This was a global declaration of Cold War, but most American actions immediately after it were defensive. Byrnes had in effect abandoned the idea of maintaining four-power control over Germany in favour of a split: the western zones of occupation would now be drawn into an Anglo-American protectorate and screened off from possible Communist infection from the east. The Marshall Plan, announced in June 1947, was a larger act in this preventive strategy. Ostensibly, Marshall Plan aid was offered for the reconstruction of all European countries. In practice, the plan was designed to be unacceptable to the Soviet Union. Its effect would be to oblige European states to choose between one economic system and the other and to erect another plague-barrier down the middle of Europe. Stalin violently rejected the Marshall Plan terms, as he was intended to. Poland was immediately the victim. At first much attracted by the Marshall Plan outline, the Polish government was soon obliged by Soviet pressure to refuse it.

In these years, the Poles learned once again that they were classified as the eggs that have to be broken to make omelettes. This time, they were learning it at American hands. It was not that American policy, before or after March 1947, was anti-Polish. It would have given American statesmen pleasure to have ratified the new frontiers of a Polish state, to have contributed to the rebuilding of the Old Town in Warsaw or to the provision of new machinery for wrecked factories. But holding Communism on the Elbe line mattered more. To this end, Germans in the western occupied zones were showered with money and nourished with ludicrous dreams of reconquest, while the Poles – who had suffered so terribly for their loyalty to the anti-Nazi coalition – were excluded.

Stalin now rapidly tightened his grasp on eastern Europe. In September 1947, there was held in Poland the founding meeting of the Cominform, the new council of the Communist movement which was to express its unity and discipline under Soviet leadership. Gomułka went to this meeting with heavy misgivings. The existence of a body of this kind, reviving in a debased form the internationalism of the pre-war Comintern, would shackle his party

---

realities of the lost war and seek reconciliation with Germany's eastern neighbours. But the *Ostpolitik* was also in large measure the result of Polish *Westpolitik*. For many years, the Poles combined friendly overtures with harsh moral pressure and a shrewd refusal to settle for anything less than total recognition of the Oder–Neisse line.

to some servile consensus. If the PPR accepted Cominform policies, there could be no authentic 'Polish Road', and public opinion would relapse into the assumption that all Communists served Moscow first and their own countries a long way afterwards.

Gomułka seems not to have expressed his dislike of the very idea of the Cominform. But when the conference was invited to pass a resolution calling for the collectivization of agriculture, on the Soviet model, he rebelled. For years, he and his colleagues in the PPR had assured the Polish peasantry that they would be allowed to keep their land. He had condemned as malevolent provocation every rumour that the private farms, many of them little bigger than large gardens, would soon be confiscated and melted down into great kolkhozes. There was a growing but still very fragile tendency amongst Poles to believe him. Now he was supposed to break his promise, to abandon the feature of his rule that, more than any other, offered a guarantee that the 'people's democracy' would respect the needs and wishes of the Polish people. He fought against the resolution, demanding an emergency meeting of the PPR Central Committee, but he was overruled.

Gomułka's rebellion had two main consequences. It showed the Communist leaders assembled at the Cominform congress that he was prepared to defend the concept of 'national' Communism even if it meant, in effect, defying Stalin. Nine months before the breach between Stalin and Tito, Gomułka made himself the first leader of a ruling Communist party to resist the Soviet Union's claim to direct the internal policies of eastern Europe.

Secondly, the row undermined Gomułka's own position within the PPR. The Party had inherited two characteristics from the old KPP: a readiness (especially among those Communists who had remained in Poland throughout the Nazi occupation) to resist unwelcome instructions from Moscow, even when they were issued in the name of the world movement, and a tendency to schism and factionalism which endures to this day. The group around Bolesław Bierut, who had returned from Moscow after the war, had never been entirely accepted by the larger body of Communists who had spent those years in Poland in the resistance; the instinctive nationalism of this 'partisan' faction worried the Bierut group increasingly as the years passed. The 'Muscovites' lacked the self-confidence of those who had fought in the resistance. In Russian exile, they had been trained to accept the infallibility of the great Stalin, and the superior experience of the Communist Party of the Soviet Union in revolutionary strategy. After the quarrels at the Cominform founding conference, Bierut and his allies laid more coherent plans for the removal of Gomułka and the return of the Party to a more orthodox course. The division in the Party leadership was evident, although Stalin was not yet alarmed enough to demand Gomułka's summary removal. But it would be wrong to explain Gomułka's fall and the victory of Stalinism as merely the consequence of external or semi-external factors, as Stalin's response to the coming of the Cold War expressed through a conspiracy by a pro-Moscow Party group in Poland. Polish Stalinism had a genuine internal dynamic as well.

Revolutions display a famous tendency to accelerate. The impatience of the Jacobins overtook the Girondins in the French Revolution, as the impatience of Russian Communists overtook the moderates of the New Economic Policy in the late 1920s. The Polish revolution, for all its initial lack of spontaneity, was no exception.

Among younger Party members, and among intellectuals especially, a fanatical enthusiasm chafed at the compromises and restraints of these early years.* Like their Soviet predecessors in the last years of the New Economic Policy, these militants feared that the revolution was moving too slowly. They were aware of the enormous surviving strength of right-wing ideology in the Polish Church and peasantry. Many of them had taken part in the civil war which lasted into 1947, and to them armed counter-revolution was no mere abstraction. They also resented the tens of thousands of late-comers in the Party, many of whom were certainly careerists or people with a negligible commitment to Marxism–Leninism. Towards Stalin, these young militants were usually uncritical. It was the Polish revolution they were worried about; they wanted to complete it and to crush its enemies, before those enemies could revive and organize themselves.

Gomułka and his inner group of supporters, most of whom were veterans of the underground partisan struggle against the Nazi occupation, survived for the moment. Not until June 1948, when Stalin's dispute with the increasingly independent Tito reached its climax and prompted him to seek full, despotic control of the other ruling parties in his bloc, did the plan to depose Gomułka move into operation. Gomułka took no evasive action. In a speech on 3 June, a few weeks before Jugoslavia was expelled from the Cominform, he stoutly repeated his heresies. It was the socialists, he said, and not the leftist SDKPiL, who had assessed the situation correctly

---

*Typical of these radicals was the young Leszek Kołakowski, later to change his views and to emerge in the late sixties as the intellectual inspiration of a moderate, 'liberal' Communism. There is a good description of Kołakowski in the post-war years in K. S. Karoi, *Visa for Poland* (London, 1959), pp. 222–4.

in 1918, because only they had understood the necessity of 'bourgeois' independence for Poland. While insisting that the bond with the Soviet Union was now the guarantee of Polish independence, he denounced those who wanted to apply abstract, ultra-revolutionary solutions to the country. This speech was a sufficient excuse for Gomułka's enemies to act. Throughout the summer of 1948, Bierut (who now commanded a majority on the ruling Politburo of the Party) attacked Gomułka for his mistaken attitudes and tried to extract from him a confession of his 'rightist-nationalist' views. Gomułka was dismissed as secretary of the PPR on 3 September, and Bierut took his place.

Polish Stalinism

The Stalinist epoch in Poland was at once sinister and grotesque, a period in which the Party ruled through open police terror. National traditions – social, cultural and religious – were challenged and violated. Economic development was distorted by a breakneck campaign for industrialization which deliberately neglected consumption; its achievements were measured by crude production targets, arbitrarily set and mendaciously reported. Poland was opened to almost uncontrolled Soviet economic exploitation, through one-sided terms of trade, while the bureaucracy was in some areas thoroughly penetrated by Soviet advisers. All this was accompanied by deafening propaganda devoted to imaginary successes and to equally imaginary espionage or subversion plots against the régime.

These were miserable and humiliating years. Under the pressures of fear or fanaticism, many Poles acted and spoke in ways they prefer to forget. In contemporary Poland, it is very much easier to hear reminiscences about the Piłsudski period or the occupation than about this time. All the same, the Stalinist episode was not so uniformly and ultimately evil as it might have been.

In the first place, it lasted a remarkably short time. Stalinism became intense in Poland in 1949; its force was rapidly dissipating by early 1954. Secondly, not all its achievements were negative: Poland emerged from the experience with a heavy industrial base of which much, at least, became of permanent value under more rational management. Society became more mobile, opportunity increased and the balance of population between the rural and industrial work-forces was vigorously and permanently altered. All these were aims that had been set by Gomułka's relatively moderate

Three-Year Plan, now carried through with very different and far more brutal methods. Lastly, the repressions of Stalinism in Poland were significantly less savage than in other states in the Soviet bloc. It was not merely that no period of terror could easily match the horrors of the Nazi occupation. It was that, in a variety of ways, the Bierut dictatorship was unwilling to drive Stalin's policies to their ultimate conclusion.

It can be argued that what Stalinism omitted to do in Poland is at least as important for the 1970s and 1980s as what it actually did. But in those years it was the dark side of Stalinism that naturally impressed the Poles. Convinced that the West was preparing for an imperialist war against the USSR, the new Polish leaders rapidly brought to an end the modest tolerance of the Gomułka period. After Gomułka's removal and before the unification congress that fused the PPS and the PPR into the Polish United Workers' Party (PUWP) in December 1948, the PPR expelled some 50,000 members. Another 100,000 were purged in 1949, many of them ex-members of the PPS. A third wave of purges removed about 160,000 more until the leadership blocked further wholesale expulsions in 1951. The management of the economy, the public services and the state bureaucracy were cleansed of all 'unreliable elements': those with middle-class origins, or with records of service under the pre-war régime, or even service with the AK, the non-Communist underground army, during the war. Those who had relatives in the West, or who had fought on western fronts during the war and returned to Poland, were also victimized. They were replaced by Party loyalists, often workers without any qualifications for their high posts beyond 'sound' class origin and a crash course of some kind at a Party training centre. Bierut stated in 1950 that he had already appointed 17,000 workers as factory directors.[15]

The armed forces were transformed and expanded. Conscription was introduced in 1949 to produce a strength of nearly 400,000 men: the largest military force in western Europe. Pre-war professional officers and many officers who had fought with the Communist partisans during the Nazi occupation – and could therefore be assumed to be loyal to Władysław Gomułka – were removed and in many cases arrested. Soviet influence and control were more effective here than in any other area of Polish life. Military organizations, training, tactics and uniforms were altered to Soviet patterns. There had been a strong Soviet presence in the officer corps of the Polish armies fighting on the eastern front alongside the Red Army (perhaps a third); many of these men were now brought back to Poland, until the positions of chief of the general staff, commander of ground forces, heads of all the service branches and commanders of all military districts were held by Soviet officers. Hundreds of supplementary Soviet military advisers were brought in. Finally, Marshal Konstantin Rokossowski, one of Stalin's senior wartime commanders, who was of Polish origin, became minister of defence and commander-in-chief in 1949.* It has been justly observed that 'the result was the transformation of the Polish army into an essentially extra-national force', as directly subordinated to Moscow as a Soviet military district.[16]

The trade unions, which had been a stronghold of socialist supporters, were taken over in 1949. Two purges, in that and the following year, changed more than 80 per cent of local union officials. A new Central Council of Trade Unions (CRZZ) was instructed that its duties were to assist the drive for increased production and to enforce factory discipline; in a society building socialism, the traditional task of unions to protect their members' interests was no longer necessary. Much play was made with carefully selected quotations from Lenin, like his remark that 'the most common and shared interest of the whole working class is the existence of a people's state, whose economic and political development guarantees the creation of appropriate conditions for the continuous improvement of the material and cultural condition of the working people'. Lenin's views of the relationship between trade unions and Party under the dictatorship of the proletariat are in fact ambiguous. They certainly do not prescribe the total and continuous control of the unions at all levels which the Party now established in Poland. Although living standards were now rapidly declining, the government set wage rates without consultation with the unions, lengthened the working week, and in 1950 passed through the limp sessions of the Sejm (the Polish parliament) legislation that in effect bound workers to their jobs and introduced an almost military code of discipline over time-keeping.

In the rush and chaos of the Stalinist industrialization drive, with thousands of raw peasants flooding into the new factories and construction sites, standards of health and safety dissolved. The government introduced a Polish version of 'Stakhanovite' competition (named after the pre-war Soviet hero of labour who had set a fashion for achieving astronomical personal production targets). Andrzej Wajda's 1976 film *Man of Marble* has recalled the sullen hatred which these 'heroes' aroused in the Polish working class. Their feats were usually followed by a general raising of production targets for each shift, and – as in the Soviet Union in the

---

* Rokossowski, an honourable man who developed doubts about the Stalinist system, was reluctant to take the post. But Bierut insisted on the appointment, apparently calculating that it would improve Poland's credit with Moscow and that he could handle Rokossowski.

1930s – there were cases of violence against Stakhanovites. A folk-rhyme records the fate of one Janusz Przyboski, who was supposed to have been battered to death by his mates in a dark mine gallery after a prodigy of coal-hewing. The workers, in title the rulers of Poland's new society, were now its most helpless and exploited section. Deprived of the normal means of self-defence, they were regularly herded to triumphant demonstrations. Their submissiveness was ensured by a system of confidential files kept by the state on their behaviour and attitudes; most personnel officers were in the service of the security police. As in other eastern European economies subjected to Stalinism, standards of work and honesty collapsed. In spite of the close surveillance and penalties, there was widespread absenteeism, theft of materials for the black market, and falsification of production statistics.

Outward appearances in Poland became more Russian. Polish soldiers wore a version of Russian uniform; hotels introduced the Russian *'dezhurnaya'*, the dragon-lady who policed exits and entrances on each floor. New architecture produced equivalents of the amazing sugar-cake skyscrapers of the Soviet Union, culminating in Warsaw's Palace of Culture, Stalin's 'gift to the Polish people', which for many years dwarfed the capital under a monolith that soared from a Palladian base through medieval Russian crenellations to a vaguely Orthodox onion spire. Polish literature, which had revived vigorously after the war, put up brave resistance to the ideological demands of Jakub Berman, the Politburo member in charge of culture, but the Soviet version of 'socialist realism' was imposed after purges of the Writers' Union leadership in 1950. Most of Poland's better writers fell silent, and little of any quality was produced in the new style. The vivid and experimental tradition of Polish painting and graphics was similarly strangled, and replaced by solemnly literal canvasses of workers with bulging muscles or chests heaving with righteous indignation. The best-known of these, Kobzdej's mighty 'Pass Me a Brick', was re-exhibited to fascinated Warsaw crowds in early 1980.

The energies of the new leadership centred on the Six-Year Plan (1950–55), guided by the State Commission for Economic Planning set up under Hilary Minc, minister of industry and trade. Gomułka's Three-Year Plan had been a striking success, and the new plan inherited much genuine enthusiasm and commitment, but its targets, hastily revised upward to meet Soviet demands, were hopelessly romantic. Industrial production was to rise by 158 per cent, agricultural production by more than 50 per cent and per capita consumption by 50–60 per cent. The proportion of national income devoted to capital investment (mostly heavy industry) actually did rise as high as 38·2 per cent in 1953, but housing, social services and the requirements of personal consumption were starved of finance. Peasant agriculture was badly neglected. Small private workshops and services were halved, and private shops vanished. The programme for reducing surplus rural population, initiated by the Three-Year Plan, ran entirely out of control: when more than three quarters of a million workers poured from the fields to the factories, this had the double result of inflating industrial work-forces far beyond economic requirements and depriving agriculture of the young and active labour needed to maintain food production.

Agriculture and the future of the private peasantry was the issue that had brought Gomułka into his first open conflict with Stalin and with the orthodox elements in his own party. His post-war land reform had given the individual peasants full ownership of their land for the first time; all estates and farms of arable land larger than fifty hectares were broken up, and six million hectares were redistributed to the peasants. Many of these new farms were exceedingly small, but in the regions taken from Germany, the Polish settlers were able to establish more viable holdings averaging between five and ten hectares.

The day after Gomułka's dismissal as Secretary, on 4 September 1948, the Party declared that Polish agriculture would now be collectivized on a supposedly 'voluntary' basis. But little was achieved. So much publicity was given to the dissolution of the collective farms in 1956 that the impression arose that the landscape had been almost wholly turned over to the 'kolkhoz' system during the Stalinist years. But the truth was that by 1955 no more than 9·2 per cent of Poland's arable land had been transferred to collectives. This did not include the areas, especially in the thinly settled Western Territories, which had been organized after 1945 into 'state farms', large nationalized units worked by paid labourers distinct from the 'kolkhoz' collective farms, which were in theory partnerships jointly owned by a community of peasants.

To have imposed collectivization on Poland would have involved something little short of an armed invasion and occupation of the countryside. For all its huge security forces and police and squads of young Party enthusiasts who might have been recruited in the cities for the job, this was too much for the régime. Instead, a modest programme of collectivization was accompanied by systematic discrimination and harassment against private farmers. Compulsory food deliveries at low prices were often enforced by violence and the imprisonment of peasants who resisted. Penal taxation weighed down the larger and more efficient peasants. Investment earmarked for agriculture either did not arrive or was mostly diverted to state farms and collectives. The countryside sank into sullen passive resistance; bad harvests and reluctance to plant crops or breed livestock reduced agricultural production, required by the Plan to increase by half again in six years.

The Six-Year Plan provoked the first of the prices-and-wages crises that were to recur, with growing intensity, until twenty years later they came to dictate the whole political process in Poland.[17] Acute shortages of food and goods in the shops began in 1951, and rationing was introduced. Then, in January 1953, a general price rise was decreed that restored some sort of balance between prices and purchasing power. There was no significant public protest at this price increase. From this episode, later Polish governments drew the fatal conclusion that inflationary pressure caused by retail shortages could be solved by sweeping overnight price increases. But as the police terror relaxed after 1956 and the population grew less intimidated, this technique became increasingly dangerous.

Terror was indispensable to the policies of the Bierut régime. At the outset, there had been something about the Six-Year Plan – its furious haste to make Poland 'catch up' with industrialized nations, its wildly ambitious targets, its contempt for the restraining pleas of experts – that appealed to Polish tradition. Polish economists, among the most original and influential in the world, have always had to grab at the stirrups of politicians convinced that economic obstacles could be stormed by a cavalry charge. The under-development of Poland was tackled like another Somosierra.* But this early enthusiasm, never universal, soon died away in the muddy reality of growing poverty, lies and official lawlessness. As Bieńkowski would put it, 'political dictatorship' gave way to 'police dictatorship'. The Security Office (known usually by its Polish initials as the UB) swelled into an elaborate bureaucracy, with agents or informers in every cell of the body public. The justifying slogan was that 'revolutionary vigilance' must be maintained against imperialist spies and saboteurs who, as the Cold War grew more bitter, were supposed to be infesting Poland. There were numerous trials, many ending in death sentences, few based on any evidence more

---

*The battle of Somosierra (30 November 1808). Commanded by Colonel Kozietulski, the Polish light cavalry of Napoleon's Imperial Guard charged a force of Spanish insurrectionaries who had blocked the pass of Somosierra with stone walls and defended it with cannon. In addition, the pass was covered with thick fog. Several Poles emerged alive at the other end of the pass. Napoleon, seeing the charge begin, is supposed to have asked, 'Are these men mad?' 'No, sire,' replied an aide-de-camp, 'they are Poles.' The Poles find Somosierra at once immensely moving and irresistibly funny. Only the English have the same habit of expressing patriotism through self-mockery.

genuine than suspicion of an individual's political views. Torture was used on occasion to extract confessions. The powers of the UB to carry through the entire pseudo-judicial process, from arrest to execution of sentence, often entirely bypassed the law. In 1952, the UB established its most intimate and powerful section: the secret Tenth Department, whose duty was to keep the Party itself – including the whole PUWP leadership, with the two exceptions of Bierut and Rokossowski – under surveillance. When required, the Tenth Department would provide material to justify the arrest of a Party member or his demotion. The proudest achievements of the UB in these years were the arrest, after much dithering, of Gomułka in July 1951 and the trials of senior churchmen on nonsensical charges which finally led to the confinement of the Primate, Cardinal Stefan Wyszyński, in a monastery.

It is time to set the period in some perspective. Stalinism was a structure pulled into various forms in the various eastern European countries that experienced it but composed everywhere of much the same elements. It was a disease – an abstract structure manifested through symptoms that vary from patient to patient. Poland, though badly infected and weakened in its very constitutional bones, displayed many of the Stalinist symptoms in far less severe form than did Hungary or Czechoslovakia. This had two results. One was good: the misery inflicted on individuals was simply less. The other was subtly disastrous: the relative mildness of Polish Stalinism meant that its traces were never entirely thrown off.

A list of the non-achievements of the Bierut years is worth inspecting. The private peasantry was not, except marginally, collectivized. The Catholic Church was not broken down to submission, although 300,000 hectares of land were confiscated and at least one bishop (Kaczmarek of Kielce) was put on trial for organizing an 'anti-state centre'. And the police terror, over the population and the Party apparatus, was never as effective as it was in many of Poland's neighbours. There were executions for political 'crimes', but fewer than in Hungary and confined to less senior offenders. There were labour camps, but less murderous than those in Czechoslovakia at the same period. Above all, the Polish revolution was reluctant to devour its own children. In Bulgaria, Romania, Hungary and Czechoslovakia, Communists were arrested by the thousand and Party leaders were submitted to torture, forced to learn their confessions and executed after show trials. The most senior Communist to be tortured by the UB, Gomułka's colleague and friend Marian Spychalski, was never brought to trial. Above all, the case of Władysław Gomułka himself showed the unwillingness of the Bierut leadership to carry the campaign against 'rightist-nationalists' to the ultimate conclusions demanded by Stalin.

Gomułka was the most obvious victim in all eastern Europe for a show trial. The UB would have been delighted to have battered Gomułka into a confession and to have cooked up any evidence against him. But after his arrest the Politburo left him untouched for a long while, apparently divided about how to handle him. When they gave leave for his interrogation, without physical methods of pressure, he refused to co-operate. He was never put in a prison, but held in a special villa on the outskirts of Warsaw. Some preparations for a trial were made; his parliamentary immunity was lifted, after the wretched Spychalski was forced to testify in a case against a group of ex-AK officers that Gomułka had connived at the admission of an agent of the émigré government into the post-war Polish army. The press screamed that the fallen Party Secretary was an ally of the class traitor Tito. But no trial ever took place. Stalin died in March 1953; Gomułka was quietly released the following year.

Why Bierut held back is a matter of speculation. The pressure for a grand trial of Gomułka and his associates, applied by the Soviet Union and the Soviet-led secret police in other countries of the bloc, was acute. One explanation is that Gomułka seemed simply too tough a nut to crack; in court, he would have denounced the Party leaders as co-responsible for the decisions for which he was being tried. Another theory suggests that even Bierut, deep in his complex personality, harboured resistance to Soviet dictation. He understood the latent dissensions within his Party and shared its trauma over the fate of the KPP leaders in the 1930s. To kill another generation of leaders would shatter the Party's morale and ensure that the victims would be avenged.

This combination of brutality and half-measures ensured that future Communist régimes in Poland would be faced with monstrous problems. The most obvious consequences of Stalinism were the distortion of the Polish economy and the reinforcement of anti-Communist and anti-Soviet passions among the people. The working class was deeply alienated. The management of the economy and the administration had passed into the hands of ignorant Party loyalists.

But beyond these effects, the very caution of Polish Stalinism had created problems without solving them. The peasantry had not been destroyed as a class, but it had been bullied and mismanaged sufficiently to establish a loathing and suspicion of the authorities that was never overcome. The Church had not been forced into surrender, but its persecution had been sufficiently intense to increase its hold on the masses. The confiscation of

Church lands in 1950, in particular, helped to complete changes that were already taking place. During the war and the German occupation, the Church had suffered with the rest of Poland – 1,800 priests, nearly a fifth of the total, were murdered – and had become a centre of popular resistance. After the liberation, the new generation of both clergy and laity had no wish to return to the class-based and often anti-democratic attitudes of the pre-war hierarchy. The fact that the Church was no longer a landowner helped to reinforce the Church's hold over the rural population – and thus, through the migration to the cities, to establish an authority in the industrial working class which it never possessed before the war.

Finally, the relative security of Party officials in the Stalinist period, especially at local level, encouraged the growth of almost immovable power cliques. This was part of a noxious but paradoxical pattern. On the one hand, the state apparatus and the management of the economy became over-centralized, regulating everything (on paper) and leaving no room for local initiative. On the other, the Party acquired a huge 'middle apparatus' of local secretaries with their own bureaucracies who rapidly learned how to impede or ignore inconvenient new instructions from Warsaw. It is hard to resist the conclusion that if this permanent apparatus had been as thoroughly terrorized during the Stalinist years as it was in most of the other states in the bloc, it would have been very much more co-operative and obedient when the time came, after the overthrow of Stalinism in 1956, to liberalize both the economy and the political style of Poland. As it was, the 'middle apparatus' survived to be a dead-weight on any project for change in the decades ahead. In Warsaw, bright young reformers would proclaim the market economy and say fulsome things about the patriotism of the Catholic hierarchy. Down in the grimy square of a provincial town, the Party Secretary continued diverting resources into useless factories and setting the police to rough up an awkward priest. The PUWP, in short, was never comprehensively purged, and suffers from it still.

The same bureaucratic fungus accreted round the supreme bodies of the Party. The staff of the Central Committee departments and the secretariat proliferated. So did their paperwork. At the same time, the dozen or so men who formed the ruling group refused – in true revolutionary style – to delegate responsibility. This was a pattern common to all Stalinized ruling Communist Parties.[18] Its results were inevitable. The Politburo members, often men of limited intellect, were faced with mountainous policy papers they had little chance to read. These documents, drafted by Central Committee bureaucrats after a concealed power struggle among themselves, offered no choices and were usually endorsed without real debate.

Politburo discussions had a dream-like quality. One witness remembers from this period how Jakub Berman, after listening to Bierut's views, would start his speech with the words: 'Comrade "Tomasz" is absolutely right ...' and then make precisely the opposite point; Bierut, nodding sagely, would then pronounce entire approval of Comrade Jakub's statement. This system survived Gomułka's return to power in 1956 and indeed survived into 1981. Another participant recalls a Politburo debate on the budget and plan, some time after 1956, in which a 3,000-page draft document had been provided for each member. Only Gomułka, an incurable work addict, had read it. After a three-hour row over some quite trivial detail, in which Gomułka repeatedly lost his temper, the rest of the budget plan was passed unexamined.

Thus it can hardly be argued that the Polish Stalinists formed an iron-willed revolutionary junta. The decision-making system they unfortunately bequeathed to their successors had three results: it paralysed Poland's official leadership; it enormously encouraged the tendency to form factions in the higher Party bureaucracy; and it placed real power in the hands of anyone – not always the First Secretary – who could pack the departments of the central apparatus with his own supporters. The government, meanwhile, was expected merely to carry out the Party policies evolved in this curious fashion.

Stalinism, in Poland and elsewhere, was not simply a phenomenon of police terror, Stalin-worship and tight rations. It was more than just an economic policy of reckless industrialization. It was also a much less easily definable set of methods of government and administration, based on an enormous bureaucracy whose careers – and privileges – depended upon group loyalty rather than upon real ability.

It was this aspect of Stalinization that the programmes of de-Stalinization in eastern Europe usually failed to root out. The failure was implicit in the fact that these programmes were carried out by the Party itself. The apparatus, central and local, was not only an executive force carrying out Party decisions; it also provided the largest single group in the controlling body of each Party, the Central Committee. If it were too brusquely attacked, it might turn against a reforming leadership and transfer its loyalty to a more conservative faction. Even Alexander Dubček, in the reform months of 1968 in Czechoslovakia, hardly made a dent in this problem, and an inordinate amount of his time was spent in the manipulation of factions within the apparatus and the Party.

In 1955–6, the PUWP threw off many of the abuses of Stalinism. But the underlying Stalinist architecture of Party and state was not greatly affected. In any small town in Poland, 'democratization' meant that the cinema manager and the director of the boot factory no longer had to keep a log-book of all their telephone calls to show to the UB. But the same Party secretary almost certainly sat at his glass-topped desk among his rubber-plants, savoured his glass of tea, and then ambled into the conference room to confront almost the same ruling group of old cronies. The agenda might include items inconceivable to them all a few years before: the formation of workers' councils, or the removal of an over-zealous public prosecutor. On the wall, a paler rectangle recalled the whiskered face with its dark, watchful eyes which had been so recently taken down. But one has to move with the times. For those who were created by Stalinism in Poland, it was often surprisingly easy to adapt and survive.

The 'Polish October' of 1956: A Last Chance

The upheavals that culminated in the 'Polish October' did not begin with Stalin's death in March 1953. For once, Poland remained calmer than other states in the Soviet bloc. Although some Party intellectuals collapsed in bereavement, Bierut could find consolation in the timing of Stalin's exit. Various show trials of 'rightist-nationalists', which Bierut had contrived to put off for so long, would probably be unnecessary now. In other countries of the Soviet bloc, these trials had acquired a frantic element of 'anti-Zionism', and Stalin himself had expired at the climax of a fresh attack of anti-Semitic paranoia. Bierut's Jewish colleagues, Berman and Minc in particular, would not now have to fear that they might share the fate of Rudolf Slánský and his fellow-victims in Czechoslovakia, or of the Jewish doctors who were accused in Moscow of plotting to kill Stalin.

The first outbreak of popular protest in eastern Europe since 1948 came soon after Stalin's funeral, but did not touch Poland at all. In late May 1953, a series of strikes led to demonstrations at Plzeň, in Czechoslovakia. In mid-June, a far larger revolt took place in the German Democratic Republic, a working-class protest which began in East Berlin and spread to other cities. Poland remained quiet and was slow to follow the 'New Course' of economic and political relaxation – a discreet release of political prisoners, a hint of criticism in the press, a little more to eat for everyone – which was prescribed by Malenkov and the Soviet collective leadership that succeeded Stalin.

When Bierut began his own 'New Course', in late 1953 and 1954, the results were uneven. Almost nothing changed for the hard-pressed industrial workers; a slight slow-down in the pace of capital investment was hardly perceived. The peasantry did rather better; the pressure on them to join collectives slackened, and cuts in taxes and in the forced deliveries of produce to the state gave them the economic incentive to grow more grain and raise more pigs for sale on the private market. For the intellectuals, however, life in 1954 became decidedly more interesting. It was possible once again to be critical. How far that criticism could go had to be established by trial and error. Censorship was still tight. For journalists, the limits meant that examples of the crassest dogmatism could be sniped at, always from the perspective of 'correcting' errors in the 'building of socialism'. Stalinist orthodoxy in the social sciences, never much more than a façade, began to show a network of cracks. Above all, the intellectuals were challenging the barriers sealing Poland off from western cultural life. The sense that a new start must be made was strong; the nation was starving for genuine discussion, fresh ideas and the intoxicating taste of the truth.

While social and intellectual unrest built up beneath them, the Party leaders wrangled interminably about the pace and scale of change. But the authority of the Bierut dictatorship was now beginning to dissolve. In late 1954, Radio Free Europe in Munich started to broadcast in instalments the memoirs of Józef Światło, a leading U B officer from the Tenth Department who had defected to the West not long after Stalin's death. Światło now proceeded to enthral and horrify the Polish public with intimate gossip about the operations of the police state. Światło described how, with torture and blackmail, heroes of the resistance and loyal Communists had been morally broken and in some cases driven insane. He named names, and the matchless rumour network of Poland constantly confirmed or enlarged on his reports. His revelations had two effects: they exposed the true extent of Soviet interference and penetration in Poland – a few months before his broadcasts began, the Soviet ambassador was still inspecting the proposed list of delegates to a PUWP congress and crossing out many names – and they concentrated attention on the fate of Gomułka and his colleagues. For years, not a word about them had been heard. Now their memory, as a coherent group standing for a more humane and democratic politics, was powerfully and probably deliberately restored (the content of Światło's broadcasts was to an unknown extent a co-production with American intelligence). Those who listened to Światło were invited to think of the Gomułka group not only as victims but as an alternative.

In the prelude to 1956, and in the flavour of 'the October' itself, the generations came to matter. It was important to be young, and the demands, defiances and exultations of the young were also a sort of programme. Those who were twenty in 1956 had memories of the Nazi occupation, but hardly of Poland before the war. Those who were in their middle or late twenties had in many cases taken part as girls or boys in resistance work or – in Warsaw – acted as runners during the Rising. Both groups had been gathered into the Union of Polish Youth (ZMP): even if they had not followed ZMP encouragement to denounce and correct their teachers, they had often laboured in the voluntary youth construction brigades which the ZMP organized.

For the older among them, especially, there was a sense of lost years. A man who had been a boy during the occupation could now be thirty and understand, for the first time, that he had never been young. The entrancing sounds of jazz, which all eastern Europeans associated with self-expression and freedom, drifted in more loudly from the West. Perhaps the chance had come to make up for that lost time.

Then, in the summer of 1955, something unbelievable happened. The World Youth Festival was held in Warsaw. For the young, this was a moment even more marvellous than the political upheaval of the following year. With the more dutiful delegations from the 'socialist bloc', thousands of French and Italian, Brazilian and African students and young people poured into the city. They brought with them not only the truth about living conditions in the industrial West, but their clothes, their music, their way of talking. They burst in like a relief force, after six years of total isolation from the non-Communist world. They left behind them a furious impatience for change and a determination that such isolation must never return.

And yet this was not at all a sceptical, hedonist, 'me' generation. In the West, socialists talked anxiously about the necessity for 'engagement' and 'commitment', a positive faith which could survive the demolition of Stalin's cult. The young Poles had commitment exactly of this type, which is one of the reasons why 'the October' moved the western left so deeply. The ZMP had taught them enthusiasm, self-confidence and a certain critical arrogance which they now turned against the Party leadership and its tired dogmatism. They had been trained to challenge 'incorrect' views, to believe that they could build the future with shovels, red flags and a guitar. This enthusiasm survived their disillusion with Stalinism. The young Poles entered the year 1956 eager to struggle for a more promising vision of Poland. To them, the opposite of Stalinism was not any return to capitalism or the pre-war system but a democratic, open socialism in which the press was free and the government did not tell lies.

By 1956 the Polish intelligentsia had re-emerged as a political force, a principal actor in 'the October' and one that was to remain active, although increasingly in opposition, until the repression and purges of 1968. Something has been said about the rising tide of protest from journalists, especially, after 1953. But the role of the intelligentsia in 1956 cannot be understood without reference to Polish history.

The Polish intelligentsia was, and on the whole remains, a distinct social group with a prominence and coherence rare in western societies. As in other eastern European countries, the word means roughly all those with a higher education, including those without such an education who share its tastes and outlook. Creative 'intellectuals' form only one element; a school teacher or research scientist is considered to be as much a member of the intelligentsia as a novelist or film-maker. In Poland, the intelligentsia originates mostly from the nineteenth-century migration to the cities of part of the *szlachta*, the petty aristocracy or 'bonnet lairds' from the Russian-ruled area of Poland. Denied a share in power, this early intelligentsia concerned itself with literature, the humanities and revolutionary politics. The crude independence of the small landowner mutated easily into the intellectuals' contempt for political authority under the partitioning powers and their disdain for the materialism of the existing middle class that produced wealth. The intelligentsia developed as a high-spirited, antinomian group with little responsibility for the society it lived in. This alienation did not really dissolve after Poland regained independence in 1918. The intelligentsia now numbered 1·4 million.[19] Although active in the professions and in education, it found no open door into politics (especially after the 1926 coup). The peasantry, the military cliques and the Catholic hierarchy all seemed enemies of enlightenment. Although many intellectuals were Catholics, the main current of their thought was leftist and sceptical, and a strong Jewish element contributed its own resistance to primitive patriotism and religious extremism.

The Nazis, well aware of the importance of the Polish intelligentsia, subjected the group to selective genocide. Half the doctors and lawyers in Poland were murdered during the German occupation, and 40 per cent of the university professors. The intelligentsia which reappeared in the years after the war was young and left-wing in its outlook, and some of its members took passionately to Stalinism. As the poet Czesław Miłosz remarked many years later, they were tired of Poland being always on the losing side. The positive promises of Stalinism, and the great attention and huge sums of money allotted to culture, offered an apparent escape from traditional alienation. And the creed's destructive impetus appealed to the ancient anarchic instincts of the *szlachta*. Miłosz commented: 'The intellectual's eyes twinkle with delight at the persecution of the bourgeoisie, and of the bourgeois mentality ... the peasants, burying hoarded gold and listening to foreign broadcasts in the hope that a war will save them from collectivization, certainly have no ally in him. Yet he is warm-hearted and good; he is a friend of mankind.'[20]

By the mid-1950s, these Stalinist intellectuals were defecting fast. Some of the most frantic devotees of the cult of Stalin now flung themselves, with equal excitement, on to the opposite course: they became the boldest challengers to Party orthodoxy and the prophets of a new, libertarian form of socialism. The 'socialist realism' dogma finally disintegrated in 1955: abstract painting and experimental or surrealist literature flourished. The Writers' Union loudly rejected an attempt to reimpose Party control.

In the 1960s, there was to be much talk about the division of the intelligentsia into 'priests' and 'jesters' – a distinction put forward in 1959 in a famous essay by the young philosopher Leszek Kołakowski (an ex-Stalinist who had met revelation on his own Damascus road). The 'priest' believes in and serves the absolute; the 'jester' stands for 'an attitude of negative vigilance in the face of any absolute'.[21] For Kołakowski, the intellectuals must remain jesters, and it was in that guise – really the mental outfit they had worn before the war – that they approached 'the October' of 1956. And yet they were very serious jesters. They wanted to open all locked doors, to break down all dogma, to be able to question everything. But the intelligentsia also felt that, in showing this 'creative vigilance', they were fulfilling the role of political leadership that history had assigned to them during the Partitions; then, they had been guardians of the high culture of Poland as the priesthood had been the guardian of popular culture and language. Their politics were an agnostic Marxism. Their claims for themselves as a group had an element of the priestly.

In the course of 1955, the Party line wavered from a commitment to reform back to a sharp reapplication of the dogmatic brake and then, in December, to concessions that allowed the first real denunciations of Stalinism to be made with impunity. But the true impetus to events in Poland came from outside, from the Twentieth Congress of the Soviet Communist Party in February 1956 at which Khrushchev denounced the crimes of Stalin. From that moment, the pace within Poland changed Bolesław Bierut died in Moscow, two weeks after hearing Khrushchev's speech, and when Khrushchev came to Warsaw for the funeral he took the opportunity to interfere, clumsily and without success, in the P U W P discussions on Bierut's successor. He appears to have pushed the name of Zenon Nowak, a reliable Stalinist, and to have suggested that the Party would be more popular if there were fewer Jews in its leadership. As many of the older leaders were indeed Jewish, this crude proposal appalled men who would normally have been prepared to follow a Soviet instruction and ensured that Edward Ochab, a shrewd politician aware of the need for reform, was made First Secretary instead. A final and complete release of political prisoners followed. The text of Khrushchev's Twentieth Congress speech was distributed throughout the Party for discussion, and the calls for radical change within the Party at once became a clamour.

It was at this point, in June 1956, that the workers of Poznań rebelled. Poznań, the main industrial city of west-central Poland, had been the centre of Polish resistance to the Prussian–German occupation in the nineteenth century, and it had a large, experienced working class with strong traditions of trade union activity. The 15,000 workers at the Cegielski engineering plant (which had been renamed after Stalin a few years before) were exasperated by long and fruitless efforts to reverse new production targets and to gain higher wages. A protest march on 28 June turned into a street demonstration; the crowds, now numbering over a hundred thousand, were unable to get an answer to their grievances and rioting began. In a day and night of street fighting with the security police and the army, nearly eighty people lost their lives and thousands were injured.

Behind the immediate crisis at Cegielski lay the boiling exasperation of the entire Polish working class, ignored by the political leadership during the intrigues of the past two years. While the Party insisted that the Six-Year Plan had triumphantly raised living standards, the masses knew better. The truth was that real earnings had fallen by something like 36 per cent between 1949 and 1955 (they were intended to rise, though not greatly) and that consumption per head had diminished by 20 per cent. Most working-class families were struggling to survive. They could now read in the papers articles that suggested that many of the grandiose industrial investments of the Plan had been unnecessary or unsuccessful, alongside reports of speeches by Hilary Minc and even Ochab which chanted improbable statistics about soaring prosperity enjoyed by the proletariat.

The shock of Poznań heaved the whole Polish situation into crisis. At the base, Party membership began to dissolve. Party groups in the factories realized that if they did not start fighting for a better standard of living, they too could be caught between worker revolts and the guns of the Internal Security Corps. Another meeting of the Central Committee, the Seventh

Plenum,* was held in July. The reformers won, less because they were in a majority than because of the fear that Poznań engendered among their colleagues, and another programme for democratization was accepted. Industrial investment would be cut, and real wages would rise. The Sejm would be given more responsibilities and freedom; the ZMP and the management of industry would be allowed to take more decisions for themselves; workers would be 'consulted'; the Party would reduce its own bloated bureaucracy.

It was an untidy package of panic measures. The reform Communists were already in close touch with Władysław Gomułka, supported by those leaders who cared little for Gomułka's views but were now convinced that he must be brought back into the Central Committee as the last chance to halt the disintegration of the Party's authority. Gomułka, however, held out for better terms: his restoration as First Secretary and the removal of his enemies from the Politburo. In this situation, his followers within the Party felt that they dared not wait to take action. Lacking a majority in the Central Committee and fearing that another, more widespread and disastrous Poznań might at any moment take place, they began to organize the factories. In September, the Party committee of the big car factory at Żerań, outside Warsaw, set up a workers' council. Encouraged by the Warsaw Party secretary, Staszewski, other plants in and around the capital followed suit. These workers' councils, which soon spread across Poland, at once became powerful arenas of revolutionary debate, challenging and criticizing the Party leaders sent to remonstrate with them. Influenced by the Jugoslav example of workers' self-management at plant level, the workers' councils also claimed the right to manage their own enterprises. Gomułka had been re-admitted to the Party in August. The workers' councils, at joint mass meetings with the students, now called for his return to power.

This was now obviously a matter of time. The Party leadership finally fell apart in early October. One faction, the 'Natolin' group (named after the chateau they used for their meetings), held out against Gomułka and 'democratization' and appealed to the Soviet Union for support. Most of the others decided to accept the inevitable. On 19 October, with public excitement at a peak, the Eighth Plenum met. Gomułka was present. But so, neither expected nor invited, was Nikita Khrushchev and most of the Soviet leadership, who had flown to Warsaw that morning.

*A Plenum is a full session of the Central Committee. Plenums are numbered beginning with each Party congress: thus the Seventh Plenum was the seventh such Central Committee meeting since the Second Congress of the PUWP, held in March 1954.

There ensued twenty-four extraordinary and decisive hours. For the first time, the threat of armed force was used against Polish Communists by the USSR. Troops moved up to the borders, and Soviet armoured and motorized units stationed within Poland emerged from their bases and converged on Warsaw. In response, the Party called the workers to armed readiness. Polish troops took up defensive positions; the Internal Security Corps, which after Poznań had been put under the command of General Wacław Komar, an officer who had been tortured and imprisoned in the Stalinist years, blocked the way to a Soviet column approaching Warsaw down the road from the west. All this time, the Soviet leaders were arguing furiously but vainly with the Polish Politburo, now reinforced by Gomułka. The Central Committee session was suspended. The Polish people waited to see if, once again, they were going to have to fight for their independence in the streets.

Early in the morning of 20 October, Khrushchev began to accept the situation. Gomułka had proved unshakeable, and the PUWP Politburo had continued to back him up. To use the Red Army would, it was becoming clear, lead to heavy fighting followed by years of underground resistance. Krushchev had received assurances that criticism of the Soviet Union in the Polish press would be suppressed, and that Poland would remain in the Warsaw Pact, the military alliance established by the Soviet Union in 1955. He chose to conclude that Gomułka would remain fundamentally loyal to the Soviet connection and that he would not permit either the basic achievements of socialism or the leading role of the Party in Poland to be destroyed. In return, he recognized that Gomułka would now lead the PUWP and that to do so he required an end to direct Soviet intervention in Polish internal affairs. Later that day, he and his boarding-party, which included Vyacheslav Molotov, Anastas Mikoyan, Lazar Kaganovich and some dozen generals, flew home. The Soviet Army units – on 'routine manoeuvres' – returned to their bases.

One of the mysteries of 'October' is what Khrushchev thought he would achieve by his descent on Warsaw. Probably he had little idea. He came, essentially, to make a scene. Accounts of the meeting are vague about whether the Russians made any concrete demands. But Khrushchev was protesting, in the first place, about being kept in the dark about the personnel changes which the Plenum intended to make. From his agents, indeed from the newspapers, he had a good idea of what these would be. But the PUWP had not informed him; it had treated the USSR as an enemy from whom secrets must be kept, rather than as Poland's mightiest and most loyal friend. (This complaint, interestingly enough, was the main reproach that

Brezhnev was to heap on Alexander Dubček and his colleagues, when they had been kidnapped and brought before him in Moscow after the invasion of Czechoslovakia in 1968.)

Behind the secrecy, Khrushchev instantly and quite correctly sensed that the real dynamic of what was taking place in Poland was Polish national-ism, manipulated and channelled by the dominant group in the PUWP. He does not seem to have tried to prohibit any of the policy changes Gomułka proposed to make. He wanted to hear that Polish–Soviet friend-ship, at the official level, would continue to be honoured and that the Party would remain in control of society. His impression of Gomułka, again absolutely correct, was that this man was willing and tough enough to deliver those guarantees. Khrushchev tried, and failed, to ensure that some of the old pro-Soviet politicians he knew personally would remain in the Politburo (this crude confidence in 'people we know' was to recur in the 1968 arguments). But after shouting abuse in Gomułka's face, he seems to have concluded that he was a real Communist in all that mattered.

With the Russians out of the way, Gomułka had to establish his own power within the Party and, with caution, to cool the furnace of popular excitement. His speech to the Central Committee, broadcast to the nation, violently attacked Stalin and Stalinism. He criticized the secret police and the collectivization programme, promising to the peasants lower compulsory deliveries and 'self-management' to the workers. He insisted that each country had the right and duty to find its own way to socialism. But at the same time, he reasserted the importance of Polish–Soviet friendship, now to be put on a sounder and more equal basis, and he warned that nobody would be allowed to question that friendship or to challenge the Party's leadership of the process of democratization.

For the moment, the mass fervour for change was useful for him. Local Party organizations, branches of the administration, trade unions and social groups of every kind threw out Stalinist leaders who had been imposed upon them, and declared their support for Gomułka. He was well aware that public opinion was reluctant to stop there, and that mass meetings all over the country were also applauding speakers who attacked the Soviet Union, who brought up the Nazi–Soviet Pact, the deportations, Katyń and the Warsaw Rising, or who attacked the Communist creed openly. But in con-trolling this pressure for a 'second stage' of 'the October', Gomułka was given unexpected assistance by the Hungarian tragedy. The revolution in Budapest began when Hungarian security men fired on a pro-Polish demon-stration on 23 October, and ended with the return of Soviet tanks on 4 November. The Poles followed events in Hungary with passionate but agonized sympathy. They sent food and medical supplies to Budapest, but they accepted their new leaders' warning that to do more would be to risk a general insurrection throughout eastern Europe which might end in world war. Brought back from his internment to Warsaw, the Primate, Cardinal Wyszyński, told the faithful on the very Sunday of the Soviet return to Budapest: 'Poles know how to die magnificently ... A man dies but once and is quickly covered with glory. But he gives long years in trouble, hardship, pain and suffering. That is a greater heroism.'

After the tanks had driven back into Budapest for the last time, there were spontaneous protests in Poland and attacks on Soviet buildings. Anti-Soviet feeling reached a new peak in November, but at the same time the final catastrophe in Hungary set limits on its expression. The danger to Poland, only just averted in October but still close, had been displayed in a way which everyone could understand. Self-restraint, as well as support for Gomułka, became matters of patriotism.

It was an extraordinary moment. The Party's control over events, and indeed over its own members, had dissolved. Instead, the only authority in the land was the direct patriotic loyalty which the masses gave to Władysław Gomułka, perceived as a national hero defending Polish independence whose own political convictions seemed hardly to matter.

Gomułka himself was well aware of this. His rhetoric became sharply more nationalistic in these weeks, as at the enormous rally of half a million people he addressed outside the Palace of Culture, on 24 October. But he realized that this phase could only be temporary. He was a clever politician and a devoted Party man. A situation in which 'Wiesław' was acclaimed as a national liberator by people who spat at the name of the Party he led could not and must not endure.

On 14 November, Gomułka, accompanied by Józef Cyrankiewicz, the prime minister, left by train for Moscow to work out a detailed agreement on the new form of Polish–Soviet relations. People prayed publicly for him when he left and welcomed him in great crowds when the train steamed back across the frontier four days later. His 'October' settlement, as it finally emerged, rested on national sovereignty. The Polish state and the PUWP gained a high degree of genuine freedom of movement in both external and internal politics. Poland largely ceased to be a 'penetrated system' in which Soviet 'advisers' directly supervised its executive. Soviet officers in the armed forces and Marshal Rokossowski were sent home, with medals and polite expressions of gratitude. The trading relationship with the USSR was scrapped and replaced by a more normal, state-to-state pattern of commercial exchanges. Poles living or imprisoned in the USSR who wished to return home were allowed to do so. The status of Soviet forces stationed permanently in Poland was regularized by a formal agreement. In foreign policy, the Poles at once reverted to a more independent diplomacy which, within the general guidelines of Soviet policies, worked to re-establish contact with the West and to reduce tensions in central Europe.

At home, Gomułka placed the security police under the control of the Ministry of the Interior and cut its numbers; some unemployed UB officers were reduced to hanging around Warsaw bars and supplementing their pensions by private blackmail. A new agreement with the Church restored its freedom to appoint its own hierarchy and the right – startling in a Communist state – to give religious instruction in state schools. Although the old pro-régime lay movement PAX, detested by most believers, was allowed to survive, there now emerged lay Catholic groups with genuine support that accepted the *raison d'état* and the necessity for the Soviet alliance but criticized the régime from a non-Marxist point of view. The best-known of these was Znak, based in Kraków, but 'Clubs of Catholic Intelligentsia' were set up in many centres. The press remained, for the moment, blissfully free; censorship became voluntary. Western films, plays and books flooded into Poland; the jamming of western radio stations ceased. The cultural liberation that had begun the year before now made Polish films, music, painting, graphics and – where it was translated – contemporary literature the centre of European attention. The young declared a permanent festival of exultant avant-gardisme, in some respects an imitation of the Boulevard Saint-Germain and its existentialist bazaar of ten years earlier. In cellar night-clubs, a girl would strip while a bearded student chanted passages from Spinoza to New Orleans jazz. Anything went. It was a happy year.

Spontaneous action, rather than planned reform, changed the face of the Polish economy. The agricultural collectives simply fell apart, without waiting for legislation, as the peasants re-divided the land among themselves and shared out the livestock. The reformed trade unions claimed some independence from the Party, but the workers showed more interest in setting up workers' councils throughout industry and these were – at first – genuinely representative. (The workers' councils often emerged from *ad hoc* 'revolutionary committees' that sprang up as centres of popular support for Gomułka and the reform programme but that were in comparison short-lived.) Through these councils, the workers demanded and won large wage rises, while the climate of confusion and political excitement meant that industrial production fell – the first example of the inflationary side-effects of working-class protest in Poland. Gomułka organized a limited revival of small private craft and service businesses, and prepared for a comprehensive decentralization of the economy by setting up a permanent advisory committee of academics to assist the government.

Superficially, there are resemblances between the events of 'October' and the explosion of 1980. Frustrated nationalism was fundamental in both cases. Other phenomena that recurred in 1980 showed themselves in 1956 for the first time: the disintegration of the Party at the base; spontaneous worker and peasant action; the reformation of all social institutions; a breakdown of censorship. But the differences are much more profound and significant.

The upheaval of 1956 was essentially brought about by forces within the Party leadership, seeking to break with the remains of the Stalinist dictatorship. Though spontaneous popular action often determined the scope and pace of events, it was secondary. Poznań certainly did not 'cause' the political changes at the Seventh and Eighth Plenums; indeed, the riots at Poznań gave momentary strength to the losing conservative faction in the leadership, and sharply checked the impetus of de-Stalinization in the Soviet Union itself. Radical political change was already taking place, and Gomułka would very probably have returned to power – certainly to the Politburo and most likely to the leadership of the Party – without the workers' revolt.

Secondly, the social force that led the 1955–6 upheaval was not the working class but the intelligentsia – in that wider, Polish sense. Here, a comparison can be much more accurately made with the 1968 reform process in Czechoslovakia than with Poland in 1980. The 'Polish October', like the 'Prague Spring', represented a rebellion of qualified and educated people against a system that denied them access to the administrative and economic élite, and that preferred to staff the senior bureaucracy and management with often incompetent figures selected for their loyalty to the Party.

The workers' movement, after Poznań, was in a sense almost irrelevant. Powerful and threatening as it appeared, it had no central structure or leadership, and in practice it was manipulated by Gomułka's supporters to strengthen his position. As a source of support for the new Party leaders, whether as physical defenders of Warsaw against the advancing Soviet columns on 18–19 October or as signatories of helpful resolutions, the workers' councils were invaluable. When they were no longer indispensable but merely a problem in the way of the Party's reassertion of control over the masses, they were gradually neutralized without great difficulty.

But for the European left, especially in the West, the 'Polish October' still seemed to be the triumphant birth of a new, democratic socialism, faithful to the ideas of Marx, purified of the distortion and tyranny that Stalin had piled on the honour of that other October in 1917. A month later, the twin atrocities of the Soviet action against Hungary and the Anglo-French invasion of Egypt felt like the dying blizzards of the Cold War which had frozen political progress in both halves of Europe. The 'Polish Road' appeared as the destined path for that 'third force' of which European socialists had dreamed for so long.

These millennial hopes died only reluctantly in the ten years of gathering disillusion that followed 1956. Two other interpretations of 'the October', in its Polish implications, survive. One, represented by the very few defenders of the ideals of 1956 left in the P U W P, like the editor Mieczysław Rakowski,* sees the episode as the great missed chance of post-war Polish history. Gomułka, for a moment, had the entire nation behind him; the Party's chief, if not exactly the Party itself, led the nation with an authenticity that no other Communist attained before or since. It was open to him to return to the experiment he had half-completed by the time of his overthrow in 1948, to carry through the principles of October until the Party exercised only a guiding role over a society allowed to express its own initiatives in almost every field. In this way, and only in this way, the Party could have overcome the original sin of its inheritance of power, the imposition of Communism on an unwilling nation by the Soviet Union.

But Gomułka did not return to his old course. A second interpretation asserts that he could never have done so, and that the hopes placed in 'the October' were based on a fatal misunderstanding. No real alliance between the Party and the nation was possible in the long run. In his book *Flashpoint Poland*, the London-based broadcaster George Błażyński writes: 'The support given [Gomułka] by the people was essentially anti-Soviet and anti-Communist ... hopes were running too high and proved to be entirely unjustified, but not because the leaders betrayed the "spirit of October". They betrayed the people's trust, but they did not betray themselves.' Gomułka retained the changes in which he believed, and withdrew gradually those which had been forced upon him.[22] In this view, the only real lesson to be learned from 1956 was that the Poles could use their own strength to rebel against the system and secure limited reforms without provoking inevitable Soviet intervention.

Expressed in mild language, Błażyński's opinion belongs to the neo-conservative ideology that has been steadily gaining ground in the West since the process of détente between the United States and the Soviet Union, so promising in the 1960s, ran into accumulating problems in the late 1970s.

---

*In 1981 Rakowski was appointed deputy prime minister responsible for negotiating with Solidarity, and became a vehement defender of the Party's political monopoly.

The essential argument is that 'reform Communism' is a myth – a dangerous myth because it encourages the populations of eastern Europe and the Third World to suppose that Marxist socialism can co-exist with basic democratic rights and a government responsive to changes in public opinion. In the neo-conservative view, this false hope must be destroyed; the struggle between liberty and Marxism knows no truce.

The Marxist leader who promises democratic socialism is thus transformed into the most insidious enemy of all. To demonstrate this point, much recent history has been reprocessed. Gomułka always intended to 'betray the people's trust'. The Popular Unity government of Salvador Allende in Chile has to be caricatured as a dictatorship more oppressive than the Pinochet junta that butchered it in 1973. Martyrs of the Hungarian revolution like Imre Nagy and Pál Maléter must have their characters blackened until they appear little less villainous than the tyrant Mátyás Rákosi whose system they demolished.[23]

Chapter Three

Years of Disillusion

From Reform to Stagnation

Gomułka's direct bond with the Polish people was a reality in October 1956 and for some months to come.* But it was not an explanation of why he had returned to power. There had been no revolution in the technical sense – the people had not given him power and neither had he picked it up like the fallen crown on Bosworth Field. He had been formally and correctly elected First Secretary by his colleagues in the Party leadership. This mattered more than at first appeared. At the last moment, his enemies in the Politburo threw their votes in his favour, realizing that he was the only man who could at once stand up to the uninvited Soviet guests and dissuade the mass of the population from a direct onslaught on Party rule. Months earlier, other Politburo members whose views were much more pro-Soviet and conservative than Gomułka's had decided to support him for tactical reasons. As a result, he assumed office burdened with political debts to colleagues who remained suspicious of the reform course.

His first test came with the parliamentary elections set for 20 January 1957. It became apparent that the voters intended to use the limited freedom of choice afforded them in the new electoral law – which provided for more candidates than the number of seats in each multi-member constituency – to cross out the names of PUWP candidates. Gomułka realized that the result could cripple the Party's authority, both in Poland and in the eyes of the Soviet leadership, and he resorted to the ultimate *raison d'état* argument: 'The appeal to cross PUWP candidates off the ballot paper is

---

*One of Gomułka's most effective allies in the October days was a young worker named Lechosław Goździk, secretary of the Party group in the Żerań car plant outside Warsaw and head of its workers' council. Goździk spoke at mass rallies and was constantly photographed with Gomułka. The American journalist Flora Lewis wrote of him, in her book *The Polish Volcano* (1959), that 'he became a quick favourite of the excited crowds, one of the few people whose words they listened to with care ... Goździk played a vital part in preventing riots then and there.' In 1957, after two minor road accidents while driving factory cars, Goździk was removed from the secretaryship and eventually pushed out of Żerań altogether. He vanished, to be rediscovered in December 1980 by a journalist on *Polityka* living as a fisherman on the Baltic coast. He had left the Party on hearing of the shooting of workers at Gdynia in December 1970.

tantamount not only to the appeal to cross out socialism. Crossing out our Party's candidates means crossing out the independence of our country, crossing Poland off the map of European states.' By reducing the election to a matter of patriotism, he succeeded in holding the anti-Party voters to 10·6 per cent of the electorate.

The awful example of Hungary still subdued the nation. The new Sejm was initially far more active and independent than its predecessor, but the elections had marked the first step to reconstructing the Party's leading role in society. By late 1957, Gomułka felt strong enough to take action against the 'revisionist' press by closing the brilliant and fearless magazine *Po Prostu*. There were riots in Warsaw, suppressed by the police, as students protested; the shutting-down of *Po Prostu* marked the end of a year's euphoria and the beginning of the breach between the régime and its most vocal supporters, the intellectuals.

While rebuilding the Party's authority over the nation, Gomułka at the same time tried to establish his own authority over the Party. No theoretician, Gomułka invented a ramshackle link between 'revisionism' (liberal Communism) and 'dogmatism' (Stalinism), which he claimed were complementary diseases. The revisionists, with their unhealthy passion for an infinite extension of democracy, had been driven to extremes by the Stalinist dictatorship and therefore were no longer relevant in the new, post-October Poland. Indeed it was only their outrageous demands which now in turn kept dogmatism alive: 'revisionist tuberculosis can only strengthen the dogmatist influenza'. Gomułka invited the Party to struggle against both maladies as if they were one. On this principle, he then endeavoured to purge the Party.

But, then as now, the PUWP was too large, too divided into factions and at lower levels too resistant to ideological instructions from above. Gomułka was able to remove some tens of thousands of Party members who were deemed to be suffering from 'tuberculosis' or 'influenza', but nearly 200,000 others voluntarily left the Party out of disillusion or indifference.

The PUWP sank to its lowest-ever membership. At around a million by late 1959, it had fewer members than at the day of its formation at the unity congress in 1948.[1] Those who remained, largely the 'apparatus' of paid Party officials, were still disunited. 'Deep differences about the ends and means of "building socialism" remained under the surface of conformity to the current Party line. The mass media, the universities, the professional organizations and the intelligentsia generally remained overwhelmingly reformist at heart, while the Party and state bureaucracy, both central and local, continued to be conservative in their sympathies.'[2]

Gomułka's own style added to the Party problem. A man of frosty, Cromwellian integrity, his opinion of his fellow human beings was not high. His temper, always short-fused, had become noticeably worse during his years of detention. He tended to gather all decision-making into his own hands; those around him, old comrades from the years before 1948 like Marian Spychałski and Zenon Kliszko, knew better than to contradict him. In consequence, Gomułka increasingly lost touch with the realities of Polish life. He heard what he wanted to hear – which, with any statesman, usually comes to mean what other people want him to hear. This suited many more indolent members of the leadership. They were content to run their own empires in their own manner while Gomułka, muttering irascibly and smoking one cigarette after another through a little glass holder, buried himself in economic statistics which, unfortunately, were often cooked.

These were years when the economy was given priority. The Stalinist approach had been romantic and political. Now, it was asserted, pragmatic planning based on realistic estimates of what Poland needed and could produce would be the Party's main concern. A grand decentralization would take place; the Planning Commission in Warsaw would no longer stipulate every detail of production, and the managers of local enterprises would be allowed to take their own initiatives.*

But the economic reform never, in the end, got much further than talk. Other, smaller countries in eastern Europe adopted some of the ideas of Polish economists and made a success of them, notably Ota Šik, in Czechoslovakia during the brief interval from 1967 to the Soviet-led intervention of 1968, and above all the architects of the Hungarian 'New Economic Model'. Even the German Democratic Republic applied a version of the Polish recipes. Only in Poland was almost nothing done. After a few half-hearted experiments in decentralization, the Polish economy always reverted to a hopelessly over-centralized system of command that planned with little regard for local initiative or public demand. And yet Poland in the middle of the twentieth century harboured Europe's most brilliant group of socialist economists; the names of Kalecki, Lange, Bobrowski, Lipiński and Brus were all famous beyond the frontiers. This failure remains the most puzzling – and fateful – mystery of contemporary Poland.

Theories have, of course, been offered to explain the failure. The most facile blames American aid. Between 1957 and 1963, the United States

* Oskar Lange observed in 1957 that there were no hairpins in Poland for the simple reason that the Plan had forgotten to order their production. See Stehle, *Nachbar Polen* (Frankfurt/Main, 1963), p. 195.

provided $529 million of assistance in various forms, including grain payable in soft-currency Polish zlotys. This support, it is argued, simply blunted the government's sense of urgency about the economy. The alternative to completing the economic reform was not after all catastrophe; somebody would always bail Poland out.

But there were two more fundamental factors. The first was economic. The Polish standard of living was simply too low, and too fragile, to be drastically re-shaped. Czechoslovakia and Hungary, several years later, started from a much higher level of personal consumption and savings; the purchasing power of Polish wages in 1957 was probably among the lowest in Europe. To end price controls or permit the closure of loss-making factories was to risk real suffering and unrest, although the new advisers insisted that the first step to a 'new model' economy must be a limited introduction of market discipline as a reliable indicator of supply and demand.

The second factor was political. The injured economists blamed the failure on the Party. Here again, the relative mildness of Polish Communism since 1945 was exacting penalties. The 'middle apparatus' saw nothing but trouble and loss of control in the new proposals, and they had never been sufficiently intimidated to ensure their compliance. Even if they supported such changes, their understanding of them was minimal: in 1959, only 30 per cent of paid Party officials had any secondary education. But the political problem lay even deeper. The PUWP had only inherited from its predecessors in government the dogma that Poland must be strictly controlled from the centre or disintegrate.

This was a much more authentic attitude than the Party's doctrinal possessiveness about its 'leading role'. It sprang from Polish history, from the experience of the seventeenth century and onwards, when all social and economic advance, even the independence of the nation itself, had been at the mercy of local magnates. The king was elected by nobles frequently bribed for their vote by foreign tsars or emperors. The Sejm could be instantaneously paralysed by its own rule of unanimity; it sufficed for one petty aristocrat, whiskered and shaven-skulled and perhaps hardly literate, to cry 'I do not permit!' and nothing could be done.

By the late eighteenth century, intelligent Poles were already familiar with the irony that small liberties could be misused to destroy a greater liberty. An elective monarchy and a parliament acting on this '*liberum veto*' unanimity were undermining the very independence of Poland. It was accordingly natural that the ideas of the Enlightenment, of the American Revolution and of the early stages of the French Revolution should have had a greater impact upon Poland than upon any other state in central or eastern Europe. The nation was already doomed – the first Partition had taken place in 1772 and only a reduced Poland remained – when the Constitution of May 1791 was adopted, making the monarchy hereditary and abolishing the unanimity rule in the Sejm. The second Partition followed only two years later, and the third, in 1795, obliterated Poland from the map. But the ideas survived. Both national independence and social progress seemed to require strong central government to overrule local interests and subdue the anarchic individualism of the *szlachta* squirearchy. The Jacobin tradition in French politics – the association of progress with centralized government from Paris, against the back reaction which was supposed to follow from devolving power to the provinces – affected Polish political thinking for the next century and a half.

It is not difficult to see such historical elements in the reluctance of the PUWP to relax its grasp on society, as the economic reform plans required it to. In the years after 1956, few even among 'revisionist' intellectuals in the Party considered their fellow-citizens politically mature. The establishment of licensed opposition parties, for example, was thought to be a suicidal idea; given their heads, the masses would probably vote for a party of the extreme clerical right – probably much like the pre-war National Democrats. Correspondingly, there were political as well as economic doubts about the abandonment of central planning; too much independence for the factories might lead to anarchy.

It was another example of the ambiguous attitude of the intelligentsia towards the problem of democracy. They were agreed that the old anti-democratic leadership and its institutions must go. But they were very much less determined about the extension of democracy downwards. Inevitably, the project for economic reform ended in a compromise: Poland remained under central direction and planning, but the planners became for a time more enlightened and realistic than they had been before.

These attitudes could also be seen in the policy taken after 1956 towards the workers' councils. It was predictable that Gomułka would resist any attempt to transform them into a system of workers' self-management on the Jugoslav model; 'heavy and medium industry,' he stated, 'is the property of the nation.' More surprisingly, the reforming economists took a similar view. Czesław Bobrowski, vice-president of the new advisory Economic Council, observed: 'Had I been an enemy of the workers' councils, I would have granted them unlimited powers and given them complete independence in their undertakings. After three months' general chaos, a serious economic crisis would have resulted.' Professor Lipiński also opposed the idea that a permanent parliament of workers could run a factory: the councils should have certain rights over how the surplus should be distributed between wages and investment, but the authority of the qualified manager must remain.[3] In December 1958, a Workers' Self-Government Act merged the councils into a new and complicated system of factory consultation. A Conference of Workers' Self-Government for each factory or enterprise composed of representatives of the workers' council, the factory Party group, the trade union and the management, was to meet every three months. Its right to supervise the factory's activities was subordinated to the requirements of the Plan. The workers' councils, already greatly enfeebled, now ceased to have any real significance.

Relations between the state and the Church soon began to decay, after the peak of patriotic co-operation in the months of national crisis in 1956. Although their biographies demonstrate that neither man was an entirely immovable object, both Cardinal Wyszyński and Władysław Gomułka considered themselves to be irresistible forces. Two millennial faiths, both assured that their historical victory was inevitable, began to grind against one another. The great monastery of Jasna Góra at Częstochowa, the most sacred shrine of Polish Catholicism, was raided by the police in 1959 in a search for illegal publishing equipment, and there were brawls between the police and pilgrims. The state refused to license many projects for new churches, and one such refusal touched off a violent riot in the steel town of Nowa Huta in April 1960.

The Nowa Huta riot was a most ominous warning to Gomułka. It showed that the new industrial working class in a town always displayed to visitors as an example of socialist achievement had in no way abandoned the militant piety of their peasant origins. But the state's gradual encroachment on the Church continued. Taxation on Church institutions was imposed, and by 1960 religious education was once more being evicted from the state schools. There were now some thirteen Catholic deputies in the Sejm, of whom five belonged to the genuinely independent Znak movement. The Znak spokesmen protested cautiously, but the main burden of Catholic retort was carried by the Cardinal. His freedom of speech remained untouched, and he used it in a succession of sermons in which he vigorously exaggerated the position. Wyszyński claimed that a 'systematic social organization has been set up to fight against God', that 'atheistic impertinence in our fatherland is grasping us by the throat', that the state provision of free contraceptives through the national health service would make of Warsaw an empty city where grass grew in the streets.

In return, the state redoubled its campaign of pinpricks against the

Church. The real penalty of the war between the Cardinal and Gomułka was paid by the parish priests, whose life and work became increasingly difficult. The feud reached a new crisis in 1966, when the Polish episcopate sent a message to the West German bishops in which they suggested mutual forgiveness for the wrongs each nation had inflicted on the other. For a moment loyal Catholic opinion in Poland was shaken. Hatred of the Germans for the atrocities of the occupation was still intense, and Gomułka's pressure on West Germany to recognize Poland's post-war frontier, the 'Oder–Neisse line', was supported by all Poles. Now the Poles were being invited by their own Church leaders to ask the Germans for pardon, to agree that the removal of the German population from lands regarded as historically Polish could somehow be equated with the five years of genocide, torture and starvation which the Germans had imposed upon Poland. Gomułka pounced on the chance. A furious propaganda campaign was launched against the Polish bishops' letter, and Cardinal Wyszyński was denied a passport. This was the year in which Poland's millennium was to be celebrated, a thousand years after the baptism of the first Polish king and the foundation of the Polish state. The Pope, who had intended to visit Poland, was now refused an invitation. Gomułka's campaign, however, misfired. As soon as the Party attacked the episcopate, Catholic opinion swung strongly back to the Church's side. The millennium became an ill-tempered shambles, with Church and state holding separate programmes of ceremonies.

But the Church–state dispute in Poland, like so many other contemporary problems in that country, cannot be understood without a little historical reflection. To a naïve Catholic, the dispute is nothing more than the survival struggle of the Church against the onslaught of an aggressively atheist Communism. One may agree that a Marxist party with the monopoly of political power and a Church commanding the loyalty of more than 80 per cent of the population were bound to collide. None the less, the collision has been relatively gentle. The Party never dreamed of attempting directly to stamp out religion and close the churches, in the manner of the early Soviet Union. Nor was there any serious effort to make religious belief a disqualification for PUWP membership; such a step would probably have lost the Party more than half its working-class members and much of its lower 'apparatus' as well. Especially after 1956, the Church–state relationship was one of rivalry rather than of mortal conflict. Cardinal Wyszyński's talk of deadly threats to the survival of Christianity bore little relation to the facts. If anybody's authority was threatened, it was on balance that of the state.

The Church–state dispute in Poland is, in fact, a chapter in European political history which was delivered so late that nobody recognized it. In almost all west European countries with Catholic populations or majorities, the battle over the frontiers of state and Church authority had been fought and settled in the nineteenth century. The Catholic Church had hotly resisted the appearance of the republican, lay state, with its claim to embody popular sovereignty and to wield an authority that needed no religious endorsement. The battle, naturally enough, had raged most fiercely over education, as the state established non-religious schools and broke the Catholic monopoly of indoctrination.

But two Catholic nations remained entirely unaffected by the great laicization movement. Ireland and Poland were both under foreign occupation, and in both countries the Catholic religion became almost totally identified with the struggle for cultural survival and national independence. Concepts like 'republicanism' or 'liberalism' either acquired a quite distorted meaning or were not understood at all. When Poland emerged into independence in 1918, a Concordat of 1925 gave the Church wide privileges and the right to give religious instruction in the new state school system. Although there was friction between successive governments and the Church, there was no effective separation of Church and state in administration or education.

So it was to the Communists that it fell, after 1945, to build the first lay state in Polish history, nearly a hundred years behind most of the Catholic nations of the West. The struggle to establish a tolerable armistice line between state and Church was as long and bitter as, for example, the Guerre Scolaire in Belgium during the 1880s. But the Communists lacked the constituency which Belgian Liberals or French Republicans had relied upon: a liberal mass movement convinced of the necessity of separating Church and state. In pre-war Poland, whose middle class had been small and weak, the ideals of tolerance and agnostic humanism had made little headway. They had been strong in the emancipated Jewish intelligentsia, but this group had perished in the gas chambers or emigrated to Palestine. After the war, the remnants of agnostic liberalism were pitilessly squeezed between the huge authoritarian creeds of Catholicism and Marxism. Following August 1980, the crucifix appeared on the wall of every office of the new Solidarity unions, signifying – among other things – that the Polish population had still not accepted the concept of a lay society.

As the years of Gomułka's second reign went by, the intelligentsia became steadily more disillusioned. Non-Party men and women did not, after all, gain the jobs and public responsibilities they had hoped for, and the direction of the economy and the administration remained firmly in Party hands. Although the arts preserved the freedom they had been granted in 1956, censorship in the press grew more restrictive until the brilliant journalism of October was only a memory. In 1962 the best cultural weeklies were suppressed and the intellectual discussion clubs closed down. In 1964, the first organized protest of intellectuals appeared, the 'Letter of the Thirty-Four', which remonstrated with the Party about the growing burden of censorship and the indirect pressures used to discourage new or critical periodicals. This was to be the first of many similar petitioning protests, signed by distinguished intellectuals and artists and leaked abroad to Radio Free Europe so that their contents could reach the Polish population. The signatories would be harassed and often forbidden to publish or to practise their professions. Official paranoia about 'imperialist' radio stations and their agents in Poland would be tautened by another notch. While the letter-signers were not put on trial or imprisoned, as they certainly would have been in most other states in the Soviet orbit, this guerrilla war between dissident intellectuals and the state generated a sinister yet strangely addictive climate of tension.

Nothing could be said straight out. Everything was implied – by a historical allusion, by a meaningful omission, by an apparently innocent choice of a word. Polish literature and film, which had been – like Andrzej Wajda's great film trilogy about the occupation and its aftermath – fearlessly direct and open, now became hermetic. No foreigner could hope to decipher the private references – cultural, historical or merely personal – through which, for example, an early Skolimowski film delivered its message to the gloating sophisticates of Warsaw. Through this semiotic jungle, the cultural gendarmerie and the intellectuals stalked each other and laid their ambushes.

This sort of opposition, although acutely annoying to the Party leaders, did not threaten them in any immediate way. Other forms of opposition alarmed them more, and they came from within the Party. In 1967, there took place the trial of two young Party intellectuals, Jacek Kuroń and Karol Modzelewski, both lecturers at Warsaw University, who had distributed a document entitled 'An Open Letter to the Party'. The views of both men, and of Kuroń especially, were to become much less radical during the opposition activities of the late 1970s and in 1980, but in the 'Open Letter' they delivered a penetrating, closely argued attack on the whole basis of Party rule in Poland from a left-wing Communist point of view. They argued that Polish society was divided between the working masses and a 'ruling bureaucracy' that exploited the labour power of the workers as ruthlessly as any capitalist system. They called for a form of revolutionary Communism in which the working class ruled directly through a democracy of workers' councils. The 'Open Letter' was never widely read in Poland, although in the West it was hailed by the far left as a rebirth of Trotskyism, but the Party considered it dangerous enough to imprison Kuroń and Modzelewski for three and a half years. Other Party intellectuals who got into trouble in this period mostly criticized the leadership from the 'revisionist', liberal-Marxist position. In 1966, Professor Leszek Kołakowski – who had journeyed far from the utopian Stalinism of his youth – was expelled from the Party for deploring in a public lecture the decay of the ideals of 1956. Especially in Warsaw, where Kołakowski taught, organized opposition groups began to form among students.

The other problem of opposition within the Party took the more traditional form of factional intrigue at the top. By now, in the mid-1960s, more and more Party members sensed that the PUWP had lost its way; Poland was stagnating politically and economically, while Gomułka's autocratic style and his deafness to all advice was becoming intolerable to his colleagues. Under Bierut, there had been a surfeit of idealism; now the balance had swung too far the other way, and many Party members sensed that 'pragmatism' had become merely a euphemism for widespread materialism and corruption throughout the Party and the administration.

But what ideal could be used to mobilize Polish society once more, to transcend egoism and indifference? The PUWP no longer had the intellectual vigour to answer this question in a Marxist way. Instead, patriotism became the slogan. The so-called 'partisan' faction, which formed at this time, set itself to rousing a formless but violent mood of resentful nationalism. For some of the faction's supporters, this reassertion of Poland's independence, coupled with invocations of the nation's heroic military past, was a sincere response to the depressed and hopeless mood around them. For others, especially its leaders, an upsurge of nationalist fervour was perceived merely as a force to overwhelm the barriers which separated them from power.

The title 'partisan' recalls the group around Gomułka between 1943 and 1948, those Polish Communists who took part in the resistance to the Nazis and whose relations with the more subservient comrades who returned from Moscow with the Red Army were always tense. Many of the leading 'partisans' in the 1960s had been in that group. General Mieczysław Moczar, their most prominent personality, had been a guerrilla commander. But these new 'partisans' were disciplinarians, determined to stamp out dissent and subversion in Poland. Their power base was in the security police, run by Moczar, which had its own curious patriotic myth.* Their influence, however, soon widened as Moczar and the journalists in his retinue encouraged a broad, ostensibly generous rehabilitation of the non-Communist forces during the Second World War. Through the Association of Fighters for Freedom and Democracy (ZBoWiD), veterans of the Home Army and the Polish armies in the West received decorations and pensions, whether they lived in Poland or in exile. Under Moczar's protection, a profusion of histories, novels and films appeared which dealt openly and proudly with the September campaign in 1939, the Silesian Rising of 1921 or the non-Communist resistance.

This opening of locked areas of history, and the glorifying of military traditions, pleased and excited many Poles. Moczar soon acquired a considerable following among a section of the intellectuals. But traditional nationalism, invoked in this non-ideological way, brought back with it three deeper and sometimes more sinister aspects of that tradition, which the 'partisans' also encouraged. The first was authoritarianism: the 'partisans' tried to represent the surviving revisionists and dissenting intellectuals as anti-Polish forces of foreign subversion. The second was anti-Russian feeling: discreetly but effectively, Moczar let it be understood that he shared this feeling and was working to reduce Soviet influence over Poland.

The third was anti-Semitism. The 'partisan' journalists, especially, tried to revive the old prejudices that associated Jews with Russian Communism and with treachery to the cause of Polish independence. Hinting at a new national Communism purged of Soviet and Jewish 'contamination', they attacked both revisionists and Jewish members of the surviving wartime 'Moscow' group. Gomułka, uncertain how to cope with this offensive, unwisely nourished it in 1967 by denouncing the 'Zionist fifth column' that was imagined to be celebrating Israel's victory in the Arab–Israeli war. This endorsement encouraged the publication of seamy books alleging, for example, that Polish Jews had collaborated with the Nazis and were now in league with the West Germans against Poland. Accusations of 'rootless cosmopolitanism' led to an outbreak of harassment

---

*One western journalist, detained by the UB in this period, was told by an officer that the real Poland, the true national ethos, had always been expressed through conspiracy and clandestinity. The various governments of free Poland had been superficial, irrelevant phenomena. Today, the officer insisted, the guardians of that ancient tradition were the security police, working unseen and unappreciated to preserve the soul of the nation.

and dismissal for Jews in official posts, and a substantial emigration began in 1967.*

The outside world watched the 'anti-Zionist' campaign with incredulous horror. It was the survivors of the Holocaust who were being persecuted, although the Jewish community which remained in Poland numbered less than 30,000. Moczar's pamphleteers were soon answered by American publications which proclaimed that primitive anti-Semitism was an inherent vice of all Poles. It was not understood – how could it have been? – that the campaign was in reality a cynical political manipulation, its effects mostly confined to the bureaucracy and the journalists' profession, or that most Poles were indifferent to it. The damage to Poland's international reputation was irreparable. In a few months, the sympathy which the nation and its new leaders had accumulated in 1956 drained away and, especially in the United States, was replaced by sharp public hostility.

The Second Breakdown

On the last day of January 1968, the government stopped a theatre production. It was a production of the poetic drama *Dziady* (*Forefathers' Eve*) by Adam Mickiewicz, the early nineteenth-century writer who is the most beloved figure in Polish literature. Mystically religious and profoundly nationalist, *Dziady* is a sanctification of the political struggle against the Tsarist occupiers which no Pole can witness without recognizing his or her own times. In this tremendous production directed by Kazimierz Dejmek, described by one girl in the audience as 'one of the culminating points in

---

*A favourite charge, retailed to me in 1968 by a senior Party official, was that Jews, unlike Poles, had not fought the Germans but had run away or allowed themselves to be meekly butchered. A not untypical case of that year involved a certain deputy minister, a pre-war KPP Communist who fought in Spain, disobeyed Party orders in 1939 by enlisting in the French Foreign Legion to fight the Germans in France, led a sabotage group in occupied France and an intelligence network, was captured and sent to Auschwitz and there took part in the attempt – suicidal for almost all involved – to blow up the crematoria. In 1968, he was removed from his post and expelled from the PUWP. In response to private remonstrations from the French and Italian Communist Parties, Gomułka suggested that his Party membership might be restored if he appealed. He refused either to appeal or to leave the country. The government then stopped his daughter, a Conservatoire student, from following her musical studies. Countless other examples showed that Jewish origins outweighed all decorations for courage in the Communist resistance or on the battle-fronts. At the time of writing, the victims of 1967–8 have not been given restitution.

the life of my generation', lines gibing at Russian power drew violent applause. The closure produced a spontaneous street demonstration by Warsaw students, which was broken up by the police.

After a month of rising tension, in which the authorities answered student and intellectual protest with abuse, threats and anti-Semitic leaflets, on 8 March a mass meeting in Warsaw University was broken up by bus-loads of Party-organized thugs. In the following days and weeks, police and student demonstrators fought on the streets of Warsaw, while in Kraków, after the police had burst into the university and beaten up several professors as well as the students they were hunting, the situation grew so serious that para-troops were brought in to occupy the city. The March student revolt led to the arrest of 1,200 students in Warsaw alone, and to the sacking of the professors and lecturers who supported them.

It was suspected at the time that the closing of *Dziady* and the violence used against those who protested were a deliberate provocation by Moczar's supporters. (Dejmek himself now believes that the provocateur was Gomułka, hoping to create a panic in which he could destroy both the liberal intellectuals and his own Party rivals.) Whatever the truth, the 'partisan' faction now launched its full offensive. While the mass of ordinary Poles watched bewildered, the Party and the entire administration plunged into a prolonged hysteria of purges, anti-Semitic slander, denunciation of supposed revisionists and 'crypto-Stalinists', and a general onslaught on the creative intellectuals.

There are few parallels to this convulsion in European history. Nobody seemed to be in control of Poland. Gomułka vainly tried to divert the avalanche by denying that 'Zionism' was any threat to the nation while joining the attack on the intellectuals and students, but he was hardly heeded. The immediate victims were the remaining Jews, or supposed Jews, in public life. More than half the remaining Jewish population, pressed to apply for exit permits, fled abroad. A height of insanity was reached in the Foreign Ministry, where junior diplomats denounced ambassadors for 'cosmo-politanism' and some officials were obliged to furnish data about the racial origins of their grandmothers. Adam Rapacki, who as foreign minister and author of the plan for military disengagement which bore his name was one of Europe's most respected statesmen, stayed away from his ministry in broken-hearted disgust, and was replaced at the end of the year. With a very few honourable exceptions, the entire press and broadcasting media joined this witch-hunt.

Bieńkowski's transition from 'political' to 'police dictatorship' was taking place. As the storm raged on through the spring and early summer,

Gomułka's position became rapidly weaker within the leadership. It seemed a matter only of time before General Moczar or one of his associates would replace him. But the international situation supervened.

This was the year of Czechoslovakia. The Soviet leaders, full of disquiet as Dubček's reform movement developed in Prague, wanted no turbulence in the rest of their alliance. They looked on Moczar with suspicion, well aware that a revival of untreated Polish nationalism and historical nostalgia would bring a revival of anti-Russian feeling with it. One of Moczar's editors told a closed meeting that the issue of the Katyń massacre should be re-opened, and a tape of his remarks reached the Soviet embassy in Warsaw. Moczar, in the Soviet view, was trying to turn Poland into another Romania, a police dictatorship held together by anti-Russian rhetoric that would take an independent line within the Warsaw Pact and Comecon. In contrast, Władysław Gomułka, so unwillingly tolerated by Khrushchev, now seemed to Leonid Brezhnev to personify the cause of Polish–Soviet friendship. Gomułka, in spite of his own experiences in 1956, had little sympathy for Dubček's experiment. Polish students were chanting Dubček's name in the streets of Warsaw; there seemed to be counter-revolution in the wind from Prague, and it was blowing his way. He willingly provided Polish troops for the joint Warsaw Pact invasion force that occupied Czechoslovakia in August.*

Gomułka's reward soon arrived. Before and during the Fifth PUWP Congress that November, the Soviet leaders threw their support vigorously behind him. Moczar was held where he was – only a candidate member of the Politburo. Gomułka was re-elected leader and kept his old team around him, with the addition of some younger and better-educated men. The atmosphere of the congress was still fanatical and strained; one woman said, 'We have the most perfect form of democracy in the history of the world,' while another delegate claimed that the congress was the 'main event in Europe'. But the 'partisan' offensive had been checked.

The grotesque events of 1968 in Poland had three results. In the first place, although he survived politically, Gomułka was fatally weakened. From being the most independent Party leader in eastern Europe in 1956, he had now become a leader who owed his position to Soviet interference

---

*Apart from intellectuals and students, many Poles were extraordinarily unsympathetic to the Czechs and Slovaks in 1968. There is traditional antipathy between Poles and Czechs, updated by recent history. The replies of Polish officers questioned in Czechoslovakia by foreign journalists illustrated the sick, contorted consciousness of those years: 'Occupation? The Czechs never knew what occupation meant, and it's time they did.' Or: 'They greeted Russian tanks with red flags in 1945, and they gave us no help in 1956. Now they can get what's coming to them.'

in Polish politics. In the mood of inflamed nationalism, this lesson was plain to read.

Secondly, the grievances which had been fomented by the 'partisan' movement remained. Poland had experienced in 1968 something not unlike the Cultural Revolution in China: even though it had been manipulated from above, the outbreak was also a genuine attack on élitism, on bureaucracy, even on wage differentials. When Moczar was blocked and the anti-Jewish hysteria died down, three kinds of unsatisfied hope remained and festered. One was this challenge to privilege, most powerful in the lower ranks of the Party. The second was the hope of the technical intelligentsia, or at least of those members of it who found Moczarism attractive, to replace the Party élite they were attacking. The third was the sort of nationalism that Moczar and the 'partisans' had evoked. This was not the 'socialist patriotism' of the 1956 reformers. It was a legitimation of the old idea of the nation as the supreme moral cause, as Roman Dmowski had preached it. The cupboards that contained recent Polish history, its glories but also all its religiosity and authoritarianism, were now open, and there was no way to close them again.

The most striking result of 1968, however, was a change in the nature of opposition in Poland. In March, the student movement had stuck closely to the ideals of 1956. In their leaflets and programme papers, the students had insisted on their loyalty to socialism. With eloquent logic, they had called for liberal reforms within the system, even sending a pathetic appeal to Gomułka in the illusion that he could not be aware of the police repression they were enduring. They wanted an end to censorship, a decentralizing reform of the economy, academic liberty. They pleaded that 'nationalism is alien to us. The attribution to the student movement of anti-Soviet slogans is baseless ...' They promised that they stood 'on the ground of socialism; we defend social control over economic decisions'.

They failed to win any active working-class support, in spite of their carefully socialist messages to factories and their appeals to the 'bond between workers and students'. Some workers, instead, were among those who came in buses to chase them off the Warsaw University campus. The March protest left the Polish intellectuals isolated in their moment of crisis. And a whole tradition of intellectual opposition – that sceptical, *marxisant*, anti-clerical tradition which skirmished for freedom and tolerance between the Goliaths of Church and Party dogmatism – died under the clubs of the police in March.

The indifference of the working class was a stunning blow. The purges of Jews and liberals from the media and every creative pursuit permanently broke the back of the old 'October' opposition, which never revived. Indeed, it was some eight years before intellectual opposition of any kind became again noticeable in Poland. And it was a very different animal that re-emerged: agnostic towards socialism but no longer towards the Church, accepting an essentially Catholic view of nationalism, servicing working-class protest rather than claiming the historic right to lead it.

None were better placed to register this change than some of those who were now forced to leave Poland and returned only many years later. Jan Kott, the critic, came back to Poland in 1979, thirteen years after he had departed into exile. The tradition of intellectual opposition he had known and been part of had almost totally disappeared and been replaced by another. In the 1960s, when one of Kott's dissident friends died, he had an agnostic burial, and Kołakowski defiantly sang the 'Internationale' over his grave. Kott returned to a Poland in which such occasions were celebrated with a funeral Mass and the singing of the national anthem: 'And Still Poland Has Not Perished ...'

Kott wrote in the unofficial literary magazine *Zapis* about a discussion with friends of several generations: 'Three names were passionately empha-sized: Dmowski, Piłsudski and Daszyński.* For a time I simply couldn't grasp what was going on. I rubbed my eyes. What did this recall? In which emigration in London, in which anachronistic Warsaw did I find myself? Before the war ... but before which war, the second? No, before the first! I had the impression that time had stood still. History was running back-wards. In the space of those thirteen years while I had been away, quite different chapters of Polish history had returned. This furious dispute, in which names were brandished like evocative signs, was about the choices and alternatives of 1979.'[4]

At the close of 1968, as the madness at last began to drain off an emotion-ally exhausted country, this transformation had not begun to show itself. That would take nearly ten years. But 'the March Events' had, although few realized it at the time, already cut the link that bound the intellectual opposition to the Party – or rather, to hopes of a democratic socialism emerging through the Party. By a sharp irony, the Polish opposition now began to explore those cupboards of history broken open by its worst enemy, the 'partisan' fanatics. And what the dissidents found there, at first mis-trustfully but then with growing fascination, was above all the Catholic Church.

---

* Ignacy Daszyński, a leader of the Polish Socialist Party (PPS) before and after 1918, briefly vice-premier of Poland.

Journalists often get things wrong. In the late 1960s, correspondents writing about Poland were well aware of this invocation of nationalist history. But we – the author was one of them – supposed that this was a manipulation, an artificial nostalgia, an exhibiting of the dead roots of the past. We were very wrong. In 1944, we thought, the tree of Polish history had been sawn down for good, and a new house had been built over the stump. In 1968, some holes had appeared in the floor of the house, and certain uninviting parts of the stump could be seen through them. But in the mid-1970s, as the floor began to disintegrate, the truth of what was taking place could no longer be ignored: the tree was growing again, shoving its huge, amputated head up through all the concrete laid on top of it. All of Poland's political and spiritual tradition was reviving, as people reconnected the present to the years *before* that 'new beginning' marked by the July Manifesto of 1944. Each successive shock – 1970, 1976 and finally 1980 – broke away more pieces of the house that Gomułka had founded a generation before. And each time, more of this buried but ominously authentic Polish consciousness emerged into the light.

In his last two years in power, between the Fifth Party Congress in November 1968 and the riots of December 1970 which overthrew him, Gomułka attempted an ambitious new start. For the first time, the PUWP put real energy into a programme of economic reform, much of it derived from the ideas which the Party had commissioned and then neglected a decade before. To provide a general staff for these changes and to hold the political balance against the 'partisans' (still the most powerful faction in the Party), Gomułka brought into the leadership a group of younger men, many of whom had expert qualifications. Józef Tejchma had some reputation among intellectuals as a man of tolerant and enlightened views. Stanisław Kociołek rapidly acquired a retinue of young technocrats and economic journalists who saw him as a man who might drag Polish management and planning into the electronic age.

The reform plans proposed to reward successful enterprises by 'economic incentives' and bonuses. A certain amount of decision-making about production would be decentralized. Above all, investment would be concentrated on a few key industries. Electronics, machine tools and the chemical industry were the main targets for this 'selective investment' programme, which aimed to attract western co-operation and equipment and thus to introduce modern technology, step by step, into the whole economy. But the guiding of the reform was entrusted to Bolesław Jaszczuk, an impetuous and aggressive personality whose methods annoyed many of his Party colleagues and spread a sense of insecurity throughout the managerial élite on whose support the reform relied.

The reform had enlightened objectives, as far as they went. But Jaszczuk's plans came too late, and were formulated too narrowly, to have any real chance of success. For one thing, they contained no promise of political change. Kołakowski had warned a few years before that a developed technological economy, above all one with market elements, could not operate properly without truthful information and open discussion – in other words, that there was a necessary link between economic modernization and a relaxation of censorship and political discipline. But such relaxation formed no part of the plans. Neither did any increased participation by the working class. The trade unions were not made any more effective or representative. Jaszczuk preferred the old practice of imposing change from the centre. He did not invite advice or criticism from his colleagues, still less from those who were going to be directly affected by his decisions.

Secondly, 'selective investment' turned out to mean the financial starvation of other spending programmes, especially social programmes. Housing was particularly badly neglected. Consumption, as usual, was given low priority, and the cost of living steadily overtook the very slight increase in real wages. Although agriculture was now supposed to have equal priority with industrial investment, most government spending still favoured the state farms, while Gomułka's personal insistence that Poland must be self-supporting in fodder, in order to reduce hard-currency spending on western gain, was making it increasingly hard for private peasants to make a living by raising livestock. Food shortages reappeared, as demand and spending power hunted diminishing supplies – especially of meat – out of the shops. Bad harvests brought this imbalance, a recurrent plague of the Polish post-war economy, into crisis during 1970.

Finally, although these limited reform plans fell short of a true 'new model' which would liberate prices and introduce elements of a market economy, they still provoked the classic problem set by all such proposals in Communist states. This was simply the class problem. Any attempt to rationalize these post-Stalinist economies, with their inflated work-forces, their indifference to demand or profitability, raised the question: who benefits? The qualified technical intelligentsia would obviously do well out of them; they would at last be given jobs and opportunities which corresponded to their talents. But the workers, in the short term, were being offered only insecurity. An enterprise that did not pay its way might now have to increase productivity by shedding labour, or even close down. This problem had arisen in Czechoslovakia as soon as market-economy proposals were accepted in 1967. The Czech and Slovak working classes remained uneasy about the implications of the economic programme devised during the 'Prague Spring', until they set about the formation of workers' councils to manage all industry. The same tensions arose in Hungary – where until now they have been contained.

The Polish workers, with their low standard of living, were especially vulnerable. As George Błażyński has put it, 'The rusty but somehow cosy factories, those "indoor-relief" houses in which enormous work-forces enjoyed total job security, in which there was no point in excessive effort and no bother about whether the product was wanted or not – all that was to vanish.'[5] Unemployment had been officially banished for a generation, and the chronic over-staffing in industry had been aggravated by a demographic 'bulge' which had obliged the government to create $1\frac{1}{2}$ million extra jobs between 1965 and 1970. Jaszczuk's reforms not only accepted the possibility of unemployment but, through the incentive schemes, threatened many workers in uncompetitive industries with an income freeze in a period of rising prices. As the decade closed, the working class was increasingly nervous, angry and – of course – impotent. The trade unions and the decay of factory-floor democracy effectively gagged the industrial proletariat. Gomułka and Jaszczuk drove heedlessly forward with their plans.

On 7 December 1970, the question of Poland's western borders was finally settled. Chancellor Willy Brandt of West Germany came to Warsaw and signed a treaty which recognized that the line of the Oder and Neisse rivers formed the western frontier of Poland, abandoned Bonn's old claim to the Reich frontiers of 1937 and agreed to open full diplomatic relations. It was a moment of moral triumph for Brandt. Kneeling before the monument to the fighters of the Warsaw Ghetto, he honoured a lifetime's dedication to making good the wounds inflicted by the Third Reich on other countries and his own. But it was a political triumph for Gomułka and for twenty years of Polish diplomacy. To reach this moment, the Poles had overcome not only the basic constitutional dogma on which West Germany had been founded in 1949, but the constant efforts by the German Democratic Republic – insistent that nobody should deal with the Bonn government before it recognized the GDR – to delay or obstruct such a settlement. And the Poles had also stuck to their purpose through two terrifying episodes in 1953 and 1964 when it looked as if the Soviet Union might be about to reunify Germany without regard for Poland's interests. The Warsaw Treaty between Poland and West Germany could in fact have been signed a few months earlier, but the Soviet Union insisted on completing its own

'Moscow Treaty' with Bonn, recognizing existing European frontiers, before Poland finished its own negotiations.

It was the Polish–West German agreement, the Warsaw Treaty of 1970, which unbolted the gates to the détente process of the 1970s. It settled the only important frontier argument which remained in Europe, and so implied that the map of Europe which was drawn by the Second World War and its aftermath could be ratified by a continental conference. This was the most important function of the Conference on European Security and Co-operation, which met in 1975 and collectively proclaimed the inviolable nature of the post-war frontiers. The Warsaw Treaty made this possible, and even the Moscow Treaty, though prior in time, was really a result of the Gomułka–Brandt understanding. The 'Basic Treaty' between the two German states, signed in 1972, was only made possible because, with the Oder–Neisse question settled, the Polish and Soviet interest in keeping the Germanies in confrontation subsided.

The Warsaw Treaty, which was essentially an agreement on Polish terms, also opened direct Polish access to the richest industrial economy in western Europe. West German industry, traditionally experienced in the eastern European market, had for years been trading profitably with Poland. Berthold Beitz, manager of the Krupp steel concern, had acted as an un-official ambassador to Poland on many occasions and knew Gomułka well. Now these connections could be expanded with full government support. It was due to Gomułka's patriotic obstinacy that this was a genuinely bilateral relationship, rather than part of some collective arrangement regulated by the Soviet Union on one side and the European Economic Community on the other.

Secondly, the Warsaw Treaty undermined the *raison d'état* argument which all Polish governments since 1944 had used to justify Poland's links with the Soviet Union. Up to 1970, membership of the 'socialist camp' had been rationalized as a necessity because 'the Germans' still asserted their right to alter Poland's frontiers. While West German school atlases showed Szczecin or Wrocław as 'Stettin' or 'Breslau' in a part of Germany 'under Polish administration', and while West German television gave nightly weather forecasts for Silesia and East Prussia, this necessity was not difficult to demonstrate. But after December 1970, this argument evaporated. What, then, was Poland's national interest in continuing subordination to Soviet strategy?

Nobody can measure how far in the long run the Warsaw Treaty acceler-ated the erosion of Party authority in Poland. Perhaps the clearest evidence was the gradual leak of content from the expression *racja stanu* (*raison d'état*). Hitherto, the words had implied the need for Soviet military and political protection against the 'German threat'. But by 1980 the expression meant only the necessity of staying in the Soviet orbit – because the alternative was Soviet military intervention. And as the year 1980 wore on, *racja stanu* lost even more of its original content and came to signify the need to be prudent over *internal* changes in order to avoid such an intervention.

In the end – and this was a measure of the awful mental bankruptcy of the Party leadership – the PUWP was in effect saying to the nation: We have to have socialism because the alternative is the Red Army. This was actually admitted in public, during the February 1981 preparatory debates for the PUWP emergency congress, by a certain Professor Grzelak: 'We now often hear it said that socialism in our country, the recognition of the Party's leading role, is today being treated as a *raison d'état*. We ourselves use this argument often ... we must restore to socialism its ideological and moral values.'

The Tragedy of December 1970

On 12 December 1970, Warsaw radio announced a series of steep and unexpected price changes. They had been decided a few days before in the Politburo of the PUWP, the Party leadership's first action after the departure of the West German guests. The average increase in the retail price of consumer goods was only 8 per cent; some domestic equipment – television sets, refrigerators – was actually made cheaper. But the central feature was a huge rise in the price of certain foods. Flour rose by 16 per cent, sugar by 14 per cent and meat by 17 per cent.

The idea of increasing the shop prices of food, especially, was in itself common-sense economics and entirely consistent with the reforms which Jaszczuk was directing. The reforms included a commitment to bring prices nearer to the real cost of production, and to reduce the already huge subsidies paid by the government to hold down the price of food in the shops; the supply of meat, in particular, was falling rapidly behind demand.

It was the method used which brought about disaster. It was not untried; at least three times before – in 1953, 1959 and 1965 – the government had proclaimed large increases in the price of food overnight. Any advance warning or step-by-step increase would, it was assumed, provoke a stampede of panic buying that would empty the shops and make black-market fortunes. The trouble in 1970 was, firstly, that the population was already mutinous and anxious about future jobs and wages, and secondly that the increases were decreed during the week before Christmas, when all Polish families accumulate meat, fish and alcohol for a feast that is looked forward to all through the year. There were protests and warnings both at the Politburo session and from the provincial Party committees, which were informed of the plan only on the morning of the announcement. But Gomułka, his closest ally Zenon Kliszko and Jaszczuk ignored them.

12 December was a Saturday. On the following Monday morning, three thousand workers from the Lenin Shipyard at Gdańsk marched on the provincial Party headquarters. They were ordered to return to work. Angry crowds began to roam Gdańsk, and stones were thrown. The city militia failed to hold the masses back and general tumult spread. The Party headquarters and other buildings were attacked, and fires were started.

On Tuesday, 15 December, the workers of the Paris Commune Shipyard in Gdynia stopped work and demonstrated in the main streets. In Gdańsk, where a general strike was proclaimed in the morning, the police opened fire on the demonstrators and men were killed on both sides. In the fighting, the Party building and the main railway station were burned down. The following day, the rebellion spread to the near-by towns of Słupsk and Elbląg, and there were reports of sympathy strikes elsewhere. The men and women of the Warski Shipyards at Szczecin prepared to strike.

The argument about who ordered the police to shoot grinds on even today. But the responsibility for the decision to use force, rather than to negotiate, plainly lies with Gomułka himself, who had already decided on the Tuesday that the fearful events on the coast were 'counter-revolution'. Kociołek was sent down to Gdańsk, followed by Kliszko, who placed himself in charge of operations and issued orders so contradictory that all cohesion between the Party authorities and the security forces on the spot broke down. The actual order to open fire almost certainly came from Gomułka on the Tuesday, and went down the chain of command through the prime minister, Józef Cyrankiewicz, to Kliszko, in Gdańsk, who passed it on to General Korczyński.* Much blame attaches to Kliszko personally, who announced

---

*Among the profuse folk-lore about December 1970 is the belief that the Polish army did not take part in the shooting. This tells more about popular nationalism and its faith in the army than about what really happened. Army units did open fire, for example at the Paris Commune Shipyard massacre. The myth, however, insists that these were militia (police) disguised by Kliszko in army uniforms. What is true is that General Wojciech Jaruzelski, the minister of defence (who became prime minister in February 1981), refused to allow the army to use force when Gomułka demanded it. Korczyński appears to have used troops without Jaruzelski's direct authority.

on no evidence whatever that the workers intended to sabotage and destroy the shipyards.

On the Wednesday, the fighting in Gdańsk died down, as the workers began an occupation strike of the factories and shipyards and drew up a list of demands. That night, Kociołek appealed on local radio to the workers to return to work the following morning; he discovered too late that Kliszko was preparing to block access to the Gdynia yards to prevent 'sabotage'. On the Thursday morning, in the darkness before dawn, the workers streaming out of the trains towards the Paris Commune yard were fired on and at least thirteen were killed. The same day, the Szczecin shipyard workers surged out into the city and street fighting, at the cost of at least sixteen lives and probably twice as many, continued through that day and the Friday.

By the weekend, Poland was close to a national working-class insurrection. The fighting had almost ceased, but work was stopping throughout the country, and a general strike seemed only hours away. On the coast, workers were in control of yards and factories; at Szczecin, they had set up a complete parallel city government, based on an elected inter-factory strike committee which kept order in the streets and organized essential supplies. Among the twenty-one demands drawn up by the Szczecin strikers there figured for the first time the call for 'independent trade unions under the authority of the working class', and for the resignation of the existing Central Council of Trade Unions (CRZZ).

Gomułka's personal position was collapsing. A message from Brezhnev, advising a political rather than a military solution to the crisis, discredited his whole approach. Frantic with rage and anxiety, he suffered a slight (but genuine) stroke which partially blinded him, and he was carted off, protesting, on a stretcher. His rivals and opponents now joined to force an emergency Politburo session, and a full Central Committee meeting was called for Sunday, 20 December.

It was evident to his colleagues that Moczar, as head of security, was aiming for the succession. But some rapid manoeuvres, probably backed by the Soviet leaders, brought forward the less contentious name of Edward Gierek, the local Party secretary in industrial Upper Silesia. Although Gomułka made one last, raging irruption into the discussions, he was bundled back to hospital and Gierek was elected First Secretary. The same night, on radio and television, the new Party leader admitted that 'the working class was provoked beyond endurance' and that the Party had lost contact with the nation.

The fall of Gomułka and Gierek's promising début put an end to the disturbances for the time being. But this was not the end of the movement. After the Christmas break, continuous mass meetings and breaks in production, especially on the coast, showed that the workers were in the mood for more definite guarantees. Gierek had already promised a wage increase for the low-paid and a freeze on prices. This was not enough, and the original economic grievances had now been compounded by the fact that Polish blood had been shed by Poles.

The Polish journalist Barbara Seidler went to Gdańsk in mid-January and found Party officials swamped with list after list of fresh demands. At meetings in the yards, the questions were not just about wages and conditions now but about basic political problems. At Party meetings, officials who began 'Comrades!' were whistled down. Above all, the speakers wanted the truth told in the press, 'how to make sure ... that all that lying never begins again'. They 'claim that the press did not live up to its task in those heated days. It only mentioned a few shops broken into by the dregs of humanity and didn't explain the motives that brought the workers of the coast on to the street.'[6]

It was a local newspaper which proved this point by detonating the next explosion in Szczecin. Workers in the Warski Shipyard pipe department were surprised one day in late January to see at one of their meetings a number of journalists and a banner promising that the department would outdo its planned production target. A picture of the banner then appeared in the local paper over a faked montage of applauding workers, with an equally faked account of their enthusiastic pledges. On 22 January, the Warski Shipyard struck, other yards and factories joined in, and a quite new strike committee, more radical than that of December, emerged. Now the workers demanded cancellation of the price rises, free Party and trade union elections, a workers' commission to take over the yard, a full correction of the pipe-shop fantasia in the newspapers and the presence of Edward Gierek and the prime minister to discuss their grievances.

A second general explosion was about to take place along the coast. Strikes were beginning to break out again in several industries at Gdańsk. Everywhere, the workers were asking for the punishment of those guilty of firing upon them, for the release of men arrested in December, for the removal from the leadership of men they associated with the repressions of December. They wanted, like the Warski staff, free elections to workers' councils and unions, and 'reliable information' in the country as a whole. They had been disappointed a few days before when the trade union leader Loga-Sowiński had resigned only to be replaced by the elderly Stalinist Władysław Kruczek, a gesture obviously designed to reassure the Soviet Union.

On the afternoon of the 24th, several taxis appeared at the gate of the Warski Shipyard in Szczecin. A tall, grey-haired man got out of one of them and had some trouble in persuading the pickets that he was indeed Edward Gierek, First Secretary of the PUWP. He had brought with him the new prime minister, Piotr Jaroszewicz, General Jaruzelski and Franciszek Szlachcic, the minister of the interior. The strike committee had been warned by telephone only a few minutes before that Gierek was on his way, and the mass meeting that gathered to debate with him in the main hall was not the elected assembly of delegates the committee had established. None the less, there followed nine passionate hours of face-to-face argument about the past and the immediate future.

Gierek's approach, repeated the next day at Gdańsk, was to appeal disarmingly to class loyalty. He was a worker, who had won coal with his hands in the pits of France and Belgium; they were workers too. He begged for their support, not on behalf of the official ideology but for himself, as an individual and a Polish patriot. 'I say to you: help us, help me ... I am only a worker like you ... But now, and I tell you this in all solemnity as a Pole and as a Communist, the fate of our nation and the cause of socialism are in the balance.'

He brought it off. The workers were impressed that he had come to them, and they were inclined to trust him. The alternative would have been to challenge the Party itself and 'socialism' – whatever that had come to mean – and they were not prepared for such a challenge. Gierek listened to their grievances and promised that the strike committee could now become the organizing body for absolutely free elections to a workers' council at Warski, but he insisted that the December price increases could not be reversed.

Normal working slowly resumed in the days after his visit. The prices question still festered, however, until the women of the Łódź textile mills – whose rates of pay and working conditions remained scandalous – struck in mid-February. Prime minister Jaroszewicz went down to Łódź but, faced by angry and resolute assemblies of women, failed to repeat Gierek's *coup de théâtre*. The following day, with reports of still more unrest from Szczecin, the government backed down and restored the old food prices.

The broad meaning of these tremendous events was obvious enough. This was the first time that a Communist government had been overthrown directly by the action of the industrial proletariat, the class which in theory ruled through the Party as the vanguard of the working class. This was also the first time since the 1920s that a ruling Party leader had engaged in open and direct debate with workers on the factory floor about the whole future development of society. (And it should be added that this was the first occasion in all post-war Europe, East or West, that a government had been destroyed by spontaneous mass protest, a feat to be repeated four years later in Northern Ireland by the Ulster Workers' Council.)

December 1970 also confirmed the split in the Polish opposition which had developed since 1956 and which had been manifest in the outbursts of March 1968. Intellectuals took almost no part in the events. In March 1968, the students of the Gdańsk Polytechnic had announced, 'We solidarize ourselves above all with the Polish working class,' but they had received no support from that class. On the first day of the December 1970 demonstrations, the shipyard workers marched to the Gdańsk Polytechnic and called on the students to join them. They stayed indoors.

This was a movement of the workers alone, which lacked any clear strategic idea of how to maintain its impetus. Religious or anti-Soviet feelings were not prominent in their demands, although one of the wilder rumours that flew across Poland after the price rises suggested that their purpose was the abolition of Christmas as a religious holiday. Instead, the strikers constantly reaffirmed their fundamental belief in socialism and in the possibility of a better Party leadership which could introduce both the economic and democratic reforms they asked for. In the early days of the revolt, some marchers sang the 'Internationale' and carried red banners. The true extent of their isolation and exploitation in Polish society had not yet dawned on the workers. In the following ten years, they were to learn many bitter lessons.

Chapter Four

Gierek and the Third Cycle

The Leap Forward

The new cycle of history which began in the flames of 1970 took ten years to revolve. The rule of Edward Gierek, that straightforward and often humble personality whose affection for working people was genuine and who initially achieved so much, ended in its turn in ruins. There should be no place for *Schadenfreude* here, even for the most devout anti-Communist. This was a failure so total, at the last, and so pathetic that it must frighten anyone who hopes that human beings can combine to chart and accomplish their own improvement. The Polish state between 1970 and 1980 did not simply fail to reach its aims. It achieved, in some detail, exactly what it set out to avoid.

The Party began by declaring that it would never lose contact with the working class again; it left the workers more alienated from the Party than at any time since 1944. The decade opened with a grand drive to raise consumption and living standards; it ended with sullen queues standing in the slush for basic staples like butter, meat and sugar. It witnessed a breakneck industrialization intended to raise technology to standards competitive with the West; ten years later, Poland stood in despair before a foreign debt of some $23 billion. The state at last conceded that private agriculture was there to stay and gave the peasantry its fair share of investment; by the late 1970s, the gap between food supply and demand had grown so enormous that nearly 40 per cent of the state budget was being spent on retail food subsidies.

In 1971, Gierek declared that the Party could not possibly regulate everything: the Party should guide, but governing should be left to the government. By 1980, the Party's interference in social and economic life had reached lengths unparalleled since the Stalinist dictatorship. He set out by inviting all intellectuals, Party and non-Party, to join a free and open debate on the 'renewal' of Polish life; by the late 1970s, it was said that there had never been a time when Poles spoke so freely in private while the mass media were so mendacious and boring. And that heavy, decent man who had put aside the pomp of his office to go and talk face to face with angry workers ended up as ignorant of their mood, as isolated from the true political situation, as Gomułka had been before him.

The good resolutions taken at the outset were almost an echo of those taken in 1956 and were to be echoed in turn by those which Stanisław Kania proclaimed after August 1980. The Party's internal democracy was to be restored to 'Leninist norms'. Workers would always be consulted: Gierek devised a system that allowed the work-forces of the largest factories direct access to him and directly elected representation at Party congresses. Intellectuals would be heard: respected experts and academics were named to a commission on modernizing the administration of the economy and the state headed by Jan Szydlak, a Politburo member, and to a commission on educational reform headed by the sociologist Professor Jan Szczepański. There was to be separation of the work of Party and state: Poland's parliament, the Sejm, was to be given the authority and the time it needed to debate and scrutinize legislation.

This new epoch was launched at the Eighth Plenum, held in early February 1971. For the first time, a member of the Politburo reported to the public on television on each day's proceedings, and the speeches were published in a special number of the PUWP's theoretical journal. From Gierek and many others came sonorous criticism of the Gomułka leadership and solemn commitments to reform. Gomułka was suspended from the Central Committee, while Kliszko and Jaszczuk, who both made sulky speeches justifying their actions, were expelled. Several other Gomułka lieutenants were allowed to resign. Mieczysław Moczar, who had survived as a Politburo member, took the opportunity to blacken further the reputations of his ex-colleagues: although still head of security in 1970, he had astutely gone to ground on the first news of the December riots, foreseeing that the crisis would ruin anyone who tried to handle it. But later in the year, for reasons still obscure, Moczar himself was removed from the Politburo and the old 'partisan' faction soon crumbled to insignificance. The Eighth Plenum, however, avoided any speculation about whether the Party structure itself, rather than its abuse, might be responsible for the collapses in 1956 and 1970. Once again, the PUWP had shied away from political change and reaffirmed that a prosperous economy would eliminate the basic sources of social tension.

Poland now took its own 'Great Leap Forward'. Jaszczuk's selective investment policy was scrapped, and the raising of the living standard became the central objective. For some years, the new plan scored real and astonishing successes. An import-led investment boom gave Poland, by 1973, the third-fastest national growth rate in the world. Even in the first year, real wages rose by more than 5 per cent and production of consumer goods by 7 per cent. In 1971, the Soviet Union provided Poland with $100 million in hard-currency credits for purchases in the West, and the United States offered $25 million credit to buy grain. At the end of the year, a Polish–Soviet agreement provided for another two million tons of Russian grain over five years, while consumer imports from the rest of the Soviet bloc increased by nearly a third. Western Europe sold Poland 100,000 tons of meat and meat products.

Quite rapidly, plans began to be outstripped by achievement, and targets were regularly raised. In 1972, national income rose by 10 per cent, nearly twice as fast as planned, and the 1973 figures were even better. This was not only an industrial boom. With a courage born of desperation, the Party decided to ignore Soviet ideological orthodoxy and accept that private farming should be treated as an essential component of the economy; compulsory deliveries to state purchasing agencies were abolished, taxes were cut and the peasants were admitted to the benefits of the welfare state. With the help of some good seasons, agricultural output began to rise.

The Polish population at last emerged from the bleak deprivation of the 1960s. The quality of life rapidly improved. Real wages rose by 40 per cent in the first five Gierek years, and at first there was much more to buy in the shops. The empty streets of Warsaw and other big cities began to fill up with small cars, as Poland started to produce the Polski Fiat under licence. It became easier to acquire hard currency, especially dollars, from relations in the West.

The Poles, who since 1956 had enjoyed the widest freedom of travel of any people in the Soviet bloc, now headed west by the hundreds of thousands. The French and Italian beaches grew accustomed to the arrival of dusty cars full of cheerful Poles, living out of cans and selling cartons of their Carmen cigarettes to save money. London hotels and restaurants gave illegal work to thousands of Polish girls and boys who equipped themselves with hi-fi gear and saucy clothes before going home. Deliberately, Gierek encouraged the creation of close links with the Polonia – the numerous and usually very anti-Communist communities of Poles or Polish descendants living in the western world. In the 1970s, some elderly American Poles began to migrate back to Poland, where they were allowed to draw American pensions at luscious exchange rates and even encouraged to build retirement houses.

With this rise in living standards, supported by a new housing programme and much more generous welfare and health benefits, went yet another attempt to decentralize industrial management. The government linked together groups of factories in the same branch of industry; known as WOGs (the Polish acronym for Large Industrial Organizations), these groupings were allowed considerable independence. In particular, they were able to vary wages, and to relate earnings to increased production and sales. This was intended to be only a cautious beginning; the WOGs amounted neither to the Jugoslav system of workers' self-management nor to the Hungarian decentralization of economic responsibility down to plant level. But in the impetuous tradition of Polish experiment, the WOGs were extended before they had properly proved themselves, until by the end of 1975, only two years after their first introduction, they accounted for 67 per cent of all Polish industrial production. Again, they worked brilliantly to begin with, their productivity outstripping that of conventional industry. But although they used their independence to invest more and more heavily, and continuously increased their wages, there was no reliable market indicator in the economy to establish how effective they were.

By 1974–5, the first signs of strain were appearing. The whole 'Leap' was, in its way, another Somosierra charge: the calculated risk of running up heavy debts, especially in the West, in order to import the components of a modern industrial base that would soon pay off those debts. Under Gomułka, for instance, the average spending on the import of western machinery was some $100 million a year. By 1972, this figure had multiplied by seven, and in 1974 it reached no less than $1,900 million.[1] It was Poland's bad luck that the Middle East war of 1973, and the colossal rise in oil prices, hit the programme in mid-stride. Although Poland's oil supplies came from the Soviet Union and were thus protected against the disaster in the world oil market, the cost of western industrial imports now soared upwards. Poland's foreign debt, around $700 million in late 1971 reached over $6 billion in 1975 and continued to climb almost vertically.[2]

Western inflation, imported in the cost of each machine-tool from West Germany or Sweden, now combined with the growing pressure of home-grown inflation. Part of the problem had been created by the workers' victories in 1970–71. The government had been forced at once to grant large wage increases and overtime concessions and to revoke the higher food prices. Once again, personal incomes were beginning to tower over the limited supplies on the market. Shortages not only of food but of many consumer goods and durables became acute. And the reckless generosity of the WOGs to their employees made matters worse.

At the same time, there was a change of heart in the state's approach to the private peasantry. The transfer of state land into private hands became more difficult, and new restrictions on inheritance, intended to assist the emergence of larger 'capitalist' farms, were regarded by the peasants as evidence that the government had not, after all, given up its campaign to destroy them and collectivize agriculture. Private farmers found it harder to get the fertilizer and other resources they required, and there were complaints that a small élite of 'specialist' farmers and market gardeners was being unfairly favoured.

Inadequate supplies to the home market were still further reduced by Poland's desperate effort to maintain exports to the West – including food exports – and to contain its trade deficit. With too little on sale, the rate of savings began to bulge ominously, and the average proportion of income put away per person multiplied by five between 1970 and 1976.[3]

In Warsaw, dribbles of blood up the stairways of apartment buildings needed no forensic analysis. Any visitor knew that a peasant woman lugging sacks of black-market veal and pork had been selling from door to door. With remarkable altruism, the East Germans agreed to help by opening their own well-stocked markets to Polish consumers. Visas for the GDR were abolished, but the inrush of shoppers (reaching seven million in 1974) eventually led to their reintroduction. East Berlin became a parking-lot for hundreds of dusty Polish buses, while in the department stores on Alexanderplatz – the stock labels and bargain announcements printed in Polish as well as German – day-trippers from all over western and northern Poland emptied the shelves. Consumer shortages occurred in many GDR cities, and the Germans began to mutter ungenerously about their neighbours.

Within Poland, the political thaw of 1971 did not last long. Public opinion, more sceptical than it had been after 1956, was not surprised to see censorship fully restored over the next two years. Gierek was even more anxious than Gomułka to enforce flattering, uncritical reporting on all matters Soviet. One motive was to propitiate Moscow for the blatantly un-Soviet relationship which was now developing in Poland between the Party and the traditionalist forces of Church and peasantry. But the restoration of censorship was also Poland's response to Brezhnev's prescient comment on the nature of détente: that as contacts between states with different social systems grew closer, the ideological struggle between them would grow more intense. Western as well as eastern attitudes in the 1970s soon confirmed his axiom. There was a sharp increase in ideological control and propaganda in the states of the Soviet bloc, but also a return to a much more militant anti-Communism in the West, especially in Britain.

Gierek's team was built around men he had worked with in his days as Party secretary at Katowice, the smoky capital of Poland's main coal-mining region of Upper Silesia. They brought with them a crude 'economistic' approach which had worked well enough in Silesia but was less suited to the incurably political atmosphere of Warsaw. Ideology seemed to bore them; they were interested in the practical application of power. Over-confident after the initial successes of the plan, they neglected the essentially political lessons of 1970. The Party daily, *Trybuna Ludu*, was able to write about the December 1970 upheaval that 'our Party, through its own strength and courage of decision, showed the way out of the crisis. It thus confirmed its right to perform the leading role in the nation's life at the moment of such difficult trial.' As George Błażyński observes, this was a ridiculous version of what had taken place.[4] But the comment seemed to justify the manner in which the Party, far from reducing its intervention in national life, was in practice carrying through a further centralization of power in the name of reform. Little soon remained of the Party's promises to share out some of its authority. The Szydlak commission on better methods of governing faded away. The Sejm relapsed into insignificance. The workers' councils that had sprung up again on the coast in December 1970 were suppressed by Party manoeuvres and police intimidation. The WOGs were deprived – not without sound reasons – of much of their autonomy.

In the same spirit, local government was radically reconstructed. Poland's seventeen *województwa* (districts) were broken up into forty-nine smaller districts in 1975, at the end of a process that abolished one of the three tiers of local government altogether. Each district had in theory been run by an elected 'people's council', but the new districts were placed under the authority of a prefect (*wojewoda*) who was directly appointed from Warsaw. There was much to be said for this reform, which simplified the system and removed at least a part of that 'middle apparatus' which had obstructed change for decades. But it also represented another sweeping act of centralization by the government – through the prefects – and by the Party, whose district secretaries now also sat as chairmen of weakened 'people's councils'.

It was another illustration of how easily the old Polish *dirigiste* tradition could accommodate to the 'democratic centralism' of a Leninist party. Except at the very summit, no official decision is final in Poland. A visit to a *województwo* headquarters usually reveals a queue of supplicants waiting with petitions or grievances, and many of them will be petitioning against a decision taken at the lower, commune (*gmina*) level of local government. In practice, there is almost no real devolution of power, no area in which a subordinate state or Party body has complete authority. Any decision at any level but the top can be overturned by the next tier, if the petitioner has a good case, good connections, or – on occasion – the resources for a convincing bribe. In this late-feudal pattern can be seen one of the reasons for the weakness of civic initiative in Poland and for the difficulty of making reform effective. It was no coincidence that the post of *wojewoda* was not an innovation but a resurrected institution from Poland before 1939.

The autocratic self-confidence that the Party displayed was, as it turned out, something of a façade. Under challenge, the nerve of the leadership – and its certainty that its course was correct – proved fragile. In 1975, when the government published the draft for a new Constitution, it provoked a storm of intellectual protest – the first such outcry since the trauma of 1968 – and denunciation by the Church. The draft was hastily rewritten. Among other formulations, a phrase defining the leading role of the PUWP in the state was softened to 'leading political force in society in constructing socialism', and a suggestion that citizens' rights depended upon the performance of citizens' duties was removed. The government had recommended a phrase about 'unshakeable fraternal bonds with the Soviet Union', but this was modified to a remark about strengthening co-operation with the USSR.

The row over the Constitution, soon overshadowed by more cataclysmic events, revealed a new and destructive trend in Polish politics. This was the sequence of gross miscalculation of public opinion, public protest and then official retreat, which in turn of course increased the confidence of the protesters. It was a sequence made possible by the workers' revolt of 1970, which had shown what the penalties of resisting mass protest could be. But it was now to be repeated over and over again, and at each repetition, political authority in Poland disintegrated still further.

In retrospect, it can be seen that March 1968 was the last contest with popular discontent that the Party won. From then on, three successive leaderships were defeated in every single confrontation with a major protest. After 1970, the people, and especially the working class, understood that they could frustrate any measure by taking to the streets with sufficient energy. The Party understood this too but, as its authority ebbed away, lacked the vigour to admit the fact and remedy matters by institutional change. Most crucially, nothing was done to restore a legitimate voice to the workers through shop-floor democracy or a more autonomous trade union system. Instead, the Gierek leadership continued to talk as if there was no challenge to the Party's leading role, although in fact it was well aware of its increasing weakness.

Meat and the New Opposition

Only this underlying lack of nerve can explain the procrastination of the Polish government and Party leaders before the most urgent problem of the mid-1970s: the growing chaos in the country's meat supply. Something had been done to encourage private farmers to produce more, but the régime was still paralysed by the memory of how price increases at the shops had been rejected by the workers in 1970–71. A gradual raising of prices over several years might have been the best policy. Instead, the issue was constantly postponed, and the 1970 price freeze, originally meant to last only two years, remained in force until June 1976. The Politburo bickered, some of its members suggesting a series of small increases, others objecting that this would redouble the incentive to over-buy and to hoard. In the end, after a few vague hints in public and some private opinion polling, the leaders decided to storm the obstacle in one single onslaught.

They were not united – some versions have Gierek himself in the minority of the Politburo that warned of the probable consequences – but on 24 June 1976 Piotr Jaroszewicz, the prime minister, told the Sejm that special allowances would be paid to low-earning workers and pensioners, with higher prices for farmers, in order to balance new and far higher retail price levels for food. Meat would rise on average by 69 per cent, sugar by 100 per cent, butter and cheese by at least one third.

The roof blew off instantaneously. On 25 June, work stopped all over the country. Strike committees appeared within hours. A demonstration at Płock, the petrochemical centre on the River Vistula, was broken up by militia. Men from the Ursus tractor plant in Warsaw blocked the main east–west European railway track and tore up the rails. At Radom, scenes developed like those of 1970, as workers from the General Walter engineering works marched to the city centre, gathering crowds of sympathizers, and besieged the Party building. Stones were flung. Then part of the crowd broke into the building and raided the well-supplied canteen; cold meat and sausages were passed to the crowd outside with yells of 'Red bourgeoisie!' The building was set alight, and a section of the crowd went on to smash shop-windows down Żeromska Street and loot the contents. The militia regained control of the streets in the evening, after a day which cost at least four lives, injuries to seventy-five policemen and about a million dollars' worth of damage.

Jaroszewicz appeared on television the same evening to announce that in view of the 'valuable amendments and contributions' put forward by the working class, the price rises would be withdrawn for further discussion. This was not quite as absurd a statement as it sounds; most workers had confined themselves to stopping work and demanding the cancellation of the decree. But it was a shattering humiliation for the Party. Gierek's common-sense told him there was no other way. His inclination was to drop the prime minister, who was already unpopular, but Jaroszewicz – like Kruczek, the trade union leader – was a Soviet confidante whose presence at the head of the government was some guarantee that Moscow would not intervene in Poland's internal affairs.

This time, there was no change of government or Party leadership. Gierek had surrendered so fast that no challenge on the scale of 1970 had time to develop. But the police were encouraged to take brutal and immediate reprisals. About 2,000 people were detained in Radom and more than 200 workers from Ursus, and many were comprehensively beaten up as they were made to run the gauntlet between files of policemen armed with batons. The arrested Ursus workers were fired and evicted from their hostels. Even in cities like Łódź, Poznań and Grudziądz, where no disorders had taken place, strikers were dismissed. Special summary courts sentenced many workers from Radom and Ursus to gaol terms. The intention was to deliver a short, sharp lesson: most sentences were soon reduced and almost all the remaining prisoners were set free the following year.

As in December 1970, the outbreak had been not just about price rises. While the coastal strikes six years before had begun as an elemental blast of anger, the 1976 strikers were at least as concerned about their work conditions as about their purchasing power. They were embittered about Gierek's betrayal of the promise that they especially – the class in whose name he ruled – would have his sympathy and his ear. They were exasperated about the way in which nobody in management, in the trade unions or in the Party groups at the factories would take their side in a dispute. There had in fact already been stoppages at General Walter earlier in June, with complaints about excessive shift quotas, refusal to pay accident compensation and bullying by the manager. All over Poland, workers protested against the special pay and privileges reserved for the Party élite. Ever since 1970, they had been quietly debating problems of justice and workers' rights among themselves: this time, they took action with a much more coherent understanding of where the sources of their problems lay.

The most spectacular consequence of the June 1976 crisis was a rapid emergence of unofficial opposition groups and of a large and varied *samizdat* publication industry. The most significant of these groups was the Committee for the Defence of Workers' Rights (KOR), originally a small group of intellectuals concerned about the victimization of workers striking at Radom and Warsaw, which issued its first manifesto, signed by fourteen names, in September. Initially, KOR confined itself to raising money for the legal defence and family support of striking workers, and to campaigning for an amnesty and a parliamentary inquiry into police brutality. But this unstructured committee, which by June 1977 included twenty-four names, rapidly developed into a political pressure group for authentic forms of workers' representation. Its most dynamic member was Jacek Kuroń, who had been imprisoned in 1967 for preaching revolutionary left-wing Communism, but KOR's approach was social-democratic and constitutional. In September, KOR expanded its activities to the general defence of civil rights and added the title 'Committee for Social Defence' to its name (becoming KSS-KOR).

In March 1977, the Movement for the Defence of Civil and Citizens' Rights (ROPCiO) was established. Although three KOR signatories also signed its founding document, ROPCiO was a noticeably more conservative and nationalist organization with a tendency to operate clandestinely. In May, after the death of a student at the University of Kraków named Stanisław Pyjas, a KOR supporter whose head injuries may have been inflicted by the police, a Students' Solidarity Committee (SKS) was established. The SKS, intended to be a focus for student activities outside Party control, spread from Kraków to several other universities but seems to have merged gradually into the wider groups supporting KOR and ROPCiO: little was heard of it during the summer of 1980. Other groups proliferated, some of them insignificant and others offshoots of the two main opposition committees; in September 1979, a press briefing by the Ministry of the Interior listed twenty-six 'anti-socialist' groups, which was probably an exaggeration.

A flourishing industry of underground publication sprang up. In April 1978, a Party meeting was told that some nineteen publications had been identified, producing a total of 20,000 copies (of which the security police claimed to be seizing about half). The most important were KOR's *Information Bulletin* and its periodical *Robotnik*, designed to be read by workers. ROPCiO produced about six publications, of which the best known was the review *Opinia*. The circulation of uncensored material was still very small, and the lack of duplicating or printing equipment meant that many periodicals were smudgy and almost illegible leaflets. Still, among other *samizdat* feats was the production of a sophisticated literary and intellectual review (*Zapis*) and the establishment of Nowa, an 'uncensored publishing house' which by 1980 claimed to have issued some fifty titles, including works by

Polish authors no longer allowed official publication and translations of – among others – George Orwell, Günter Grass, Osip Mandelstam and Joseph Brodsky.

To the surprise of the outside world, the Polish authorities made no decisive move to suppress this opposition. Its members were constantly harassed and threatened, and from time to time detained (for example, nine KOR members were arrested in May 1977 but released again without trial three months later); there were numerous police raids on the 'uncensored' press, and the appearance early in 1978 of the Association for Scientific Courses (TKN), in effect an unofficial university resembling the courses organized by the resistance during the Nazi occupation, produced many instances of violent disruption by police agents. But Gierek was unwilling to use the full repressive force of the state against this intellectual opposition, and it continued to grow.

KOR publications in particular began to reach political activists in certain large plants, many of whom were disaffected Party members. This led to two important developments. One was the appearance in 1977 of the first 'free trade union' groups, which were usually connected indirectly to KOR through local supporters of *Robotnik*; in April 1978, the 'Free Trade Unions of the Coast', numbering less than a dozen devoted members, issued their first declaration from Gdańsk. The second development was the formation – decisive for the events of 1980 – of an informal alliance between the new opposition and the Catholic Church. In May 1977, St Martin's Church in the old heart of Warsaw, which already contained a sanctuary to the memory of men and women who fell defending it during the 1944 Rising, gave shelter to fourteen hunger strikers protesting against the arrest of the nine KOR members. The strikers included two prominent lay Catholic intellectuals. The same month, a group from the opposition took part in a 'week of Christian culture' attended by the Primate, Cardinal Stefan Wyszyński, who received them afterwards and encouraged them to 'defend the cultural values of the nation'.

After the June 1976 disaster, Gierek and the government rapidly applied the brake to the régime's ambitious economic programme. In late 1975 the targets of the economic plan had been reduced, and in December 1976 the so-called 'economic manoeuvre' reduced the invested proportion of the national income from 35 per cent to about 30 per cent; the emphasis of investment switched to the production of consumer goods for the domestic market. Some eight million tons of grain were imported in 1977, and another seven million tons the next year. Yet another fresh start was made in the approach to private farming, in the hope that higher production would close the gap between the apparently insatiable consumer demand for pork, especially, and the market supply. (Bad harvests had contributed to a fall in pig numbers of nearly a quarter between 1975 and late 1976.) A fifth of all investment was now channelled into agriculture. With some ideological misgivings, measures were taken to allow private peasants to acquire more land and to own tractors; as in France or West Germany, the government was moving to encourage the disappearance of the smallest farms (in 1978, 90 per cent of Polish peasant holdings were less than ten hectares in size) and their replacement by efficient medium farms of some twenty-five hectares.[5] Foreign journalists were not thanked for exclaiming that Poland was trying to introduce elements of capitalist farming into the countryside, but they were not wide of the mark.

Imports of food helped to achieve a 15 per cent increase in supplies of meat in the first few months of 1977, but in spite of the new inducements to the farmers, domestic food production rose only very slowly. Earnings meanwhile continued to rise, and so did the gigantic subsidy paid to hold down the price of food in the shops, estimated at 70 per cent of the retail price by the end of 1977.[6] There was something irrational, even aggressive, about the carnivorous obsession that now gripped the Poles. Their per capita meat consumption was higher than that of several western countries, and their insistence on pork at the expense of more plentiful meats like beef or lamb led to queues and shortages. In an act of subconscious aggression, the population was literally eating away the foundations of the political structure.

With the brakes firmly applied, the boom slowed down and stopped. On the eve of the Eighth Congress of the PUWP, in February 1980, the Central Statistical Bureau published a candid and frightening set of figures that revealed that national income had actually fallen by 2 per cent in 1979, agricultural production had fallen by a few percentage points, and principal industrial output was showing a 'negative growth' for the year of nearly 5 per cent. From experiencing one of the highest growth rates in the world, Poland had become a stagnating economy in only five years. This violent reversal, which went much further than its planners intended, was exaggerated by Poland's growing dependence on the capitalist banking world. Many of the short-term debts run up in the early 1970s began to fall due at the end of the decade, forcing the Polish government to seek fresh loans partly intended to service these earlier borrowings. In December 1979, the deputy finance minister, Marian Krzak, admitted that Poland's foreign debt stood at nearly $18 billion, and in spite of the fierce deflation of the economy and a slowing-down of imports from capitalist countries, this indebtedness continued to balloon upwards. The immediate result of this diversion of resources was a disastrous shortage of funds to invest in the domestic economy.

To satisfy its creditors, Poland had made a far more radical change of course than a western state might have done in a similar position (compare the relatively slight adjustments enforced on Britain by the International Monetary Fund in 1977). But Poland was now caught fast in a trap which awaits all backward economies attempting rapid industrial transformation. Imports of advanced technological goods financed by hard-currency loans have to continue, if for no other reason than that they are now required for the production of export goods that alone can raise the hard currency needed to service the previous debts. Thus the whole purpose of an industrialization programme is transformed: originally conceived as a means of raising domestic consumption and living standards, it becomes a means of repaying foreign creditors – but a means that ineluctably runs up further debts to those creditors. Poland's natural wealth in raw materials – coal, copper, sulphur – was not enough to cover the deficit, while the export of Poland's other traditional hard-currency earner, food and especially meat products, could not be expanded for fear of provoking further popular unrest.

The Gierek leadership announced in 1979 its intention to expand 'socialist democracy', defined as an improvement in the workers' self-management system (the ineffective Conferences of Workers' Self-Government) and some reform of the trade unions. The government made more concessions to the private farmers, and in an attempt to improve distribution permitted private individuals to lease many categories of shop and small enterprise from the state. But these measures did not halt the steady dissolution of political authority. Gierek himself, an increasingly exhausted man, would have preferred a cautious and systematic democratization. But he was trapped between the mass discontent generated by the economic crisis and the resistance of the usual hard-line faction in the leadership who were opposed to any relaxation of Party control and shocked by his tolerant approach to the unofficial opposition groups.

Although Gierek was personally responsible for allowing the showing of Andrzej Wajda's film *Man of Marble* in 1977, a pitiless attack both on Stalinism and on the moral corruption of post-Stalinist Poland, censorship remained oppressive. In November 1977, Poland became the object of worldwide derision when a copy of its secret censorship directives was published in the West, a catalogue of grotesquely detailed restrictions designed to make truthful reporting impossible – which at once explained the growing circulation of the opposition press. This did not prevent a steady extension of the régime's 'success propaganda', entirely counter-productive because it contradicted the daily experience of the population – it especially annoyed industrial workers. A television series, *Tu Jedynka* (*First Programme Calling*), set out to prove that life in the imperialist West compared badly with conditions in People's Poland. Again, this infuriated the millions of Poles who had visited the West in the past twenty years.

Television, which in the early 1970s had run programmes in which politicians were confronted with genuine phone-in questions, was now stifled by the jaunty Maciej Szczepański, a Silesian acquaintance of Gierek's who developed a life-style of spectacular corruption and debauchery on state funds. The Szczepański scandal, which did not explode until 1980, was an extreme but far from isolated case. Throughout the decade, Poles – again, especially industrial workers with their own pooled sources of information – were increasingly aware that corruption among Party and state officials, never rare, was spreading on a pandemic scale. The combination of local power, inflated rewards, market shortages, and the total absence of press scrutiny encouraged the élité to feather its nest abundantly from restricted-access shops and to plunder for its own use every kind of supply from meat to building materials for its country villas. The official responsible for dealing with this problem was none other than Mieczysław Moczar, who since his fall from the Politburo in 1971 had been in charge of the state anti-corruption bureau, the Chamber for Public Control (NIK). Characteristically, he contented himself with a silent amassing of files on the sins of hundreds of public figures in the state and the Party.

A word should be said about public reaction to this plague. Corruption in itself, the misuse of state resources for private purposes or the paying of bribes, is regarded with surprising tolerance by many non-Party Poles. Even the Szczepański revelations about yachts, Swiss bank accounts and call-girls of many colours seemed to entertain rather than to shock. 'Who wouldn't, if he could?' was a common response. What aroused anger was the way that corruption seemed to become associated with the privileges of a whole institution. It was assumed that the Party, the police and the security police were collectively maintaining a high and in some ways illegal standard of living for their members. There was much truth in this. Real fury was generated not so much by the corruption of an individual as by corruption arising from his membership of one of these collectives. In the Lenin Shipyard at Gdańsk, all workers knew that Party members were being put higher up the housing waiting-list than families with more children and more years on the list. In the same way, the discovery in 1980–81 of a building programme of hospitals and clinics for employees of the Ministry of the Interior, apparently at the expense of the desperately under-equipped National Health Service, again and again provoked strikes and occupations up and down the country.

Jacob and the Angel: Church and State

Church–state relations in Poland have always resembled the wrestling of Jacob and the Angel – 'I will not let thee go, except thou bless me!' At first, Gierek's prospects of gaining this blessing seemed fair. The Church had not played a prominent role in the 1976 disturbances, and its initial reaction had been a moderate condemnation of both police brutality and 'a few anti-social elements'. Answering workers' questions in September 1976, Gierek was encouraged to suggest that no real conflicts remained between state and Church and that 'fruitful co-operation' on national object-ives was possible.

Gierek's intention, sincerely held, was to reach a détente with the episcopate that could be cautiously developed into limited co-operation. The Church would accept that Poland was legitimately a socialist state and would use its influence to encourage hard work, honesty and the notion that the prosperity of the nation was the joint responsibility of Catholics and Com-munists. In return, the state would recognize the authority of the Church in the moral field and, as long as Church leaders refrained from attacking the political leadership of the state, would avoid harassing its legitimate activities. At the same time, Gierek made a fresh effort to reach a settlement with the Vatican through direct contacts in Rome.

The Church appears to have taken this offer as a sign of weakness, and the Primate and the episcopate began to escalate their demands on the state, including the right to broadcast Mass and the restoration of religious education in schools. This escalation continued through most of 1977, as the Church established contact with the new opposition groups and criticized the government for the food shortages, the 'godless mass media' and the persecution of the strikers from Radom and Ursus. In December 1976, Cardinal Wyszyński had encouraged church-goers to give money support to these workers, and it was he who opened the door to contact with KOR, especially, in the following year.

There was an element of bluff in this escalation. The Church was not in principle averse to the sort of co-operation in the national interest that

Gierek was proposing, and relations with the state were more intimate than these defiant public statements suggested. But the Church was eager to have its position and its demands secured in a formal agreement recognizing the legal status of the Church in Poland, and suspicious that Gierek was seeking an agreement with the Vatican behind its back. This fear that the government might insinuate a wedge between Rome and the Polish bishops, by persuading the Vatican that Wyszyński was an old reactionary out of touch with the epoch of détente, had been endemic for many years. The Church wanted its own legal recognition by the régime to precede any such treaty between Warsaw and the Vatican.

In October 1977, great publicity was given to an unprecedented meeting between Gierek and the Primate. The communiqué spoke of the 'unity of Poles in the work of shaping the prosperity of People's Poland', which suggested both Church–state co-operation and acceptance of the Communist régime's legitimacy. In December, Edward Gierek was received by Pope Paul VI in the course of a visit to Italy, but official propaganda about triumphant reconciliation with the Vatican was answered by a bucket of cold water from the episcopate. After a sharp attack on the government, the bishops repeated all their previous demands and added a claim for the re-establishment of an independent Catholic press.

The wrestling went on. Gierek refused to let the Church go; concessions of a minor sort were made over religious education, while government officials paid Cardinal Wyszyński compliments on his patriotism and sense of national responsibility. The Church continued to insist upon constitutional recognition, yet again raising its ante by giving support to the unofficial 'flying university' (TKN) courses and by demanding the outright abolition of censorship.

It was in the course of 1978, with Jacob signally failing to prevent the Angel continually improving his holds, that discontent with Gierek's religious policy surfaced in the Party. At a Central Committee Plenum in May, Tadeusz Grabski, a Party district secretary, criticized the leadership's economic management but also complained that the Church was being allowed to push the Party around. Once the episcopate had asked politely for favours; now the Catholic hierarchy simply came to the government and gave its orders. Grabski was removed from the Central Committee and lost his job, but this was the first appearance of a new grouping that became centrally important in 1980: a faction of well-educated men with a background in economics who wanted sweeping economic change without any reduction of the Party's power monopoly. This coterie of 'enlightened despots', whose most prominent member was Stefan Olszowski, a former foreign minister who had now advanced to a position of great influence within the Party secretariat, felt that Edward Gierek was now following the worst possible combination of policies: while cutting himself off from the advice of the technical intelligentsia, he was at the same time frittering away the Party's authority by unnecessary tolerance of dissent and by concessions to the Church which only created an appetite for more.

On 16 October 1978, the Angel received unexpected and devastating assistance from his master. Cardinal Karol Wojtyła, Archbishop of Kraków, was elected Pope. While the population rushed to the telephone, opened bottles, hung out Polish flags or merely sat happily weeping in front of the television screen, the Party leadership went into emergency session. This was no moment for Grabskian anti-clericalism. A handsome message of congratulations was despatched to Rome, sounding the only note available to the Party at such a moment: nationalism. 'For the first time in the history of the papal throne, it is occupied by a son of the Polish nation, which is building the greatness and prosperity of its socialist fatherland with the unity and co-operation of all its citizens.'

This extraordinary event, which amazed the Poles even more than the Catholic faithful in continents that had never heard of Cardinal Wojtyła, changed overnight a number of proportions in the Polish political situation. By transferring the leadership of Polish Catholicism from Warsaw to Rome, the election of Pope John Paul II brought to an end the almost absolute authority of old Cardinal Wyszyński. Recovering from the shock, the government could hope that its policy of improving relations with the Vatican in order to outflank the stubborn resistance of the Polish episcopate might now be more effective. But, on the other hand, the supersession of Cardinal Wyszyński also meant that Poland's spiritual leadership was now setting up its standard in the western world. A great source of authority in Polish society was now no longer in Poland and, of course, no longer subject to direct influence from the government.

This was a situation with some precedent in Polish history. The 'Great Emigration' after the failure of the 1830 Rising had in effect transferred the moral leadership of the nation to Paris, and Poles were familiar with the concept of legitimate governments-in-exile from the Second World War. (Indeed, the husk of the wartime London government survives in London today, although it is many years since it commanded any perceptible allegiance within Poland.) The election of a Polish Pope now repeated this pattern, more in the manner of 1830 than of 1939. The authority was formally only spiritual, yet the intimate part the Church had played in Poland's patriotic struggle against the Partitions, in resistance to the Nazis, and of course in defending traditional values after 1944, ensured that this authority would also be sensed in Poland as political. The Pope would surely shield his own flock against the storm.

The election of John Paul II thus had an immediate political effect. Poland's unofficial opposition groups were, not unexpectedly, vastly heartened. Active participation by young Catholics in Church life increased, and so did their concern for political change. In Kraków, the Pope's home city, Cardinal Wojtyła had been the friend, contemporary and protector of many lay Catholic groups, especially the Znak organization, with its journals and publications; these old allies now found themselves involved in the outside world of international Catholic politics (which was not always appreciative: the theological conservatism and the total rejection of any ideological compromise with Marxism which came naturally to these Polish lay activists soon made them objects of suspicion to liberal Churchmen and advocates of a revolutionary 'theology of liberation'). Within the Polish Church itself, the event slowly brought to the surface discontent with the Primate's increasing readiness to strike bargains with the government, and his reluctance to endorse a more uncompromising support for the opposition groups. The overriding imperative to show a united front with Cardinal Wyszyński against the government had lost much of its force.

As for ordinary Poles, they reacted with unaffected, incredulous delight. Given their history and their beliefs, no other honour to the nation could have satisfied them so completely. Non-Catholics and many rank-and-file Party members whose religion was nominal shared in this exultation. Believers naturally saw in this triumph a sign of divine favour towards faithful and tormented Poland. Many at once turned to a familiar poem by the early-nineteenth-century writer Juliusz Słowacki, which now acquired prophetic force:

> *Among the quarrelling, the Lord struck*
> *On a mighty bell;*
> *Lo, for a Slav Pope*
> *He provided the throne ...*
> *He shall spread love, as today the Powers*
> *Spread weapons ...*

Negotiations were at once begun by the Vatican for a papal visit to Poland. Gierek was convinced that the best policy was a generous and welcoming approach to the new Pope. Nothing was to be gained by an appearance of embarrassment or alarm. The arrival of a Polish Pope could, he thought, be used to enhance the unity of the nation on the basis of a simple, patriotic spectacle: the socialist fatherland receiving its most distinguished son. The publicity and the influx of western journalists which would accompany the visit also offered an occasion to display the achievements of the régime and its understanding with the Church on the importance of those achievements. In this hopeful approach, not shared by the whole leadership, Gierek was supported by Stanisław Kania, a steady and cautious apparatus man now in his forties who carried responsibility in the Politburo for security and religious affairs.

Gierek took pains to keep the Soviet leadership fully informed about these plans. To some extent, the Pope's election may have strengthened his position in Moscow; for all their ancestral dislike of crusading Polish Catholicism, which Russians associate with repeated invasions and threats to Russian unity in earlier centuries, Brezhnev and his colleagues recognized that this was a specifically Polish episode best left to a Pole to handle. They asked only that the visit should not be used to stir up anti-Soviet feelings – a condition which the Pope accepted and honoured.

The visit took place over eight days of furnace heatwave in June 1979. No such manifestation of love and loyalty was ever seen in Poland, or, perhaps, will ever be seen again. Between a quarter and a fifth of the population of Poland turned out in person to meet John Paul II on the stations of his pilgrimage, and the crowds on the Kraków Meadows at his farewell numbered close on two million. The disorders that the government may have feared did not take place, and its decision to leave the organization and policing of these colossal gatherings to the Church was well justified. National television recorded the meeting at the Belvedere Palace in Warsaw between the Pope, Edward Gierek and the leaders of Party and state. Gierek, ill at ease, spoke earnestly of the importance of national unity. The Pope, not without a faint twinkle of relish in his eye, accepted his point and said that he rejoiced in all the social achievements of Poland 'whatever the inspiration from which they come'. He added, however, that all forms of colonialism were bad and that all alliances must be based on the individual interest of their member nations.

Inevitably, this demonstration of Poland's solidly Catholic allegiance rendered the country's political situation still more fragile. But in the short term the régime could console itself with the Pope's readiness to accept the socialist nature of the Polish state so long as it observed certain norms of human rights and decency. There had been no anti-Soviet or anti-Communist outbreaks. Indeed, the masses treated the authorities with an ominous indifference rather than with hostility. The Pope's attitude at the Belvedere was that of a person speaking from a position of strength so overwhelming that he could afford magnanimity and concession towards an authority that was, in comparison, so insecure.

Authority Dissolves: 1980

The visit of the Pope temporarily distracted public attention from the irritations of daily life. The sombre streets, strewn with fresh flowers over which the Papal motorcade advanced, lost their outline behind a mass of bunting – yellow and white for the Vatican and red and white for Poland. The government enjoyed a brief respite. But the general consensus in Poland both before and after the visit remained that another great crisis of the régime was approaching. The basic economic situation and shortages of food and other consumer goods grew worse. Work stoppages, usually minor breaks in production but occasionally more serious, like the strikes over inadequate meat supplies that had hit the Upper Silesian coal mines in October 1977, were common and also – although the official press did not report them – common knowledge.

In November 1978, a study group named Experience and the Future (DiP, in its Polish acronym) was recruited from about a hundred prominent people to prepare an inquiry into the problems of Poland. DiP, which included non-Party and Party members and several Catholic intellectuals, enjoyed an ill-defined semi-official status, and was supported and encouraged by Stefan Olszowski. Its report, completed just before the arrival of the Pope, was refused official publication and eventually appeared in October 1979 as an 'uncensored' product of the Nowa publishing group.

The DiP report consisted mostly of responses to questions put to individual members of the team. Its criticism was all-embracing and scathing. The fundamental problem, it declared, was that 'during the entire post-war period, Poland did not develop any universally accepted or truly workable rules and norms to govern its social life. No agreement was reached even on issues of a most general nature ...' The population had not accepted the Party's approach to the exercise of power, the implications of Poland's *raison d'état*, the way wealth was distributed, the legal and labour systems or the interpretation of history. In other words, DiP was asserting that the entire Communist project had so far failed to win authenticity and was still governing an unwilling and alienated citizenry.

DiP drew attention to popular resentment of the privileges for the élite, and suggested that a new class differentiation was rapidly emerging. This bureaucratic class sought 'not only to preserve its numerous and almost feudal privileges for the rest of its own life, but also – again in keeping with the rules of the feudal order – to pass on these privileges to its heirs and descendants'. The report pointed out that wage differentials now ranged from 1:20; the group that monopolized power in society was acquiring a corresponding monopoly of wealth.

Much of the report was devoted to attacking the use of censorship and the habitual mendacity of public information. One respondent composed an almost hysterical litany of alienation when he wrote, 'We are faced with sham planning and the sham implementation of plans, sham accomplishments in industry, science, the arts and education, the sham declaration and fulfilment of pledges, sham debates, sham voting and elections, sham concern for social welfare and the appearances of government, sham socialism and social work, sham freedom of choice, sham morality, modernity and progress, the opening of ostensibly completed factories and social facilities with great pomp and circumstance, the sham struggle against wrongdoing and the sham contentment of all citizens, sham freedom of conviction and sham justice. The playing of this game ... has become so widespread that no one, not even the highest levels of government, can distinguish any longer between what is real and what is unreal.'[7] Unless there was fast and radical improvement, 'negative changes ... may reach the avalanche stage that would threaten open social conflict'.

But after delivering this murderous analysis of hegemonic failure in Poland, the DiP intellectuals rather surprisingly proposed a relatively moderate reform of the very system they had shown to be inherently unsound. Much in the spirit of 'liberal' proposals in 1956 and 1971, they suggested more independence for the Sejm, a restriction of the Party's direct control over society and the state, a decentralizing reform of the economy and a reduction of censorship. (Stefan Bratkowski, a journalist member of the group, expressed these conclusions in sharper form in August 1979, and added a proposal for trade unions independent of the Party.) But the DiP prescription was acceptable to reformers within the Party, whereas its diagnosis most certainly was not. No severe steps were taken against the authors of the report, who remained in close contact with Olszowski up to the Eighth Congress of the PUWP, held in February 1980.

A Party congress is preceded by the issuing of 'guidelines' some months in advance, which are then discussed exhaustively by local Party meetings and conferences. In October 1979, as these pre-congress discussions began, it at once became clear to district Party secretaries that the mass membership was dangerously exasperated. In factories, the Party meetings often turned into unruly protests that concentrated on the chaotic food supply, the growth of corrupt privilege in public life, the infuriating effect of official 'success propaganda' on working-class families and the lack of effective workers' representation in the plants.

This shock-wave of criticism was taken seriously by the most powerful group in the PUWP beneath the top leadership: the forty-six district Party secretaries and the three Party secretaries of the urban districts of Warsaw, Łódź and Kraków. Many of them were now impatient for a change of leadership and a reform of economic management before it was too late. Theirs was the most influential level of authority in the Party, for they could manipulate the choice of delegates to a Party congress and thus affect the balance of the next Central Committee which the congress elected.

Gierek's opening speech at the Eighth Congress, which met in Warsaw on 11 February 1980, was disarming. He confessed the gravity of Poland's economic position and, while he acknowledged that contrasts of wealth had appeared, he denied that this implied any class struggle of a new kind. Solemnly warning against corruption and the abuse of power, he repeated in very dilute form some of the DiP solutions. In the vaguest terms, he spoke of a renewal of 'socialist democracy' that would give the Sejm more responsibility, invigorate the media and somehow – reconciling an impossible contradiction – render the trade unions at once more obedient to government and more responsive to the needs of their members.

As the congress proceeded, several district secretaries delivered carefully coded but damaging attacks on the shortcomings of Poland's economic management. Gierek at once offered a back-stage compromise that would leave his own position and the performance of the Party immune from criticism by diverting all blame to the failures of the administration and the government. This was disingenuous. It was of course the Party that determined the policies of the government, and in the pre-congress discussions the critics had not spared the Party. However, the deal was struck. Prime minister Piotr Jaroszewicz was forced to resign and hand over his office to Edward Babiuch, a close collaborator of Gierek's who had been in charge of Party organization and staffing.

Gierek had anticipated this sort of trouble. His opening speech had already drawn a distinction between the correctness of Party strategy and failures in its execution for which the government was responsible. He probably intended to drop Jaroszewicz at some later stage anyway; the prime minister was intensely unpopular both as the author of the 1976 price rises and as the father of a son notorious for shady deals (he had been put in charge of the state agency for importing western cars). But the strength of the protest took him by surprise. He was in any case preoccupied with the international situation, which was rapidly changing to Poland's disadvantage.

NATO had taken the decision in December 1979 to deploy a new generation of American theatre nuclear weapons, Pershing II and Cruise, ending the tacit truce on rearmament in Europe which had made détente and the 1975 Security Conference possible. At the end of December, the Soviet Union had sent its armies into Afghanistan. The Poles, remembering the last glaciation of the Cold War, feared that a repetition would again induce the super-powers to tighten their hold on their respective blocs – in the Polish case, putting in danger the limited but precious degree of independence and internal tolerance that had been achieved in the 1970s. Gierek accordingly used the congress platform to propose that a European disarmament conference should be held in Warsaw. The whole European security process was now blocked by the linkage which the Security Conference had established between disarmament and the intractable complex of human rights; Gierek's suggestion offered a way of treating disarmament on its own.

Internally, the political manoeuvre at the Eighth Congress had two results. One was that the deal freed Gierek's hands to reinforce his own position within the Party leadership. Stefan Olszowski, whom Gierek now perceived as a dangerous rival, was removed from the Politburo and sent as ambassador to the German Democratic Republic (Polish embassies have always been used as shelves for distinguished losers in Party disputes). As well as Olszowski, Jaroszewicz, the liberal Józef Tejchma and the elderly hard-liner Józef Kępa lost their places in the Politburo. They were replaced by Alojzy Karkoszka; the natty and ambitious Jerzy Łukaszewicz, who now became responsible for propaganda and the media; Tadeusz Wrzaszczyk, head of the planning commission; and Andrzej Werblan.*

The second result was that thousands of Party activists and ordinary working-class members now finally ran out of hope and patience. The pre-congress campaign of 1979–80, the most genuine and plain-spoken for years, had been their last attempt to push change through the existing Party structures from below. Now they concluded that their voices had been

* Werblan had been in the ruling bodies of the Party for nearly a quarter-century. His intimacy with the Soviet Union was always assumed, and this was the point of appointing him to the Politburo in 1980 when Jaroszewicz, equally close to the Soviet leadership, was removed. In June 1968, Werblan wrote a long, 'theoretical' article published in *Miesięcznik Literacki* attributing many of the historical weaknesses of Polish Communism to the high proportion of Jews in the movement. The article caused great scandal abroad, especially in the Communist Parties of western Europe.

ignored and their anger manipulated. The congress had merely repeated that the Party's basic strategy was correct, and had sought to placate them by lopping off a few official heads. They had wanted a change of policy, and now, in their frustration, they began to debate the need for changes in the very structure of the Party. By introducing free elections to Party posts and rotating jobs in the apparatus, they hoped to tear away all the successive filters which had suppressed their criticisms and – in effect – to reverse the whole power flow within the PUWP.

Immediately after the congress, Edward Babiuch, as the new prime minister, made a courageous début before the Sejm and admitted the disastrous condition of the economy. He offered the customary promises of cleaner government and a more effective voice for working people, and warned that another effort would have to be made to bring shop prices closer to production costs and incomes. In April, he repeated his warnings more plainly: the Poles should prepare for times of austerity, and there would be gradual price increases which might lead to a fall in the standard of living. By June, there was already evidence that the cut-backs were hitting working-class incomes, while the state banks were ordered to reduce the wage funds available to each industrial ministry.

The old Stalinist Kruczek was finally removed from the chairmanship of the trade unions (CRZZ) after the Eighth Congress and replaced by Jan Szydlak, a younger but not very effective member of Gierek's inner leadership. This did not impress a small band of men and women, obscure workers whose names were known to nobody outside their own city, who were trying to hold together a much-persecuted group called the Free Trade Union Committee of the Coast, at Gdańsk. Several of them had been members of the 1970 strike committees. In December 1979, they had organized a rally to commemorate those strikes which collected several thousand people outside the Lenin Shipyard, much to the alarm of the authorities who arrested many of the participants. At the Elektromontaż works, about twenty-five workers who had taken part were fired. On 25 January, the factory set up a five-man Workers' Commission, including a certain electrician named Lech Wałęsa, to fight for the reinstatement of the twenty-five. At the Lenin Shipyard, the crane driver Anna Walentynowicz, a member of the Free Trade Union group who had also been prominent in December 1970, was removed to another job outside the city. On 31 January, about a hundred of her workmates stopped work for four hours until she was brought back and given her old job in the yard.

The government's skirmishing with the opposition groups hotted up in the early months of 1980. Kuroń and some of his associates were detained, and then released again, for urging a boycott of the Sejm elections in March and then on suspicion of planning to attend a service in a Warsaw church commemorating the Katyń massacre. (The twentieth anniversary of Katyń impelled one man to burn himself to death on 21 March, in the main square of Kraków.) Mirosław Chojecki, who ran the Nowa publishing house, was fined for illegally acquiring a mimeograph machine, and several other dissident centres were charged with various offences. In May, the episcopate condemned this increase in 'repressive measures' and suggested that the government would do better to put its energies into reforms for the benefit of the public.

On 1 July 1980, the government introduced a new price system for meat and meat products – a complicated, rather modest measure. For some years, the government had been increasing the number of so-called 'commercial' shops, at which good meat was sold at much higher prices than in normal stores. The July measures merely transferred another 2 per cent of the cheap meat to the expensive 'commercial' outlets. It was true that this affected the best-quality cuts, and bacon, and that their prices would rise by as much as 100 per cent in some cases. But the measure was not nation-wide; local authorities were left to apply it when they saw fit. It looked as if, at last, a Polish government had managed to learn from experience.

So, however, had the workers. There were no demonstrations, no riots. But as soon as the new price system was understood – it was not announced until the following day and then in the most obscure terms – work began to stop in major plants. Departments of the Ursus tractor works outside Warsaw struck; so did the workers at the big aircraft factory at Mielec in south-eastern Poland and a vehicle parts factory at Tczew, near Gdańsk. This was a spontaneous movement, and yet these first reactions set a pattern which was followed closely for the next six weeks. Men and women would leave their machines, and a strike committee would at once appear to press for a compensating wage rise. The government, aware of the underlying peril and desperate to avoid any repetition of 1970 or 1976, ordered factory managers to concede. But as the days and weeks of July passed, the scale of the pay settlements steadily rose, and workers who had accepted a 5 per cent increase in the first days of July would return to strike action as the awards to individual plants crept up to an average of 10 per cent and then reached 15 or even 20 per cent in isolated cases by early August. While there was no general strike, by the end of the month the stoppages – usually only for a few days – had affected every region of Poland except for the Silesian coal basin. At first, official news of the stoppages was suppressed – 'breaks in production' was the euphemism preferred by the censors. But KSS–KOR instantly set itself up as an information exchange, and the working class soon became aware of all the major strikes and settlements. A co-ordinated movement now began to emerge. By 18 July, fifty-one plants had successfully fought for pay rises, and another seventeen were on strike. By 8 August, KOR estimated that 150 plants and enterprises had taken industrial action since 1 July. The power of the movement was made very plain in mid-July at Lublin, between Warsaw and the Soviet border, when an eight-day strike was joined by railway workers and one of the main rail routes to the Soviet Union was blocked by parked locomotives and wagons.

Gently but inexorably, the régime's control over society was dissolving. In Lublin, new elements were introduced into the crisis: workers there, although they did not form a joint strike committee for the whole city, brought forward a long list of demands that went far beyond matters of wages. These included parity in family allowances with the police, work-free Saturdays, the end of press censorship and trade unions 'that would not take orders from above'. The Lublin strikers did not press these points home and settled simply for a pay increase on 20 July, but they had revealed how rapidly the self-confidence of the working class was growing as the government, day by day, failed to offer them any determined resistance. As the Polish-born journalist Daniel Singer wrote afterwards, Lublin was a 'dress rehearsal' for Gdańsk.

Gierek attempted to hold the line with a television speech on 10 July. He refused either to drop the price increases or to consent to a national wage rise, and ministers followed him before the television cameras to confirm that the shortages were growing worse. But the argument that Poland could not afford the strikers' demands went unheeded. So did a more ominous warning by the Politburo at the height of the Lublin rail strike that these actions could 'awaken fear among Poland's friends'. Meanwhile, KOR went from strength to strength, acting as the only source of news about the strikes for both Poland and the outside world, and helping to transform the strikes from a scatter of local disputes into a self-aware and co-ordinated movement of national protest. In early August, KOR declared that it would henceforth function not only as an information exchange but as an active contact bureau to link the factories.

KOR's achievement in July and August was made possible only by Edward Gierek's last and most extraordinary display of forbearance. The committee could easily have been knocked out in the six weeks before the Gdańsk strikers made KOR's protection their concern. For much of the time, its nerve-centre consisted only of Jacek Kuroń and one faithful girl assistant burning up the telephone in his father's small flat on Mickiewicza Street, in Warsaw. Yet, apart from the usual threats and harassments, nothing worse befell the leading KOR figures in this period than two brief detentions. The tougher members of the Party leadership, out of the Politburo since the Eighth Congress, watched this ineffectual behaviour on the part of the régime with growing fury.

The escalation took its course. Gierek, inexplicably, left for a holiday in the Crimea on 27 July, where he met President Brezhnev the following week. On 29 July, there was a public transport strike at Gdańsk, and four days later a short stoppage in the shipyards and the port. An apparent lull followed. Then, at dawn on 14 August, the morning shift at the Lenin Shipyard refused to start work. A mass meeting began, with the manager arguing from the top of a bulldozer. A few minutes later, Lech Wałęsa was hoisted over the tall steel fence, went straight to the improvised platform and, with the matchless impudence of a natural leader, took charge. The entire shipyard declared an occupation strike and presented a first list of demands.

On 15 August, the other shipyards at Gdańsk and Gdynia and the dock workers joined the strike. The actors of 1970 had now taken the stage again, and the Polish authorities never doubted that a new and infinitely more dangerous situation had arisen. Gierek, telephoned in the Soviet Union, cut short his holiday and flew home. The Poles, not knowing what to expect, were aware that another cycle of their history was ending and that some huge trial of their strength must lie ahead.

Poland on the Eve

Poland in the 1970s, for all its sickness, was very much more than a place of economic blunders, tortuous manoeuvres and petty repressions. It was also the most peculiar political structure on the European continent. Outwardly, Poland affected to be just one member of a community of nations 'building socialism'. But the Polish reality was an eccentric balance of compromises, in which the Catholic hierarchy was less dangerous to the Communist Party than the proletariat. This balance earned astonishment, but also admiration. Poland, it must be emphasized again, was in many ways far the most tolerant and open society in eastern Europe. Its standard of living was below that of most of its neighbours, and the sheer stress and tension of a Polish existence was greater than that of – for example – a

Hungarian. But the opportunity for a Pole to follow a way of life which had little or nothing to do with the state ideology had no parallel in the rest of the Warsaw Pact.

In the West, Polish society was usually referred to as 'pluralist'. A better word might be 'corporative'. Formally, the political order consisted in a monopoly of power held by the PUWP, ruling in the name of the working class and through the state bureaucracy, which acted – under the Sejm – as its executive. The reality was quite different. The Party's exercise of power had become conditional and limited. A number of huge social bodies had come to impose limits on how Party and state could govern. If these limits were ill-defined, their sanctions were not. Any one of these groups was, it was assumed, capable of putting up the sort of resistance that could destroy the régime's authority and – almost certainly – precipitate a Soviet military intervention.

The first and second of these groups, the Catholic Church and the private peasantry, had been identifiable from 1944 onwards. As we have seen, even the Stalinist dictatorship treated them with caution, especially in the matter of collectivizing the land. Both emerged enormously strengthened from the crisis of 1955–6. By ending collectivization and offering a compact with the Church, Gomułka had transformed them from dangerous enemies of People's Poland into indispensable allies who made his own victory possible. Given that a return to all-out Stalinist terror was unthinkable, it followed that the post-1956 régime would not survive if those allies withdrew their essentially contractual consent. Rivalry remained, of course. The ensuing two decades of wasteful squabbling between Church and laicizing state proved that no final peace treaty is possible between two forces each of which knows, on *a priori* grounds of dogma, that it will triumph in the end. But the underlying compact held.

The working class joined this power-balance only in 1970, and at once rendered it far more precarious. Its late arrival was not surprising. While the Church and the private peasantry had a 'federal' relationship with Party authority, operating through the episcopal hierarchy and through the peasantry's complicated and rather corrupt institutions, the workers were kept under 'direct rule'. The PUWP founded its own structure on the proletariat, through basic cells and branches in every place of work, while the trade unions remained entirely directed by superior Party authority. The workers were theoretically already in power through their 'vanguard', the Polish United Workers' Party. In contrast to Church and peasantry, they were not even recognized as a group that required distinct representation. They lacked the means to draw attention to their feelings by nicely calibrated pressure, so expertly used by the Church. In the end, the workers were forced to choose between acquiescence and open rebellion.

The state had much to offer the three great blocks of vested interest, each of them prepared for limited co-operation with government in the national interest. But three fundamental difficulties kept the balance unstable. The first was the sheer impossibility, in times of such economic strain, of satisfying the workers and the peasants simultaneously. To hold urban food prices down to the level the workers wanted, to pay the price for agricultural produce the peasants wanted and to ensure adequate food supplies to the shops was entirely beyond the government's means. The second difficulty was that the institutional machinery was utterly inadequate for such a neo-corporatist structure. The Church alone was fully equipped, interacting through formal and informal representation with the state. The peasants had no reliable means of negotiating collectively; the United Peasants' Party (ZSL), which in theory defended their interests, had been for thirty years an almost lifeless body which transmitted PUWP instructions to the countryside. Above all, the industrial workers had no genuine institutions of their own.

Gierek was aware of this, and intermittently talked about trade union reform. There was even some discussion about creating a 'workers' parliament' in which direct dialogue between the state and the factory shop-floor could take place. Savants wrote papers about conflict resolution techniques in capitalist societies. But even after the 1976 explosion, nothing of any significance was done.

The third problem, underlying all the others, had been identified by the DiP report. It was that the common ground shared by the three great interest blocks and the Communist state was simply too narrow to support a system of this kind. They all agreed that the Polish nation must survive in independence, and that too much turmoil in Poland risked extinguishing that independence by bringing in Soviet tanks. That, however, was where the common ground ended. Thirty-five years old, the régime had still not imposed its own view of society and politics on the nation; with so little consensus, it could maintain its relationship with the three 'partners' only by buying them off with ever-rising concessions rather than by genuine co-operation. The Church continuously raised its price for counselling popular restraint, as Gierek's requests for Church support became more urgent. The private farmers saw no reason to show the slightest gratitude for a stream of highly expensive favours from the state, and were soon to assail the régime with a ferocity unmatched by any other section of the community. The workers were left in no doubt about the self-destructive consequences of insisting on simultaneous wage rises and price freezes, but three times in ten years made precisely that demand.

It was not surprising that morale in the PUWP was rotting away. What, now, was the nature of the Party's mission? Ideological commitment had paradoxically declined as the educational level of the Party bureaucracy improved. Gomułka had found the Party talking feverishly about ideas and left it a party so overwhelmingly preoccupied with economic management that it scarcely understood that politics still existed in Poland. Thus, the terrible economic failure of the later 1970s shattered the Party's self-confidence as completely as the thrilling surge in consumption a few years earlier had made the comrades feel infallible. At the same time, the post-Stalinist decay of ideology had rendered the PUWP incapable of any penetrating self-criticism comparable to the great Marxist self-examinations of 1955–6. The reaction to failure became mere formula: Leninist norms of Party life have not been observed, certain personalities have not lived up to the trust the Party placed in them, the links with working people have not been polished recently ... A few heads would fall. Crises were dealt with by tactical 'fixing', usually by manipulating the factions within the apparatus.

Tension increased between the ruling élite of the Party and the local bureaucrats – the regional officials and secretaries who burst into protest at the Eighth Congress in February 1980. As the economic and political situation worsened through the late 1970s, the Gierek style of buying off trouble with concessions decided at the supreme level frustrated and compromised this 'middle apparatus'. The 'corporatist' pattern, which depended not only on placating the three great interest blocks at the national level but also on conciliating individual factories or districts, took power out of the hands of the local apparatus and created wide, irrational contrasts between different industries and even different regions of the country.

The leadership made efforts to conciliate the apparatus itself, mostly in ways that made the general political situation still worse. Changes in Party statutes allowed these permanent Party bureaucrats to win a majority (53 per cent) in the Central Committee, the very organ that was supposed to regulate and discipline them, and a blind eye was turned to many corrupt practices at the local level. But the disaffection of the apparatus continued to grow.

And there was a gradual decline in the quality of the people at the top. It is enough to glance back at one's notes from press conferences almost two decades before to register this change: what had become of those tough, witty men, confident that Marxism was resilient enough to be adapted to any situation, who held leading positions in the early 1960s? Twenty years of faction-fighting, always at the expense of the original minds and individualists and – at the end of the decade – of Jews, carried out a negative selection. The leading personalities by 1980 were limited, pragmatic men, often with a background in the peasant youth movement or in local Party bureaucracy, whose talent was for survival rather than innovation. The increasing pressure of this factional struggle narrowed recruitment to leadership until each change merely rearranged the same old names, the reshuffling of a greasy, familiar pack of cards.

At the same time, the industrial working class was steadily discovering a new sense of independent identity. It was in two senses a young class. Physically, nearly one third of the industrial work-force was under twenty-four years old by the mid-1970s. Historically, it had little in common with the relatively small pre-war proletariat whose leading figures had in any case been removed into Party, trade union or administrative jobs after the war. By 1976, some 40 per cent of the population were 'workers' in the broadest sense, including employees in all nationalized enterprises, state agriculture and forestry; perhaps only 15 per cent were employed in industry. The older workers were often of peasant origin, part of the torrent of labour drawn off the over-populated countryside into the first industrialization programmes after the war, but the link with the peasantry persisted in another form: the distinctive feature of the Polish working class is its high proportion of 'peasant-workers' who commute to factories from small farms and often remain part-time peasants. (In 1968, 10 per cent of industrial workers were part-time farmers and nearly 25 per cent of them travelled daily into the cities from the countryside.[8]) Locally, these proportions could be very high; in 1980 at the sulphur mines of Machów, near Tarnobrzeg, nearly three quarters of the miners lived on small farms in the district.

The appearance of independent militancy in the working class was not just a matter of resistance to high prices and low wages. Another factor was the great expansion of higher education. By 1975, nearly half of all students in higher education were workers or of worker origin. But at the same time, the chances of social promotion were narrowing. The industrial 'leap forward' of the previous years had absorbed another wave of educated young workers into management, which was now saturated: by the mid-1970s, nearly one employee in eight was in some form of managerial post. The Party, a traditional social escalator, was also blocked as its bureaucracy became a self-perpetuating and to some extent a hereditary élite. Ambitious, educated young men and women who would certainly have been recruited upwards ten years before now stayed on the factory floor; they were the natural leaders of discontented workers and were soon to emerge as local Solidarity activists.[9]

Industrial workers, especially in the biggest factories, were far more sophisticated than their predecessors in 1970. The protests of the new, raw working class of the Stalinist years had been violent, but without organization. In the 1970s, sallies on to the street had often ended in bloodshed and looting, some rioters well inflamed by vodka. Once the workers had seen a solution in taking control of production on the spot through workers' councils, but these were institutions that proved easy for the authorities to neutralize; they atomized the strength of the original rebellion instead of providing it with a united and independent direction.

These lessons had been learned by 1980, when the workers at once produced effective *ad hoc* negotiating committees, at the plant and later at the city level, answering to mass democratic assemblies. Order was strictly kept, and the possession of alcohol in the striking plants was banned. There were almost no street demonstrations; instead, the workers returned to the old technique known to the world between the wars as the 'Polish strike' and occupied their places of work.* Finally, and most significant of all, they deliberately rejected the temptation of a 'workers' council' solution and stood out for a permanently independent representation which accepted no responsibilities under the existing régime: free trade unions. The vestigial loyalty to what still claimed to be a workers' state, which had hampered workers' class-consciousness and actions in 1956 and 1970, had finally dissolved.

Lechosław Goździk, forgotten hero of the 1956 workers' councils, watched Solidarity on television in 1980 and told a Polish reporter: 'It's a different style. Beard and sweater. We used to put on suits and ties, and shave carefully ... You can see this is the second generation of workers. At FSO [the car factory where Goździk worked in 1956] the lads were mostly from the countryside and the older skilled men had come from the railways – from the pre-war industrial development area, the worker-élite which was

---

*The occupation strike, which became common in western Europe after the Second World War, has many advantages. It protects the workers against police violence on the streets (which also makes picketing extremely dangerous), it holds valuable machinery hostage, it prevents lockouts or the employment of scab labour, it holds the strikers together and maintains morale under siege conditions, and finally it symbolizes the workers' claim to own the means of production. Occupation strikes occurred in Poland from 1931 onwards. (As an illustration of pre-war militancy, there were 2,056 strikes involving 675,000 workers in 22,016 factories in the course of 1936, with the loss of nearly 4 million man-hours.) See D. Lane and G. Kolankiewicz, *Social Groups in Polish Society* (New York, 1973).

pretty good before the war. Both lots behaved much more carefully, showed much more restraint, than they do now.'

It seemed eccentric, at first, that in late 1980 one of the Solidarity centres began to distribute copies of Lenin's classic *What Is To Be Done?*, written in 1902. In fact, few books could have been more significant at that point. Solidarity still claimed to be a purely trade union movement, without political aims. But *What Is To Be Done?* is about the transformation of workers' movements into political forces. After defining 'trade union consciousness', the self-awareness of a workers' movement which is spontaneous and limits itself to workers' problems, Lenin suggests that such a movement will always fall into the hands of 'bourgeois ideology'. The task of revolutionaries is to give trade unionists the socialist consciousness they cannot achieve by themselves. 'The consciousness of the working class cannot be a truly political consciousness if the workers have not been trained to respond to *all* and *sundry* cases of arbitrariness and oppression, violence and misdeeds, *whatever classes* may be affected by these cases.'

This is exactly the training that KSS–KOR tried to give the workers before and after August 1980. But it was not a Marxist group, and it avoided any definite ideology just as it avoided any formal structure. Among its thirty-four members in 1979, the most obvious unifying element was that they all bore the scars of recent history: thirteen had fought in the resistance, mostly in the AK, many had experienced imprisonment for their views during the Stalinist period or – like Kuroń and Adam Michnik – in the Gomułka years, while five were old enough to have taken part in the 1920 Soviet–Polish war.[10] KOR included several well-known intellectuals of the older generation: the writer Jerzy Andrzejewski, the actress Halina Mikołajska, the economist Edward Lipiński. But its political imagination came principally from survivors of the student struggles at Warsaw University in the 1960s: Jacek Kuroń, Adam Michnik and Jan Lityński. Their inspiration remained Marxist, but they had moved from a conventional revolutionary perspective to original, gradualist ideas for a democratic transformation of society based upon independent social organizations.

KOR did not make Solidarity. The revolt of August 1980 would almost certainly have taken place without its existence, and would probably have generated the idea of independent trade unions by itself. New, independent unions had been suggested briefly at Szczecin ten years before, and in fact KOR, while arguing in its 1978 Workers' Charter that free trade unions were indispensable, saw them as a long-term objective and was taken by surprise when Solidarity emerged. But KOR decisively influenced the *nature* of Solidarity as it developed, especially through its journal *Robotnik* and its local support groups, filling the ideological vacuum with encouragement to fight 'all and sundry cases of arbitrariness and oppression' and ensuring that the new union would be committed to wider demands that were not just industrial but political.

Kuroń started from a perception astonishingly close to that of the discontented 'middle apparatchiks': that nothing in Polish life functioned properly because there were no generally accepted rules. If society was to work through bargains between authorities and groups, then those groups must be allowed to form organizations of their own that could guarantee that the bargains would stick. Kuroń looked forward to a 'Poland of social movements', created by a 'struggle for pluralism' in every area of life.

He accepted that the state would continue to be led by the Party. But the present chaos threatened the Party's position with collapse. Only a Poland with internal freedom of association could, through a 'historic compromise', rescue the Party and grant it legitimacy. With political authority on this new and solid footing, the fear of Soviet intervention would recede. Kuroń insisted that the Russians would accept almost any internal reform or change in Poland so long as the Party was not in danger and the fundamental alliance with the USSR – military, political and economic – was preserved. In the end, the Soviet Union could accept the 'Finlandization' of Poland, as a partner all the more reliable because it was a society founded on free consent.

This was a seductive argument. Subtly put, it none the less appealed to a popular vein of optimism: to the notion that it was the external relationship, not the internal details of the régime, which mattered to Moscow. KOR's tactics, as prescribed by Kuroń and Michnik, were also gradualist. Formal strike committees or workers' councils should be avoided; they were too easy to crush or subvert at this stage. Instead, workers in each factory should form tightly knit associations that posed no demands on their own, but infiltrated existing bodies – the union branches or the workers' self-government structures – and gradually rendered them representative. (The inspiration here was the unofficial 'workers' commissions' organized by the Communist Party in late-Franco Spain, which successfully infiltrated the state unions (*sindicatos*).) At a later state, real demands could be put. Then these demands 'must be supported by the expert advice of economists, engineers, lawyers and sociologists. The demands must be publicly proclaimed in Poland and abroad.' These last suggestions were eventually followed at Gdańsk, where the workers recruited an advisory team of intellectuals and insisted on publication both of their demands and of the negotiations.

Kuroń and Michnik were well aware of the discontent in the 'middle apparatus' of the PUWP. They framed their arguments carefully to appeal to this group, putting great emphasis on the stability of a 'durable compromise' between Party and people. To a hard-pressed local PUWP secretary or district prefect, vainly trying to enforce Warsaw policies through trade union branches that the workers regarded with contempt, or through agricultural 'circles' (state-run peasants' co-operatives) that the farmers distrusted, the plan had some attractions. KOR hoped that these groups in the Party would eventually enter into dialogue with the 'social movements'.

Great publicity was given in the West to all these 'dissident' movements – a title which KOR especially always rejected, preferring to be seen as an unofficial opposition. Though the membership of such groups amounted to only a few hundred, the 'uncensored' press created a far wider circle of supporters who distributed the publications, collected money or organized their own discussion clubs. Influence on the mass of the working class remained very slight. But the little Free Trade Union groups gathered nuclei of politicized workers in key plants – Ursus in Warsaw, some of the Silesian coal mines, the Baltic shipyards – while *Robotnik* provided basic advice on how to organize and run a strike. Other opposition groups, like ROPCiO or the nationalist Confederation for an Independent Poland (KPN), found their audience among older intellectuals and in Catholic circles.

Opposition among the peasantry took organized form in 1978, with a spontaneous campaign against advance payments demanded by the state for an old-age pension scheme. Beginning in the poorer eastern districts, a scattering of 'farmers' self-defence committees' appeared, often supported by the village priests and assisted by advice and publicity from KOR. A particular centre of resistance was the village of Zbrosza Duża, south of Warsaw, which became the object of continuous police harassment and political pressure. In 1979, the 'peasants' centres for knowledge' appeared, unofficial colleges organizing not only debates on all the assorted grievances of the private farmers but courses on the history of peasant politics in Poland. It was this aspect which most alarmed the authorities. They concluded that what they were seeing was an ill-disguised revival of the old independent Polish Peasants' Party. Although, again, the total numbers involved in the 'self-defence committees' was minute, the Peasants' Party was still proudly remembered by older peasants, and a hidden foundation on which to revive organized peasant politics existed throughout the country.

The Church's deep attachment to the 'spiritual values' embodied in a private peasantry, reaffirmed by the Pope on his visit in 1979, helped to bring about its own *rapprochement* with lay opposition groups. Even K O R, whose most active spirits had been formed in revolutionary Marxism and several of whom were of Jewish origin, found reasons to welcome the Church as an ally. As we have seen, it was in May 1977 that contact was effectively made with the Catholic hierarchy over the Warsaw hunger strike. In the same year, Michnik published a famous and much-disputed essay in which he reviewed the whole history of opposition in Poland, and concluded that its weakness had arisen from the division between the Church and the anti-clerical, Marxist intellectuals who had fought for democratic socialism in the 1950s and 1960s. The repressions of 1968 had destroyed that opposition (of which of course Kuroń and Michnik had been part) for good. Now the common interests between Catholics, intellectuals and workers could no longer be ignored. As Kuroń put it, the Church 'had to oppose the system that placed restrictions on the liberty of the individual, which is a fundamental Christian value and a value of our entire culture'.

The barriers between different sections of the population – the Church, the intellectuals, the peasantry and the working class (which had renewed the deep emotional loyalty to Church and nation inherited from its peasant origins) – were falling. Poles were coming together again, although on the basis of a mythical view of the past: Kuroń's assertion that even before the war the Catholic hierarchy and the working class had put individual liberty as their supreme value hardly stands historical examination. But the convergence towards a more conservative, religious conception of liberty was real enough. Especially after the election of a Polish Pope, the lay Catholic groups – already involved in opposition projects like the 'flying university' (TKN) – became more active and influential. Two Catholic journalists, Bogdan Cywiński, editor of the Kraków periodical *Znak* (*Sign*) and Tadeusz Mazowiecki, editor of the rather more radical *Więź* (*Link*) and a leading figure in the Clubs of Catholic Intelligentsia (KIK), were to make decisive contributions to the politics of Solidarity.

More must be said about the Pope's visit to Poland in June 1979. These were days that once revealed and changed the nation, bringing forward the maturing of all these historical processes. For anyone who travelled round Poland with John Paul II, it took time to become normal again. In dreams, one walked still over strewn flowers, in the glare of the sun. On the screen of closed eyelids, one saw again those long, long Indian files of men, women and children walking through waist-high green meadows on their way to meet this man, carrying their crosses and their banners. The curtains rustled in the wind; one started awake, hearing the soft, vast rippling which is the sound of a million human beings clapping their hands.

This was called a pilgrimage, a papal journey to honour the martyr St Stanisław, slain by a Polish king 900 years before. (The king lost his throne; the martyr became Poland's patron saint.) It was a demonstration that after thirty-five years of Communist rule the Church was still an overwhelming force in the nation. But it demonstrated not so much defiance of the régime as the truth about positive feelings. The people poured out these emotions in public, rejoicing that through the election of 'our Jan Paweł' their nation was famous throughout the world, surrendering to the catharsis of hearing the Pope at last give public voice to their private hopes and sorrows. It was important, too, that he said these things in a crystalline, literary Polish which had not been heard from official platforms for a generation. The cycle of more than thirty sermons, prepared as a single cumulative work of argument, was not least a revelation to those Poles who wanted to be proud of their own language. The effect on the young of hearing truth spoken in true words would be hard to exaggerate. It was well put by one boy: 'Now I realize that nobody has ever talked to me before ...'

The Pope, it soon appeared, took an almost Calvinist view of his election. God, rather than the Conclave of Cardinals, chose him, and chose him because he was a Pole. But why, he asked himself, did God decide that this was the hour for his Church to be led by a Slav? His conclusion was that Heaven required certain special strengths of Polish Catholicism to be made universal. The Church in Poland rested upon a unique mass loyalty almost unaffected by social class. This rock-like base meant that it could claim moral sovereignty over society. But it meant also – to this Pope, relying on his long experience as a Polish bishop and cardinal – that the Church was strong enough to afford general endorsement of any régime, including a Marxist one, which respected what he called 'the cause of man' and did not violate man's dignity, either as an individual or as a member of the collective nation.

This implied, too, that the Church should not be anywhere committed to a particular political party: a view almost totally incomprehensible in Catholic western Europe. But the Pope also laid before world Catholicism the highly traditionalist social views of the Polish Church: emphasis on a patriotic, united, independent nation, insistence on the unlimited family in which men labour for just reward and women raise children in the faith, belief in the virtue of the private peasant on his own inalienable strips of earth. Finally, there was the passion to see Europe united and at peace, a universal Polish interest so urgent that it can be classed as a transcendent form of patriotism.

Much of this could be welcomed without hypocrisy by Edward Gierek and the government. They could not share the Pope's views on sexual morality or the sanctity of small farmers. But, as the Belvedere meeting between Poland's civil leaders and the Pope showed, they were delighted that he should be preaching patriotic unity and that he should be repeating – with grief and indignation – that Poland was entitled to an honourable place in the world. Although warier of John Paul's meaning when he talked about European unity, they rejoiced in his cry at Auschwitz: 'No more war! Never again war!' and felt real gratitude that in the same sermon he left his text to add a special salute to the Russians who had died there: 'We know how great was the part of that nation [a Polish word never confused with 'state'] in the last tragic war for the liberation of the peoples.'

While the Pope did not exactly say that the régime was legitimate, he was prepared to concede that it was not illegitimate. The Church did not challenge the Party and state's right to rule, only their offences against human rights and dignity. This at least discarded the opinion of many older Polish Catholics, at home or in the emigration, which was that Communism was an imposed foreign occupation which could never be entitled to obedience. At the meeting in the Kraków Meadows, one group released a gas-balloon painted with the crowned eagle of pre-war Poland and the rune of the Warsaw Rising – symbols of total rejection, total defiance. It was that view which the Pope's visit consigned to the past.

At the time, the authorities drew much comfort from these hints of partnership and co-operation. This was quite mistaken. In many ways, the régime had been very much better off when the Church was in sullen opposition. That at least meant that it did not interfere. In those days, contacts between the Church and the state had mostly been effected in Rome, through the skilful Cardinal Casaroli, the Vatican's unofficial foreign minister. Now the collective Episcopal Conference in Warsaw negotiated directly with the government. The result was not only continuous leverage to extract more concessions, applied at every moment of weakness (which the bishops could spot much more accurately than Casaroli), but frequent and increasing intervention by cardinals, bishops and even abbots in the political process. The closer the wrestling embrace of Jacob and the Angel, the more intimate and effective became the Angel's fingers. The Church grew so confident that in early September 1980, when the government was looking for a successor to prime minister Babiuch, the Church intimated to the leadership that Tadeusz Grabski would not be acceptable to the episcopate because of the anti-clerical remarks he had made in the past. This was the sort of penalty the Party had to pay for trying to enlist the Church as a shock-absorber in social conflicts.*

* A slighter but more baroque example of the new mood was provided by Bishop Tokarczuk of Przemyśl, who found several microphones in his palace wall. The bishop summoned a high legal official from Warsaw to explain this outrage, but no meeting took place because the bishop insisted on receiving the official as a penitent at his palace, while the official demanded that the bishop call upon him at his hotel. Tokarczuk – it is said by a friend of his – then sent one of the microphones to the Pope, by parcel, and hung another one as an offering on the altar of Our Lady of Jasna Góra at Częstochowa, where for some months it dangled among the model hearts and limbs and rosaries offered by thankful pilgrims. Eventually the Abbot of Jasna Góra removed it and put it in a cupboard reserved for especially valuable votive gifts.

Chapter Five

Solidarity

At the Lenin Shipyard

The strike at the Lenin Shipyard in Gdańsk which began on the morning of 14 August was not entirely spontaneous. Few strikes are. In this case, the little Free Trade Union of the Coast decided to strike a match and see if the 17,000 employees of the shipyard would burn. The pretext was a renewed attempt by the management to get rid of Anna Walentynowicz, the crane driver whose appearance – small, middle-aged, a worried expression behind cheap, thick spectacles – disguised the most powerful orator in the whole strike movement. 'Anja' was liked and admired in the yard for her battles with authority, and her political activities in the Free Trade Union group were respected.

The opposition in Gdańsk at this point consisted of two groups, ideologically remote from each other but in practice driven into a certain intimacy. One was the Young Poland Movement, essentially a nationalist and anti-Russian circle. Young Poland was middle-class and tended to extremes; its Gdańsk members included the medical student Dariusz Kobzdej, the considerably older intellectual dissident Tadeusz Szczudłowski and a young girl named Ewa Ossowska. A few months before, in May, the Young Poland people had organized an illegal demonstration to commemorate the Third of May, the anniversary of Poland's enlightened constitution of 1791; Kobzdej and Szczudłowski had been beaten up by the militia and given three-month prison sentences.

The other element was the Free Trade Union, built around its publication *Robotnik Wybrzeża* (*Worker of the Coast*). This was a much more working-class formation. Its guiding nucleus contained names that were to become famous through the strike and later in the leadership of Solidarity: Lech Wałęsa; a serious, bearded engineer in the laboratories of the Elmor plant named Andrzej Gwiazda and his wife Joanna; Bogdan Lis, who was a worker at Elmor and a Party member; Anna Walentynowicz; and the young nurse Alina Pieńkowska from the Lenin Shipyard. The Free Trade Unionists also numbered one man who was more the type of the opposition intellectual. This was Bogdan Borusewicz, a graduate of the Catholic University of

Lublin and a KOR supporter who acted as the chief editor of *Robotnik Wybrzeża*. Borusewicz had a long record of conflict with the authorities, beginning with a three-year gaol sentence in 1968 for handing round illegal leaflets in Gdańsk, and in earlier years he seems to have been close to the conspiratorial nationalist position of Young Poland. He maintained this contact and also provided the trade union group with a direct link to KOR. There is a report, unverified, that Borusewicz arranged a secret meeting between Jacek Kuroń and the nucleus of the Free Trade Union of the Coast some time in August.

Early in August, Young Poland and the unionists met for a party to welcome Kobzdej and Szczudłowski back from prison, and there seems to have been, on the fringes of the celebration, discussion of the possibilities of a shipyard strike. The following day Borusewicz gathered three young workers from the Lenin Shipyard – probably distributors of the group's paper – and held a serious briefing with them on the details. They had experience to learn from. In July, they had attempted to call a strike but failed. As one of the three later told the British journalist Christopher Bobinski, 'We didn't really believe we could bring the yard out. We tried to get a strike going last month when the meat prices went up, but then it didn't work.' This time, the Free Trade Union resolved to light a much more ambitious match. Some six thousand single-sheet leaflets about Anna Walentynowicz's sacking were run off, most of them to be put around the city itself.[1]

At 4.30 a.m. on 14 August, the three arrived at the yard gate weighed down with posters and leaflets. Nobody stopped them. The first posters went up. The first arguments began around the leaflets. A banner appeared: 'We Demand the Reinstatement of Anna Walentynowicz and a Cost of Living Rise of 1,000 Zlotys'. At first hesitantly and then with growing interest, men gathered round. A march began from one department of the yard, then from another. Party officials who tried to stop them were shouted down. Workers already up on the hulls of vessels under construction stopped work to watch, then began to climb down and join in. By about quarter past six, a mass meeting had begun inside one of the gates.

From the top of a bulldozer, Klemens Gniech, the manager, argued with the workers. He hoped to prevent the formation of a strike committee – the three boys with Borusewicz's leaflets were already calling for volunteers – and he told the crowd that if they went back to work, there could be negotiations. But as he spoke, willing hands were helping Lech Wałęsa over the twelve-foot perimeter fence.

Unlike Anna Walentynowicz, Wałęsa had not worked at Lenin since 1976.

An electrician by trade, he had been on the 1970 strike committee at the yard and one of the delegates who met Edward Gierek when he came to confront the workers in January 1971. Wałęsa hung on as a member of the shipyard's trade union 'works council' until 1976, when he was sacked after a provocative speech. He found a job at a repair station for building machinery, was dismissed for agitation in January 1979, hired by Elektromontaż and sacked again in January 1980.

Wałęsa's irruption into the meeting, on that August morning, was not the entrance of some unknown Messiah. Most people except the young apprentices knew 'Leszek'. He meant trouble, but trouble of the right kind. They liked him for his fast-talking, infectious patter, but they also recognized his underlying decency: a good Catholic, a loyal family man with six children at the age of thirty-seven, a comrade who had paid a heavy price for standing up for his friends. Wałęsa's real obsession was with the memory of the dead of 1970. He had twice been involved in illegal commemoration meetings in December 1978 and 1979, and it was this which had brought him into contact with the circle around *Robotnik Wybrzeża*. By his own account, he had been detained about a hundred times by the police since 1976. No intellectual, he possessed a telepathic grasp of workers' emotions and a deep-seated, driving anger. The morning shift on 14 August welcomed him as the man for this moment.

The meeting was running out of steam as he turned up, and men were drifting away. Wałęsa jumped up on the bulldozer roof and furiously attacked the manager, Gniech – actually a liberal personality with much sympathy for his employees. The crowd clustered back around him. 'Remember me? I gave ten years to this shipyard. But you sacked me four years ago!' He turned to the men and women in their grey overalls below, and shouted that an occupation strike would now begin. They cheered him. Soon they were asking for his reinstatement too, and that of others. After two unsteady hours, the strike had lifted off in earnest.

They went indoors to talk, and settled in the hall of the yard's health and safety centre: two hundred shipyard workers in work denims (many had brought in a spare set, knowing that a strike was on the cards) facing Gniech and his colleagues. Wałęsa and members of the Free Trade Unions of the Coast at first dominated this strike committee, and it soon became clear that the demands were not going to be exclusively economic. The strikers now asked for a 2,000-zloty rise (about a third of the average monthly wage), the reinstatements, family allowances on the scales enjoyed by the police and security service employees, earlier retirement and better food supplies, including abolition of the 'commercial' meat shops. Gniech, after telephoning 'higher authority', was also forced to concede that a monument to the victims of December 1970 could be set up outside the main gate. And on Friday, 15 August, as a strike began at the Paris Commune Shipyard a few miles away at Gdynia and spread throughout the Gdańsk conurbation, the demands broadened yet again to include free access to the mass media, the release of political prisoners and the right to establish free trade unions.

These first days were angry and nervous. The government at once cut telephone communications between the coast and the outside world, in a futile attempt to contain the strike. The shipyard workers were frustrated that they were negotiating only with Gniech and the local authorities; well aware of their own significance, they wanted Party and state leaders to come down to Gdańsk as they had done in the crisis of 1971. Gniech, however, kept his head and calculated that the political demands, though sincerely felt, could be treated as deliberate over-bidding. By Saturday, he had brought the negotiation down to a wrangle about pay levels, and in the afternoon the Lenin Shipyard strike committee agreed in principle to settle for an extra 1,500 zlotys a month, the reinstatements, and a promise of no victimization. In Warsaw, the official news agency Interpress telephoned foreign correspondents to tell them that the Baltic strikes were over.

But they were not. In the first turning-point of the Gdańsk strikes, the 50,000 other workers in the city who had stopped their machines now intervened. Smaller, lower-paid and more exposed to police reprisals, these other enterprises had been relying on the Lenin Shipyard as the flagship of Gdańsk industry to win a settlement which they could adopt. At about noon, as the negotiations were ending, a delegation from the Gdańsk public transport garage arrived at the yard and its spokeswoman, a tram driver named Henryka Krzywonos, accused the shipyard of selling itself too cheaply and leaving its comrades in the lurch. 'If you abandon us, we'll be lost; buses can't face tanks!'[2]

Although the strike committee split, a majority voted to settle. Wałęsa used the yard's public-address system to announce a return to work, but he was clearly uneasy, and when the mass of workers outside greeted him with noisy barracking he sensed that he had misjudged the mood. This time, the Gdańsk workers were ready to play for the highest stakes, and they were supported by a large crowd outside the gates which hissed men who began to leave. Ewa Ossowska, the girl from Young Poland, was standing on a barrel and begging the workers to stay on strike. Wałęsa, on the instant, changed his mind.

There was a time of total confusion. Wałęsa was swung on board an electric trolley and rattled round the yard appealing for the occupation strike to continue. Bogdan Lis and the two Gwiazdas, assuming the battle at Lenin was lost, went back to the Elmor plant and started organizing an Inter-Factory Strike Committee there, with a fresh list of demands. Alina Pieńkowska set off round the city to prevent other striking enterprises surrendering. More delegations converged on the Lenin yard. A few hours later, the radical minority of the Lenin strike committee and representatives from twenty other plants were gathering again in the same conference hall and forming an Inter-Factory Strike Committee (MKS). The MKS scribbled out a list of sixteen demands and issued it the same evening. The strike would go on, it said, until they were satisfied.

These had been hours governed by instinct and emotion, rather than anyone's plan. But although it was not understood until afterwards, the crisis had been a necessary stage in the strike at Lenin. Those who voted to end it, so reluctantly followed by Wałęsa, had been older and more cautious workers brought into the committee at Gniech's suggestion. When they left, and when the majority of the shipyard strikers opposed a settlement, the defeated radicals in the committee simply formed a new strike committee more in tune with rank-and-file feeling and broadened its base to include the whole Gdańsk conurbation. The dragon shed its milk teeth, as a sharper set emerged beneath them.

Loyalty to the memory of the dead was probably the most powerful slogan at this point. Father Jankowski, the parish priest, had agreed to celebrate a Mass at the yard next day, Sunday, but he called it off when he heard the strike was ending. Desperate efforts went on into the small hours to get him to change his mind, even – it is said – including a suggestion to kidnap him. Meanwhile, yard carpenters constructed a large wooden cross – this idea came from Szczudłowski, one of the Young Poland people – and hung it on the gate. A pit was dug outside on the spot where four men had been shot down by the police in 1970. And at nine the next morning, before a crowd of several thousand, Father Jankowski said his Mass and blessed the cross as it was bedded into the ground. People around it looked at the cross standing there and thought of all that its presence meant, and wept. The place instantly became a shrine which the townspeople surrounded with fresh flowers and, by night, with glimmering candles. Thousands of Lenin workers who had gone home returned to see this marvel, and went on past it through the gate to take part in the occupation strike. Draughtsmen in the yard had already designed a permanent monument for the site; the following week a maquette appeared on the table of the MKS presidium.

The sixteen points of 16 August turned out to be only a first version of the strikers' demands. But the demand for free unions was there in a preamble: 'After the end of the strike is proclaimed, the MKS will not dissolve but will carry through the execution of the demands; it will organize free trade unions, acting as the district council of free trade unions.' Now and in future, the MKS did not demand the abolition of the official unions (CRZZ), but asked for 'the end of interference by the administrative organs in the functioning of trade unions'.

With the sixteen points, the real struggle for the future of Poland began. Several points amounted to universal political demands lodged on behalf of the entire nation; there was no way that this challenge could be 'managed away' by cash bonuses to this trade or double meat allocations to that factory. The third Polish cycle, that of Edward Gierek, ended when the sixteen points were passed through the shipyard gates to the crowd outside.

The points, later expanding in a new formulation to twenty-one, obviously derived from several sources. Free trade unions had been proposed by Wałęsa and his comrades and were now fervently supported by the mass of strikers. Other 'political' points – the abolition of censorship, the exercise of free speech and expression under the Constitution, the right to strike and the right of access to the media for the MKS – all echoed workers' demands from 1970–71. Only a few seemed to have stemmed directly from the opposition groups: immunity for the unofficial publishing houses, application of the provisions of the International Labour Organization on trade union liberty and the freeing of three activists connected with KOR.* One could add to that the new point which requested access to the media for churches 'of all denominations'. All these points were now added to the original demands which Gniech thought he had dealt with, including the 2,000 zlotys, and made applicable to the entire strike movement in the conurbation of Gdańsk, Gdynia and Sopot.

When local KOR activists entered the MKS hall, they were cheerfully greeted as allies. The assistance of intellectuals in strikes was no new idea; back in 1970, the Szczecin lawyers had helped the strike committee with legal and drafting advice. But the idea of actually handing over details of negotiation to opposition intellectuals had not yet arisen. In that sense, the MKS in this first week had a working-class character which to some extent it lost when the 'experts' arrived from Warsaw later. It was uncompromising

---

*They were: Edmund Zadrożynski, a regional contributor to *Robotnik*; Marek Kozłowski, a KOR supporter at Słupsk, not far from Gdańsk; and Jan Kozłowski (no relation), an activist among private farmers in south-eastern Poland.

in its demands, although aware that the movement was strong enough to destroy the régime and provoke Soviet intervention, and must therefore show restraint in its means. It was egalitarian, still showing the instinct to level out rewards and wages that had been evident in 1970. With the exception of the points about the Church and the release of KOR detainees, its programme was not 'symbolic' but practical, even the attack on censorship being seen as a guarantee that the central points – free unions and an improved standard of living – would not be eroded. And this was meant to be a one-way deal, the workers asking and the authorities giving. The notion of a grand political and social contract with the régime, involving assurances from the workers' movement as well as from the authorities, was not yet part of this position. Nothing illuminates this independent stand more clearly than the absence of any movement to take over the factories and run them through workers' councils.

Warsaw responded fast to the emergence of the MKS. Tadeusz Pyka, one of the government's team of deputy prime ministers, was sent down to Gdańsk at the weekend to lead a negotiating team, while Cardinal Wyszyński, in alarm, observed that the workers' demands were legitimate but called for 'calm and honest work'. On Monday, 18 August, Gierek held a Politburo meeting and then spoke to the nation on television, promising better food supplies, pay and welfare allowances and a special commission to look into workers' grievances. He offered reform of the CRZZ unions and, while warning 'enemies of socialism' not to exploit the strikes, gave an assurance that force would not be used to solve the crisis.

This speech was entirely ineffectual. Next day, another MKS appeared in the industrial town of Elbląg, near Gdańsk. Then the revolt spread to Szczecin, in Poland's north-western corner. Szczecin had been the most radical strike centre in 1970–71. Now, after an occupation strike began at the Adolf Warski Shipyard, 25,000 people all over the city and district stopped work. Kazimierz Barcikowski, another deputy premier but also a full Politburo member, at once set off for Szczecin to treat with the MKS, which had set up its headquarters in the Warski administration buildings. Gierek's mild tone in public was in any case not shared by all his colleagues; a frantic letter from the secretariat to all Party members claimed that the strikers' demands were a conspiracy by subversive forces to overthrow the workers' state.

Wednesday, 20 August, was another decisive day at Gdańsk. Pyka's negotiations collapsed. He had been endeavouring to split the movement by offering separate deals to each enterprise. Out of 261, the strikers at seventeen workplaces initially agreed to separate negotiations, but broke them off when Pyka insisted that any deal was conditional on their withdrawal from the Gdańsk MKS.

The strike in the Gdańsk region was still expanding day by day. Some 500 delegates were now packed into the main hall at the Lenin Shipyard, and had evolved a 'presidium' of fifteen to negotiate with the government. Exasperated by Pyka's tactics, the MKS now took another step which was crucial for the eventual emergence of Solidarity. It had originally intended to negotiate on behalf of the 261 enterprises only on the twenty-one points, leaving other, local demands to be handled by individual strike committees. Now the MKS became the sole and exclusive negotiator, and all additional bargaining at factory level was stopped until a central settlement was reached.

Gierek recalled Pyka to Warsaw and replaced him with Mieczysław Jagielski. This was an altogether more impressive envoy, a senior deputy premier and full Politburo member who had been head of the state planning commission and, since 1971, Poland's permanent representative to Comecon, the economic organization of the Soviet bloc. Suave and metropolitan as he liked to appear, Jagielski was in fact the son of a peasant from eastern Poland; he had spent almost his entire career in the rural bureaucracy until he became Gomułka's last minister of agriculture. In Comecon, he had grown accustomed to the niceties and the polished tables of economic diplomacy. Now, suddenly, his chief was pushing him off the sledge to reason with the wolves.

The negotiations did not begin in earnest until Saturday evening, 23 August. Jagielski, his face grey with distaste, came striding down a lane of shouting, laughing shipyard workers and hustled his delegation into the conference building. He found that the talks with the MKS presidium were to be held in a room at the back of the building with one glass wall, through which huge boilermakers chewing green apples and western photographers with long hair stared and made faces at the negotiators. Worse still, every word Jagielski spoke was broadcast to the large hall where the full MKS sat listening, and to the thousands of shipyard workers lying on the dusty grass or clustered round loudspeakers outside.

Wałęsa, as the two groups settled in their chairs, was still not sure what to make of Jagielski. Although Jagielski may not have known it, Wałęsa had offered his resignation the day before on the grounds that his own past record for conflict with authority might hinder an agreement. His presidium colleagues turned the offer down, but this was a second token of how anxious Wałęsa really was, underneath his truculence, to strike a quick bargain. The killings of December 1970 seem to have haunted him; the other MKS leaders, perhaps less imaginative, were more resolute.

He decided, as he had done with the shipyard manager, to hit Jagielski hard and fast, to gain the initiative and learn more about his adversary. Within moments, Jagielski was on the ropes, with Wałęsa shouting at him about faked political trials and demanding the release of KOR prisoners (another fourteen, including Kurón, had been detained on Wednesday). As the shipyard workers cheered under the loudspeakers outside, one MKS presidium member after another flung himself at Jagielski: the first was being hunted by the police and asked whether the war against Germany hadn't been fought for freedom; another said the press had been proved to lie and the Ministry of Justice probably lied too; a third said that the local authorities abused their power; a fourth complained that strikers couldn't reach their children in holiday camps because the telephones were still cut. Finally Andrzej Gwiazda moved in on the wretched minister: Jagielski knew, he said, that the precondition for negotiating was that the telephones should be restored, so when would the lines be opened?

Jagielski, though shocked, soon pulled himself together and gave a long, coherent reply to the twenty-one points. It was not encouraging. On free trade unions, he would only offer new legislation for a thorough overhaul of the old CRZZ unions. He rejected the 2,000-zloty all-round pay rise, arguing that it should be a percentage increase to maintain wage differentials, and gave only cautious assent to the principle of linking wages to price increases. He denied that the militia and security police had unfair family allowances. Other 'social' demands, like improvements in the state health service and a five-day working week, were in outline possible, but needed far more study and funds that would be difficult to raise. (Jagielski ignored point 3, which asked that the press freedom guaranteed in the Constitution should be respected and that all religious denominations should have access to the media.) Only once did his resentments break through, when he suddenly exclaimed that he, too, had been through hard times in the occupation. 'I was beaten and tortured in a prison for a year ... They murdered my father and two brothers. My mother went mad for three years because she was inhumanely tortured. I can show you all my scars!' It was a protest that he was as good a Pole as anyone in the room.

The Soviet Union's press comments on the events were still brief and neutral, but Moscow's underlying fear that the 'Polish infection' might spread was shown on 20 August, when for the first time since 1973 the jamming of western radio broadcasts to the USSR was resumed. The strikes, now proclaiming their solidarity with the Gdańsk demands, spread back across Poland all through this week. In Warsaw, most people assumed that

Gierek must resign within a few days. But he staved off the end with one more feat of manoeuvre. The Central Committee met for its Fourth Plenum on Sunday, 24 August, the day after Jagielski's first round of talks at Gdańsk, and performed a hasty re-shuffle in Party and state.

The senior victim was prime minister Babiuch. This tiny, fatalistic man had done his best against hopeless odds, but he was now replaced by Józef Pińkowski, a mild figure whose acquiescence seemed his main quality. In the Party leadership, the faction around Stefan Olszowski broke through, loudly proclaiming that they had predicted this crisis. Olszowski himself was hauled back from East Berlin to the Politburo; and his lieutenant, Tadeusz Grabski, was made a deputy prime minister and Andrzej Żabiński, a forceful young district secretary from Opole, became a deputy Politburo member. Gierek's old ruling team was massacred. Among those who fell were Łukaszewicz, the author of 'success propaganda'; the failed negotiator Pyka; Szydlak, as the head of the CRZZ unions; and – this Olszowski made sure of – Zdzisław Żandarowski, the man in charge of Party appointments who had in his time brought down both Olszowski and Grabski. Finally, the Plenum took relish in firing Gierek's disastrous choice as head of broadcasting, Maciej Szczepański, and all Party cells were invited to discuss his gaudy sins.

Gierek himself survived. Again, he spoke humbly and self-critically about 'our own errors, inconsistencies, delays, and hesitations', and promised that citizens would have more say in the running of the country. He went as far as to promise that there could be free elections in the old CRZZ unions, and that he would accept the election of strike leaders to union posts, but he would not concede the right to create an entirely independent trade union confederation. It was not enough. At Gdańsk, Szczecin and Elbląg, the strikers agreed to fight on until they won.

But this Fourth Plenum, one of the most complete leadership changes in the post-war history of eastern Europe, had in effect terminated Gierek's reign. He was now quite isolated. Two other powerful figures were emerging. One was Stefan Olszowski. The other, very much more discreet, was Stanisław Kania.

Olszowski, the 'enlightened despot', was far the better known. He was highly educated and, at forty-eight, relatively young. The son of a schoolmaster, Olszowski set off up the Party ladder as a student politician in the Stalinist ZMP youth movement and was rewarded by being made Polish representative to the International Union of Students in Prague. In 1963, he became director of the Central Committee's press office, a brilliant career achievement at only thirty-two, entered the Central Committee itself the next year, and in 1968 became Party secretary in charge of press and propaganda.

This was the year when General Moczar was in the ascendant and when the régime's propaganda concentrated on the frantic denunciation of 'Zionists'. Olszowski did his job without apparent reluctance, but avoided too close an identification with Moczar; when the general fell in 1971, Olszowski lost his Party post but was consoled with the position of foreign minister. For the next five years, his intelligence and affable manner won him a high reputation both in the West and in Moscow. But when he came back to Warsaw in 1976 as Party secretary in charge of the economy, his deep differences with Gierek emerged.

Olszowski, not unlike Janos Kádár in Hungary, was a cynical and ambitious realist, but he lacked Kádár's slightly melancholy streak of humanity. He saw that a radical decentralization of Poland's economy was required and envied Hungary's 'New Economic Model', but he also insisted that such a huge reform must be accompanied by a tightening of political discipline – exactly the opposite approach to Gierek's combination of centralism and tolerance. As we have seen, at the end of the decade Olszowski was able to collect an intellectual following of reformers and to some extent to overcome the ugly reputation he had acquired in 1968. When the summer crisis of 1980 opened, he was at first attracted by the chance of seizing the leadership of a reform programme which would be under the Party's control. But within two weeks of the first occupation strike at Gdańsk, he became convinced that the workers' movement was falling into the hands of 'anti-socialist forces' and that only harsh, decisive action could save the Party from being overwhelmed.

He and Stanisław Kania were both of the same square, heavy-faced build. There the resemblance ended. Kania, like both Jagielski and Barcikowski, came from the poor peasantry. He began work as a blacksmith's apprentice and had almost no education beyond two years at the Party college during the Stalinist period; his grasp of economics and his direct knowledge of the outside world were slight. His career in the Party was that of an apparatchik dealing with rural and agricultural policy until he became secretary of the district surrounding Warsaw in 1960. It was Babiuch, that shrewd student of Party personnel files, who spotted Kania's potential and in December 1968 had him elevated to head of the Central Committee administration department – a neutral term, which in practice meant that he was the political second-in-command of security.

His chief was General Moczar. When Gierek managed to get rid of Moczar, Kania was given his job. He became Party secretary responsible not only for security but for the armed forces, and – a few years later – for the supervision of Church–state relations. Some idea of the reticent Kania can thus be formed from the generally forbearing treatment of dissent during the 1970s and from the decision – which Kania supported – to risk the Papal visit. Tough and independent as he was, he stayed out of faction-fighting and remained loyal to Edward Gierek. Kania was a bad formal speaker, inclined to fumble and lose his page, but could drop jargon and be endearingly direct when he chose. Although he was not a 'liberal' or a man of ideas, the killings of 1970 had deeply shocked his patriotism and his old-fashioned, uncritical belief in the working class. Nothing is known of his relations with Moscow, which as head of security he must have cultivated, but the western press was wide of the mark in calling him 'Moscow's man' when he became First Secretary. Like his friend General Jaruzelski, minister of defence, he was a loyal Communist determined that Poland could solve its own problems without resort to force.

Over the weekend of 23 August, a new element entered the situation at Gdańsk. A group of intellectuals arrived from Warsaw, invited to serve as expert advisers to the MKS in the negotiations. This intervention, which was to have long consequences in the politics of Solidarity, had begun when sixty-four prominent figures in cultural life, soon joined by several hundred other signatories, issued an 'Appeal' on 20 August in support of the strikers and their demands. 'In this struggle, the place of the entire progressive intelligentsia is at their side. That is the Polish tradition, and that is the imperative of the hour.' The appeal went on to insist that the crisis must be solved by negotiation, not force, and for the first time suggested that a political settlement affecting the whole of Polish society could emerge. 'Only caution and imagination can today lead us to an understanding in the interests of our common fatherland.'

The moving spirit behind this Appeal was Tadeusz Mazowiecki, editor of the Catholic periodical *Więź* and a central figure in the clubs of Catholic Intellectuals (KIK). The following day, Mazowiecki brought together a small group of friends in Warsaw and suggested that a few of them should go to Gdańsk and give the appeal to the MKS and to Jagielski. They could even act as a 'mediating' team of experts. Some, like the writer Andrzej Kijowski, hesitated; support, rather than mediation, seemed to be what the workers needed. But Mazowiecki and the historian Professor Bronisław Geremek set off for Gdańsk, while a circle composed mostly of Catholic laymen from KIK, from the 'flying university' (TKN) and from the DiP research team stayed in Warsaw to recruit advisers for Gdańsk and Szczecin. In both places, but with rather less enthusiasm at Szczecin, the offer was accepted. The team that settled in at Gdańsk consisted of Geremek, Mazowiecki and Wielowiejski, from KIK; Waldemar Kuczyński and

Tadeusz Kowalik (both economists); the sociologist Jadwiga Staniszkis, a representative of the student generation of 1968 who had been imprisoned with the other student militants in that year; and Bogdan Cywiński, editor of the Catholic periodical *Znak*, in Kraków. They were followed by scores of uninvited enthusiasts from Warsaw and Kraków, eager to help, some of whom provided an 'outer circle' of advisers. Among them came members of various opposition groups, from KOR to the nationalist Young Poland movement.

On Monday, there was a pause. The MKS refused to talk until the telephones to the rest of Poland were reconnected, and this was finally done the same night (although international telephone and Telex lines remained blocked). In the afternoon, the MKS team took the chance to test its own resolve: at the suggestion of some of the new experts, part of the presidium, including Wałęsa, went off with them to one of the machine-sheds which they knew was not bugged and briefly went over their position on free trade unions. The experts wanted to be sure where they stood. Would the presidium accept something less – a reform of the CRZZ official unions? The strike leaders were firm: a trade union with genuine independence was essential.

On Tuesday, a third round of negotiations with Jagielski proved almost completely barren. While giving way a little on social and economic points, he would not even discuss free trade unions. As the exasperated presidium tried to make the government delegates understand that they were talking about free, independent unions of their own, Jagielski replied that he quite agreed that the existing unions needed overhaul and that absolutely democratic elections to their branches should be held at Gdańsk as soon as possible. It was a dialogue of the deaf.

But Jagielski was playing a game. When the closed working party met the same day, composed of the experts of both sides with three men from each negotiating team, the atmosphere was entirely different. In private, the government side was perfectly prepared to discuss the technicalities of establishing independent trade unions. Led by the earnest young prefect of Gdańsk, Jerzy Kołodziejski, the officials agreed to look at methods of legal registration for a new structure. But they were reluctant to include in any agreement a statement that workers had the *right* to set up independent unions. Candidly enough, they said that it would look as if the authorities were encouraging such a development 'from above', the sort of behaviour that in Czechoslovakia in 1968 had fatally discredited Alexander Dubček's leadership with the Russians. The MKS side were left with a strong impression that the government preferred the appearance of being driven into conceding independent unions, even though this could – and in the event did – mean that workers elsewhere in Poland would have to strike to win the same rights as Gdańsk.

The best account of these private talks has been left by the young sociologist Jadwiga Staniszkis, who was a participant. She wrote afterwards: 'During the first meeting of the working party, a peculiar, semi-relaxed atmosphere, gentle and even ironic, prevailed. One reason was that experts on both sides ... were more or less members of the same Warsaw milieu. The government experts were rather critical but basically loyal professionals; we were more openly critical, but still acceptable within the framework of Gierek's 'window-dressing' liberalization. If it had only been a matter of our political attitudes, we could very easily have changed places. This atmosphere made negotiations easier: the element of mutual trust already existed, and leaks from both sides helped things to move more smoothly. And the surreal nature of our joint situation made bargains more possible. It created a curious detachment from the real context in which we were talking ... But on the other hand, this climate dangerously increased our mutual loyalty to each other as we bargained. It was one of the main reasons why, in order to keep the negotiations going, the workers were not informed about crucial details and choices established by the working party. We ended this first meeting in an optimistic mood.'[3]

The great strike had now settled into the spectacle which became so familiar on the world's television screens in the last weeks of August. When the visitor had wheedled and bribed his way into a taxi at Gdańsk airport – petrol was severely rationed in the region – he drove into a silent, Sabbatical city whose empty tram-rails were already crimson with rust. People moved about on foot or by cycle, clustering round the few open shops for meat or bread. Outside the closed gates of the Lenin Shipyard, encrusted with fading flowers wedged in the railings and with portraits of Pope John Paul II, a permanent crowd stood waiting for news. Through the gates, the visitor passed through a scrappy park around the conference building, where thousands of workers in frayed grey overalls and little black berets stood listening to the negotiations relayed over loudspeakers or dozed in groups on the grass. Some six thousand men had been sleeping in the fabrication halls on blankets and air mattresses for two weeks now, separated from their families – nobody was allowed to leave except on compassionate grounds, although husbands and wives could talk through the fence and parcels of food could be pushed through. The possession and sale of alcohol was strictly banned in the yards and in the district as a whole, and any worker found with a bottle had his name read out over the loudspeakers and the contents spilled on the ground.

In the hall of the health and safety building, the hundreds of delegates who formed the MKS sat at long tables loaded with mineral-water bottles, flowers, tape recorders and assorted papers. In the corners, typists laboriously hammered out blurred copies of bulletins – there was no luxury like a Xerox machine – or prepared open sausage-sandwiches with glasses of tea and gritty black coffee. At one end was the empty dais for the MKS presidium, backed by three symbolic objects: a crucifix, a Polish flag and a life-size statue of Lenin in white plaster.

For almost all of the strike's interminable hours and days, the task of the delegates was simply to listen and to wait. Many men and women were scribbling; it became a fashion to pass the time by composing verse, and after the strike a brochure of poems and doggerel entitled 'Give Over Telling Us You're Sorry' was selected from their ingenuities. At the gate or in the hall, there would be an occasional flurry as somebody flung out copies of an opposition newspaper or leaflet. Another break from the monotony was Mass, as a polished Church limousine – flowers on its bonnet and a crucifix on the windscreen – nosed into the yard. Father Jankowski, splendid in lace-edged vestments, would hear confessions and take the hundreds of kneeling workers through the old responses they knew so well. And once or twice a day, Lech Wałęsa would rush through the hall scattering votive cards of the Black Madonna of Częstochowa and scrawling autographs, on his way to report on the day's progress to the cheering crowd outside the main gates.

At the glass wall of the inmost room where the negotiations took place, foreign television crews and photographers fought noisily for space.* This was true transparency; Jagielski was to protest: 'I have often negotiated in my life, but never about Polish issues with the participation of the foreign press!' Every few minutes, a gigantic bald engineering worker would emerge from the room and bellow *'Cisza!'* (Silence!) at the mob. Each word and facial expression of the negotiators could be registered through the glass, and their working conditions – low easy-chairs crammed round what was really a coffee-table, so that only a few inches separated the nose of minister and striker – were wretched. Between sessions, anybody could slip into the room and button-hole presidium members; Wałęsa would sit in a corner, joggling a

---

* The government gave visas to almost every western journalist who applied at this time; after the settlement, they were gradually squeezed out again as their visas ended. The intention may have been that a publicity barrage might deter the Soviet Union from an immediate intervention.

baby daughter on his knee and discussing the next day's tactics for anybody to overhear.

Lech Wałesa and the Leading Role

In Warsaw, there was now intense excitement as the newspapers abandoned caution and began to give fuller coverage to what was happening at Gdańsk, Szczecin and elsewhere. The government daily *Życie Warszawy*, for example, published a dialogue with its own printers, who were allowed to say that their trade union 'produced only shit', was run by 'bonzes feathering their own nests', and recruited 'no trouble-makers, only conformists'. Tragic cries of alarm rose from the authorities. The journalist Ryszard Wojna warned on television that the tumult might end in another partition of Poland (an incredible remark for a member of the PUWP Central Committee to make about Soviet intentions), while Mieczysław Rakowski, editor of *Polityka*, told the viewers: 'Things are taking place in Poland that are the source of all my hopes – but also of my unease, and of my deepest fears.'

It was at this point that Cardinal Wyszyński, the Primate, put a foot wrong. In a sermon delivered on 26 August, pounced on by state television and the papers, he supported the workers' demands but suggested that there were faults on both sides and that long strikes were a threat to the nation. Reports of this sermon shocked the strikers in the Baltic ports, who had expected full-blooded encouragement from the Cardinal, and appalled the more radical wing of the hierarchy. In Gdańsk, Bishop Lech Kaczmarek sent emissaries down to the yard to tell the strikers that the government had censored the sermon and twisted its meaning. When the full version finally appeared, days later, this was seen to be almost entirely untrue, but the MKS meanwhile accepted the bishop's excuses and angrily accused Jagielski and the government of bad faith.

On Wednesday, 27 August, Jagielski did not return to the yard. But the working party on trade unions held a second, crucial session. Even the intellectuals on the MKS side had been astonished by the workers' insistence that free trade unions were the central, non-negotiable point; in Warsaw, this had at first sounded like a wildly provocative demand that the régime could never accept and that might soon subside. Now, after the encouraging first session of the working party, the government experts were grim. They hinted that the leadership, possibly Moscow as well, had put them under pressure. Free trade unions formed an 'ideological precedent' that could not be accepted, because it shattered the fundamental link of the Party with the working class. The only way out was to neutralize the precedent with some declaration of loyalty. It was suggested that the preamble to the agreement should state that the new unions recognized the Party's 'leading role' in the state and Poland's existing alliances. This would allow the authorities to declare that the 'ideological orientation' of the new unions was socialist – that their independence would be only qualified, and ultimately subordinated to the P U W P as the rightful vanguard of the working class.

Jadwiga Staniszkis was one of the few experts who saw that this wasn't just a matter of words but a departure from the whole spirit of the movement. But her colleagues, eager to settle and perhaps dazzled by the idea that the régime was even contemplating the acceptance of free unions, advised the workers from the M K S presidium to make this declaration. Such a formula 'doesn't mean anything … Let's use their double talk.'[4] A drafting group was set up. Staniszkis stayed out of it. It all smelt of manipulating the workers, a smell marvellously absent in the Lenin yards until then. She would have preferred to re-call the presidium and leave the decision to their vote. In the event, nobody voted on the preamble, which was now worked out and rapidly accepted by the government experts. In its final version, enshrined in the Gdańsk Agreement of 31 August, the wording ran: 'The unions endorse the principle of social ownership of the means of production, constituting the foundation of Poland's socialist system. Recognizing the leading role of the Polish United Workers' Party in the state, and without undermining the established system of international alliances …'*

On Thursday, 28 August, Jagielski came back in the morning for a third round. Some progress was made. He conceded that liberty of the press in theory protected by the Constitution should be made effective. He gave some ground on the right to strike and the release of political prisoners. But although he now had the experts' draft on free unions in his pocket, he was still not conceding this key point in public. The night before, on local television, he had repeated yet again that 'this crisis of confidence can and must be overcome within the framework of existing trade union institutions'. He and Wałęsa now, essentially, had a deal. But they had yet to get their own masters to ratify it. Jagielski had to face a Party ruling group already badly split and now increasingly panicky as workers in the great industrial centres like Wrocław, the steel city of Nowa Huta, and finally the last bastion of loyalty, the coal-mining basin of Upper Silesia, each struck and set up its

---

* See Appendix 2, p. 280 for the texts of the Gdańsk and Szczecin Agreements.

own MKS with its own demands. And Wałęsa had to face his own strike committee, waiting in the hall.

Friday was a day of waiting. The shipyard workers entertained themselves by tuning the loudspeaker system to listen to the police radio net. Then, in mid-morning, the presidium announced that the government team would not come that day. There had been a hitch; the government felt that not everything could be decided at once.

As it turned out, there was a political crisis in Warsaw. At a meeting of the Politburo, Olszowski and his supporters were declaring that the revolt must be stopped before it was too late; a state of emergency should be declared, and the armed forces should be used to open the ports and break the Baltic strikes.* Gierek, standing on his public promise that this crisis must be solved by negotiation, resisted. He was firmly backed by Kania and by General Wojciech Jaruzelski, the two men directly in charge of the police and the armed forces. At Gdańsk, where the Party secretary, Tadeusz Fiszbach, called a district Party meeting, Admiral Janczyszyn, commander of the navy, refused to allow his men to be involved in any confrontation with the workers. Fiszbach, himself strongly committed to reforms, was relieved to hear it. In Warsaw, the battle in the Politburo finally swung against Olszowski, and the way was open to a settlement on the terms that Jagielski was reaching – an almost complete acceptance of the strikers' demands.

In the Lenin yard, where little of this was known, Wałęsa tried to appease the growing unease he sensed in the MKS. From the platform of the main hall, he assured the delegations that there was nothing sinister about the working parties behind closed doors. The final verdict remained with the MKS. 'We will rely on your opinions. We have no competence to take decisions, only to draft a text that will be put to the plenary session of the MKS.' Another speaker summarized the results of the talks so far and gave the first account of the vital preamble on free unions: 'We don't question the leading role of the Party or Poland's alliances; we just want the workers to have the means to defend themselves.'

Message after message was read out and cheered: that an MKS was

* Curiously enough, in view of the bitter argument over the text of the new Constitution in 1974–5, it contains no provision for a national state of emergency or state of siege. The only relevant provision is for a state of alert when war seems imminent. There is no obvious explanation for this gap. Probably the drafters simply forgot it. While a strike in western countries occasionally leads to the declaration of a state of emergency, without any grave consequences, the Polish assumption is that such a declaration implies the eventual use of force against strikers, either directly or by decrees 'conscripting' key sections of the labour force.

formed at Wrocław; that a poll at Elbląg showed that 90 per cent of the strikers wanted to stay out; that workers in the Lubin copper mines were striking in support of the twenty-one points; that negotiations were beginning with the coal miners at the MKS at Jastrzębie in Upper Silesia;* that an MKS was formed at Bydgoszcz. At eight in the evening, Wałęsa was back on the platform. The first demand for free unions had been almost solved by the experts. 'Everything is going well now! We are moving forward. There's hope that we'll finish quickly, though probably not tomorrow. We are near the finish!'

The next morning, Saturday, 30 August, Jagielski and his team reappeared. They were almost jovial. The thunderstorm in Warsaw had cleared the air; now the negotiations could be concluded. Andrzej Gwiazda, for the MKS presidium, read out the draft preamble to point 1, with its formulation on the leading role of the Party. Jagielski immediately welcomed this sign of 'ideological and political orientation'. Point 1 was initialled, and then point 2, on the right to strike and immunity for strikers and their supporters. Here Jagielski, understanding very well that 'supporters' was a euphemism for opposition groups like KOR, suggested that the word could be dropped, and was drowned out in an angry babble of voices. 'I accept, I accept!' he could be heard shouting.

He was in a hurry. Another special session of the Central Committee – the Fifth Plenum – was gathering in Warsaw that afternoon to ratify the Gdańsk and Szczecin agreements. But at Gdańsk there was a good deal still unsettled. To save time, both sides agreed that the proposals on wages and social or working conditions should be drafted in greater detail and presented to the government by the end of September. The rest of the agreement could be drawn up in the next few hours by the experts. Jagielski hopefully suggested that they might issue an advance communiqué stating that a settlement had been reached, and that work could resume on Monday. But the MKS declined to be railroaded. Jagielski, unabashed, said he would be back for the final signature that night or on Sunday. Thirty-five years a Communist, he ended: 'I'm a farmer, and I believe Saturday's a lucky day. Yes, the day of Our Lady, that's right, Our Lady, when my parents always started the harvest ...' There was a roar of ironic applause and laughter.

Jagielski set off once again for Warsaw. The agreement, the great victory, was almost complete. And yet it was only the foreign press and the Warsaw

---

*It now seems probable that it was this news that an MKS was forming at Jastrzębie, meaning that the free trade union movement had flooded into Upper Silesia, that in the course of the day made the course advocated in the Politburo by the hard-liners seem impractical.

intellectuals who seemed to see the situation like that. The workers, inside the MKS hall and outside, had only now digested the deal that had been presented to them. They began to argue among themselves. After more than two weeks of majestic self-restraint (the delegates had even added a ban on smoking, and that in one of the most cigarette-addicted societies in Europe), their solidarity was cracking at last. The whole atmosphere changed. Suddenly, there were strike guards with red-and-white armbands in and around the hall, checking everyone's credentials. There were provocateurs slipping in, they said, who were trying to sabotage the talks.

The argument first exploded in the presidium room. A group of young protesters from a local opposition group (perhaps the Movement of Young Poland) walked boldly through the door and accused the presidium and its advisers of selling out the strike by accepting the Party's leading role. The words 'Treason to the working class!' were heard. Wałęsa saw that this reaction might prove infectious and said foolishly: 'Never mind, we still have a chance that the Central Committee will reject it.' The MKS presidium itself broke into two quarrelling halves. Eventually, a majority agreed to call Kołodziejski, the prefect, and get him to tell the Central Committee that another phrase must be added to the preamble, guaranteeing full independence of the unions from Party interference. This was futile, and if the request ever reached Warsaw it was ignored.

Although the loudspeakers had been switched off, dismayed MKS delegates gathered to watch the waving arms and contorted faces through the presidium window. Experts hurried in and out, distraught. The presidium was trying to go back on its own signature, they said; the whole agreement was in peril; 'these people just aren't responsible!' It was not long before the uproar spread into the main hall. Groups formed, shouting in one another's faces. There was more talk of secret alterations to the text, of shady deals behind the delegates' backs, of *agents provocateurs*.

Wałęsa appeared, half-running down the hall towards the microphone. 'We can't go back on our word. We have agreed, after all. And this is just a matter of words. It's practice, only practice, which will tell how this agreement will work. If we prolong the whole thing, we may lose everything we have gained. (*Applause.*) Who disagrees – anyone? Nobody's going to manipulate these unions. Look, we're going to have a building of our own, with a big sign outside saying "Independent Unions". If anybody tries to manipulate us – then we strike . . .'

The hall roared for him. Only on a few young faces was there the stunned expression of an intelligence which has been insulted. But it was time for a performance of music and recitation by the best professional talents of

Gdańsk and Warsaw. For an hour, the delegates were able to forget their doubts by listening to the great nineteenth-century poets speaking for the Polish nation, laughing at political satire, standing to sing patriotic hymns in the discordant voices of men whose work keeps them slightly deaf. The smudgy duplicator which had been turning out copies of the strike bulletin *Solidarity* ran off sheets of Słowacki's 'Hymn of the Confederates'.

> *Never will we league with kings,*
> *Never bow our heads to force . . .*

But after the performance, the arguments returned. This time, they centred on the release of political prisoners and opposition members, specifically named in point 4. Most of the KOR activists were now in prison, and reports of other arrests were coming in by the hour. Jagielski had been evasive about their release, and the MKS presidium had not insisted on a detailed assurance. But the fate of the KOR members was less worrying for most workers than the lack of clarity about the scope of the new unions. The negotiations seemed to be talking about regional unions, perhaps confined to the coast. Surely the final text should make it clear that such unions could be founded all over Poland, and join together in a single confederal structure.

Gwiazda read out a declaration mentioning KOR and naming nineteen dissidents under arrest: there could be no mutual confidence between government and workers until they were set free, he said. The MKS applauded and was about to vote for Gwiazda's statement when Wałęsa stormed up to the platform, grabbed the microphone from a girl who was about to speak and counter-attacked. 'Don't name names. We don't want to be accused of supporting any organization. We respect these people who have done much for us but we are trade unionists, nothing but trade unionists ...' He, too, was acclaimed.

The debate whirled on. Wałęsa dominated the struggle for the microphone; when he reached for it, nobody would deny him. He kept coming back to the Party's leading role: 'It's we who are creating trade unions, and if you and I are there, we won't allow anyone else a leading role in them' (passionate applause). He talked of the agreement that had finally been signed that morning in Szczecin, and said loftily that at Szczecin they had made too many concessions. Then he reverted to the matter of the prisoners.

It was his final, and most dazzling, release of demagogic genius that day. Suddenly he was offering a fresh position: why not give Jagielski an ultimatum? 'Will we tell him we don't negotiate before the prisoners are free?' The ultimatum won a massive vote of support. Wałęsa announced that in consequence there could be no more talks that night. Somebody said doubtfully that an ultimatum was too heavy. At once, Wałęsa suggested that they should forget the ultimatum and instead ask for a declaration before signing the agreements. 'Right, so we require his written declaration that he will free them!' The MKS, its wits numbed, voted for that, too. And in the event, Wałęsa next day did something quite different. He told Jagielski that if the prisoners were not freed there could be another strike, but set no time and demanded nothing in writing. The government released them almost at once.

For the first time, the main strike committee was debating the shape of the emerging agreement – but at a moment when it was too late to make any significant changes without destroying Wałęsa and the presidium and choosing new negotiators. The delegates were not prepared to go that far, but the arguments dragged on until a worker from the Ursus plant, in Warsaw, begged the MKS to come to its senses. 'We are about to win the greatest victory in thirty-five years – our victory. I appeal to the maturity of all delegates not to raise obstacles. Will you let one or two per cent of you hold everything up?' This was a generous under-estimate of the opposition, but the crisis slowly blew itself out. It was too late, everyone was too weary, the day had shattered all senses of proportion. In the end, people wanted to believe the serious, haggard Gwiazda, when he said, 'These concessions are not our final word, and we shall carry on the struggle for our rights. We have only one real guarantee, which is ourselves.'

The strikers began to drift back to their mattresses; the MKS delegates yawned and went for a smoke in the summer darkness. By midnight, nobody was left in the hall but a tiny, fanatical student group that had taken over the presidium table and was insisting to a red-eyed strike official that there must be an annex to the agreements, permitting the union to raise money from Poles in America. But elsewhere in the block, the working party had settled down for a last all-night session on the remaining points.

Significantly, the three workers from the presidium – Gwiazda, Bogdan Lis and Zdzisław Kobyliński – decided that after the uproar over the point 1 preamble, they might be better off without their experts and intellectuals. They went into the working party alone and, with the exception of the question of the 2,000-zloty pay increase, wrested adequate solutions from the government on almost everything else.

Sunday, 31 August, was the climax. For much of the morning, the Lenin yard was unapproachable. The crowd outside the gate had grown to many thousands, packed into a narrow street and a waste ground of rubble, and was listening to the open-air Mass being conducted within the yard. The people heard the episcopate's declaration on the crisis (a much firmer message than Wyszyński's sermon), which insisted that social peace could not be restored without freedom of speech, of belief, of education in those beliefs, and of association. The episcopate quoted the Second Vatican Council: 'The right to establish free trade unions is one of the fundamental rights of a human being.'

For the last time, Jagielski, Fiszbach, the prefect Kołodziejski, and Zbigniew Zieliński, from the Party secretariat in Warsaw, hurried between that waiting file of workers. Through a swaying scrum of reporters, they were propelled into the conference building, and the final negotiations began at 11.40 a.m. Point 1 and its preamble were already home and dry, accepted by the Central Committee the afternoon before. Jagielski and Wałęsa briefly sparred over the release of political detainees, Jagielski pleading that he had no control over the public prosecutor and Wałęsa delivering his own deliberately imprecise threat to go back on strike, until Jagielski admitted that he was hopeful that action could, after all, be taken ... the workers round the loudspeakers clapped vigorously.

After that, it all ran smoothly, the drafted points accepted and initialled one after another with brief discussions. The last ceremony was to bring the document and the two negotiating teams through to face the MKS delegates, those worn men and women who had waited eighteen days to see this moment of signature.

It was just after 4.20 in the afternoon. Wałęsa, unused to reading from prepared notes, spoke awkwardly. To the MKS presidium, he recalled that they would be going back to work the next day, 1 September, the anniversary of the outbreak of the Second World War. 'We think about our country and our national cause, about the common interests of our family which is called Poland. We have thought a great deal about it during our strike ...' They hadn't won everything they wanted, but they had achieved as much as the situation would allow for the moment. 'We shall also achieve the rest of it, because now we have the thing that matters most: our independent, self-governing trade unions. They are our guarantee for the future.'

Then they all marched through into the big hall to meet the applause of the MKS and the blaze of Polish television lights – this scene was shown to the nation the same night. Wałęsa thanked and congratulated the delegates and the strikers. 'And now, with the same determination and solidarity that we showed on strike, we shall go back to work. As of tomorrow, the life of our new trade unions begins. Let's take care they always remain independent and self-governing, working for us all and for the good of the country, for Poland. I proclaim that the strike is over.' For the last of so many times, the delegates swung to their feet and sang the national anthem.

Lech Wałęsa had a few more words to say. When the cheers died down, he pointed out that the dispute had been settled without force, 'through talking as Poles talk to Poles' (a phrase that was to become a catchword throughout the country). But some – he seemed to mean the hard men in the Politburo rather than the Soviet Union – had felt that force could be the answer. They had not won. 'What have won are common sense and prudence, represented, as I think we all realize, by deputy premier Jagielski and a certain rather sensible group . . .' Jagielski replied, remarking optimistically that there had been no winners and no losers here. Then the texts of the agreement were spread out, under the Christian cross and the Polish eagle and the plaster Lenin, and they signed. Wałęsa, back in high spirits, used a pen the size of a police truncheon which bore a picture of the Pope. The applause began again. It was over.

Szczecin: Workers on Their Own

Szczecin had signed the day before. The thirty-three points raised by the Szczecin M K S, which had settled into the production management building at the Warski Shipyard, were in effect subsumed into the Gdańsk Agreement. But in a few respects the workers at Szczecin had gained more and conceded less. And the whole atmosphere was a contrast to that at Gdańsk.

Szczecin is a big, hard-living city, a mixture of ugly German red brick and grimy post-war concrete, in Poland's extreme north-west corner where the River Oder runs out into the Baltic. The district of West Pomerania, twice as far from Warsaw as Gdańsk, still has the air of a distant colony established to guard the new frontier with the German Democratic Republic. Some 55,000 people work there in jobs connected with the sea, 12,000 of them in the Warski yard and another 13,000 work in the new chemical plants.

'It was a very authentic business, a pure workers' movement,' said one writer who acted briefly as an adviser to the M K S. 'There was no exaltation, no kibitzers, no cameras. The Szczecin strike had no connection with the Warsaw intelligentsia. I admired the purity of these leaders, who denied themselves tempting publicity.' Throughout the strike, which lasted thirteen days, foreign correspondents and television crews were kept outside and told sharply that what was happening in Szczecin was between Poles and none of their concern. As a result, the outside world knew little of the negotiations there, and some of its details still remain obscure.

The strike began later than at Gdańsk, but initially set a higher price for agreement. The demands, which went up on the gates of the Adolf Warski Shipyard on the evening of Monday, 18 August, numbered thirty-six, and the first of them demanded the formation of independent political parties. That was a high-water mark of all the demands made in Poland in the summer of 1980, and it was soon dropped. But it was a token of the spontaneous militancy of Szczecin, controlled only with difficulty by the workers' leaders. The news drifting along the coast from Gdańsk was at first fragmentary. Then, on the Saturday after Gdańsk stopped work, the whole staff of the Warski yard were given an unsolicited pay rise of 10 per cent. One worker recalled: 'This made us realize that something very big was happening in Gdańsk, something unique. There was a very unusual atmosphere in the shipyard. Everybody remembered 1970, and felt that the time had come to settle accounts over what had been going on in the country ...'[5]

There was a Free Trade Union group in the city, but at Szczecin none of the opposition organizations was as influential or as prominent as at Gdańsk. On Monday, 25 August, a large, formless crowd simply coagulated by the gate telling each other that they must do something to show support for the Gdańsk comrades. They decided to call for the director, Stanisław Ozimek, and the local secretary of the Party, Janusz Brych, but for some time the workers did nothing more coherent than fling accusations at the pair until Brych suggested that they would do better to choose delegates. A worker took the microphone and proposed that three to five delegates from each department should meet within the yard, for their own safety.

As had happened at certain moments at Gdańsk, the engine of activity now went into frantic overdrive. Within a few hours, the separate Warski departments had drawn up lists of demands, the department delegates had met and elected a presidium for themselves and the mass of grievances had been edited down into an initial thirty-six points, which were posted on the gate and broadcast over the loudspeakers. The strikers chose for chairman Marian Jurczyk, a forty-eight-year-old storeman who had been on the old strike committees of 1970 and 1971. Most of the men on those committees had been hounded into exile and even death, or had been absorbed into good jobs in the provincial bureaucracies. But Jurczyk remained in the yard, a calm, courteous, steadfast, infinitely angry man. The writer Andrzej Kijowski, who met him now, thought that with his 'quiet, powerful hands' this slight figure was 'a real worker'. He was certainly no Wałęsa. He lacked both the demagogic intuition and the fascination with fame which made Wałęsa so spectacular. But he was a far harder bargainer. When the rest of the city began to stop work next day, and Kazimierz Barcikowski flew from Warsaw to get talks going, he found himself facing a small man who would not even return his greeting, only repeating in a voice so soft that it was hard to hear, 'These are our demands ...'

The negotiations roughly followed the Gdańsk model. The MKS for the Szczecin region, by the end representing 380 enterprises, sat in the upstairs management hall where the old strike committee had sat in 1970–71. The presidium negotiated in a small room on the ground floor until the final night, when the strikers overcame their suspicions and agreed to meet Barcikowski in the main administration building, which stood outside the Warski gates and beyond the protection of the occupying shipyard workers. But there was less 'transparency'. Not only were journalists banned, but the actual negotiations between presidium and government were not transmitted live to the waiting MKS. The presidium kept a tape, in case of disputes, but the main strike committee was obliged simply to wait and to trust. They could gain some idea of what was being achieved through briefings from the presidium and reports in the strike bulletin *Jedność* (*Unity*). All other unofficial publications and uninvited opposition figures were banned. The presidium briefly accepted an offer of legal advice from one visitor who was later discovered handing round brochures for a new political party of his own. He was taken firmly by both arms, run to the gate and inserted into a taxi for the railway station.

A small team of advisers from Warsaw was none the less taken on. As in 1970, the strikers had already accepted drafting and legal assistance from a group of radical lawyers in Szczecin – for some reason associated as the Club of Szczecin Bibliophiles. The arrivals from Warsaw were welcomed under the mistaken impression that they were economists, although Andrzej Kijowski was a well-known fiction writer whose work had been banned for years (not a contradiction in terms in Poland), while Professor Tymowski, a zealous, bouncing figure, was a sociologist.

Kijowski was surprised to find the workers' leaders so politically aware and so intelligent. His original misgivings that he would be cast as a mediator were allayed. They only wanted his opinion. What did he think of the demands? He said that, in his view, the moral basis of the strike was provided by the 'political' elements: free parties, the broadcasting of Mass on state television, the release of political prisoners. This was very much the answer of a 'Warsaw liberal', but the workers went on to ask him, very gravely: 'Please tell us if you think that free trade unions are compatible with the organic unity of our nation!' Kijowski may well have been one of the opposition intellectuals who set off for the Baltic thinking that the call for free trade unions was preposterous. But he soon recognized that the core of the strike was 'their absolute determination for trade unions, for elementary justice: that was what lay behind that incredible waiting, that patience'.[6]

Barcikowski did not imitate the diplomatic gloss of Jagielski's negotiating technique. He, too, was a peasant-Communist who had made his career in the Party youth movement and in agricultural administration. But he was more at ease with the workers than Jagielski; their refusal to be impressed by flattery or courtesy did not break his stride. Barcikowski, who was backed up by the local first secretary and prefect and by Andrzej Żabiński, the keen new recruit to the Politburo, took nine negotiating sessions to reach agreement. His brief, like Jagielski's, was to stall on free trade unions as long as he could, but to be generous on points touching pay and social conditions.

The Church was much less in evidence than at Gdańsk. The main gates of the Warski yard bore a reproduction of the Black Madonna icon from Częstochowa and there was a cross, but the railings did not become the open-air altar for offerings which had arisen at the Lenin yard. A suggestion that Mass should be held inside the yard on Sunday was accepted only after a long debate among the Warski occupiers and then on the grounds that it would not be compulsory. While it is not easy to be certain about such figures, at least five of the fifteen presidium members were Party members, a higher proportion than at Gdańsk. This did not prevent the strikers from sticking to their point about access to broadcasting for the churches. When Barcikowski objected that the government could not impose something which the Church had not directly requested, the strikers broke off talks and sent two men up to the bishop's palace to get his confirmation.

The strain was damaging. Outside, the city was entering the second week of a general strike. Essential services and food supplies were kept going, the staff in these enterprises hanging out banners which read: 'We are working, but we support the demands of the strike' (there was such a banner on the city hall). Inside Warski, the negotiators in the final week were getting only two or three hours' sleep a night, while even among the waiting strikers there were four nervous breakdowns.

The crisis of Friday, 29 August – the day when the hard-line faction in the Politburo tried to force the declaration of a state of emergency – was especially nerve-racking in Szczecin. Kijowski recalled: 'There was a sense of panic. Everybody vanished: the government delegation, the presidium members ... We experts sat alone in the presidium room. The government experts told us that free trade unions had proved unacceptable to Poland's allies, which was the government's last-ditch argument. When a report came that there were strikes at Warsaw, a presidium member said to me: "This is a disaster! Now there will certainly be a state of emergency."'

A meeting set for 4 p.m. was cancelled. But then, later in the evening, the green lights went on again as better news came from Warsaw. Barcikowski appeared on television at 8.11 and gave a tense but encouraging picture of the state of the talks. Only six points remained to be settled, while twenty-seven had been disposed of. Barcikowski, whose speech was broadcast by all national television stations, warned the Poles in plain language what the result of further huge pay claims could be: 'A further explosive increase in purchasing power would rapidly and inevitably produce chaos and galloping inflation.' The supplies to the market, already inadequate, could not possibly stand up to another surge in demand. The next few months were to show how right he was.

In the small hours of Saturday morning, the two teams met for the last session, in the main administration block outside the gate. The strikers took no experts with them except Professor Tymowski. At 3 a.m., Barcikowski suddenly accepted the remaining points, without further argument. Four of the MKS presidium voted against the settlement, but the majority were in favour. Żabiński, sitting beside Barcikowski, could not hold back tears of relief.

The formal signing took place later the same morning. The ceremony was laconic, in the Szczecin manner. Jurczyk read out the text of the agreement, and then thanked the strikers and especially the workers' guards, in their red-and-white armlets, whose bearing 'testifies once again to the great wisdom and sincerity of the working class'. Barcikowski made a short, shrewd speech, reminding his audience that Poles, especially, needed a strong state if they were to survive and prosper in competition with nations 'that often conquered other nations by means of their statehood, while we were among the conquered'. After the signing, everyone in the hall and the thousands of dirty, weary workers occupying yards and factories throughout the city rose to their feet and sang the national anthem. The Warski manager, Stanisław Ozimek, suggested everybody took a day off; he would meet them at the first shift on Monday morning. Marian Jurczyk went to the microphone as the meeting began to disperse: 'A last word to the workers' guard. Take that picture of Our Lady off the gate, but give Her all the honours. She kept us going.' A group of strikers turned to one of their advisers from Warsaw and asked her, 'Well? Have we been cheated or not?'

The Baltic Agreements

The same question was being asked at Gdańsk the following day. Behind the applause and singing, the strikers' mood had turned heavy at the end. When Wałęsa made his last procession to the gate to tell the crowds outside that the strike was over, journalists noticed that the workers seemed to withdraw from him as he passed, to evade his eye. Later, the economist Waldemar Kuczyński, who had been one of the MKS experts, said cryptically, 'We won the strike, but we lost the negotiations. We tried to stop an avalanche with a piece of paper.'

To outsiders, including most Poles, this mood of disappointment seemed perverse. They saw that intellectuals and the Church had combined to support the rebellion of the working class, and that this uniting of Poland behind its workers had brought the most glorious victory for human dignity and liberty since the 'Polish October' of 1956. Indeed, this victory promised – if there were no Soviet invasion – to be more profound and durable. There had been no violence; the workers had acted like statesmen as well as heroes. In insisting on free trade unions, the workers had shown that their faith was greater than that of the intelligentsia; the most powerful force in the nation had at last taken responsibility for the nation. The coming of Solidarity, as the new union was to be called, meant that for the first time there was an independent institution to ensure that the promises of the authorities would be kept.

This was too rosy a view. But the two agreements were astounding documents all the same. The Gdańsk Agreement, much the longer of the two, rambled along without any logical order, at times going into details as minute as the demand that back-pain should be recognized as an occupational disease for dentists. The Szczecin Agreement was in some ways tighter. After the storms over the preamble to point 1, the Gdańsk militants were dismayed to discover that at Szczecin the strikers had got away without paying homage to the 'leading role of the Party'. All that the Szczecin text says is: 'It will be possible to establish self-governing trade unions that will have a socialist character in accordance with the Constitution of the Polish Peoples' Republic ...' (The new Constitution, it will be remembered, included a vaguely formulated statement that the PUWP was the 'leading force in society in the building of socialism' – not the more orthodox Soviet phrasing which the Gdańsk experts had persuaded the strikers to accept.)

The Gdańsk Agreement carefully spelled out the need for new unions, 'which would be an authentic representation of the working class'. It recognized anybody's right to stay in the old CRZZ unions, and added that 'in future there could be a possibility of co-operation between the unions'. But registration of the new unions was to be distinct from that of the CRZZ unions. (Although it does not appear in their agreement, the strikers at Szczecin seem to have accepted that they could simply associate themselves with the existing registration of the CRZZ, a dangerous concession.)

The right of an MKS to become the organizing nucleus of a new union, and to arrange free and secret elections to it, was recognized. But the Gdańsk text, especially, still left the geographical extent of the agreements unclear. The wording seemed to suggest that free trade unions might be a privilege only for the inhabitants of the cities along the Baltic coast. This ambiguity made it inevitable that industry in the rest of the country would remain in turmoil until each regional MKS had won the right to establish its own branch of Solidarity.

The new unions were to have their own research centre and 'issue their own publications'. They would be guaranteed the opportunity of expressing their views on all major decisions affecting earnings, prices, investment strategy and the balance between investment and consumption. This clumsy formula avoided the appearance of a formal corporatist partnership with government, which neither side wanted, but it omitted to explain whether Solidarity would be heard before or after such decisions. It did not even amount to a 'right to consultation'.

In both texts, the government agreed to build the Solidarity unions into new laws on trade unions that were already being prepared. The Gdańsk text here used the historic words: 'The right to strike will be guaranteed in the new trade union law ...'

The Gdańsk provisions on the press were ambitious. The government engaged to present a bill to the Sejm within three months defining and limiting censorship, restricting its bite to the protection of state and economic secrets, 'the security of the state and its vital international interests', the protection of the feelings of believers and atheists alike, and the prevention of morally offensive material. While the semantic loopholes here were wide, the point was that for the first time censorship would be not only legally defined but subject to appeal. A citizen could challenge a censor's decision in the supreme administrative court.

The government finally conceded that Mass could be broadcast on Sundays but only on radio. (The German Democratic Republic had been carrying Lutheran services over the state radio for years.) Two further provisions stated that the media should express 'a variety of thought, views and opinions', and that all official documents should be open to public inspection unless they fell within the areas defined for censorship – a 'freedom of information' proposal much more liberal than the law in many western countries.

One paragraph in the Gdańsk text, calling for a rapid economic reform, also specified that trade unions would help to draft the sections of the reform that dealt with workers' self-management and internal democracy in enterprises. This passage may have been inserted at the wish of Jagielski. Now and in the ensuing months, the government was desperately anxious to involve the new unions in a moderate 'workers' control' movement, which would have the side effect of drawing the unions into just that co-responsibility they wished to avoid.

The strikers had demanded free Saturdays, and their famous all-round increase of 2,000 zlotys on the basic wage. But these, like the demand that pay should in future be index-linked to inflation, were evasively answered. The government merely promised that by the end of the year studies would be ready on 'ways of compensating for the cost of living' and 'principles and means of introducing free, paid Saturdays'. The all-round increase, the core of the economic sections of the twenty-one points and the plainest statement that the workers wanted equality as well as liberty, was diverted into a marsh of separate pay-bands and industrial agreements.

Above all – and this was perhaps the most serious mistake the workers and their advisers made – the arrangements for pay rises were to be made on a 'branch' basis. As Solidarity was organized as a horizontal organization of all workers grouped region by region, this came to mean that the pay details were negotiated between the government and the old CRZZ unions, which were 'vertically' organized industry by industry on a national scale. The wage question, seen by the strikers as compensation for price rises, thus slipped out of Solidarity's hands altogether. The weakness of the strikers' negotiators here is difficult to explain. According to Staniskis, who was present, Wałęsa decided to accept 'branch' pay settlements against the advice of several of his colleagues, whereupon a worker sitting next to her commented, 'We made a mistake giving Leszek so much power!' The delays and inadequacies of the pay settlements and their anti-egalitarian spirit (the government tended simply to jump salaries up by one grade, which of course gave the better-paid more than the low-paid) were to be the greatest single cause of tension between Solidarity's mass membership and its leaders in the months ahead.

But the levelling instincts of the workers bore fruit in reforms of pensions, family allowances and wage minima. The strike had not just been a revolt against the economic privileges, real or imaginary, of the Party, state and police bureaucracies. It was a blow aimed at the whole corporatist style of Polish government in the 1970s, which had opened wide gaps between different categories of workers. It is important to realize that the shipyard workers, bad as their conditions were by western standards, were aware that they had been treated as part of the aristocracy of the Polish working class. In this sense, August 1980 was a rebellion of the better-paid on behalf of the lower-paid, in which the better-paid tried to divest themselves of the wage differentials which preserved their own special status. Such acts of collective altruism are rare in history. But the strikers' instinct, absolutely sound, told them that the régime's ability to control the working class depended upon its ability to hold that class divided.

The Gdańsk Agreement, unlike the Szczecin text, included a number of important concessions to working women: a programme to build enough pre-schools and nurseries for all the children of working mothers and a three-year maternity leave period. Lowering the pension age to fifty for women and fifty-five for men was the only demand which the government flatly rejected as 'impossible to fulfil in the present economic and demographic situation'. In the days of the strike, it was women who were doing the typing and keeping the delegates fed, even though many other women were sitting at the MKS tables. But the MKS presidium included three quite exceptional women among its eighteen members: the tram driver Henryka Krzywonos, the crane operator Anna Walentynowicz and the young nurse Alina Pieńkowska. The strike had begun over Walentynowicz; without Krzywonos and Pieńkowska, it might well have petered out as a mere round of wage bargaining. Pieńkowska, in particular, secured the acceptance of a very long and detailed schedule of improvements for the state health service.

The original twenty-one points had referred not at all to the countryside, unless one counts the request for meat rationing. But the Gdańsk Agreement raised several peasant grievances. In a 'stipulation' by the MKS, neither accepted nor rejected by the government, the strikers asked for assurances of a stable future for private family farms (in other words, an end to the ultimate threat of collectivization), equal rights to buy land for state and private farms, and 'the restoration of conditions for the development of village self-government'. But not a word was said about the notion of a private farmers' trade union. Nobody predicted Rural Solidarity, whose emergence later in the year was to face the régime with one of its most difficult political problems.

Another slow-burning fuse was lit by the government's acceptance of the twelfth Gdańsk point: that 'leading and managing cadres' should be selected on the basis of ability rather than party affiliation. Superficially, this was an obvious demand for efficiency and common fairness. But – as the experts especially were aware – it struck at another crucial element of the Party's leading role, its right, universal in the Soviet system, to appoint its nominees to all commanding posts throughout Polish institutions (A list of these posts, known as the 'nomenklatura', is appended to Denis Macshane's invaluable book *Solidarity: Poland's Independent Trade Union*, published by Spokesman, Nottingham, 1981.) In the late summer of 1981, the régime fought a desperate action to defend the 'nomenklatura' principle when Solidarity finally adopted the principle of workers' self-management, including the right of employees to select or veto their directors.

Stanisław Kania and the 'Social Contract'

The eruption of a volcano has commonly two phases. The first explosion is the blasting-out of the old, hardened plug of rock which chokes the volcanic pipe. Then the lava wells up and flows outwards across the countryside. The settlements at Gdańsk and Szczecin at the end of August were the initial blast. From then on, for the rest of the year and into 1981, rivers of lava poured slowly over the institutions of Poland, changing and destroying. At intervals, when a lava-flow was checked, pressure would build up until another, annihilating explosion threatened.

But the men and women who had to struggle with the consequences of those first agreements could not afford to think about any inevitable process. Acts of will were required of them, as the rest of Poland beyond the Baltic coast entered the struggle to establish its own 'independent, self-managing trade unions'. A brief strike in the anthracite mines of Wałbrzych brought victory to the local MKS there, and on 3 September a major agreement was signed at Jastrzębie covering the whole Upper Silesian coal basin. Throughout the country, this pattern was repeated: a factory or group of factories would strike, occupy and form a joint committee, presenting a list of demands that were essentially local but that ended with a final demand to be associated with the twenty-one points of the Gdańsk Agreement. It soon appeared that in one respect these local *postulaty* were more radical than those set forth at the Baltic ports. Many of them called for the dismissal of the local Party secretary or the prefect. At Jastrzębie, the strikers' so-called 'thirteenth demand', which wasn't published, was for the removal of Zdzisław Grudzień, Party First Secretary at Katowice and one of the most powerful provincial magnates in Poland.

A scene typical of Poland in these weeks was provided by the striking sulphur miners near Tarnobrzeg, on the middle Vistula. Outside the Machów opencast pit, with the reek of brimstone on the air, a few men were standing outside the gate. There was no religious display, only the Polish flag and a huge 'Occupation Strike' placard facing the main road. Here, where most of the workers were commuters from smallholdings, the list of twenty-eight demands was almost entirely local and practical. The men wanted protection against lung corrosion by sulphur, danger money, the same rights as coal miners and a 33 per cent wage rise. 'You have to work for a day to earn two pounds of sausage!' But they also asked for limits on the arbitrary power of the militia and the security police, for local funds earmarked for the police to be transferred to building schools and pre-schools and for 'the extension of the Gdańsk twenty-one points throughout the land'.

The pickets at the gate thought their demands were modest. They hadn't asked for officials to be fired or for any religious concessions, 'although every Pole, believer or non-believer, wants religious education in schools'. They had not yet decided to affiliate to Solidarity, but instead wanted to join the existing miners' union (they were now classed as chemical workers).

There were no intellectuals here. But the miners were waiting for some local lawyers to come and help to draft a settlement with the government negotiators, and they were getting advice from a doctor – who had been employed at Machów until he was fired for protesting at the lack of precautions against sulphur disease.

The very structure of the new unions had now to be invented. The MKS at Gdańsk and Gdynia adopted the proud name Solidarity, from the title of their strike bulletin, and this example was followed at Szczecin. It was intended that Solidarity should be a nation-wide confederation, but new unions were sprouting that at first denied having any connection either with the old CRZZ or with Solidarity. In many cases, the entire trade union membership in a plant, complete with officials, would simply re-name itself an independent, self-governing union (NSZZ, in the Polish initials).

The CRZZ was composed of 'branch' unions, trade by trade, each governed from central headquarters in Warsaw. Solidarity emerged with precisely the opposite structure: it consisted of *regional* groupings of workers, including every trade. This gave it two advantages. In the first place, a regional union could apply pressure at the point where, in Polish administration, the immediate decisions were usually taken: at the level of the district (*województwo*), with its prefect and its powerful Party secretary. Secondly, a territorial union leadership was very much harder to manipulate and to isolate from its members than a national executive of elderly full-time officials based in Warsaw. But these advantages, which thoroughly suited the democratic spirit of the new unions, threw into glaring relief their failure to conduct wage bargaining, which under the Gdańsk text was to be decided branch by branch, not region by region.

Officially, the Solidarity unions declared that they would co-exist with the CRZZ federation. Unofficially, there was doubt in both Solidarity and the Party whether the CRZZ could long survive, and many predicted the mass defection to Solidarity which soon began. Under Szydlak's successor, Romuald Jankowski, the CRZZ made promises of reform to which little attention was paid, but all across Poland workers found leaflets apparently produced by the CRZZ warning that Solidarity would be a union with no funds and no benefits to offer its members. This funds question was not, however, so serious as it looked. Money that could be used for cheap loans to workers (Assistance Fund), or for holidays and for collective benefits (Social Fund), was almost entirely held in the accounts of each factory or enterprise. The trade union had not owned this money (except for 40 per cent of each membership fee, which disappeared to pay 'administration costs' at the CRZZ in Warsaw); it had merely acquired the right at plant level to distribute it. It was obvious that these rights could easily be transferred to a Solidarity union, or shared if both unions co-existed in the same enterprise.

After the first week, Solidarity moved from the Lenin Shipyard into the shabby old Hotel Morski in the Gdańsk suburb of Wrzeszcz. As Wałęsa had promised, the door displayed a brilliant new sign: 'Independent Self-Governing Trade Union.' Outside, crowds stared and smiled. Inside, the stairs and corridors swarmed with messengers and delegates, as the old MKS presidium, now the 'Presidium of the Inter-Factory Founding Committee,' (MKZ) drafted provisional union statutes to be presented to the Warsaw District Court for official registration.

Wałęsa, who had set up his office in a corner bedroom complete with a desk to put his feet on, an outsize potted palm and a wash-basin to use as an ash-tray, at once sent for Jacek Kuroń. Within hours of his release from detention, Kuroń was furnished with an MKZ *laisser-passer* and – much to the horror of cautious spirits – appointed chief adviser on union organization. The Gdańsk presidium, which after all had not been elected by anyone, was now acting as the leadership of Solidarity throughout Poland. It was not until 17 September that an all-Poland meeting of Solidarity representatives was held at Gdańsk and established the nucleus of a 'national co-ordinating committee' (KKP). Meanwhile, thousands of visitors travelled to the Hotel Morski to study the 'Gdańsk model' and take it home to copy.

The conclusion of the Gdańsk and Szczecin Agreements finally pitched the Party into the crisis of confidence which Gierek had staved off for so long. Throughout Poland, Communists were playing star parts in their local strike committees, and it seemed likely that the great majority of the Party's 1½ million worker members would join Solidarity or at least forsake the CRZZ unions. Even before the shipyards struck, elections to works councils in August had shown how matters were going: in Lublin, after the main strike wave there, many Party members were elected to these councils but not one single candidate *nominated* by the Party.

In the first weeks of September, the vigour and optimism of the new union organizers contrasted horribly with the paralysis and demoralization of the Party. What sort of Party would this be, if the working class abandoned it and left only the permanent bureaucracy, the Party apparatus, behind? What could be the leading role of a Communist Party separated from the proletariat by a non-Communist – perhaps even a formally Christian-Democrat – trade union movement? For the shorter term, anyone could see that without regaining confidence in itself, the Party could not regain the confidence either of the working class or of Poland's allies, especially of the USSR. It was the Party's weakness and divisions, not the existence of free trade unions, which was more likely to provoke a Soviet military intervention.

For days after the agreements, Edward Gierek was not heard from. He was expected to go to the television cameras and call the turbulent nation to order, but he did nothing. The total failure of his speeches and appeals in late August had broken his nerve. His paralysis allowed other Party leaders to move fast. Intrigues aimed at Gierek's replacement, already simmering during the last week of August, now came to a point. Already a 'line' of sorts was evolving. The upheavals of August, it ran, had been an authentic, justified workers' movement. It was not anti-socialist, although there were certain anti-socialist circles (KOR was especially meant) that hoped to exploit the movement for their own parasitical ends. Therefore the protest could be treated objectively as a call for the reform and renewal of the Party, as well as of the unions and all Polish institutions. By refusing to use force against the strikers, the Party had taken the first essential step towards this renewal. An article in *Trybuna Ludu*, the Party daily, published in the first days of September, went further. It stated that workers were entitled to set up any union they wished, and added that 'The principal duty of our Party is to be present wherever the working class finds itself.'

In other words, the new unions were there to stay, and Party members should join and work through them rather than against them.

A plenary session of the Sejm was due on Friday, 5 September, to confirm the appointment of Józef Pińkowski as prime minister. The day before, as the various party groups of deputies met to discuss their speeches, the anger and anxiety began to boil over.

At the PUWP meeting, usually somnolent, Andrzej Werblan began by suggesting that the crisis had three sources: genuine workers' grievances, 'anarchistic elements' in the population and 'anti-socialist groups'. He was at once challenged by deputies from all over Poland: the port manager from Szczecin, a worker from Warsaw and a coal miner from Wałbrzych were among those who protested that no 'anti-socialist elements' had been needed to provoke the entirely justified revolts in their constituencies. One woman burst out desperately: 'I want to be able to be *proud* of my Party ...' A deputy who was present said afterwards: 'I have never heard people speak so freely since 1956!'*

The following day, a small knot of jeering workers watched as the deputies arrived for the debate. Rumours were traded in the polished marble corridors of the Sejm: all non-Communist deputies would vote against Pińkowski's confirmation, it was said. Pińkowski himself, a dejected figure, trudged off on a long speech about economic retrenchment. Edward Gierek was absent, which seemed odd: the convention is that the Party's First Secretary introduces to the Sejm the PUWP's candidate to head the government. The other ministers were present, squeezed into the narrow roller-coaster car of pews which is reserved for the cabinet. At a little after half past ten, thirty minutes into Pińkowski's speech, a message was delivered to General Jaruzelski, the minister of defence, and to the minister of the interior, Kowalczyk. They clambered over their colleagues and left the chamber.

There was an intermission. The Sejm, which has far less security than a western parliament, is one of the few places in which foreign journalists can brush sleeves with Poland's leaders. Ministers and Politburo members paced the lobbies or huddled urgently over black coffee. Still no Gierek. 'Groups are forming to take over the leadership,' said a Central Committee member. 'Great changes are coming in a few weeks. We must move from opposing the workers' movement through accepting it to finally taking the lead of it.' Stanisław Kania, a square, unruffled figure, sauntered past with his slightly rolling walk.

---

* A poll conducted that week by the magazine *Polityka* revealed that less than 1 per cent of the sample believed that 'anti-socialist' or 'anarchic' groups had been the cause of strikes.

The debate began again. Andrzej Żabiński, still under the spell of his incredible days and nights at Szczecin, spoke out for a thorough democratization of Party life, for full and enthusiastic acceptance of the agreements. The Sejm was beginning to stir on Frankenstein's slab. One speaker after another began to attack Gierek's régime, and at least three speakers used the ugly word *stempel* (rubber stamp) to describe the Sejm itself. Professor Jan Szczepański, a sociologist who enjoyed wide licence for his opinions, complained that everyone had known what was going to happen but had affected ignorance. The government could learn something about sound, clean, effective organization from the strike committees, while the Party must find a way to purge itself without 'palace intrigues'. The journalist Karol Małcużyński made the speech of the day, explaining to laughter and bursts of clapping how official propaganda had become so absurd that the population had stopped believing even bad news, let alone good. The censorship of Sejm proceedings in the press was a scandal. 'Polish society is an adult society, and it has a right to proper information about what happens here and in the outside world; a Polish journalist, for his part, must have the right honestly to carry out his profession and his civic duty.'

The Sejm was alive and excited for the first time for many years. Afterwards, one deputy called it a *Noc Wigilijna* – the night of Christmas Eve when, the legend tells, beasts in their stalls are given the power of speech.

The debate was still in magnificent flow when – in the late afternoon – the news came that Edward Gierek had been struck down by a heart attack. The speeches went on, but senior Party members bolted from the chamber. Gierek, they said in the lobbies, had been on his way to the Sejm in the morning when he had been taken ill and managed to divert his driver to a hospital. Soon followed news that an emergency Central Committee plenum was being summoned that night, after the Sejm session. The Party can move cruelly fast, in emergency. Everyone knew that this was Gierek's political end, whether or not he survived physically. The betting was that Stefan Olszowski would succeed him. One deputy produced a sinister cyclostyled letter 'from a worker' she had received that morning, slandering Gierek and praising Olszowski as the man of law and order. And yet Gierek's fall, inevitable within the next few weeks, seemed to have come slightly too early for the factions preparing to replace him. Olszowski's campaign, checked by the conclusion of the agreements, had hardly got under way again.

In the chamber, the journalist Męclewski said that the Sejm had become a true parliament again, thanks to the workers. The actor Holoubek said that official propaganda showed contempt for the nation, which had shown its thirst for truth during the Pope's visit. For the PUWP, Mieczysław Rakowski, editor of the reforming magazine *Polityka*, wound up the debate with an opening sentence that stunned the deputies: 'It isn't easy for me, as a member of the Central Committee of the party that bears the main responsibility for the country's development, to say anything here ...'

There was a happy sense of honour won back, of power driven to hang its head. In the end nobody voted against Pińkowski, but there was a spatter of abstentions on nominations to the new cabinet. The Marshal (Speaker), unaccustomed to this, peered in confusion around the chamber as members laughed and pointed out dissenting hands. The voting was a small naughtiness, no more. Behind the attacking speeches a very Polish sense of patriotic responsibility had remained, forbidding extreme actions or words which might suggest that Poland was a nation divided against itself.

The deputies flocked merrily out into the night, impatient to watch themselves on the evening television news. Between the grey ribs of the Party's Central Committee building, rows of lights were on and the first black cars were arriving at the main entrance. The political leadership of Poland was about to change. And yet nobody gathered on the moist pavements, nobody even stopped to watch. In 1956 the masses had turned a face of hope towards the Party. In 1970, they had turned towards the Party in anger and reproach. In the summer of 1980, the Poles simply turned their backs.

The meeting began at eleven on Friday night and broke off only three hours later, at two on Saturday morning. Olszowski's supporters made no move for the leadership, for in the past two weeks a much wider consensus had been constructed, they realized, for Stanisław Kania. Many in the Central Committee still found Olszowski's tone too aggressive. Kania seemed solid, imperturbable. Only a man of the centre like Kania could lead the nation and the Party on a course of moderate renewal (*odnowa*) which could satisfy both the workers and the 'Socialist Community'.

So it was Kania who was elected First Secretary of the PUWP. He caught the mood of the Party and the population well. In the Central Committee debate, he told aghast provincial secretaries who asked what would happen if 90 per cent of the workers joined independent unions: 'Better a step to the right than a step over the precipice!' There was simply no alternative. He would never permit the Polish armed forces to shed the blood of Polish working people. To the Party, he offered modesty rather than political *machismo*. He didn't regard himself as a leader, he said; he was not sure that a leader was what the Party needed at that point, and his duty would be to use the whole Party to 'put the collective wisdom of the people to work'. These were words meant to reassure defeated rivals, who might now be fearing that he would banish them from power altogether. With the same lack of rancour, he paid respect to Comrade Gierek's fifty years of work for the movement and wished him a rapid recovery.

Olszowski, at this Sixth Plenum, proposed a two-track policy. After a gruesome description of the anarchy waiting to engulf Poland, he suggested that the Party should simultaneously welcome the new workers' movement in its socialist aspect and strike hard against the 'anti-socialist forces' which were trying to misuse it. In practice, no other policy was open to the leadership, caught between the hammer of Solidarity and the Soviet anvil, and Kania only repeated Olszowski's recipe in more cautious terms. The strikes had been 'a manifestation of worker protest in its main, pure worker form', directed not against socialist but against deviations from socialist principles. But at the same time there must be a 'sharp struggle' against the anti-socialist adversaries who were still exploiting discontent for ends 'running counter to the aspirations of the workers'.

The public greeted Kania's election without strong feelings either way. He was not well known as a personality, and his long connection with security prompted some doubts. Those who had been in contact with him reported that he was simple and honest, and that he had done a decent job in restraining the extremism of the security police during the 1970s. But the Saturday reports of his speech made many Party veterans lay down the newspaper and shake their heads ironically. Kania's speech was, in so many ways, a repetition of Gomułka's rhetoric in 1956 or Edward Gierek's in December 1970.

Once again, the workers' revolt had not really been directed against the Party, only against its mistakes. Once again, it was only a wicked little swarm of 'wreckers' who tried to give it the appearance of a protest against the nature of the régime. Once again, the answer lay in a 'return to Leninist norms of Party life' – whatever they were – and a more honest, humble style that would restore the bonds between Party and society. This might be best achieved by holding an emergency Party congress in the next few months. Gomułka and Gierek had promised early Party congresses too. Stanisław Kania was repeating his predecessors when he said that such tensions would never be allowed to repeat themselves. In proclaiming the end of one cycle, he seemed to be performing the traditional launching rites of the next one.

The Sixth Plenum, called so suddenly, decided to resume its work a week or two later when the new leadership had been able to assess the situation. Kania's election was followed by the appointment of Żabiński and Barcikowski to the Politburo (Barcikowski had been only a candidate member), and of Olszowski's ally Grabski, Zdzisław Kurowski, and Jerzy Wojtecki to the posts of Central Committee secretaries. If anything, this made Olszowski's hand within the Politburo stronger. Kania might have the loyalty of the Central Committee, which meant the loyalty of much of the provincial apparatus too, but Olszowski, Grabski and Żabiński would have great influence in the making of day-to-day decisions. Kania and Olszowski seemed to be in accord over the 'two-track' strategy towards the new unions. But their approaches both to discipline and to a fundamental democratization of the Party through the emergency congress remained far apart. The PUWP leadership was still fragmented, even under this new commander.

It was this lopsided alliance at the top that set up a pattern mystifying to the outside world. The Kania–Olszowski team would for a time move along a path parallel to that of Solidarity, designing economic and political reforms and tolerating the steady expansion of the new unions. Then, without apparent reason, the authorities would swerve across and attempt to block Solidarity's advance. For the first eight months after the Gdańsk Agreement, almost all these challenges ended in a humiliating retreat for the régime, a needless increase in tension, and a dangerous loss of the meagre authority the Party and government still retained. No rational explanation fitted these fiascos, except for Poland's favourite theory of 'provocation'. Assuming that Soviet agents were hardly in a position to dictate government policy, this could only mean that the hard-liners in the Politburo, Olszowski and his allies, wanted to goad Solidarity into the sort of extreme action that would justify the use of force by the authorities – ultimately, Soviet force. A more likely source of these mad confrontations was the 'Thomas-à-Becket' syndrome of most authoritarian systems: the tendency of eager, stupid officials and policemen to take precipitate actions that they fancy will please their masters. The muddles produced by Olszowski's control of many policy levers and Kania's support in the Central Committee encouraged this. The Party's decisions were often less the result of deliberate choice than the random 'resultant' of multiple bureaucratic collisions.

In the first weeks after Kania's election, however, there was some optimism to be found within the Party, as well as despair. Kania himself, with much sympathy from older men and women who looked back wistfully to the ideals of 1956, still hoped that the great schism between workers and Party might quite rapidly be overcome. The troublemakers from KOR could be pared away like a fringe of mould, and the healthy core of Solidarity would soon make its peace with a reformed and liberalized Polish United Workers' Party. The natural unity of the working-class movement would reassert itself.

This 'myth of social unity', which implied that the schism was of recent origin, could not resist any serious historical test. It did not long resist the realities of the present, either. The last thing that Solidarity wanted was a *rapprochement* with the Party. On the contrary, the whole movement was agreed that the Party as a structure must be kept out of the union, which it would certainly try to infiltrate, and eventually to recuperate.

The End of a Myth of Unity

Within a few days of the Gdańsk Agreement, Warsaw itself began to develop into a major and often impetuously radical centre for the new unions. Based at first in the Huta Warszawa steelworks north of the capital and at the Ursus tractor plant, a Solidarity union known as Mazowsze (Masovia, the province round Warsaw) opened an office in an overcrowded apartment a few hundred yards from the Central Committee. A second, swarming nucleus of activity appeared in the Warsaw offices of KIK, the Club of Catholic Intelligentsia, which Mazowiecki and his friends had converted into an information exchange for independent trade unions. Here, in a press of workers collecting smudgy 'make your own union' leaflets, *grandes dames* typing out advice on how to strike, ancient intellectuals exchanging rumours with foreign journalists in verdigris-encrusted Kraków French, and young men passing out tiny medals of the Virgin of Kozielsk-Katyń, a visitor could struggle to the window and see right across the street the portals of the official CRZZ building. As portals, they seemed to be a failure. Nobody went in or out of them, and the building appeared to be inhabited only by potted plants.

Over at the Mazowsze office (the kitchen of a flat, where strike delegations shouldered pots and pans off the wall and the wooden stair thundered to the boots of a ceaseless two-way torrent), the first draft union statutes were being distributed. The provincial chairman was the young engineer Zbigniew Bujak from Ursus, and the Mazowsze presidium at first consisted entirely of shop-floor workers. Now and in future, their best adviser and organizer was Janusz Onyszkiewicz, a young mathematician with an expression of dreamy detachment who had been associated with KOR.

These draft statutes were the best evidence that the Party's hopeful 'social unity' strategy was not going to be successful. Sketches of these statutes, which had to be approved by the Warsaw District Court before a new union could be registered, had been completed in Gdańsk and Warsaw as early as 5 September, less than a week after the Agreements. The two drafts were nearly identical. After professions of intent to 'encourage active commitment to the good of the Fatherland and of all working people', and regulations for free and secret elections to all posts, the statutes banned 'from holding office in the union any person occupying a post of authority in the state or economic administration or in the leading positions of political organizations at the place of work'. In other words, the Party group in the factory could never take over the factory's Solidarity branch. As if this were not enough, Solidarity was also contemplating in early September another clause that would lay down that a member 'of any party' who joined the union must place obedience to the union before obedience to his party's discipline. This clause, in the end not added to the statutes, would have defied the fundamental principle of Communist Party discipline, which cannot be effective unless it claims absolute priority over every other obligation a Party member may acquire.

This was far from the only sign that the Solidarity unions took their independence literally. A good example of how they saw the distinction between co-operation with the state and 'social unity', was provided by a row which blew up at Gdańsk at the end of the second week in September. In defiance of the agreements, the local newspapers were refusing (which meant that somebody was forbidding them) to print an important Solidarity communiqué. Lech Wałęsa, who could now brandish something like 750,000 signed applications for Solidarity membership in the Gdańsk region alone, went to prefect Kołodziejski and talked the language of power until the prefect agreed to pull the necessary strings. The following day, the communiqué was published. It turned out to be quite conciliatory. After laying out the structure of the union in Gdańsk and its programme for internal elections, the document ended with a warning against wildcat strikes. The right to strike existed, even though no law had yet been passed to embody it. But strike action should be treated as a last resort, and never undertaken without prior consultation with the MKZ at the Hotel Morski. 'The decision to strike may be taken only by a vote in which more than half the total number of employees is in favour. The enterprise strike committee must then approach the MKZ in order to obtain approval for strike action.'[7]

This incident, which had many parallels in other parts of Poland, also showed up the reluctance of the government to carry out the provisions of the Gdańsk Agreement on censorship and the mass media. (But one was strictly honoured: on the morning of Sunday, 21 September, millions of Poles gathered round radio sets and listened for the first time to a broadcast Mass from the old Church of the Holy Cross in Warsaw.) The main bill to set legal controls on the censorship began a leisurely amble through drafting committees, versions and debates, under the invigilation of the minister of justice. But fair reporting, let alone direct access to the media, was often denied to Solidarity.

The 'uncensored press' continued to circulate. More importantly, many of its more radical commentaries on the situation were taken up and reprinted in the three trade union periodicals which had begun as strike bulletins and were now reaching huge local readerships: *Solidarność* at Gdańsk, *Jedność* at Szczecin and *Niezalezność* (*Independence*) at Warsaw. The censors themselves had become erratic. Towards weekly magazines and periodicals they were for a time much more tolerant. The daily press, on the other hand, although far more informative and critical than it had been before August, remained under close surveillance. As one writer put it, 'In Czechoslovakia in 1968, the Party had everything under control except the press. Here, the press is the only thing the Party still does control.'

The Gdańsk and Szczecin Agreements did not end the tension; they spread it to the rest of Poland. The government was allowed no respite. On 20 September, three weeks after the agreements, there were some sixteen strikes in progress in various parts of the country and this was becoming an average. Two issues constantly recurred in these protests, beyond local demands and support for the twenty-one points of Gdańsk: wages and complaints against the behaviour of local authorities. The MKZ at Gdańsk summed up this feeling that the agreements were not being respected with a protest on 19 September: 'In many centres, the activities of independent unions are being sabotaged by the authorities, and people who want to join these unions are being intimidated.' The committee knew nothing about 'anti-socialist' elements in the unions but plenty about 'old, discredited union leaders' who were intriguing to block the development of Solidarity. The same day, Zdzisław Grudzień, the Party chief at Katowice, resigned 'on grounds of health' and was replaced by that ever-rising star Andrzej Żabiński. Grudzień, notorious for grandiose building projects and his own luxurious private country houses, had been allowed to save face; in reality, the 'thirteenth demand' of the Silesian strikers was now being granted, and he was pushed out of the Politburo two weeks later.

The delay in paying out wage increases now led to the first serious trial of strength between government and unions, just a month after the agreements. In August, the strikers had not prevailed in their demand for an all-round increase of 2,000 zloties as compensation for price increases; instead, they had been offered unspecified rises to be negotiated 'branch by branch'. The only concrete gain in that clause was the promise that these would be complete by the end of September. This had not been kept. Local

Solidarity leaders were not only angry but worried; wage increases were the first solid evidence they could offer their worker members that the new unions were more effective than the old. Already, especially in the Gdańsk Shipyards, sceptical men muttered that all power structures were much the same.

On 29 September, the second meeting of the provisional national committee of Solidarity took place at Gdańsk and decided to play it very tough indeed. The committee announced a one-hour protest strike for the whole country on Friday, 3 October. The government's hasty announcement later the same day that eight out of the twelve million public-sector workers would receive their pay rises by the end of October did not mollify the unions. With some three million members, they felt ready to show their muscle. For the first time, but not the last, the Solidarity membership had shown its radical impatience – and pushed its regional leaders in turn to put pressure on Lech Wałęsa and his advisers, who would have preferred a negotiated compromise.

The strike call caught the Party leadership at a bad moment. The previous week, on 26 September, the Politburo had rejected drafts for the resolutions of the Sixth Plenum, still in adjournment. The next session was again put off. Kania was rumoured, wrongly, to have flown to Moscow for consultations. Arguments about the way forward were breaking out again, and the leadership – in the traditional fashion – had been too preoccupied with faction-balancing to pay attention to details like the progress on pay talks. Barcikowski, the Szczecin negotiator, went on television to reproach Solidarity for pursuing a strategy of tension and breaching the Gdańsk spirit; Jagielski hastened up to Gdańsk and spent seven fruitless hours on 1 October remonstrating with the Solidarity national committee. Wałęsa and his colleagues faced Jagielski with three demands: an end to the harassment of independent unions and their founding committees, defined access to the mass media for Solidarity and a more equal distribution of the funds set aside for the pay rises. The talks got as far as outline agreement, then collapsed as the government refused to tie itself to specific dates, times and sums of money.

On Friday at noon, the one-hour strike was inaugurated by the wail of factory sirens all over Poland. It was to some extent a symbolic affair: the Mazowsze union, for example, required only certain shops in selected large plants to stop work, while other workers were allowed to support the gesture simply by hoisting Polish flags or wearing red-and-white armlets. It was better followed in the main industrial centres, especially Gdańsk, than in small towns. But as a proof of the new unions' control over the Polish labour force, it was solid enough to appal even the most liberal Party officials.

The long-halted Sixth Plenum resumed the next day. The shock of the strike turned it into one of the most desperate, ill-tempered and prolonged sessions that anyone could remember. Opening on Saturday, the Central Committee endured no fewer than seventy speakers and finally ended its meeting at dawn on Monday morning. In the cycle, it corresponded to that resounding Eighth Plenum in 1971, a settling of accounts with the discredited team from the last period. But this was much more bitter. The onslaught was led by Olszowski and pressed home by the faithful Grabski, who read out an indictment, name by name, and demanded that the accused be expelled from the Central Committee.

The Plenum was supposed to be analysing the causes of the summer's upheaval, 'the deepest crisis in the history of post-war Poland', as Kania named it. There was recrimination, and the removal of seven leading members of the Gierek team, but little lucidity. A Party member from the Szczecin shipyards penetrated to the heart of the problem when he pointed out that the strikers' demands were actually little different from the ideas thrown up by Party cells in those anguished debates before the Eighth Congress back in February: why had those warnings been suppressed and ignored?

Two conclusions could be drawn from the meeting. The first was that Kania's line of democratic renewal within the Party still prevailed but that it was slowing down perceptibly. The Plenum's resolutions talked in guarded terms about reforming the PUWP's internal elections, limiting the number of terms in office that a Party functionary could serve, and reducing the number of officials who held both state and Party jobs. But no date was named for the emergency congress which was to bring these changes about; it was left to the next meeting to set the day. This was an unmistakable sign that resistance to Party 'renewal' was stiffening up in the hard-line faction of the Politburo – and probably in the Soviet Union as well.

The second conclusion was that the optimistic 'myth of unity' had finally been dispelled. After Friday's strike, nobody was still naïve enough to talk about a natural convergence of this 'pure' workers' movement and the Party. Instead, the more intelligent speakers tried to point the Party towards a 'social contract' policy, a recognition that Polish politics were now plural and that the only chance was for a regulated, honest partnership between the state and the new unions. Tadeusz Fiszbach, the wise First Secretary from Gdańsk, who, with his round skull and metal spectacles, resembled the young Gomułka, made this point: 'The independent unions are increasingly to be understood as one of the guarantees for the stabilization of our public life.

Although our Party did not bring about their creation, it is in these new organizations that it has the best chance to find today the conditions for an active participation in national life by the vital forces in the nation.'

The Plenum resolutions took a similar 'contractual' line when they reaffirmed that the Gdańsk, Szczecin and Jastrzębie agreements must be carried out, but that the best guarantee that they would be put into practice was a return to normal work. Mieczysław Rakowski, the Party's best-known exponent of a liberal 'Eurocommunist' approach, called directly for coresponsibility in power with the new unions; this would at once separate them from elements which only wanted to make trouble.

In reality, the 'social contract' course was almost as unlikely to succeed as the 'unity' approach. The lava was still flowing, and nothing permanent could be erected until it had stopped. The one-hour strike had succeeded only as a show of force. It had not brought a solution on pay or access to the media, neither had it won any guarantees that local obstructions would no longer be laid in the way of the new unions. It ensured only that the mass membership would continue to chase their regional union leaders into more radical demands. But without an internal revolution for which the PUWP was quite unready, the Polish leaders could not offer the Solidarity militants the degree of press freedom they wanted, while they dared not call off the campaign against KOR in case the Soviet Union concluded that they were losing control. The gap between the two sides was simply too wide to allow a 'social contract' on the basis of the Gdańsk and Szczecin Agreements.

The government, for its part, was helpless in the face of the worst economic failure suffered by any European nation since the war. To give the unions the increases in pay, better food supplies and improved social services they were pressing for what would have meant abdication. The concessions the government did make were damaging enough; there was a 12 per cent increase in the national wage fund, only three quarters of which could be covered by increases in goods and services. An inflationary flood of purchasing power was submerging the Polish market just as domestic production was falling steeply: by November, industrial production was to be $2.6 billion behind the planned target and had already declined by 12 per cent in August. It was known that crop losses of potatoes and sugar beet from frost and floods were going to be severe, and as potatoes vanished from the shops, the demand for bread and flour rose by 25 per cent.

The foreign debt crisis remained apparently insoluble. However, the world continued to provide fresh loans. The Soviet Union offered credits equivalent to $550 million between May and August and, with other eastern European countries, provided an emergency programme of food exports to Poland after the summer strikes. West German bankers put together a new loan package worth $670 million in October. The following month, Secretary of State Edmund Muskie recommended that United States agricultural credits to Poland should be increased to $900 million, while the Poles beseeched American banks for a further loan of $3 billion. How Poland was going to pay the interest on these loans – interest had cost the country some $8.4 billion in 1979–80 alone – was a mystery. The export trade had been devastated by the summer agreements. Food was being diverted to the insatiable domestic market, while the production of coal, which had provided about 12 per cent of Poland's export earnings, was 14 per cent below its daily production targets. By November, Poland was thought to owe the rest of the world a total of $21 billion, perhaps more, and the upward curve was growing steeper.

It may well be asked why international bankers, supposedly a hard-headed crew, continued to provide more finance. Poland was not a member of the International Monetary Fund, and the efforts of private banking consortia to impose guidelines of a rough-and-ready kind on the Polish economy were fruitless. (In 1979 a western bank group lent Poland $550 million on the understanding that the trade deficit would be around $600 million: it turned out to be $1,400 million.) To insist that the Polish government 'put its house in order' by increasing exports and cutting imports was quite vain, an invitation to commit political suicide, until the régime reached a stable accommodation with the Polish workers.

There were two main reasons for this meek martyrdom of the bankers. One was an old fragment of common-sense; they had lent so much already that they could not afford to write it off. The second was political. Chancellor Helmut Schmidt and, more hesitantly, President Carter considered that the economic collapse of Poland would eventually lead to a restoration of political tyranny and probably to Soviet occupation. Prosperity, on the other hand, or what passed for prosperity in Warsaw, would relax all political tensions and make it easier for a durable compromise between the Party and the population. To this end, Chancellor Schmidt especially leaned heavily on his bankers, whose Polish bad debts were already big enough to be dragging down the Deutschmark against the dollar. The argument was again heard that, if everything else failed, the USSR and Comecon would pay Poland's debts. There is no shred of evidence for this theory. But it may have comforted the bankers, and it gave rise to the foolish speculation that the USSR would never invade Poland because Moscow would then have to pay off Poland's creditors.

As the first snows of late autumn arrived, it was the home economy that preoccupied the Polish government. Incredible as it seemed, a European industrial state with a large farming sector and a wealth of raw materials was coming – in peacetime – within sight of hunger. Already many people were spending up to four hours a day standing in line for supplies. Meat apart, butter, sugar, potatoes, cooking oil, all kinds of chocolate, and biscuits had become rare or unobtainable. The gap between the consumption of one harvest and the reaping of the next might seem a medieval anxiety, but the authorities were now wondering whether even bread might not disappear from the shops in the spring of 1981. Meanwhile capital investment was being cut back, in a transfer of resources to the purchase of goods to stock the shops. In November, state investments were reduced by 17 per cent, and work on sixty-seven out of 250 projects was stopped.

The economy was empty. The political reforms in the Gdańsk Agreement, even if they could be assimilated by the Soviet Union, could only come about after a slow and stealthy process of democratization. But militant workers had set up new unions on the assumption that there could be immediate changes, which the August agreements had seemed to confirm. The régime's inability to deliver the impossible stoked up fires at the unions' base. Transmitted up through the regional leaderships, this heat soon reached Wałęsa and the Solidarity negotiators. It narrowed their room for compromise and tempted them to fight symbolic battles which they could win, rather than battles for concrete gains which were unattainable.

The next conflict was already on the way. On 22 September, the Warsaw District Court rejected the first application for registration by a new trade union, lodged by a founding committee in Katowice. Among other points, the court objected to the union's intention to operate throughout Poland. Two days later, several other independent unions, including Gdańsk's Solidarity, handed in their applications and draft statutes. One of these, a union for the national airline LOT, became the first new union to win legal registration, and eleven others soon followed. But Solidarity, far the largest, only received a letter from the court with a list of complaints about the statutes. These boiled down to three: the court objected to Solidarity's claim to operate nationally rather than regionally, its ban on Party members and managers holding union office and its attitude to the Party's 'leading role'.

At first, the national committee of Solidarity did not take this too seriously. The leading role had been dealt with in the Agreements; why repeat this in the statutes? It soon became clear that it was the Party that was insisting – through the supposedly independent court – on getting this phrase into the text to be registered. But after a series of meetings, Anna

Walentynowicz and a delegation reported on 16 October that the judge would no longer stipulate a 'leading role' clause.

On the following day, a most 'contractual' occasion took place. Wałęsa, who had required a great deal of persuasion to sit with an official planning body, appeared with Andrzej Gwiazda in Warsaw and took part in the first session of the committee drafting the new law on trade unions. It was typical of the dislocation of the leadership that, on the same day as this striking first gesture of partnership, the District Court judge – obviously on Party instructions – changed his mind. Registration, which had seemed so near, was suddenly off again. Wałęsa left for a tour of southern Poland in a rage.

The next meeting of the Solidarity national committee was held at Jastrzębie on Monday, 20 October (the Silesian workers were impatient to show that Gdańsk was not the trade union capital of Poland), and an angry, confused debate ended with a call for a general strike. Wałęsa managed to hold back militants who wanted to give the government an ultimatum: a strike on 4 November if Solidarity had not been registered. Wałęsa's view was that nothing should be done until and unless the court finally rejected Solidarity's statutes, and then only after consulting all the union's regional groupings. But he was sufficiently stirred to tell an audience in Katowice that night: 'They have often threatened us in the past with rockets and tanks. But we won't let ourselves be slapped in the face.' And he made it clear that the union would carry on its work with or without legal registration.

Chapter Six

Towards a National Tragedy

The Registration Crisis

The first phase of Solidarity's existence was over. The Party's new leadership had recovered from its initial shock, and although the chaos and demoralization in the PUWP rank-and-file was still spreading, the Politburo under Stanisław Kania felt that it was possible to take action. Illusions about an easy settlement with Solidarity had dissolved; the economy was drifting towards worse disasters, while production fell and the government failed to offer any plan of recovery. The Soviet leaders' alarm was growing week by week, and they required at least some evidence that the PUWP was not going to abdicate power without a struggle. Pushed on by Olszowski, the Party now began a series of sudden challenges to Solidarity which were to bring Poland to the verge of civil conflict and foreign intervention.

The threatened general strike offered the régime only catastrophic alternatives. It could try to ensure victory by using force against the unions, or it could lose what remained of its authority by allowing the strike to take place and win. Either choice would probably provoke a Soviet military intervention. Yet the authorities now behaved with an inconsequence that made the situation rapidly worse. At first, the workers' threat to strike brought results: the unhappy Judge Kościelniak of Warsaw District Court let it be known that he would allow Solidarity to affirm the Party's 'leading role' in a separate annex to its statutes. The Solidarity rank-and-file disliked this solution, but it was a compromise the Solidarity negotiators thought they could accept. On Tuesday night, however, Rakowski went on television to argue that the 'leading role' should be in the main text of the statutes: this would 'help the fate of Poland' (that is, placate the Russians) and make Solidarity's commitment to a socialist system finally reliable.

Solidarity in turn refused to budge. Hopes of another compromise were raised on Wednesday, 21 October, when Kania met Cardinal Wyszyński for the first time since becoming Party leader. But the Cardinal only signed a communiqué that observed blandly that good relations between Church and state were essential, and flew off for a two-week visit to Rome, leaving the fuse of crisis still burning. The decision of the District Court was to be given on Friday, 23 October.

When the day came, Wałęsa strode into the Warsaw court through a large and excited crowd. After the exchange of some formal statements, Judge Kościelniak announced that the court accepted the statutes for registration. His words were cut off in a storm of cheers and clapping which spread to the crowd outside. The judge suspended the sitting, and many of the spectators poured out into the street laughing and singing in triumph.

But the judge was not finished. Wałęsa and the few who remained in the room froze in disbelief as he began to speak again. The statutes were accepted, he went on – but they would be modified. He ordered the insertion of a long clause repeating that Solidarity recognized the socialist system and Poland's alliances and 'recognizes that the PUWP exercises the leading role in the state'. And there was more. The judge struck out the cautious provisions for the use of the strike weapon and inserted another clause of his own, which declared that 'the organization of a strike must not contradict the legal regulations in force'.

The furious Solidarity petitioners filed out of the courtroom and drove across Warsaw to the KIK offices for a council of war. That the judge's action was a legal monstrosity – his task was to accept or reject, not to amend – and that the judgement had been forced on him by political pressure was accepted by all of them. It was harder to decide how to react. Wałęsa and his Catholic advisers hesitated until telephone calls from all over Poland revealed the depth of anger and disillusion among Solidarity branches. Many local union leaders demanded a general strike. Some – at Gdańsk and at the mining town of Wałbrzych down on the Czechoslovak border – had heard false news that their negotiators had accepted the judgement, and they accused them of treason to the movement.

Most of the regional founding committees (MKZ) represented on Solidarity's national committee preferred to go through the legal channels of an appeal to the Supreme Court before taking direct action. The difficulty was that the Gdańsk MKZ – large, touchily militant and still inclined to regard itself as the source of all wisdom – continued to dominate the committee. Its members, especially the original nucleus from the Lenin Shipyard, were wary both of Wałęsa's talent for compromise and of his Catholic counsellors (now including an emissary from Cardinal Wyszyński who seldom left Wałęsa's side). Twice during these few days, on the first news from the Warsaw court and at the national committee meeting three days later, this suspicion had boiled over.

The national committee, which met at Gdańsk on 26 October, at first struck a theatrical pose. The Gdańsk regional organization declared that it would revert to the strike committee from which it had sprung and return to its birthplace in the Lenin Shipyard. There it would expect the arrival of the prime minister, Józef Pińkowski, within twenty-four hours. If he did not show up, a strike would begin.

The meeting calmed down when Pińkowski offered by telephone to receive a delegation in Warsaw on Friday, 31 October. Jagielski arrived in Gdańsk and, after talking to Wałęsa in the prefecture, persuaded Solidarity to prepare a list of demands for the talks with the prime minister and to postpone the decision to strike. But a warning was issued that a general strike would take place on 12 November if the meeting with Pińkowski was not a success.

The temperature throughout Poland was now running dangerously high. For most of those who had joined or supported the new trade unions, this was the hour of trial. The régime, it seemed, had judged its moment and was now about to revoke the whole Gdańsk Agreement. There could be no surrender on registration, even though the government was expected to respond to the general strike by declaring a state of emergency and using force. In Warsaw and elsewhere, Solidarity headquarters prepared to go underground with all the inherited skill of a people that had organized resistance in every generation. But this was a misperception. Kania genuinely wanted the union registered. Judge Kościelniak's 'insertion' had certainly been an act of criminal stupidity or provocation, forced upon him. But the régime was genuinely surprised that Solidarity would not repeat its August assurance that it respected the Party's 'leading role'. Kania and his supporters were even more shocked at what they considered the union's 'overreaction' to the judgement. None the less, the situation was growing so dangerous that Kania resolved to concede.

He took the necessary precautions to protect himself against rivals who might accuse him of capitulation. On Wednesday, 29 October, he extracted from the Politburo a declaration that his *odnowa* (renewal) programme for Party and state should move more quickly. It was agreed that a permanent disputes commission would be established to take from the cabinet and Politburo the burden of acting as a labour appeal court.

The next day, to the surprise of the world, he and Józef Pińkowski flew to Moscow. They talked to President Brezhnev and Nikolai Tikhonov, the prime minister, and were back the same day. Kania had asked for this meeting – his first encounter with Brezhnev since he became leader of the PUWP – in order to gain Soviet approval for the change of course he was about to make. Most of Poland's other allies were already in consternation.

Both the GDR and Czechoslovakia that week closed their frontiers to all but a trickle of Polish travellers (the State Department in Washington accused them of breaching the freedom-of-movement provisions of the Helsinki Final Act, the declaration by the participants in the European Security Conference). Bulgaria and the GDR sonorously proclaimed the organic unity of the socialist community and the duty of its members to rescue each other's régimes. In comparison, the Soviet leaders remained calm and allowed Kania to do what he must. The announcement after the meeting expressed confidence that 'the Polish workers will find a way to resolve their acute problems'.

On Friday, 30 October, Wałęsa and two coach-loads of Solidarity delegates arrived at Pińkowski's office. They brought with them the demand for registration without insertions and five other *postulaty* as well: access to the media (again), faster pay rises, better distribution of consumer goods to the shops, an end to 'repressions' and – significantly for the future – recognition of the peasants' right to form a trade union. It was a long day's struggle, in which the government finally contrived to out-manoeuvre Solidarity. The first question was soon settled: both sides would abide by the results of an appeal to the Supreme Court on 10 November, and it was hinted that the result would satisfy Solidarity. But the other five points, which Solidarity at one moment thought had been accepted in principle, faded out of reach again as a drafting committee sat down to work out a final communiqué. In the end, there was no written communiqué at all. The government did not want to be tied down to details. The trade unionists, who had developed a jovial intimacy with some of the government team while things were going so well, left at around midnight wondering what exactly they had achieved.

They had a verbal agreement on the registration formula, and another on preparations for a Solidarity weekly newspaper. But the government was not ready, on paper or off, to grant immunity to members of the dissident groups or to those it considered 'anti-socialist'. Neither would the government tolerate a peasants' union. It was all too vague to give anyone much confidence that even the registration assurance would hold. Solidarity went ahead with staff work for the general strike on 12 November. And in this oppressive, nervous atmosphere, a Warsaw crowd held an open-air commemoration service on All Souls' Day for the victims of Katyń. The Moscow visit should have cleared the air. It had not.

But in the event, all went smoothly. A discreet private deal with Solidarity, swallowed with some resentment by the Politburo, allowed the Supreme Court to strike out all Judge Kościelniak's insertions and to tack on the first paragraphs of the Gdańsk Agreement, those recognizing the Party's 'leading role', as an annex to the statutes.

And yet the week leading up to the hearing had been one of intolerable tension, culminating with official menaces about the conscription of workers in the event of a strike, the summary expulsion of several foreign journalists and a meaningful few minutes on television showing Soviet tanks lurching about on manoeuvres. In spite of Kania's declarations that the new unions were in Poland to stay, industrial trouble began to erupt all over the country. Health service workers, exasperated at their failure to win a pay increase, occupied a room in the Gdańsk prefecture and stayed there for eleven increasingly turbulent days, joined half-way through by theatre and museum workers. On the very day of the Supreme Court settlement, a dangerous conflict exploded at Częstochowa, the town which contains Poland's most sacred shrine of pilgrimage, with the prefect ordering all his factory managers to protect their enterprises against Solidarity and the new unions demanding that the prefect and most of his assistants be fired.

The registration dispute was a disaster. It violently increased mistrust and combativeness in the unions, and did great damage to Kania's position within the Party. Since the end of the Sixth Plenum in early October, he had managed to fortify himself a little. Outside the Party bureaucracy, support for 'renewal' was spreading. He was able to replace a number of ministers who were incompetent or worse: Milewski took the interior post, while the liberal Józef Tejchma, who had gone off to be ambassador in Switzerland earlier that year swearing that he would never be dragged into Party intrigues again, was recalled to Warsaw and given his old job as minister of culture. The Sejm, after recovering the gift of speech in September, was now almost unruly. The satellite political parties and groups became unpredictable in their orbits. Thirty-eight members of the Democratic Party, supposedly representatives of the self-employed, voted against the government in the Sejm on a minor point. The official Peasants' Party attacked its own hierarchy. Most amazing of all, the pro-régime Catholic formation PAX exploded on 20 October and replaced its old leadership with younger militants who professed to be vibrantly critical of the régime's errors – an event as unnerving as the ripening of wax fruit.*

---

*PAX had arisen from a squalid post-war deal between Stalinists – possibly Russians rather than Poles – and Bolesław Piasecki, who before the war had been the leader of an anti-Semitic group of the ultra-right called the ONR-Falanga. In exchange for immunity from prosecution for his political past, he was instructed to set up a pro-régime organization for lay Catholics, a sort of filter to catch old National Democrats who might accept the Soviet alliance but could never stomach Marxism. Piasecki, who became quite rich through PAX publications and the

All this helped Kania. Moderate, responsible unrest was exactly what he needed. With pleasure less unalloyed, Kania also watched the return towards power of General Moczar, whom he had replaced in 1971 as head of security. As courts all over Poland tried corrupt officials on the evidence of documents collected by Moczar's Supreme Control Chamber (NIK), he was not to be trifled with. At the beginning of November, he managed to recapture his invaluable old position as chairman of the main Polish veterans' organization (ZBoWiD). But this, it appeared, was to be a re-formed, liberal Moczar. The same night, he was to be seen on television gravely extolling the patriotic achievements of the Polish Jews: a new soul indeed. A government spokesman, Józef Klasa, assured the press that Moczar was one of the soundest figures in the nation. (This was not strange, as Klasa had been the head of what was politely called 'personnel policy' in the foreign ministry during 1968.)

Moczar, who was taken back into the Politburo on 2 December, was signalling friendship to Kania. He would support him and the *odnowa*, and use his phenomenal net of personal contacts to pick up signs of approaching conflict. Moczar still had many acquaintances in the intellectual and artistic world, and he now quietly offered his patronage to forces as diverse as the rank-and-file movement appearing at the Party grass-roots and groups on the fringes of KOR.

Ferment in the Party

The registration crisis of early November completed the disaffection of the Party's provincial apparatus. These men and women had come a long way since August. Few of them still imagined that the Party could take the lead of this workers' movement. By mid-November, one third of the district first secretaries and prefects in Poland had been replaced; as the uproar at Częstochowa showed, the people's appetite for bureaucratic blood was growing. Few Party officials, except for steadfast reformers like Fiszbach, had much faith left in any 'social contract' or partnership. Their view was increasingly crude: if Solidarity was not checked, it would continue attacking

---

sale of religious *bibelots*, was deeply hated by independent Catholics. The Vatican placed all PAX publications on the Index, and in the 1960s Piasecki's son was murdered – plainly for political motives. PAX survived all political upheavals; it was assumed that the Soviet Union regarded it as indispensable.

until the Party had no authority left. There would be anarchy. Then the Russians would come: the 'national tragedy'.

Not all 'middle apparatchiks' translated their fears into active opposition to Kania. But the dethroned officials, like the dismissed government ministers, were still sitting in the Central Committee, a substantial 'cemetery vote' to which Olszowski or Grabski, Kania's hard-line rivals, could appeal when the right time came. And there was not much time left. The emergency Party congress, whenever it came, would elect a new Central Committee. If congress delegates really were to be chosen freely and without 'guidance', the old Central Committee members would probably all be thrown out and replaced by revolutionary workers wearing a Solidarity badge on one lapel and the Black Virgin on the other. If the choice was between that sort of 'renewal' and the old-fashioned Party the apparatchiks had grown up with, accustomed to full control and full obedience, they felt increasingly old-fashioned.

Down at the bottom level of the Party, among the cells and especially the factory shop branches, a movement was growing that alarmed Kania and the middle apparatus equally. Many workers had left the Party, perhaps several hundred thousand by December. The trouble was coming from those who stayed and who combined their membership with the badge and principles of Solidarity. The total enrolment of Solidarity at this point may have been about 8½ million. Perhaps 750,000 of these – including many local union leaders – were Party members, accounting for about one third of the PUWP's membership.

This rank-and-file movement was at first a protest against the slow pace of 'renewal'. In particular, these Party members wanted an emergency Ninth Congress as soon as possible (the longer the delay, the better the chance for conservatives and apparatchiks to reorganize). But the real scandal this movement gave was organizational. It was not just that Party groups in factories were calling their own meetings to discuss the congress without higher Party permission. They were reaching out to other groups in other factories, making direct contact and short-circuiting the strictly vertical flow of authority and decisions in the Party. This was the sin of 'horizontalism', a fundamental breach of Leninist discipline, and it had been caused by the sharp political mistrust that had developed between the Party's local full-time officials and its working-class membership.

The first focus of organized rank-and-file pressure was the old university city of Toruń, on the lower Vistula river. Here an alliance had developed between Iwanów, the Party secretary in the Towimor factory, and radicals in the Party group at Toruń University. On 27 October, an 'illegal' meeting of Party members from eight local enterprises was held, to which regional Party officials were invited. On 17 November, there was a much larger and more determined 'horizontal' meeting. And when the Party expelled Iwanów a week later, the Toruń workers refused to recognize the decision.

The November meeting set up a standing presidium and voted for a programme – basically, a warning to Kania to hurry up. The Toruń workers wanted free and secret elections in all Party organizations at all levels by 15 January; as the Towimor staff said, 'a compromised apparatus cannot offer the people a concrete programme'. The Ninth Congress must meet before the end of January 1981. New laws on trade unions, censorship and a new electoral procedure for the Sejm and local government must be ready by the end of the year. All the 'guilty in recent years' must be punished. All the proceedings of the Eighth Congress in February 1980 and of the Central Committee meetings since then must be published at once.

Behind this demand for speed lay radical, distinctly *gauchiste* principles. A Toruń document dating from November demands rotation in all Party posts, separation of the Party from the government, and all political decisions to be taken by elected Party bodies rather than by individual officials. Party elections should have no limit on the number of candidates (for First Secretaries, at least two candidates must stand), should be secret, should not accept nominations from persons not present at the meeting and should – for higher posts – permit only elected delegates from below to vote. This revolutionary, anti-bureaucratic platform was obviously intended to smash the domination of the Party by local and national apparatchiks. These proposals would break the hold of the apparatus over the Central Committee (of which they formed 53 per cent) and strip it of much local power by reserving 'political' decision-making for democratic assemblies.

By December, 'horizontal' Party bodies were meeting in seventeen out of Poland's forty-nine districts. The Fonika radio factory at Łódź, for example, became the centre of such a movement in the whole region, raising demands similar to those of Toruń but going even further. The Łódź, radicals wanted a 'verification' (a complete member-by-member purge of the Party), and an immediate congress prepared only by 'those who had the courage to oppose totalitarianism, who can be integrated with the Solidarity movement'. Fonika produced a scathing analysis of a Party 'so compromised that transformation is not possible; it can neither regain the confidence of society nor renew itself'. Undemocratic election practices had compromised the whole socialist system in Poland: 'In Poland it is not socialism which rules, but a system of "mandatism" (substitution).' The Fonika document suggested that a remedy would be to change the Party's name from United

Workers' Party to Socialist Workers' Party, a return to 'the good old traditions of the Polish Socialist Party and the Polish Workers' Party before the unification of 1948'.

This was not so naïve as it seems. It must be emphasized that the ideas behind the rank-and-file movement were not liberal, but close to those of the Soviet 'workers' opposition' in the 1920s. It was sensed that in becoming a gigantic, universal administration the Party had almost completely lost its political character. These rebels wanted a lean, highly political, revolutionary Party of the working class, which would give ideological leadership and leave the drudgery of administration to the government.

For Kania, the rank-and-file rebels were a dangerous embarrassment. Although they talked as easily about 'Leninist norms' as anyone else in the Party, they were acting in a manner which suggested to the rest of the 'socialist community' that the PUWP had lost the power to maintain democratic centralism among its own members, and was therefore entering a terminal phase of disintegration.

With the Supreme Court judgement, hope revived that Solidarity and the state, having taken their rivalry to the cliff-edge, might now feel that honour was satisfied and learn to live with one another. The registration crisis had been about words, in western eyes an absurd reason for so dangerous a quarrel. But the shipyard workers in August had already understood how important those formulations were. To accept the Constitution, with its fuzzy mention of the PUWP's leading part in building socialism, was tolerable. To inscribe into Solidarity's statutes direct acknowledgement of the Party's right to lead society and the state was entirely different. Within Poland, everyone understood that one day the Party might refer to this phrase as if it were an oath of loyalty to whatever policy the PUWP might adopt – and if that 'oath' were broken, the union might plausibly be dissolved for breach of its own rules.

Slowly, the sky began to clear. Wałęsa celebrated his triumph on 11 November, the night after the Supreme Court judgement, guest of honour at a special gala performance of song and recitation at the Warsaw Opera House. He was still the man for whom people waved placards reading: 'Don't be frightened! The whole nation is with you!' At the end of that week, at short notice, Kania asked to see him and they spent two hours alone together. Kania was concerned to get Wałęsa back into the official committee planning the trade union law; at all costs, Solidarity must be made to carry a share of responsibility for state policies. Wałęsa was evasive, and declined to sign any statement about the talks. He shrewdly used the occasion to press the case of the obstinate nurses, teachers, museum workers and the rest who were still occupying a room in the Gdańsk prefecture. In the familiar way, this dispute was now turning septic as the government refused to negotiate; medical schools and faculties all over Poland were being taken over by students, factories were holding sympathy meetings and the Gdańsk Solidarity M K Z was preparing for a strike call if there was no solution.

If their meeting had no formal results, Wałęsa and Kania seem to have reached some tacit understandings. Speaking two days later on 16 November, Wałęsa suggested that now that the union was legal there should be an end to wildcat strikes. 'It may indeed appear that unrest is rampant in the country, with stoppages here, sit-ins there, and hunger strikes somewhere else ... Even when there is just cause, there are other ways to settle our grievances without striking.' The next day, the health service workers and their comrades won a respectable settlement and thankfully stumbled out of the Gdańsk prefecture. On 19 November, after such government prevarications that the Częstochowa unions had to send a delegation to Warsaw, the city's prefect, Wierzbicki, finally resigned. The Sejm began a vigorous two-day debate on the economy; the non-Party deputy Bukowski enchanted his colleagues by demanding the resignation of two ministers for tolerating disgraceful conditions in slaughterhouses.

The 'Naroźniak Affair'

The ironies in Polish chronicles being neatly stitched, it had to be on the evening of 19 November, that hopeful, lively day, that the police raided the offices of the Warsaw Mazowsze branch of Solidarity. They were looking for a confidential circular on how to deal with dissidents, issued by the public prosecutor's office – and they found it. Zbigniew Bujak, the young worker from the Ursus plant who was chairman of Mazowsze, was questioned on the spot. Next day, an unknown lad named Jan Naroźniak, a print worker who helped Mazowsze with duplicating, was called to explain certain matters to the police. They did not let him go, but served him with a ninety-day detention order, the first Solidarity activist to be arrested. They also arrested Piotr Sapielo, a clerk in the public prosecutor's office, and charged him with passing the circular to Naroźniak.

The fat was in the fire again. This time the issue was symbolic, rather than a matter of the union's life or death. But Mazowsze blew up at a touch, and on Sunday, 23 November, it warned that there would be a strike if the two men were not freed within twenty-four hours. It was a sign of how high passions were rising in Poland, and of how deeply the registration crisis had outraged and alarmed the population. A few days before, at Szczecin, after addressing a mass rally, the national Solidarity leaders had been chilled by the questions the audience threw at them: when would the Communist leaders who had brought Poland so low be punished? When would the union become a political party? Was it true that a new mass grave had been discovered in Katyń Forest?

The police thought they had a case. An official document classified as secret had been stolen, a crime in any country. They refused to release Naroźniak and Sapielo. On Monday, 24 November, half a dozen Warsaw factories, including Ursus, stopped work. Wałęsa, jerked along by the blast of Mazowsze's instant militancy, warned that there might be other strikes in the rest of Poland unless the two were freed.

The crisis had returned with a new accompaniment: railway workers, at the peak of an interminable pay dispute, now contrived to prick the Soviet Union on its most sensitive nerve. Their strike this Monday lasted for only two hours and affected commuter lines at Gdańsk and Warsaw rather than the international rail routes. But *Izvestia*, in Moscow, wrote of 'activity aimed at heightening the tense situation in Poland' and warned that a rail strike could 'affect Poland's national and defence interests and disrupt transit rail links across Poland' – a plain accusation that Solidarity was trying to block communications between the USSR and the twenty Soviet divisions in East Germany. During the Lublin rail strike in July, the Russians had made no such complaint. The Polish authorities knew that they were being given a most ominous sign of Soviet impatience.

Matters grew far worse on 25 November. At a press conference in the Ursus factory, Bujak threatened the government with a general strike in Warsaw on Thursday (27 November), if it did not instantly agree to negotiate on a list of demands. This was becoming standard Solidarity practice: when a strike threat was made, the union would deliberately package several other issues with the original grievance. The difference this time was that Bujak was asking for things that the Gdańsk and Szczecin Agreements had never mentioned.

The most sensational of these was the demand for a commission to investigate the methods of the Polish security police and the public prose-cutor's office, and to devise safeguards against unjust police harassment. For the first time, the régime's coercive power was being directly attacked. The union asked for cuts in the police budget, for the punishment of those responsible for the brutalities of 1970 and 1976, and for the release of political activists including the right-wing nationalist Leszek Moczulski and other members of his group – all in addition to the freeing of Narozñiak and Sapielo.

Before, it had always been Gdańsk or Wałęsa's group that led the attack. Now the Warsaw workers were charging ahead with an *élan* that pulled Solidarity's national committee along in their wake. Mazowsze was not impressed by warnings that in plunging beyond the Gdańsk text and trying to maim the security police it was demolishing the whole image of the union as a non-political organization whose charter was the Gdańsk Agreement. Bujak and his followers wanted to break the power of the public prosecutor, Lucjan Czubiński, for good, and to justify themselves they published the stolen circular. Prepared by Czubiński the month before, it was a strangely unconvincing and inaccurate account of opposition groups active in Poland. Its burden was that these groups contemplated the overthrow of the socialist system, by force if necessary, and that it was they, rather than the workers, who had originated the idea of independent trade unions as a step towards their plans for counter-revolution. There was nothing new in the circular to any Pole familiar with police propaganda, except for its weird mistakes of fact. But Mazowsze was entitled to argue that it showed that part of the state apparatus, at least, was refusing to accept coexistence with Solidarity.

Solidarity's national committee met at Gdańsk and decided to back the Warsaw action, accusing the authorities of provoking the collision. In Warsaw itself, the strike began to break out long before the deadline of noon on 27 November. A rally held at the Ursus works on the very day Bujak gave his press conference – the tractor plant was already on strike – revealed that at least four large enterprises had already stopped work, and the big Huta Warszawa steelworks on the northern fringe of the city announced that work would stop at 6 a.m. the next day, 26 November. The central streets of Warsaw, and many trams and buses, were now decorated with 'Free Naroźniak' posters. At a meeting at the Ursus works, the audience burst into what the United Press correspondent called 'wild, rhythmic applause' when a union speaker repeated the ancient battle-cry: 'It is better to die on our feet than to live on our knees!' For the first time since August, the sharp smell of insurrection was in the air. This was an offensive that Wałęsa did not control, and it was galloping into territory that Solidarity had not entered before.

On 25 November, the State Department told journalists that Soviet troops near the Polish border had been put on a higher state of alert than normal. Even in the western press, this remark rated only a paragraph or two. The next day, the Americans spoke of an 'unusual series of Soviet military moves' in the western border districts of the USSR, which could be designed to give the option of a rapid invasion. Again, the guarded language brought little response in the European media.

On Thursday, many things happened with great rapidity. While the workers were pledging themselves to die on their feet, hectic negotiations had been in progress behind the scenes. A small group of liberal journalists, all Party members, had for some time been acting as informal counsellors to Stanisław Kania. In this extremity, they attempted to use this contact and their stock of credit in opposition circles to mediate between the strikers and the régime. Before dawn on Thursday, 27 November, Naroźniak and Sapielo were released – against guarantees given to the government by Stefan Bratkowski. Bratkowski, chairman of the Association of Polish Journalists – a black-bearded, stubbornly optimistic enthusiast for change – had been one of the driving forces behind the DiP (Experience and the Future) study group in 1978–9. For him the releases were a triumph of personal diplomacy. With only eight hours to go, Solidarity lifted the deadline for a general strike in the capital. There remained the matter of the other demands, above all the question of a commission to investigate the police.

It was now that everyone's calculations went astray. The striking workers at Huta Warszawa were told that Jagielski, the deputy premier who had nego-tiated at Gdańsk, would come to the steelworks before noon to open talks on the police inquiry; his arrival would be the signal for them to resume work. It seems, however, that nobody had shared this plan with Jagielski, who, when he woke up in the morning, flatly refused to accept this penitent's role. He told a delegation from Huta Warszawa that he would be prepared to discuss the matter but not until after the next Party plenum, due within a few days.

The strikers took this answer badly. In the words of Bernard Guetta, correspondent for *Le Monde*,* '"They are making fun of us!" retorted the mass of workers, and the strike went on, threatening to detonate the powder-keg for no good reason; everything, after all, had been won, short of the arrival of the Politburo dressed in sackcloth with ropes around their necks – which perhaps was the factory's unconscious wish-fantasy.'

Those who had hoped that the Warsaw strike could be turned on and off like a tap were learning a terrifying lesson. The Huta Warszawa works were out of control, and the strike was threatening to spread back to the rest

---

* *Le Monde*, 27 November, 1980. Guetta, a young journalist who spoke no Polish when he became the paper's eastern European correspondent in 1979, was throughout the crisis of 1980–81 an indispensable and incomparable source of information for the outside world. Here and in other passages, I have relied upon his narrative.

of the city. Zbigniew Bujak remonstrated, the exhausted Jacek Kuroń was brought in to speak to the workers, Stefan Bratkowski – who had staked the release of the two prisoners on his ability to deliver the end of the strike – collapsed. The government booked an aircraft seat and flew Lech Wałęsa down from Gdańsk. For hours, the peacemakers beat in vain against the spreading flames, until, after frantic negotiations the government made an announcement on television that the talks on the police would take place. Even then, the Huta Warszawa strikers would not be convinced, until the producer of the programme had been dragged out of bed and relieved of the actual text of the announcement. Finally at 4 a.m. on Friday, 28 November, the strikers voted to go back to work. Twenty-one abstained; two were against. Guetta, who like all the participants in the scene had hardly slept for two days, asked a steelworker: 'Why are you all so mistrustful here?'

'Well, you know how it is, we have had thirty-five years of it . . .'

The Shadow of Invasion

As the Naroźniak crisis deflated, there arose from all over Poland a chorus of voices begging for a breathing-space. Wałęsa appealed to his followers to concentrate on building up their organization – elections at the factory level were now beginning to take place in Solidarity – and to give strikes a rest. Jagielski told the Huta Warszawa delegates that the government would not tolerate another strike confrontation. Mazowsze stated that 'Our country and Solidarity require peace, organizational work, an atmosphere that permits the rebuilding of the economy and the consolidation of the gains that have been made.' To frustrate provocations, it stopped distribution of all posters and leaflets in Warsaw. In many provincial union branches, un-forgiving post-mortems on the Naroźniak affair took place. There was a feeling among less radical members that Solidarity had gone beyond its proper limits as a trade union in striking for two unknown young men who – outside Warsaw – were imagined to be activists in some opposition group or other.

Abroad, alarm about imminent Soviet intervention in Poland was rising just as tension within the country was collapsing into a mood of relief, even of battered optimism. These western warnings, first expressed around 25 November, grew to a clamour during the weekend of 29–30 November. But the Poles were at first distracted by the Seventh Plenum of the Central Committee, which was held on the first two days of December.

At the Seventh Plenum, Kania managed to coax the Central Committee to take another laborious stride towards 'renewal' of the Party. A provisional date was set – around the end of March 1981 – for the emergency Party congress, and a commission was set up to prepare it. Once again, Kania made a steady, moderately reformist speech emphasizing his readiness to co-operate with Solidarity and his satisfaction that the union was now legally registered. He gave the customary warnings to 'imperialist' and 'diversionist' groups, but also told Solidarity that some of its leaders were pushing for political strikes which were unjustified and outside the union statutes. 'Dual power is not tolerated in any state, and it will not be tolerated here.'

On Party matters, Kania tried to follow a path between the local apparatus and the rank-and-file radicals. He agreed that the congress should change the rules for Party elections and examine ideas for rotation in executive posts. Lenin had called for 'unity of action, freedom of discussion and criticism'. But it was not the moment, he thought, to elect new officials at the local level or to hold a general 'verification' of all PUWP members. He and the Party would not tolerate the 'horizontal' agitation of the rank-and-file campaign, which was 'factionalism and splitting activity'. The Party must have some discipline; it was 'neither a debating club nor a vague association of like-minded people'.

Kania said nothing about several of the most dangerous questions of the hour: the censorship law, or the growing demand for peasant trade unions. In spite of his calm, encouraging manner, his freedom of manoeuvre within the ruling group was slight. The hurricanes of November had driven more of the regional Party leaders, who had at first welcomed Solidarity as a lever to break up the remains of the Gierek régime, to take refuge in the far tougher and more pessimistic interpretation personified by Stefan Olszowski. An excellent example of this change was Andrzej Żabiński, the new Politburo member and First Secretary at the Upper Silesian capital of Katowice. The man who had wept when he saw the agreement signed at Szczecin, and who had spoken like an angry tribune of the people in the Sejm debates a few days later, now regarded Solidarity as the enemy. Just before Kania held out that hand of friendship and trust towards the new union, Żabiński had suggested to a private meeting of Party activists in Katowice that there were three ways to bring Solidarity to the ground. The first was to flatter its leaders by constant meetings with the greatest in the land, which would give them an illusion of power and gradually corrupt them because – as Żabiński put it – 'corruption is naturally associated with power'. The second was to drive its leaders out on a limb by provoking them into taking action in cases which were controversial or even unpopular – for instance, striking to secure the release of Moczulski and other leaders of the ultra-rightist Confederation for Independent Poland (KPN). The third was to exploit the latent tensions between Solidarity's territorial and 'branch' organizations.*

It was lucky for the country that this speech by Żabiński did not become generally known for a month or so. Kania wanted to convince the nation that the leadership accepted Solidarity and remained committed to honouring the Gdańsk Agreement. The existence of a Politburo faction with views like Żabiński's made this less credible.

When the Seventh Plenum came to make personnel changes, Olszowski again led the chase after scapegoats. Moczar and Grabski became members of the Politburo, and Tadeusz Fiszbach a candidate member. The casualties were older men associated with a conservatism much more traditional than Olszowski's: Alojzy Karkoszka, Stanisław Kowalczyk, Władysław Kruczek and – after so many years – Andrzej Werblan left the Politburo. (The last two had generally been considered to be Soviet confidantes.) Now only four out of the fourteen members elected to the Politburo by the Eighth Congress in February 1980 survived, but the new intake did not greatly change its balance of forces. Fiszbach and perhaps the enigmatic Moczar were good for Kania. Grabski would back Olszowski, and the appointment of Roman Ney, rector of the Mining Academy, as a Central Committee secretary reinforced the disciplinarian position. It mattered most that Olszowski now became the Politburo member responsible for ideology, which involved influence over the media, while Grabski supervised the economy.

In spite of the strength of his rivals in the Politburo, Kania's position elsewhere was reviving. The Naroźniak affair had revealed wide structural cracks within Solidarity and had induced some of its central leaders, Wałęsa in particular, to seek a truce with the régime. There was nothing like a coalition yet. But the two moderates, Kania and Wałęsa, needed each other's support against their respective extremists. If Wałęsa could deliver a moratorium on strikes which might weaken the arguments of the Politburo hardliners, Kania could strive to prevent any more of the provocative blunders which sent militant workers and provincial Solidarity chiefs stampeding through Wałęsa's appeals for restraint.

Both sides could agree to use the same language of 'national unity'.

---

* While most Solidarity organizations were regional, some 'vertical' or 'branch' structures had begun to appear. For example, the Solidarity groups in steelworks across Poland established a 'steel industry committee', which met every eighteen days and entered tariff negotiations both with the relevant industrial ministries and with the Sejm commission on heavy industry. See: *Report of International Metalworkers' Federation Mission to Poland*, Geneva, 1981, p. 38.

Indeed, Kania had already, in his Plenum speech, looked forward to the December anniversary ceremonies in the Baltic ports and declared that 1970 must be 'a memory which does not divide but unites'. On 5 December, Solidarity was able to report that there was not a single strike in progress anywhere in Poland. The Church was delighted to bless this germ of reconciliation.

But the strongest pressure for national unity did not arise from these internal pacts at all. Western alarm about a Soviet invasion of Poland reached its peak while the Seventh Plenum was still sitting. On 2 December, the German Democratic Republic closed its districts bordering on Poland to foreign military attachés. The United States announced that 'several' Warsaw Pact countries had put their forces on alert; Anatoly Dobrynin, the Soviet ambassador in Washington, was called to the State Department and warned against the consequences of his country's taking military action against Poland. There was a chorus of protest from other western countries and from the European Community in Brussels. Lord Carrington, the British foreign secretary, said that an invasion would mean the end of the entire détente process, and make it impossible to proceed further with the Madrid review conference on European security and co-operation.

There were angry denials from the Soviet Union and Czechoslovakia in the course of the day. But western alarm was based on the evidence of spy satellites and the intelligence-gathering techniques not only of NATO and its members but of neutral Sweden, in particular. Soviet forces in the GDR, Czechoslovakia, and the western USSR (apparently not yet the other Warsaw Pact armies) were moving forward to start-line positions around the eastern, western and southern borders of Poland. The two Soviet armoured divisions stationed in Poland – one at the main supply and communications base at Legnica, in Silesia, the other at Drawsko Pomorskie, near Szczecin, covering a group of Soviet military airfields near the Baltic coast – remained where they were.

There could be no mistake about this movement, far too large to be concealed, or about its significance. All that was unknown was whether the final decision to invade had been taken. The NATO governments were determined not to repeat the failure of August 1968, when the preparations for the invasion of Czechoslovakia had not been clearly identified and proclaimed to the world. Equally, it was felt in all western capitals that the Soviet leaders must not be allowed to think that East–West relationships would be patched up as rapidly as they were after the Warsaw Pact occupation of Czechoslovakia. They must be left in no doubt that an attack on Poland would lead to a violent rupture. The whole network of contacts woven since the early 1960s might be severed, and a new Cold War would begin.

The western governments encouraged their mass media to pull out all the stops. 'Poland On The Brink' was the headline in every newspaper and the lead to every broadcast bulletin. To a certain extent, this was a deliberate 'prophylactic' barrage, designed to train on the Soviet Union a glare of publicity so blinding that it would deter a final decision to intervene. There is evidence that it may have been successful. The barrage apparently so upset the Soviet leadership that it was decided to call an emergency summit meeting of the Warsaw Pact at the end of the week – a meeting which, rough as it proved for Kania, was to give Poland a chance to bring the situation under control.

The West was not concerned to score merely a propaganda victory over the Soviet Union. NATO, which had been taken by surprise when the Warsaw Pact used force against Czechoslovakia in 1968, had for some years considered that Poland was close to another explosion which might well end in anti-Russian insurrection and Soviet invasion. NATO planners had not the slightest intention of assisting the Poles if that happened. But at the same time they realized that this might not be a conflict confined to the Soviet 'backyard'. Fighting in Poland – it was thought likely that the Poles would resist, unlike the Czechs and Slovaks – could present a threat to European peace. There would be Polish 'boat people' trying to cross the Baltic, and possible conflicts between rescue vessels and Warsaw Pact navies. There could be an isolation of East Germany, possibly encouraging the population to rebel and precipitating East–West military confrontation in Berlin and on the River Elbe. Just conceivably, prolonged resistance and bloodshed in Poland could bring internal pressures within the whole Soviet bloc, even inside the USSR, to the point of explosion.

The West's supreme fear was disorder. A matchlessly English diplomatic comment in late 1980 went: 'There are three scenarios. The first: Poland avoids collapsing into chaos, and there is no invasion. Second: Poland does collapse into chaos, but there is no invasion. Third: Poland collapses, and invasion takes place. The first scenario is of course the best. But the second, chaos with no invasion, is the worst from the point of view of Her Majesty's Government ...'

The Polish reaction to this tremendous shout of warning was mixed. For the first few days, people tended to pay little attention or to respond angrily. The danger of a Soviet invasion was remote, they said, and this 'alarmist hysteria' in the West was harmful to the reform process in Poland; it merely reinforced those in the Party who wanted to halt change by pointing to the danger of a 'national tragedy'.

The truth was that the Poles – again, unlike the Czechs and Slovaks – had been vividly aware of the possibility of Soviet military intervention ever since August. But there was tacit agreement not to talk about it, in case fear began to paralyse the national nerve. A common Polish retort was that the Russians would never invade because they knew the Poles would fight. That was mere self-reassurance, a refusal to think. Underneath irritation at western warnings was a deep-laid Polish cynicism about bold talk from the West which reached back to the trauma of Poland's abandonment by her allies to the Nazis in 1939 and to Stalin in 1944.

The Polish leaders, on the other hand, showed signs of desperation – either because they believed western signals or, more probably, because they were receiving private warnings from the Soviet Union. Kania's speech at the end of the Central Committee session on 2 December harshly criticized the opposition groups, and he quoted Lenin to the effect that 'the only revolution worth anything is the one that knows how to defend itself'.

Two days later, the newspapers of 4 December carried an 'Appeal' to the nation from the Central Committee, drawn up in haste as the plenary meeting was ending, which began: 'Fellow-countrymen! The fate of our nation and this country are in the balance! The persisting unrest is pushing our fatherland to the brink of economic and moral annihilation ...'

If Kania had wanted to shock the Poles by this, he succeeded. The tone of the Seventh Plenum had not prepared them for this agonized language at all. On the contrary, Poland was cooling off. Solidarity issued a puzzled, resentful statement pointing out that nobody was on strike. That same Thursday, the Party spokesman, Józef Klasa, briefed the western correspondents. He intended to speak about the Plenum, guiding them towards a line of cautious optimism about the future, but he turned out also to have prepared himself on the only topic they really wanted to hear about. The correspondents drove Klasa into a corner. He insisted that the Soviet troop movements were normal manoeuvres, that no invasion was imminent, that the PUWP was perfectly capable of solving the crisis by itself. But in the end he replied to the question whether, in certain circumstances, the Polish leadership would appeal for Soviet military assistance.

In a way, this was a ridiculous question. Everyone knew the answer. As Klasa put it, 'If the threat to socialism were to become real ... Polish Communists would have the right and duty to ask for aid from other socialist countries.' The important question was a different one: how far could socialism be modified away from the Soviet design without either collapsing or provoking foreign invasion? But it was significant that Klasa, a senior official with a highly developed survival instinct, was willing to answer the 'invasion' question at all. Afterwards there was a grand fuss, with the Polish government papers accusing the western press of scandalously distorting Klasa's words. This was all pantomime. Klasa had acted cleverly and deliberately. By stating that the *Polish leaders* had the right to decide when socialism was in danger and required international rescue, he implied not only that the Russians should not pre-empt that decision but – almost more important – that it was the constituted Party leadership alone, and not some small conservative faction of 'healthy true Communists', which had the monopoly of invitations. The Poles had watched the Soviet Union accept the 'invitation' offered by a minute splinter group of hard-liners to intervene in Czechoslovakia in 1968. Already, the Soviet press was beginning to croon over 'healthy' nuclei in Poland: veterans, officials of the old C R ZZ unions, and so on. The Polish leaders were not having any of that.

The bad news from the borders continued to squawk from the western radio stations. This bitterly cold week brought the Poles two celebrations to which the news gave special meaning. One was the 150th anniversary of the 1830 Rising, that 'November Night' on which cadets from the Infantry Academy had marched through the frosty darkness to attack the Russian cavalry barracks and the Belvedere Palace. The other, special to the mining regions of southern Poland, was the 'Barbórka', the festival of St Barbara, patroness of miners. For the first time in the memory of most Poles, the feast was restored as a great religious occasion. Black-plumed columns of miners marched along steep streets behind a crucifix, cradling in their arms the image of the saint. In the church at Wałbrzych, packed to the doors, Archbishop Gulbinowicz of Wrocław bound both commemorations together. After prayers for Maurice Thorez (who turned out to be a colliery named after the great French Stalinist), the archbishop asked his congregation to remember 1830 and 'our young men who gave their lives for freedom against the Tsar of Muscovy'. He bound the congregation to pass on good Polish–Catholic traditions to their children, like the shirt slashed by a Cossack sword which had been passed down from generation to generation ...

Saturday was the tenth anniversary of the Warsaw Pact. The day before, on 5 December, the Pact had held an emergency summit meeting in Moscow, which was only announced to the world that evening when the participants were already on the way home. A communiqué recorded merely that there had been an exchange of views on the 'international situation' and spoke at some length about international tensions and the threat to peace. At the end, a paragraph revealed that 'representatives of the PUWP' had informed the meeting about developments in Poland, and that the meeting had expressed confidence that 'Communists, the working class, and the toilers of fraternal Poland' could overcome their problems. The Poles were assured of fraternal solidarity and support; 'Poland has been, is and will remain a socialist state, a permanent member of the family of socialist countries.' But the truth was that the Warsaw Pact meeting had been summoned precisely to discuss the Polish crisis. Both Poland and the German Democratic Republic had brought their ministers of the interior, which hardly suggested a foreign-policy agenda. Almost all the time was devoted to Poland, the peace-and-security bulletin being speedily carpentered together at the very end of the meeting.

The form of the meeting had been that of a trial. Erich Mielke, GDR minister of the interior, acted as prosecutor, standing at a table behind a stack of documents from which assistants fished out relevant papers. The documents were nothing less than an East German archive of every anti-socialist remark published in the last few months in the Polish 'unofficial' press or in the Solidarity weekly newsletters. Mielke's line of argument was triumphantly simple. A Party that does not seize such publications or punish their authors must objectively agree with their contents.

The Russians, presiding like judges, apparently said remarkably little. They probably thought Mielke's performance overdone: to suggest that the PUWP supported anti-Communist or anti-Soviet views, even 'objectively', was a terrible charge that did not correspond to the facts. In any case, they had not called the meeting to declare that Poland must be invaded but, on the contrary, to remind the Polish Communists how they must behave to ensure that intervention never became necessary. A secondary purpose seems to have been to allow the angry and insecure lesser brethren, Czechoslovakia and the GDR particularly, to blow off steam. Finally, with the West's warnings echoing round the world, it was not enough for the USSR simply to deny that it meant to interfere. The Soviet attitude to Poland had to be defined in public.

Was this the real Soviet thinking at this point? All is guesswork, based on sparse evidence. The rather restrained behaviour of the Soviet leaders at this meeting was accompanied – intelligence data make this quite clear – by military movements which entered their most menacing phase in the next few days. A call-up in the Ukraine and the Baltic republics caused disturbances to normal life which needed no orbiting satellites to be noticed; even civilian vehicles were mobilized. According to a report from Stockholm,[1] there were unusually many military ship movements in the Baltic on 6 December, the day after the Moscow meeting. The following day, several Soviet divisions moved out of Kaliningrad and camped on the Polish border in tents. This unambiguous advance took place over the whole weekend of 6–7 December and lasted into Monday. On Sunday night, apparently referring to this move-up and possibly to reports that an airborne division was embarking troops in western Russia, the United States informed the world that Soviet preparations for military intervention in Poland were 'complete'.

They were not quite complete. But this weekend was far the most dangerous moment for Poland since the first strike wave developed in July. For the first time, a realization of the peril in which the nation stood seemed to flow over the population. On Monday, appalling rumours began to flash from one corner of the country to the other. Russian troops had been seen passing west through Rzeszów or Przemyśl. East German armour had crossed the River Oder and was advancing towards Gdańsk from the southwest. These was nothing in any of this. But in the evening, a report with a much better source was heard in Warsaw: four Soviet divisions – far less than a full invasion force – were entering Poland in a 'normal movement' to relieve units stationed in the GDR. A grain of truth seems in retrospect to have been hidden here. Strange things were going on, and western military attachés were among those who thought that an intervention would be executed by 'creeping invasion' – the gradual introduction of unit after unit – rather than by the simultaneous bursting through the frontiers by thousands of tanks on the 1968 precedent. It is possible that such a movement was actually initiated and then – for whatever reason – withdrawn.

Monday, 8 December, had already brought a sharply nervous reaction from Poland over a story from *Tass* which alleged that Solidarity supporters at the Iskra factory in Kielce had disarmed works guards and imprisoned the manager. There was no word of truth in this. But it stank to the Polish authorities of the sort of pretext which the Soviet media had scattered over Czechoslovakia in the weeks before the invasion there. A man from the official Polish news agency was rushed down to Kielce, and next day's papers ran a story – mystifying to those who had not heard about the *Tass* report – describing production at the Iskra ball-bearing plant as rather better than usual. (More tales of this kind were put out by Soviet journalists in the months ahead.)

Slowly, the tension began to ebb a little. It may be that the Soviet Union's rulers were pursuing, as they often had before, a two-track policy of negotiation and military preparation at the same time. The Warsaw Pact meeting in Moscow enabled Brezhnev to postpone any final decision about Poland. The troops took up their final positions, and it was no bad thing from Moscow's point of view that the Poles should hear about it, but the Soviet leaders had already agreed that the time had not come for military action. The world realized that the immediate emergency was over when Brezhnev left on Monday for a long-planned trip to India. His soldiers stayed where they were, freezing in temporary tents and huts through the December frosts, prepared to move into Poland when the order came. They were condemned to wait there for many weeks.

This knowledge changed the atmosphere in Poland. People drew together. There was, none the less, no great transfer of trust to the nation's political leaders; few Poles doubted that some of them, at least, were capable of calling in Russian troops if they thought it necessary. In this lay the most obvious contrast between Warsaw in 1980 and Prague twelve years before. The Poles could not say to Kania and Olszowski, as the Czechs had said to Dubček and Svoboda: 'Be with us: we are with you!'

Conciliators and Radicals

If the Poles now understood that they were under siege, they gave no collective signs of despair. On the contrary, although spokesmen for the intellectuals or the Church, for K O R or the private peasantry would earnestly assure a visitor that a period of discretion and sobriety must now ensue, the Polish people remained in strikingly high spirits. Among the most invigorating events of recent months had been the award of the Nobel Prize for literature to Czesław Miłosz, a compliment to Poland as delicious, in its smaller way, as the election of the Pope. Miłosz, who received his prize in Stockholm at the most perilous moment in these December days, had lived in exile since 1951, and few Poles had been allowed to read what he had written. Some of his verse printed abroad had been passed around among the younger generation, while in the Party's upper reaches his marvellous and intimate analysis of Polish Stalinism, *The Captive Mind*, was furtively devoured as a form of political pornography. But his poems now appeared in a variety of 'unofficial' versions on the streets, and the workers' committee in charge of the 1970 monument at Gdańsk asked his permission to inscribe some of his verses on the plinth. At a meeting of the Warsaw Co-ordinating Committee of Gastronomic and Hotel Workers Affiliated to Solidarity, the chairman proposed to make contact with the Solidarity actors' group 'in order to prepare artistic evenings in our cafés and restaurants, for example with readings from Miłosz and Norwid* and cabaret performances. This will be our and the actors' protest against the pseudo-entertainments offered to gastronomic clients at present.'

Another ground for national pride and self-satire was offered on 9 December, in a field just off the main road between Szczecin and Koszalin. Two workers on a drilling-rig wondered why it had started raining out of a clear sky. They had barely time to notice that the rain was a queer colour before – with a blast that shook the landscape – the Karlino gusher ignited. Poland had struck oil at last. The gusher blazed on for over a week, a pillar of smoke by day and of fire by night, while the Polish Army vainly endeavoured to shell it to extinction. Karlino provided good material next day for the first night of the Warsaw cabaret 'Under the Aegis', which had opened and shut over the years like a snuff-box and now gathered *toute Varsovie* – the smart editors, the best actors and film directors, the novelists, the KOR actress Mikołajska and the man who had persecuted her friends so vigorously, General Moczar – all into one suffocatingly overcrowded room. 'This house in which we all live and which bears the name of Poland ...'

They laughed and cheered and laughed and wept, and at the end sang with a special passion, something to do with the steel hulks waiting at the other end of the night, the cabaret's own hymn: 'Let Poland be Poland'.

The world of the intelligentsia was changing out of recognition. Censorship was now very fitful indeed. Although the brakes were reapplied for a few weeks after the leadership's return from Moscow – a documentary film of the Gdańsk negotiations in August was suddenly denied general release, for example – newspapers and reviews were full of lively controversy and penetrating reporting. Queues began to form at newspaper kiosks in the darkness before dawn; a copy of Rakowski's weekly *Polityka* could find a buyer at nearly a hundred times its cover price. *Życie Warszawy*, the government daily, which had become unreadably dull, blossomed into a perfect tree of knowledge under its new editor Jerzy Wójcik, with the black-bearded Stefan Bratkowski singing loudly in its branches. (Its previous editor was passed to *Trybuna Ludu*, the Party daily paper, with the suggestion that he might make them a safe Prague correspondent.)

There were some compensative drives operating here. Polish journalism, given its head, is as dazzling and intelligent as any in Europe. But for many

* Cyprian Kamil Norwid (1821–83) wrote a close-textured, intellectual poetry which even highly educated Poles find difficult. He, like Miłosz, produced much of his work in exile.

years, ordinary Poles had come to regard journalists as liars paid to defame their hopes and ignore their suffering. At the Lenin Shipyard in August, Polish journalists had the greatest difficulty in gaining admittance, and when they did, were often abused by the workers. Indeed, there is some evidence to suggest that, next to the police, journalists had by 1980 become the most detested section of the community. Now the Journalists' Association became 'independent and self-managing', and its club provided a forum for discussions on every aspect of political or economic reform.

Neither journalists nor other intellectuals could hope to regain the glory that had surrounded them in 1956. This time, they were content to act as ancillaries to the revolt of the working class. But university and research staff soon followed the example of Gdańsk and established new unions. Something like a parallel Academy of Sciences emerged in the Society for the Support and Propagation of Science, a carefully selected pantheon of a few score savants.* Schoolchildren in many cities demanded 'pupil power'. Warsaw University followed the pattern of the Lublin works council elections and chose as Rector a man who was in the Party but not the Party's candidate. And yet this intellectual spring-cleaning was remarkably tentative compared – for example – to the same process in Czechoslovakia twelve years before. There, every association from the small-town chess club to the greatest learned society had summoned an emergency general meeting to throw out its old officers and elect a new, reform-minded committee. The old Czech unitary youth organization had fallen apart like a husk, as new, busily militant student bodies sprang up.

But in Poland, matters had never been so bad as in Czechoslovakia. Good men and women had held a multitude of posts, even if they were unable to achieve much in them, while the placemen and stoolpigeons were seldom in the majority. And there was in 1980 this faintly deferential air about the Polish intelligentsia, aware that its role was to hold the door open for the working class, which contrasted with the confidence of Czech and Slovak intellectuals that the 'leading role' was theirs. A symptomatic feature of Poland in 1980 was the almost total absence of student militancy. Although Polish observers predicted that the situation would blaze up out of control as soon as the universities reopened in the autumn, nothing of the kind happened, and by December some Solidarity leaders were both puzzled

---

* The organizers were determined both to exclude those scholars who were 'compromised' and to avoid recriminations over the past. They accordingly devised an ingenious selection procedure: an original nucleus of eighteen persons with mutual confidence in one another met, and each of them was permitted to nominate three further suitable names. But any of the other seventeeen could veto any of these nominations – without offering a reason.

and worried at the apparent reluctance of students to join the union.

This diffidence, which was at the heart of all of Poland's post-August 'renewal' process, seems to have been entirely overlooked by many neighbouring Communist Parties, especially that of the Soviet Union. All their historical training, from Marx's analyses of nineteenth-century France to experience of events in both halves of Europe in 1968, taught them that the confluence of student protest and worker protest was the most inflammable of all mixtures. To avoid such a confluence, they – and the PUWP – had given much attention since the death of Stalin to segregating these two social elements and even to encouraging their mutual suspicion. In 1968, Gomułka's régime had been able to isolate a student rebellion without great difficulty and even to recruit workers to break up student gatherings.

The political insurrection of 1980 short-circuited the analytical equipment of these post-Stalinist parties. The Polish industrial proletariat was lodging not only demands proper to toiling masses – wages, conditions – but also blatantly political demands that would drive a wedge between the Party and the working class. As it was established *a priori* that no working class could spontaneously make so shocking a suggestion, it followed that somebody was putting the workers up to it. This 'somebody' could only be disaffected intellectuals, known to abound in Poland. Thus if all the members of the Committee for the Defence of Workers' Rights (KOR) and their associates were locked up for attempting to subvert the socialist polity – surely a simple measure to arrange – the proletariat would escape their spell and return to healthy obedience.

As the true course of events since the summer showed, this was a hopelessly faulty approach. In the first place, it quite misunderstood the part which KOR and other opposition groups were playing in Solidarity. By December 1980, KOR had almost ceased to function in any recognizable way, apart from the issue of occasional public statements and the continued publication of its periodicals. The younger and more dynamic members of the committee were mostly separated from each other, working as advisers in various regional Solidarity centres: Jan Lityński in Wałbrzych, for example, or Jacek Kuroń himself at Gdańsk, or Janusz Onyszkiewicz in the Mazowsze offices in Warsaw. Karol Modzelewski, co-author with Kuroń of the famous 'Open Letter to the Party' of 1967, had not been associated with KOR but became a central figure in Solidarity at Wrocław and later press spokesman for the whole union. Kazimierz Świtoń, another free-lance veteran of opposition, became a key figure in the new union headquarters at Katowice. In all these cases, the political activists were in secondary positions, providing invaluable advice but never political leadership. This was retained by the presidium of each local 'founding committee' (M K Z), which had previously been the inter-factory strike committee in the district. The chairmen of these committees were generally young workers, but the presidia usually included one or two intellectuals and professionals: the deputy chairman at Wrocław was a twenty-six-year-old historian; the Kraków presidium included civil engineers and lawyers; in Radom the secretary was an archaeologist; and so on.[2] Secondly, the advice offered by the opposition members was frequently on the side of moderation and, as such, frequently rejected. (The classic case here was Kuroń, who had argued in both Gdańsk and Warsaw against precipitate strike action.) Third, any systematic attempt to round up and suppress these opposition members, especially those working inside Solidarity, would provoke all-out resistance by the union, probably in the form of a general strike. There had been no room for misunderstanding about that since Wałęsa's exchanges with Jagielski on the last day of negotiations at Gdańsk in August.

Thus the assumption by the Warsaw Pact neighbours that 'dissidents' were at the root of the trouble in Poland was not only wrong but put the Polish leadership in an impossible position. If Kania and his fellows denied that KOR and the rest were setting the pace, then they were obliged to admit to the international Communist movement that the Party itself – not just under Gierek, but now – was in some way to blame. This they were not yet prepared to say; in 1980, they still hoped to keep the institutional Party reforms due at the emergency congress to a minimum. So they were reduced to assenting to the 'anti-socialist, counter-revolutionary forces' diagnosis. At first, the PUWP leadership did no more than sponsor furious press attacks on KOR in general and Michnik and Kuroń in particular. But after the Moscow meeting, which committed the Polish government to taking some definite action, the leadership set off in loud pursuit of Leszek Moczulski and the Confederation of Independent Poland (KPN), in the pathetic hope that the Soviet Union would take the arrests of these insignificant extremists as a substitute for the suppression of KOR. *Trybuna Ludu*, the mouthpiece of the Central Committee, published a remarkable article on 11 December which argued that many who had been driven into so-called illegal opposition during the Gierek years could now be regarded as loyal to the new system, whereas 'uncompromising struggle' must be waged against those who attacked Poland's socialist system and her alliances. In other words, it was KPN and the nationalist right who were the enemy, not a social movement like KOR. But none of these ingenious evasions cut much ice in Moscow.

The need for a social truce was obvious to everyone. But in their haste to reach this truce, the leaders of the Church once again overreached themselves and offered concessions to the civil government which divided the faithful and even the hierarchy. A conference of the episcopate on 10 and 11 December issued a statement whose 'positive attitudes' towards the régime astounded even members of the Central Committee. It was the closest the Church had ever come to full recognition of the Communist state since 1944. It gave powerful endorsement to Kania's policy of 'renewal' and appealed for co-operation with the state authorities. 'The efforts of all Poles should be directed to carrying out the process of renewal which has been begun and to creating conditions for the implementation of the social contract between state and society.' The episcopate warned, 'None may act in such a manner as to drive our fatherland into danger of losing its freedom or its existence as a sovereign state,' and again, 'A decisive will is needed to counter-act all attempts to slow down the progress of national renewal, to inflame society or to exploit our present difficulties for aims alien to the interests of our nation and our state.'

Even at the height of a national emergency, this was much too conciliatory for a section of the clergy, and bitter arguments followed. It was alleged on one side that the episcopate, which was now regularly meeting the government in a new Joint Commission, had been promised the right to build two more seminaries and had received a hint that the state might relax its power of veto over the appointment of bishops. The statement brought protests from Catholics in a variety of opposition groups, and expressions of alarm from Solidarity. A 'Gang of Four' was identified as the party of conciliation: Bishop Dąbrowski, secretary of the episcopate; Bishop Kaczmarek, of Gdańsk; Archbishop Stroba, of Poznań; and Father Orszulik, spokesman for the episcopate. Their critics were led by Bishop Tokarczuk (of the microphones) and Archbishop Gulbinowicz (of the slashed shirt).

This quarrel became far worse a few days later when, on 13 December, Father Orszulik held a briefing for the foreign press. His exact words are disputed. But he devoted part of his remarks to a direct attack on KOR in general and Jacek Kuroń in particular ('those in the ranks of KOR and in dissident circles who don't know how to show a sense of responsibility') and on 'noisy and irresponsible declarations aimed against our eastern neighbour'.

A foreigner might find this line of argument reasonable enough, in a country now walled in by foreign tanks. The Poles, on the contrary, asked what matters had come to when the Catholic Church felt obliged to protect the Soviet Union. This was not a response born only of anti-Communist bigotry. Behind it was the essential spirit of the movement that had taken the form of Solidarity: not a refusal to co-operate with the authorities, but a refusal to be blackmailed into such co-operation by the threat of *raison d'état* – Soviet intervention.

It was all evidence of how the cohesion of the Church in Poland had begun to break up in the two years since Cardinal Wojtyła's election to the Papacy. Cardinal Wyszyński, as Primate, was still venerated and formidable, and the prestige of the Church in general had never been higher (on a radio discussion at about this time, listeners could be heard suggesting that bishops should act as arbitrators in labour courts because they alone were impartial and respected!). But Wyszyński was in his eightieth year, ill-adjusted to an entirely new Church/state context. The episcopate was losing touch with its own followers as it made closer contact with the government. Authority was draining away to Rome, to the great Pole beyond the Alps who had not been passive in this crisis. This same week, an official from the Communist Party of the Soviet Union, Vadim Zagladin, had arrived at the Vatican for discussions. Their content remains a secret, but a few days later two different sources reported that the Pope had told Zagladin that if Poland were invaded he would simply fly home to be with his own people.

Another, much more impetuous movement was making itself felt during December. The peasants' protest was moving rapidly beyond the few villages and districts of its origins and acquiring national form as Rural Solidarity (Solidarność Wiejska).* On 14 December, a Sunday, the farmers came to town, marching through the empty streets of Warsaw behind banners to the hall of the Polytechnic (the technical university), where they held their first congress. The issue was registration as a union, so far denied to them by the authorities. Their style was turbulent and uncompromising. Andrzej Gwiazda, the second man in the main Solidarity, argued that their movement should focus on a general defence of agriculture rather than higher farmers' profits; even before registration, they could organize locally and put an end to village corruption. But the delegates were much more stirred by Father Sadlowski, the leading figure of the Farmers' Defence Committee at Zbrosza Duza, who spoke of the land which 'belonged to your fathers and your ancestors' and of the need for village schools to teach 'the spirit of the nation, of patriotism' rather than 'traditions imported from outside'.

Rural Solidarity was soon claiming half a million proprietors as members, out of some 3·2 million smallholdings in Poland. But the government remained deeply unwilling to concede legality to a 'union' of non-

---

* There was orginally another private farmers' union, which called itself Peasants' Solidarity (Solidarność Chłopska); it was unwilling to accept landless workers from the state farms as members. The union finally named itself 'Solidarity of Individual Farmers'.

wage-earners, although Kania was prepared to repeat that private farming could be regarded as a permanent feature of Polish society. Fear that the union would simply act as an anti-Communist political party was one element; intense Soviet disapproval was probably another. But the peasants had strong allies. The Church intimately supported the long sit-in for registration that began in January 1981 at Rzeszów in the south-east of Poland, and in February refused to go on acting as a mediator in industrial disputes until Rural Solidarity was registered.* The other ally was the main body of Solidarity, which supported the peasants with extraordinary resolution. There can be few cases in the history of peasant countries when industrial workers have been repeatedly prepared to take strike action on behalf of farmers – and in this case the satisfaction of peasants' ambitions would in the short term probably mean higher shop prices. Rural Solidarity did not win official assent to registration until April 1981, and then because of industrial Solidarity's readiness to go to the brink on this and other issues.

The Christmas Truce

The week of commemorations, the tenth anniversary of the 'December Tragedy' of 1970, had arrived. It was presented, as both Party and Church wished, as a ceremony of national unity. A precarious Christmas spirit was encouraged: Wałęsa forgave his militant critics in the Gdańsk section of the union while resolving to discourage any further strikes. Kuroń consented to keep an even lower profile, to spare the authorities embarrassment. Stanisław Kania went off, once the Baltic commemorations were safely over, to talk with shop-floor Party members in the Płock petrochemical works and found them fizzing with rank-and-file radicalism. 'I hope this renewal will be the last,' one woman told him. 'It's certainly the last I intend to live through as a Party member!' Rationing was introduced for Christmas, in the hope of ensuring everyone a fair share of good meat, carp and herring, but 150 delegates invaded and occupied the prefecture at Piotrków Trybunalski asking for more.

And the Russians, as the year closed, began to talk to the West about Poland. What they said was not reassuring in any final way, but it was at least

---

* At Rzeszów, the peasants brought an altar into the room, which was decorated with papal and Polish flags. Mass was celebrated daily at this altar and a priest was on hand to hear confessions at the side of the dais. See the eyewitness report by Tim Garton Ash, *The Times* (London), 22 January 1981.

encouraging, delivered in tones much more relaxed than the East German or Czechoslovak hubbub about counter-revolution. The message was that the Polish leadership could still deal with its own problems. Valentin Falin, who had been Soviet ambassador in Bonn, told the West German magazine *Der Spiegel* that anarchy was not reigning in Poland, that nobody in Poland apart from a few groups was challenging socialism or the Party's leading role and that, in his view, the New Year would have a peaceful beginning. When reporters asked him if he didn't see some contradiction in the existence of independent trade unions in a Communist state, Falin replied amiably that they should never underestimate the possibilities of socialism. And Boris Ponomarev, one of the Central Committee secretaries of the Communist Party of the Soviet Union, remarked in Paris, 'The Poles are big enough to sort out their own affairs. The USSR is in no way contemplating intervention.' Lesser Soviet diplomats conveyed the same message to western colleagues. They did not deny the right of the Poles to ask for military support in an emergency, and an article in *Pravda* (signed by 'Petrov', one of the *noms de plume* of Soviet officialdom) sharply criticized the West for trying to deny the Poles that right, but all Soviet sources in late December were emphatic that no such request had been made and they did not expect that it would have to be made.

The West remained unconvinced. This relaxed tone belied the presence of the thirty Soviet divisions positioned around Poland's borders, and it belied what was generally thought to be the Soviet Union's unyielding rule: that reforms which brought the leading role of the Communist Party into question could not be tolerated. It might be that no full invasion was planned for the moment. But the view in NATO and in most western foreign ministries was that Soviet intervention some time in 1981 was almost inevitable, whether it was done by a single *coup de force* or, as NATO analysts thought, by a slow, osmotic introduction of forces into Poland. Even if the USSR had decided that it could live with Solidarity, and there were signs that it might be thinking that way, the threat to the PUWP's leading role embodied in the coming emergency congress would be too much. Even if the leaders of Solidarity and the Party could reach an understanding, their followers were certain to provoke further collisions until the Polish government concluded that it must use force or go under. Even if the Russians could put up with new unions and a reformed Party, a free association of the private peasantry would be too seditious, too seductive to the Soviet rural population.

This was a pessimism that most intelligent Poles refused to share. As we have seen, there was a sense in which they could not afford to do so. But their own reasons were often impressive. In the first place, living all their lives in the shadow of Soviet power politics, they were more interested in a decision to intervene than in the deployment of the tanks, which hardly surprised them. The elaborate political preparations – the 'counter-revolutionary incidents', like the Iskra hoax, or articles like that of 'Petrov' which accused NATO of encouraging subversion in Poland – were predictable too. Russians liked keeping several options open. But many Polish observers were convinced, at the end of 1980, that the option of using force against Poland was still much the least popular in the Kremlin.

Solidarity members, especially, stood firmly by the old Kuroń–KOR theory that a 'Poland of social movements' was to the advantage of both the Party and the Soviet Union. The real lesson of 1980 had been that Poland was not governable under the model of socialism imposed since 1944. To prolong or to restore by force that old model was only to make sure that Poland would be a source of political upheaval and economic catastrophe for the indefinite future. The Gdańsk Agreements had been reached peacefully and they challenged nobody; if they were only put into practice, they would help to guarantee a more contented, industrious Poland, easier to live with as an ally and a trading partner.

Economists put it another way. Poland had now become a sort of plague-ship in the Comecon fleet. The whole eastern bloc was paying for dilettantism in Poland's economic management in the 1970s. The German Democratic Republic, for example, was now short of the Polish coking coal, sulphur and copper on which her industry relied and was spending precious hard currency buying these raw materials in the outside world – and had just been obliged to lend Poland an additional $125 million. The only way out of this absurd situation was a radical economic reform with the emphasis on private agriculture, decentralization and market forces. Admittedly, nothing had been achieved with this reform in the four months since Gdańsk except magniloquent chatter. But outside intervention to halt the political process in Poland would ensure that this potentially rich country would hold back the development of her neighbours for another generation.

The Poles were also scornful about the 'Polish flu' theory, initially popular in the West. On the whole, other Communist countries had not been infected by working-class unrest. The Polish explanation was that they were not interested in exporting revolution. Foreigners were less charitable; they pointed out that few proletariats in the Warsaw Pact states had been treated with such a mixture of negligence and corruption, and that the workers' standard of living in Czechoslovakia, Hungary or the GDR was much higher than in Poland. Romania was the exception, but there the Ceausescu régime had made rapid economic concessions to the workers after August and tightened up its repressive apparatus. In the GDR, Czechoslovakia and especially Hungary, some care had been taken to overhaul the existing trade unions and make them more responsive at shop-floor level. No doubt workers in all these countries would like 'independent, self-governing unions'. But in most of them, the critical combination of relative political freedom and acute economic discontent had not existed. And, lastly, there was a degree of national prejudice operating in Poland's immediate neighbours; older Czechs and Germans were inclined to regard Poles as people who didn't know how to work and who drank too much. They were not disposed to adopt Polish models of industrial organization.*

In the popular mind, grounds for optimism about Soviet policy towards Poland were often less rational. Many boiled down to faith that a nation of 35 million people with a grand tradition of civil and military resistance was unconquerable and the Russians knew it. There was an assumption that no Polish collaborating régime could emerge after a military intervention, and that the Soviet Union would be reduced to controlling Poland through direct and indefinite military occupation, much as the Germans had done. This would be the end of Polish Communism; the Party would not survive the trauma of foreign intervention. Some voices, but perhaps fewer than in the West, predicted that the Polish armed forces would resist a Soviet incursion; a few even claimed that they would win.†

But all these Polish attitudes had one element in common. Whereas

---

* Curiously enough, there was a more distinct echo of Polish developments in China. For some time, Chinese press accounts of Solidarity were sympathetic, because it was an embarrassment to the Soviet Union. No direct link can be demonstrated, but in late 1980 and early 1981 reports of worker revolts in China began to filter out. The best-known was a long-lasting movement among steelworkers at Taiyuan, in Shanxi; supported by a local *samizdat* publication, the workers struck, elected a committee and presented ten demands. In general, the Chinese response was to improve the system of elected workers' councils in factories, to encourage trade unions to talk about improving living standards and to publish rather less glowing accounts of Poland. See the article by Isabel Hilton in the *Sunday Times* (London), 3 May 1981.

† Western military analysts were more sceptical about armed resistance. The Polish officer corps were well-trained, well-paid, and efficient. As far as European war was concerned, they were politically closely integrated into the Warsaw Pact. But the experiences of 1970 and 1980 suggested that, in times of civil crisis, their first instinct would be to stand aside and preserve the army's integrity rather than to act either for or against a Soviet intervention in Poland. If fighting between the city populations and Soviet forces developed, the army would probably refuse to send conscripts, especially, into such a conflict. Such neutrality would be unlikely to survive if the fighting endured for more than a few days. These were the melancholy reflections of military attachés in Warsaw.

western spectators tended to take a determinist view – 'changes in structure are taking place that are fundamentally unacceptable to the Soviet Union, and will therefore sooner or later be suppressed' – the Poles placed the responsibility for foreign military intervention upon themselves. If matters grew no 'worse', they were satisfied that the USSR would probably stay its hand. If, however, popular aggressiveness and official obstinacy made no compromise with one another, they would eventually bring down in ruins the entire state structure and the economy as well. At this point, it was recognized, the Soviet Union could hardly be blamed for intervening.

The ideology of patriotic compromise was thus, in the end, more compelling than any other. It certainly presented difficulties. Practically, compromise with the state kept breaking down because of the government's reluctance to carry out all the engagements of the Gdańsk Agreements. Theoretically, it made no allowance for the enormous tensions of what was really a political revolution crammed into the constricted form of a trade union. But the decision to accept this constriction, which was the decision for a 'self-limiting revolution', in itself implied such a patriotic compromise.

This was the sense of a famous article by the journalist Daniel Passent which appeared on 6 December. Under the title 'Chance for a Centre', Passent argued that there must be a state that had the authority to act as a social arbiter. But on what base could it be founded? 'What we need here is a new "historic compromise", this time a Polish one, which is supported by a grand coalition of trade unionists, Communists and Catholics, the sort of coalition which has often been discussed but has never yet been achieved. This coalition can be lasting only if it sets itself realistic objectives, which means that it must act within the bounds of the socialist idea and that every member of it must be interested in a joint victory . . . In such a coalition, there is no place for extremists of any wing, for people who want conflict for conflict's sake. Only a coalition and the construction of a centre position will let us take advantage of the great chance before which we stand.'[3]

This was a vision which most of Passent's readers could share. But where in the unknown territory of the year 1981 would 'trade unionist, Communist and Catholic' agree to pitch their historic compromise? The truth was that their struggle against one another was not nearly completed and that the leaders of all three powers, however devoutly they longed for a grand coalition, were being driven by forces which they did not yet control. The Polish lava was still flowing. Until it came to a halt and began to cool, no 'Centre' built upon it could survive.

Chapter Seven

Antecedents and Analyses

Workers' Revolts under Socialism

The revolutionary strikes on the Baltic in the summer of 1980 do not belong only to Polish history. The ancestry of what was done at Gdańsk and how it was done is the lineage of the entire labour movement since the industrial revolution. But more specifically, these strikes belong to an inner, tragic family of struggles: the conflicts between industrial workers and socialist régimes that began soon after the Bolshevik Revolution of 1917.

Gdańsk, Gdynia and Szczecin were not mere repetitions. They introduced something quite new into this series: an ambiguous attitude towards socialist theory and practice, which made the workers initially refuse to claim control of production and to accept a programme with 'liberal' points alien to the stereotype of a proletarian manifesto. But the situation was still, in outline, a familiar one. The class was in rebellion against those who were supposed to be its vanguard. For the participants, the precedents stretched back as far as 1921.

In that year, workers in the big industrial plants of Petrograd had launched a series of strikes and demonstrations against the Bolshevik government. This episode was the immediate prelude to the better-remembered insurrection of revolutionary sailors at Kronstadt, the island fortress at the mouth of the River Neva. Faced with the choice of tolerating what looked like an ultra-left 'Third Revolution' or using force, Lenin and Trotsky decided reluctantly to use the Red Army. On 16 March, Bolshevik forces made their final assault across the ice. The fighting probably cost over 4,000 lives.

Kronstadt was a personal and political tragedy for the Revolution. But it was also a formidable and significant workers' movement. At the outset, the Petrograd workers were demonstrating for better food supplies, but their demands broadened to include free speech for other revolutionary groups and the liberation of working-class prisoners. The loyalty of these strikers to the October Revolution was beyond question – they had brought it about. Their protest was against 'War Communism', the one-party Bolshevik dictatorship established to haul Russia through the Civil War. There was no food, the peasants who alone might have fed the cities were being terrorized off their fields, and the original revolutionary democracy of the 'Soviets' had become a sham. The workers were, in effect, saying that War Communism was no longer required and that the Revolution must return to its true form.

Well before the Kronstadt sailors joined in, the Bolsheviks had reacted to these strikes with force. Troops had been sent to break up demonstrations, and a state of siege was proclaimed in the city on 24 February. It was two days later that a delegation came in by boat from Kronstadt to find out what was going on. On the 28th, the crew of the battleship *Petropavlovsk* voted for a list of fifteen demands, in effect a political programme for an open, plural revolutionary régime in which the Bolsheviks would no longer have a monopoly of power. There should be press freedom (which in this context meant freedom for supporters of the Revolution), liberation of all left-wing detainees, and the abolition of 'political sections' in the forces (which gave the Bolsheviks an 'unfair' advantage). Peasants should be allowed to work their own land, and small craftsmen who did not employ wage labour should be tolerated. The *Petropavlovsk* programme said very little about direct workers' grievances beyond demanding 'equalization of rations' for all workers, and politically Kronstadt probably went further than the Petrograd strikers would have wished. Although the subsequent Bolshevik excuse that the Kronstadt sailors were in league with the 'Whites' and the counter-revolution was a conscious lie, the spirit of Kronstadt owed much to anarchist ideas which Lenin and Trotsky regarded as almost equally dangerous to the survival of the Revolution.

The Kronstadt uprising achieved little, except to harden within the Bolshevik leadership that intolerance of dissent that cost Lenin his hopes and Trotsky his life. While the soldiers and sailors of the Revolution were killing each other on the ice, the Tenth Party Congress was already meeting in Moscow, and a few days later Lenin used its platform to announce the 'New Economic Policy' and the restoration of incentives to private entrepreneurs and the peasantry. The NEP, prepared before the February upheavals, made at least some of their sacrifice in retrospect unnecessary.

Petrograd and Kronstadt took place within revolutionary limits. The movement was directed against the Bolshevik power monopoly, but it implied – Kronstadt especially – a deeper, decentralized revolution which would end the rule of a vanguard party 'substituting' for the workers and replace it by the direct self-management of all producers. But the successors of Kronstadt, in this genealogy of Gdańsk, all took place in the socialist states set up in the Soviet-controlled zone of Europe after 1945, and they occupied a very different political context. They broke out in societies whose revolutions had not, with a few qualifications, been authentic but had been imported in the wake of the Red Army. To varying extents, the workers who took part in them were influenced by injured nationalism as well as by economic exploitation. The relationship of these post-war outbreaks to socialist ideology varied too, but all took a broadly 'positive' attitude towards socialism and offered their support to a reformed Communist régime. All, that is, until 1980, and perhaps one should put that date back to the Radom and Warsaw outbreaks of 1976. And yet neither of those episodes was precisely 'anti-socialist'. They would have been easier to deal with if they had been. They are better described as 'asocialist' – indifferent.

The first of these movements occurred in Czechoslovakia in 1953. The 'February Revolution' of 1948 in Czechoslovakia had been the most genuine and least 'imported' of the post-war Communist accessions to power (except for that of Jugoslavia). If its form had aspects of an extra-parliamentary coup, the campaign astutely steered by the Czechoslovak Communist Party was none the less supported by the great majority of the Czech working class. There ensued a period of Stalinist terror, best remembered for the grotesque political trials of Rudolf Slánský and his associates. The workers also suffered severely: 39 per cent of those in prison for anti-state offences in 1950 were classified as workers, and they remained the biggest single group of security-police victims.[1] In 1953, shortly after the death of Stalin, open protests against the régime took place. The living standards of the Czech working class, which had risen immediately after 1948, now fell sharply. In June, the government carried through a sweeping and sudden currency reform that was intended to destroy the bank resources of the bourgeoisie but that in practice abolished the life savings of hundreds of thousands of workers and their families. Widespread strikes culminated in demonstrations and disorder in Plzeň. But the rebellion was harshly repressed, and the Czech and Slovak working classes soon relapsed into an apathy from which political agitators – liberal reformers or neo-Stalinists – found it almost impossible to rouse them.

A much more spectacular explosion took place in East Berlin a few weeks later. A protest by construction workers building the Stalinallee touched off a strike which, on 17 June, reached more than 250 towns in the German Democratic Republic. For many years afterwards, West German propaganda presented it as a great demonstration against the division of Germany, and 17 June became an official holiday as Day of German Unity. But this was false: 17 June was a spontaneous but on the whole disciplined workers' protest primarily against the régime's new system of increased work quotas, and only secondarily for free elections and the liberation of political prisoners. The intellectuals took no part in it, and even technical staff in the factories often refused to join the strikes.

It was the confusion of Soviet policy following Stalin's death in March that brought about this crisis. It was decided in Moscow that in order to persuade the West not to integrate West Germany into the Atlantic Alliance, an extraordinary gesture must be made. The Politburo of the Socialist Unity Party (SED), which ruled the GDR under the supple but implacable Walter Ulbricht, was accordingly instructed by Moscow to put its entire policy into reverse by returning much of the economy to private hands, cancelling price rises and adopting a sunny liberalism towards the class enemy. The SED Politburo did as it was told on 9 June, but decided – not quite unreasonably – that increased work norms, which had already been decreed, must stay in force in order to pay for these concessions. The building workers, however, did not see why they should carry the burden when private farmers who had bolted to West Germany were in effect being offered bribes to come home and take their farms back. On 16 June, a strike developed into a large and angry march around the public buildings of East Berlin. The workers, with the help of a loudspeaker truck they had encountered, put forward four demands: a return to the old work norms, a cut in the cost of living, free and secret elections, and an assurance of no victimization for strikers and their spokesmen. The government at once promised to withdraw the new norms, but the workers, who had no coherent leadership, decided that they would carry on the protest next day and called for a general strike.

The next day, the protest burst out all over the GDR. The scenes in East Berlin had been relayed throughout the country by radio stations in West Berlin, and there was an astonishing similarity in the events of 17 June wherever action was taken. The historian Arnulf Baring identifies two stages. In the morning, the workers gathered together, chose a strike committee at random* and then marched into the town centre, ripping down Party posters along their route. The town hall and perhaps other buildings would be occupied (only the Dresden workers thought of trying to take over the telephone exchange), and the marchers would go to the prison and demand the release of political prisoners – especially of workers they knew.

In the second stage, matters often ran out of hand. The general public

---

* 'At several of the larger works, most of the men elected to serve on the committee were those who happened to have been standing near the microphone' (Arnulf Baring, *Uprising in East Germany*, Cornell, 1972, p. 70).

would mix with the demonstrating workers, swamping the discipline of the strike leaders, and looting and arson in many cases broke out. There were some instances of physical attacks on Party officials. Meanwhile the original strike committees had usually given over their authority to a 'central strike committee', which often turned out to be chaotic and dominated by extremists. In most strike centres, the rebellion culminated in the afternoon with a mass rally, after which the strikers marched back to their plants and the rest of the population went home. In this sense, the 'rising' of 17 June brought itself almost tidily to an end; Soviet tanks and the police did not intervene until the end of the day in most places, and when they did so they were relatively restrained in their use of force. The whole episode, which might have ended in massacre, cost twenty-one lives.

Inevitably, the SED afterwards suggested that the strange uniformity of the revolt signified imperialist plotting. But there was almost no co-ordination between strike centres. This was a spontaneous demonstration whose pattern seems to have derived from older German working-class traditions of solidarity and action. It was consciously an attack on the SED but not anti-socialist; the political tradition of this part of Germany was Social-Democratic and to a lesser extent Communist. Its demands were modest, its ideas of what further action to take non-existent, and its isolation from other social groups of the population almost total. Afterwards, there was much heart-searching by the East German intellectuals.

The next cluster of worker revolts appeared in the crisis year of 1956 in Poland and in Hungary. In contrast to the events of 1953, both movements evolved an institution to express their purpose: the workers' councils, directly elected factory committees which avoided the existing Party and trade union structures. Their economic and political instincts were strikingly close to those displayed by the Paris Commune in 1871 and catalogued by Marx, Engels and Lenin as marks of working-class rejection of the bourgeois 'state machine': the levelling of wages, for example, and the insistence that all representatives should be elected, closely mandated by their electors and revocable at any time. Both in Poland and in Hungary, the workers' councils functioned simultaneously as the instrument of workers' self-management and as revolutionary political centres, another echo of the Paris Commune's refusal to distinguish between industrial and political democracy.

The differences between the movements in the two countries were, however, very great. In Poland, after the spontaneous mutiny at Poznań on 28 June, the reforming forces in the PUWP and the intellectuals were able to use the workers' councils as a source of political mobilization against the old

Stalinist clique. When they had achieved these ends, the new Party leadership under Gomułka was able to tranquillize and eventually to anaesthetize the whole movement. In Hungary, where revolutionary intellectuals had paid relatively little attention to the working class, a whole array of workers' councils sprang up in response to the second Soviet intervention on 4 November and – unsupported by any other class – carried on political resistance for another month. The relative independence of the Hungarian councils allowed them to formulate a programme for a provisional republic of workers' councils; this never emerged in Poland.

Workers' councils were nothing new in the Polish labour movement or in recent Polish history. In 1944–5, as Polish migrants moved in to take over the industries abandoned by the Germans in the Western Territories, the factories were in practice run by the workers for want of any trained managers. A decree of October 1944 had formalized the workers' collective right to supervise and participate with management, but these rights were largely withdrawn in May 1945 when full control of production was reserved for managers and the workers' role in deciding pay levels was cancelled. In 1956, the new workers' councils were much more political. They demanded control of management and production, ignoring proposals for a trade union reform, but they also – the Warsaw car plant at Żerań especially – became both discussion clubs for anti-Stalinist revolution and potential bastions of armed force to fight for revolutionary gains.

The Party extended the rights of the workers' councils in July and agreed to give them full legal recognition in November 1956. *Trybuna Ludu* called this 'a new inspiring movement ... originating in our country, a movement that inscribed on its banner: Workers really are the masters in their own factories.'² A Party delegation went to study workers' self-management in Jugoslavia. But in reality, Gomułka had little more enthusiasm for workers'-control socialism than did Khruschev. The principles of abolishing wage differentials and of dual power within the state (respectively *uravnilovka* and *dvoevlastie*, in pejorative Russian newspeak) would undermine the authority of any conventional Leninist party, and Gomułka considered that workers' self-management, factory by factory, would make central planning impossible and restore the laws of the market: 'All the laws governing the capitalist economy would come into play, only with worse results.'

The Polish workers did not want to understand the reality of their isolation as a class, and submitted to the slow grinding-down of the councils into purely economic bodies and finally in 1958 into the bureaucratized impotence of the Conferences of Workers' Self-Government. Hannah Arendt

wrote: 'The fatal mistake of the councils has always been that they themselves did not distinguish clearly between participation in public affairs and
the administration or management of things in the public interest.'[3] This,
precisely, was the mistake the Polish workers did not make in 1980.

In Hungary, both factory workers' councils and district-based workers'
or revolutionary councils sprang up during the first phase of the 1956
revolution. Their main task was to maintain the general strike. Their
demands were closely similar: freedom for other political parties, withdrawal
of Russian troops, Hungarian neutrality, the right to strike. (A few leftist
factories stipulated that only political parties supporting public ownership
should be licensed. Fewer still asked for religious instruction to be restored
in schools.[4]) But no coherent ideas about how to enforce these demands
emerged.

After the second Russian intervention in Hungary, the most bitter fighting
of all took place in the working-class districts of Budapest. When it died
down, the general strike held on throughout the country. The workers'
council movement now became radicalized. At the suggestion of Miklós
Krassó, one of the very few intellectuals involved, a central workers' council
for all Budapest was set up. Its main job was to negotiate with the Russians
and the new Kádár régime they had installed, but its programme was one of
democratic socialism. As weeks of vain political struggle passed, the
workers began to organize a nation-wide political system based on the
councils, centring on a national council with mandated, revocable delegates
and advised by a 'workers' parliament', a society based on the direct rule of
producers. Once again, the old features of working-class revolution were
emerging, features that Lenin overlooked in *What Is To Be Done?* (1902) but
recognized in his maturity with *The State and Revolution* (1917). Little could
be achieved, however, against hopeless odds. The main strike leadership
was arrested in early December, and the last workers' councils dissolved
themselves in January 1957.

The Poles in 1980–81 detested being compared to the Czechs and Slovaks
in 1968. The allusion could only be ill-omened, but it was also true that
they knew remarkably little about what had really happened then. Like
westerners, the Poles were hardly aware that there had been two main phases
in the Czechoslovak experiment: the 'Prague Spring' of liberal experiment
which ended with the August invasion, and the working-class upsurge which
began only shortly before August and reached its height in late 1968 and early
1969 while the Soviet tanks were already in occupation. This second phase
in Czechoslovakia, acutely relevant to the Polish developments after August
1980, is worth describing in detail, as the most elaborate but at the same time

moderate programme for introducing workers' councils that has been seen in Europe.

The reform process in Czechoslovakia, which began in January 1968 with the replacement of Antonín Novotný by Alexander Dubček as leader of the Czechoslovak Communist Party, did not at first greatly affect the working class. As Vladimir Kusin has written, 'The Czechoslovak reform movement had been called to life by the intelligentsia and was led by a coalition between the intelligentsia and some change-oriented groups in the Party.'[5] The workers, who formed more than half the Czechoslovak population, were accustomed to a secure, not ill-rewarded life in an industrial economy that was comfortably stagnant. They were inclined to see in the changes after January a development that either did not concern them or that might even be threatening. Economic reform, especially, might at last give the meritocracy and the educated the jobs they deserved but would certainly lead to the closure of factories that did not pay, to wide differences in pay levels and to a condition of general insecurity which the working class had not experienced for decades.

Dubček and the reformers realized that this apathy was dangerous. In this mood, the working class might well listen to the defeated Novotný and his conservative followers if they campaigned against political liberalization. Accordingly, the new leadership set out to mobilize the workers, beginning with the trade union federation (ROH).

Little came of this in the first few months. The Party secured some personnel changes at the top of the ROH, and persuaded its enormous, sluggish bureaucracy to redefine its purpose as an advocate of higher living standards, rather than as the transmission belt of state production plans. But it was not until the early summer that ROH began to break up, as the component trades within began to fight their way out of the twelve megaunions into which they had been herded. The twelve soon became thirty-two. (The old Transport and Communications Union, for example, broke up into three, for road, rail, and air, but the locomotive drivers – a proudly maverick group – refused to join the Railway Workers' Union and set up their own Federation of Locomotive Crews. The ROH refused to recognize them and they were eventually denied registration.)

This was not enough for the Party leaders. Under increasing ideological pressure from the Soviet Union and their Warsaw Pact allies, they had to demonstrate in some way that the Czechoslovak working class was an active participant in the reform process. The notion of workers' self-management in some form was discussed in a proliferation of schemes which finally took shape in June 1968 as guidelines for the establishment of 'enterprise councils'.

These councils, as devised mostly by Dubček's economics adviser Ota Šik, were to be directly elected bodies in each plant supervising its management and its total financial strategy (for example, the decision on how much of the surplus to invest and how much to distribute as bonus). The majority on the councils would be composed of workers, but there would be some elected experts from outside and a representative of any bank or ministry that might have invested in the factory.

The whole plan was an implant from above. But it was accepted. Power at the factory level was, after all, a very substantial compensation from the insecurity that Šik's wider plans for the introduction of market forces would bring. It was none the less a moderate affair, and enterprise councils could only be set up with leave from the appropriate ministry. (Railways, telecommunications and forestry were among the sectors of employment exempted from the project.) But there were soon signs of real interest and commitment from the shop-floor. The council statute of the big Škoda works at Plzeň, for example, was amended to adjure its members to 'arrive at decisions independently, without accounting for them to any other social or political organization'. Here was just that attempt to limit the duties of Communist Party membership which Solidarity was to contemplate in Poland twelve years later.

The Soviet invasion on 20–21 August 1968 transformed the Czechoslovak workers' movement. The apathy dropped away. 'In the train of the invasion came patriotism. Patriotism accomplished what democracy and socialism had failed to do – convert the generally passive support among the workers for the revival (of Czechoslovakia) into active support.'[6] Especially in the main cities, thousands of workers were at once pitched into the hectic activity of resistance: the production and transporting of protest literature, the diversion of Soviet military and surveillance supplies, the establishment of clandestine broadcasting networks. On 22 August, with the streets of Prague full of Russian tanks, the survivors of Dubček's leadership group managed to summon the Fourteenth Congress of the Czechoslovak Communist Party. Given shelter and protection by the workers of the ČKD works at Vysočany, the congress strongly reaffirmed the enterprise councils as a component of socialist democracy. At the same time, the resolutions – drawn up before the invasion – made it very clear that there was to be no Paris Commune or Kronstadt in Czechoslovakia. The councils were not organs of 'dual power' but subordinate to 'society as a whole', and they must 'furnish a firm and dynamic base for expert, technically and organizationally skilled management'.[7]

The central feature of this second phase of the Czechoslovak reform was the emergence of these workers' councils, now wide awake, militant and determined to save what they could of 'socialism with a human face'. Some nineteen enterprise councils came into being during September and by the end of the year another 260 had appeared. By mid-1969, there were probably about 300 such councils operating – almost all of them in Bohemia and Moravia; only a dozen or so appeared in Slovakia, where the approach to the whole reform had been more cautious and more preoccupied with winning full federal status for the Slovaks.

But the councils were not, in the end, very effective either in preserving their own existence or in defending the gains of the Dubček period. Essentially called to life by Dubček and his group, they could not acquire a life of their own that would have enabled them to join together and fight independently after August. A meeting was held in Plzeň in January 1969, which in theory represented 890,000 employees gathered in enterprise councils, but no effective national organization emerged. The Soviet and conservative pressure on the Dubček leadership was now suffocatingly heavy. A draft bill to establish enterprise councils was published at the end of the month, but it was a primary Soviet objective that it should never become law. By the time that Gustav Husák finally replaced Dubček in April 1969, the workers' movement was too enfeebled to offer any real opposition. The mopping-up that followed was elaborate: the councils were gradually abolished and some 63,000 ROH office-holders were purged from their posts in the ensuing year – almost the entire elected or appointed cadres from the shop-floor upward. (The Federation of Locomotive Crews refused to bow the knee, and was closed down.)

In the course of 1968, an ironic change had taken place in the mutual attitudes of workers and intellectuals. In the spring of 1968, the sense among liberal reformers was that the workers were suspicious of their enthusiasm for a free press and open democracy. Several factories in the industrial region of Ostrava set up Committees for the Defence of the Freedom of the Press in April and May, but this initiative did not spread further. Following the Soviet invasion, however, there was a surge of hope among intellectuals that the working class might now save the situation. Dubček's leadership, although restored to formal authority, was now in effect the hostage of the Soviet Union; only the workers, fortified in their enterprise councils, seemed to be an independent power in the land. As late as January 1969, at the Plzeň congress, a speaker urged that the movement could 'preserve a breeding ground for democratic socialism'. A month later, the writers' periodical *Literární Listy* announced desperately: 'All Power to the Workers' Councils!'

It was much too late. And in any case, the real political energy in the second half of 1968 had come not from the enterprise councils – still finding their feet – but from the reorganized trade unions. It was through the trade unions that a formal offensive and defensive alliance between students and organized labour, a political rarity, had come to birth in December 1968.

This was the year of student militancy throughout Europe and North America. In France, West Germany, West Berlin, Italy, Jugoslavia and Poland, the student revolutionaries had sought a common front with the working class. Except in Czechoslovakia, their success with the trade unions themselves had been very limited, but student militants from Paris and Berlin had been visiting eastern Europe since the beginning of the year to exchange experiences with university rebels in Warsaw or Prague.* The Czech students (there was hardly any corresponding surge in Slovakia) began on conventionally liberal grounds: their first concern was to break out of the unitary Party youth organization (ČSM) and indeed to get away from the artificial yoking with working-class youth that the ČSM had imposed on them. In May 1968, the ČSM finally disintegrated and the students established their own union (SVS).

But the interest of student leaders in attacking the roots of bureaucracy had already led them back towards the workers; in March, a group of students at the philosophical faculty of the Charles University in Prague had addressed an 'open letter' to the workers, denying that Dubček and his reforming supporters planned to restore capitalism and blaming the Party bureaucracy for deliberately setting workers and students in opposition to one another.

The same faculty became the centre of a distinctly *gauchiste* leadership of the SVS. After the Soviet invasion in August, the SVS became a source of vigorous resistance to 'normalization' (the liquidation of the reforms), and in November staged a four-day sit-in strike that attracted great sympathy. Factory delegations arrived to help the students, many enterprises passed resolutions of support for the students' demands and one aircraft factory in Prague voted to strike if any attempt were made to silence them.[8] Contacts with the unions, once established, now became intense. At this period, all unions were holding special congresses in order to adopt new federal structures, and SVS leaders were invited to the foundation congress of the

---

* Rudi Dutschke and other members of the Sozialistischer Deutscher Studentenbund (SDS) in West Berlin visited Prague in the spring. Western papers reported that the Czech students had been shocked by Dutschke's ardent Marxism and treated him as an enemy, but the truth is that both sides liked each other and were intelligent enough to learn from each other's experiences.

Czech Metalworkers' Union, numbering a million members, in December. On 18 December the SVS and the metalworkers signed and published an 'Agreement on Co-operation'.

The Agreement was a common platform for political struggle. Its basis was the defence of the principles adopted by the Party after January and the 'Action Programme' of the Prague Spring. Students and metalworkers committed themselves to a strike if Josef Smrkovský, next to Dubček the most trusted man in the reform, were removed from his post as chairman of the National Assembly (parliament). Other points condemned the National Assembly's delay in passing the 'Law on Socialist Enterprises' (covering the enterprise councils) and demanded that 'a team of workers' deputies from enterprises and of Czechoslovak economists be given the chance of working out an alternative economic programme'. In the winter of 1968–9, the SVS concluded a series of similar agreements with other unions of which the most significant were the printers, the power-station workers and, outside the ROH, the embattled Federation of Locomotive Crews.

In the end, the pacts had only limited effect. Smrkovský was removed but the metalworkers, by now worried that resistance might provoke Soviet repression on the Hungarian scale, did not go out on strike after all. The print-workers, who had promised to resist the return of censorship and not to print attacks on the 1968 policies, stopped only one number of the anti-reform magazine *Tribuna*. Heavy pressure was exerted on the SVS in 1969 to join the National Front, the official alliance for all political or social bodies, but the unions felt that they could not support the students' refusal to give in, which seemed to them unrealistic. They were not prepared to renounce their winter agreements with the SVS, but when Husák finally banned the SVS in June 1969, they did nothing.

The students had been able to give a certain amount of help to the workers in late 1968, especially in the establishment of communications between factories and in organizing joint worker–student action committees in Czechoslovakia's cities. But the main results of the worker–student pacts were intangible: the breaking-down of social barriers and the understanding of why a dictatorship had found it necessary to erect them. In May 1969, three of the radical leaders of the SVS wrote a letter to the Bertrand Russell Foundation in London, aware that they now faced long years of exile or imprisonment. It was a bearing of witness to what the last year had taught them. 'All of a sudden, the original slogan "Society is not free because the intellectual is oppressed" has changed into the completely new and perhaps more accurate "Only when the immediate producer enjoys the full and democratic rights of a citizen in society, only then may the intellectuals have the right to talk about their freedom."'

In March 1968, when the Prague Spring had scarcely begun, the Polish students demonstrating in Warsaw and Kraków had hoped that their spark would leap across to the workers. Jan Walc, a Warsaw student then, recalls as a supreme moment the appearance in the packed main hall of the university of 'a man in a faded grey *fufajka* [work-jacket]' who called out that the working class were with the students. Everyone burst into the 'Internationale'.[9] But this was a mirage. The workers stayed neutral or even hostile. The Gdańsk students who 'solidarized "themselves" with the Polish working class' in 1968 refused to join the workers in their hour of agony in December 1970. It took ten more years for Polish students to comprehend that final message of the Czech SVS leaders back in 1969.

The strikes of December 1970 in Poland were in one sense a 'pure' workers' revolt. Except for legal experts, especially at Szczecin, there were no intellectual advisers. The revolt was neither provoked nor exploited by the Party, although it gave Gomułka's rivals the opportunity to overthrow him. The demands raised by the strikers were in embryo those of 1980: economic relief, publication of their grievances, a genuine system of workers' representation. All that was missing was the conception of independent trade unions as an instrument for wider political change.

The idea of independent unions was certainly around. The first of the twenty-one demands lodged by the strike committee at Szczecin in December 1970 was 'the resignation of the present CRZZ, which never defended the working masses. We demand independent trade unions under the authority of the working class.' But, interestingly enough, this demand had disappeared by the time of the second strike at Szczecin on 22 January 1971, when the new, more radical, strike leadership asked instead for free elections to workers' councils, trade union committees (*rada zakładowa*, literally 'works council'), Party basic organizations and youth groups. Faith in free workers' councils and in participation at factory level had survived the disillusion that had followed 1956. The December demands at Szczecin had ended:'We shipyard workers distance ourselves from all political and anti-state activity. The character of our action is solely economic. After the fulfilment of our demands, we will return to conscientious and honest work.' The remaining issues were mostly matters of wages and prices, or of the punishment of those responsible for the orders to open fire upon the workers. And the old ghost of *uravnilovka* irrepressibly returned: 'We demand that the earnings of the Party and government apparatus should be limited to the level of average industrial earnings.'

A closer look at Szczecin in 1970–71 reveals the trial-and-error way that the awareness of the Polish workers developed. The structures evolved in December were not very effective in the long term, although they were democratic enough. Each department of the Warski Shipyard, focus of the strike, elected three representatives who then chose a strike committee, later joined by the Repair Yard strikers. There were many Party members among the department representatives, and four of the strike committee at Warski, including Jan Dopierala, the chairman, were in the Party. The main body of strikers seems to have conceived a distrust of Dopierala and, as negotiations with the government produced little result, began to look for a more dynamic leadership. On 22 January, this leadership emerged. In the turmoil which followed a meeting at the pipe-works of the Warski yard, a group of men jumped on to the roof of a snack kiosk and one of them – Edmund Bałuka – managed to make himself heard by using a roll of corrugated iron as a megaphone. The crowd of workers turned towards him, and he was able to convince them to start another occupation strike.

This new strike command, thrown up by the impatience of the Warski labour force, was composed of tougher, more marginal individuals than its predecessor. Bałuka had been a seaman who had served two gaol terms: one for attempting to escape to the West, and another for striking a policeman. Adam Ulfik, who stood beside him on the roof, was a little older. As a boy, Ulfik had been deported to a Nazi concentration camp for resistance work; after liberation, he murdered the Kapo* of his hut at Mauthausen and was imprisoned by the Americans. He returned to Poland, where he was jailed at Szczecin for the same offence as Bałuka's – punching a cop.

These were real men of their times. They stood alone, social maquisards who belonged to no great ideological army. They were not devoted Communists like Lechosław Goździk, the workers' leader in 1956, and neither were they pious sons of the Church like Wałęsa. The shipyard liked them because of this simplicity: they were loyal to their comrades and they hated authority. Unfortunately, they were not by themselves a match for the régime.

Their initial success was spectacular enough. They summoned Gierek, Jaroszewicz and Jaruzelski to the shipyard, and they came; the ruled spoke to their rulers in that debate as they have seldom done in human history. Bałuka and his comrades also understood – and this was a quite crucial perception – that the success of the movement in the longer term demanded

---

* A Kapo was a prisoner set over other prisoners by the SS guards. Often professional criminals, Kapos could behave as ruthlessly as their masters.

that the actual directing bodies of the strike must be kept in being and must go on to acquire some officially recognized authority. By itself, an agreement with the government was just a scrap of paper. It was Bałuka's strategy which was used in 1980, when the Inter-Factory Strike Committees were transformed into local organizing bodies for the new Solidarity trade union. But in 1971, with localized 'workers' control' still seen as the traditionally more radical and 'left' solution, the strike committee at Szczecin demanded from Gierek the right to turn itself into the organizing committee for free elections to the existing workers' councils and shipyard trade union groups.

The strikers were both surprised and delighted when Gierek readily agreed to these free elections and to the strike committee's new role in them. But in the weeks which followed, the Party was able to whittle down the effects of what the régime had conceded that night. The elections were finally held on 12 February. The London-based writer Bolesław Sulik, who has studied the whole episode closely, points out that Bałuka and his group, whether from innocence or ineptitude, did not campaign effectively, while the Party loyalists – supported by management – put in many hours of persuasion and pressure. 'The workers' leaders showed their deplorable lack of political experience ... As a result, while the vote was favourable for some of the old committee members ... whose popularity got them elected to departmental councils, at the level of the enterprise only Bałuka, whose name had become famous, was admitted to the main workers' council.'[10]

After the elections, the strike committee automatically dissolved. If it had won, it would have dominated the new bodies but, as it was, the authorities were now free to deal with the individual strike ringleaders at leisure. What became of them has never been either explained or, in Szczecin, forgiven. The youngest member of the strike committee, Bogdan Golaszewski, was found gassed at his home in August 1971. Galaszka knocked a policeman's cap off in May, and was given several years in prison. Bezia only just escaped a long sentence after a fight in a restaurant. Urbański, Ewa Zielińska and Jola Jakimowicz – everyone remembered her voice, because she had acted as 'announcer' on the strike loudspeaker system – all lost their jobs in the yard.

Adam Ulfik, the 'giant with the child's grin', worked away for a time on his own private contribution to international law: any occupation strike lasting longer than five days and involving more than half the work-force should, he thought, automatically become a concern of the United Nations and be adjudicated by a UN commission. But suddenly queer things began to happen to him. He was attacked by men who tried to chloroform him. Then he was tried, convicted and gaoled for raping the mentally handicapped daughter of a concierge. Ulfik's friends at Warski refused to believe this;

they scented a frame-up, and protested. Ulfik was moved to the prison hospital. After his release he was not allowed back into the shipyard, but granted his pension rights. In February 1976, for no reason anybody could explain, he suddenly died.

Edmund Bałuka survived for a time as a member of the shipyard workers' council. But everyone who had been on the strike committee was now being raided and harassed; the police had been ordered to find all the tape-recordings made of Gierek's debate with the strikers. At the end of 1972, he was offered a reasonable job elsewhere as regional chairman of the metal-workers' union. He accepted. Six weeks later, he was sacked. When he went back to the Warski yard, there was no job for him any more. Bałuka did not need the message to be repeated. He managed to get back his old seaman's card the following year, and some months later jumped ship in Majorca.*

Jacek Kuroń summed it up: 'Through all of 1971, the Party concentrated on breaking up the workers' representation in Szczecin. This finally succeeded with the use of brutal violence, persuasion, corruption and provocation. But the entire country had learned a lesson: these people who formed the new government were not to be trusted in negotiations.'[11] The point he was trying to make (in an essay written before 1980) was that any attempt to set up an authentic structure to act as a formal negotiating partner with the régime was bound to fail. The authorities would always cheat and always win in the end. Kuroń was contrasting the failure of the Szczecin strike committee and workers' councils to bring about the lowering of the December 1970 prices with the success of the women textile workers at Łódź, who had not done anything so foolish as to elect a negotiating committee but had simply struck and threatened until they won. Then they had gone back to work, leaving no vulnerable representatives behind as hostages.

In 1980, Kuroń's warnings were ignored. The workers, more confident than he had anticipated, returned to the tradition of setting up permanent representation. They avoided the danger Kuroń spoke of in a very simple way: by making that representation so extensive and powerful that the régime would hesitate to break any pact negotiated with it. The workers'-council

---

* Bałuka wandered about western Europe for many years, at one time running his own magazine in Paris. He too developed rather eccentric political views, demanding that the agreements of Teheran, Yalta and Potsdam should be abrogated. In late 1980, Szczecin Solidarity requested immunity for all members of the 1970–71 strike committees, including Bałuka, and asked that he be allowed to attend the dedication of the monument at Szczecin on 17 December. But it was not until April 1981 that Bałuka appeared, having crossed the Polish frontier under some disguise or other, and took refuge inside the Warski yard. He was now open to prosecution for both illegal exit and entry, but it was only in May 1981 that Solidarity persuaded him to report to the authorities – who took no action against him.

form was at last abandoned – or, more accurately, relegated to the status of a democratic reform of industrial relations. It was no longer seen as a grand political solution, except by those surviving working-class Marxist thinkers who knew that a co-operative republic of self-managing producers was the final destination of all genuine socialism.

How far workers' councils can provide a route to that destination remains bitterly disputed. But these post-war episodes from eastern Europe help to suggest some conclusions.

– Workers' councils are the most radical expression of spontaneous working-class action. Even today, when workers occupy their places of employment with the intention of taking them over permanently, the same old instincts press towards the surface: direct democracy with revocable office-bearers or leaders, and the levelling of rewards. The more radical the occupation, the more strongly these features emerge. But the less spontaneous the workers' council (as in Czechoslovakia in 1968), the less radical it will be.

– Workers' councils and factory councils are probably most effective when they are part of a revolutionary movement against a crumbling capitalist order. The Soviets in Russia, the *Räte* in the German revolution of 1918–19 and the factory occupations during Allende's presidency in Chile offer examples. By establishing 'dual power', an authority over workplaces and perhaps cities or districts that parallels the authority of the state, they decisively weaken the state's power to resist.

– A spontaneous movement of workers' councils is not, in the end, likely to survive without a political movement to support its aims and exploit its victories. When the political movement collapses or defects, the councils have proved unable to maintain their political impetus and independence. In Poland after October 1956, the councils rapidly became impotent when the PUWP lost interest in them, and their reappearance in 1970–71, with no organized political support, was very short-lived. In Hungary in 1956, there was an attempt to set up something like a *Räterepublik*, a republic of workers' councils, as a revolutionary political structure, but against the Soviet troops and the hostility of the new Party leadership under Kádár it stood no chance.*

* Sheer topography helped to make workers' councils vulnerable. Modern factories are mostly built on the periphery of cities, remote from the centres of political struggle and easily isolated from one another by armed forces. The workers' resistance to the 1973 putsch in Chile against Salvador Allende was ineffective for this reason. In 1871, most Paris workers were artisans who lived and worked in the city centre; if they had been commuters from peri-urban housing schemes to factories as distant as Renault at Boulogne-Billancourt, the Commune would probably never have arisen.

Where the councils are backed or sponsored by some national political organization, on the other hand, they may endure. The best example is Jugoslavia, where 'self-management' was not spontaneous but installed in 1950 by the Jugoslav Communist Party. One can also assume that the councils in Czechoslovakia, enticed into existence by Dubček and his colleagues, would have maintained themselves if the Warsaw Pact intervention had not taken place.

The contradiction here is painful and obvious. In order to survive initially, the councils need the protection of a conventional, structured political party. But workers' councils, if they are not technocratic shams, must look forward to a society given over to the decentralized, anti-bureaucratic democracy that they themselves practise. If they are truly revolutionary, as they were at Kronstadt, they can only regard all centres of political and state power as their enemies. This problem was recognized very early by the fathers of Marxism–Leninism, and their successors evolved the familiar Communist sketch of how events should develop: the workers' councils help the vanguard party to seize power, then surrender their autonomy during the period of proletarian dictatorship, and, in the end, are reborn in the glad light of a Communist society in which central state power has withered away.

The attraction of workers' councils in eastern Europe has been that they were working-class organizations beyond the control of the Party. It was for this reason that the Poles kept coming back to them. But the Party proved able to regain control as soon as the elected delegates of the councils ceased to be mandated by shop-floor workers who could recall them at any moment. By the late 1970s, Polish workers had understood that the councils could not survive adverse political conditions. And, as their view of their problems became increasingly political and less limited to economic grievances, they became open to new suggestions.

The Poles were not the first in eastern Europe to attempt to form independent trade unions. In western Romania, wage cuts and increased production targets led to a long strike in the Jiu Valley coal mines, in which some 90,000 workers took part. Two years later, in February 1979, a Free Trade Union of the Working People of Romania appeared in the same region. Several thousand people are reported to have joined in the next few months, but the union appears to have been more of a human-rights committee; its members were mainly drawn from the Hungarian and German minorities whose grievances were cultural and political as much as economic. The security police arrested most of the union's leading figures.[12]

The Polish workers had been sceptical about a trade union solution, dismissing unions as structures so closely meshed into local and national Party decisions as to be unreformable. But this generalization was not always true, even in Poland. In November 1956, at a special meeting, the CRZZ had torn up its agenda, thrown out most of its old executive and passed a resolution 'proclaiming the democratic character of the unions, the abolition of the administrative influence of the Party apparatus on them and their full independence of the state'.[13] It had been the Czechoslovak trade unions, rather than the workers' councils, which had most stoutly defended the democratic reforms of 1968, and in the late spring there had been a period when some of the ROH radicals raised the slogan of 'trade unions without Communists!'

Generally, however, it was fair to see trade unions as extensions of the power structure. After the end of Stalinism, they mostly ceased to act directly as 'transmission belts' of Party instructions to the workers, but – through their alliance with management and their control of the distribution of social funds – they retained close control over the behaviour of individual men and women at work. In theory autonomous, they were in practice an important instrument through which the state attempted to achieve its production plans. But there was great variation in the way that trade unions in eastern Europe fulfilled their duty to protect their members' interests at the shop-floor level. In the GDR, for example, unions utterly conformist at the national level often fought hard for their members in the shop or 'brigade' context. In Poland, on the other hand, union shop-stewards were usually expected to back management in a dispute.

The PUWP leadership found itself in a dilemma here. On the one hand, it was terrified of relaxing control over the union movement, especially after 1970, in case this instrument of control over the mass was snatched out of its grasp altogether. On the other, it realized that the unreformed unions were losing touch with the workers in a dangerous way. After the 1976 upheaval, Gierek urged the CRZZ to stay close to the moods of the workers, to identify their problems and solve them before they reached the point of explosion. The trouble was that the unions could regain contact with their members only if the Party were prepared to allow free and open elections to the trade union 'works committee' (*rada zakladowa*), as had briefly taken place in 1971. But here Gierek's nerve failed. The opposition writer Karol Modzelewski wrote him an open letter in November 1976 which defined the weakness: 'It would be a good idea to change the electoral practices ... But experience suggests that up to now the autonomy of trade unions has always been liquidated in the name of the administrative security of the Party – in other words, because of the bureaucratic terror of political officials at the prospect of independent representatives of the work-force.'[14]

It was above all through the trade unions that the Party was supposed to carry out its leading role in relation to the working class. A 1977 handbook, typical for most states in the Soviet sphere, described this relationship for the CRZZ: '[Party activity within the unions leads to] wide political control by the Party over all union activity. The essential channel for this is control over the activity of Party members who are union activists. The forms of political leadership by the Party in trade unions are essential elements of the trans-mission mechanism between the Party and the masses ... The trade unions are thus the connection between the Party and the working masses. The bond between the Party and trade unions (personifying the masses and represent-ing their interests) is the corner-stone of the whole theory and practice of building socialism. Lenin frequently refers to the importance of this link.'[15]

As in the matter of 'Leninist norms of Party life', Lenin is constantly invoked to support established practice between Party and trade unions. In historical fact, Lenin's views on the relationship were slightly inconsistent and all – after 1917 – responses to crises rather than Papal Bulls binding for all times coming. His best-known definition, given at the Tenth Congress in 1921, sought a compromise position between the extremism of Trotsky (who wanted trade unions to be fused into the state structure in an almost military posture of obedience) and the views of Tomsky and the Workers' Opposition (who wanted the trade unions to replace the entire economic and state administration of Russia). Lenin preferred the trade unions to be closely subordinated to the government in policy matters but not to become 'statified', in Trotsky's expression. They should be a voluntary organization, and the Party (which then had only half a million adherents among the seven million trade unionists) must make its way to leadership through the individual merits of its candidates. Then the trade unions could gradually become a 'school of Communism' for the rest of their mass membership. Lenin agreed that the unions should take a more direct part in controlling production – by participating in planning, by supervising wage-rates and production norms, and by enforcing labour discipline.

This could be justly called a fair-weather programme. Nothing here gave guidance to a union official – unless he was a Party member – trapped be-tween the interests of his members and the instructions of the state. Between the lines of Lenin's Tenth Congress resolution, there was room for coercion of the unions by the state, and even more for coercion of the workers by the unions. But Lenin's longer-term plan for the unions was that they should be nothing less than the instrument of the 'cultural revolution'. The state must in the end wither away, and as it did so every individual would be learning the art of administration until there was no need for any permanent bureaucracy at all. 'If we fail to convert the trade unions into organs educating the masses, on a scale ten times larger than at present, for the immediate participation in the direction of the state, then we shall not achieve our objective of building Communism.' [16]

It is a very long, downhill track from thoughts like these to the shabbily totalitarian view of trade unions that prevails in eastern Europe today. The Party's position in union posts is hardly achieved on merit. The bureaucracy shows no intention of withering away or handing over its functions to union-trained citizens. The unions' only dignity, to put it cruelly, is that of a production gendarmerie for the state. Yet in Poland, during the 1970s, opposition thinking veered away from workers' councils towards the idea of some new institution that would do what the trade unions were blatantly incapable of doing: acting as a genuine defender and representative of workers' interests. There was talk about a 'workers' parliament', an assembly of elected delegates from all the major plants – which was to give life to Gierek's spasmodic practice of making direct contact with the biggest industrial work-forces. Some opposition intellectuals, like Modzelewski, thought that an enterprise might elect an *ad hoc* committee for discussions on one subject at a time, dissolving when the topic was settled. The idea of establishing 'free trade union' nuclei in industrial cities was thus only one scheme among many others.

What were the subjective motives of these east European workers' movements? No single answer could be given for any of them. But three elements seem always to have been present, although in very different mixtures.

The first is the element of political protest against cruel and unjust government. The outbreaks in the GDR, Hungary and Poland in 1956 were all associated with a revolt against an oppressive régime that was either falling or assumed to be falling. The Czech workers were not so closely associated with this overthrowing phase. But the three subsequent Polish explosions, in 1970, 1976 and 1980, were increasingly 'political' in that attacks on the Party and state authorities and on institutions like the judiciary, the press and the censorship occupied each time a relatively larger part of the total protest.

The second element is economic interest. Here there are two rough sub-categories. There were motives of desperate material self-defence by workers who could no longer stand the deprivations being inflicted on their families: this was true in 1953 in both Bohemia and the GDR, at Poznań in 1956, in Hungary the same year and in Romania in 1977. But there has also been the fear of *losing* an existing degree of security, however low-level. The

Czechoslovak workers in 1968 were nervous about the effect of a market-economy reform on their standard of living, and – although no open protest movement developed – so were the Hungarians following the introduction of the 'New Economic Mechanism'. The 'Polish December' revolts two years later had elements of both sub-categories: the price increases devastated the consumption levels of a very poor population, but at the same time Jaszczuk's reforms threatened to introduce unemployment and wide variations in earnings.

A third, inescapably important component was nationalism. It is many years since the argument was heard that only the remnants of the old bourgeoisies of eastern Europe harboured patriotic resentment against the treatment of their countries by the Soviet Union. There was certainly some truth in this in Bulgaria, and in Czechoslovakia during the first decades after the war. But the events of 1956 showed that many elements of the old nationalist political cultures of central and eastern Europe had been mediated to the new working classes, especially those recruited from the peasantry.

Nationalism acted as a sort of hormone in these revolts and movements. When released into the bloodstream, it dilated arteries; political processes did not so much change their form as take place faster and more radically. The Hungarian workers'-council movement existed before 4 November 1956, but the second Soviet attack on Budapest sent it into its decisive phase. The Czech trade unions, relatively discreet in the first half of 1968, were transformed into the major source of reforming and resisting energy by the Warsaw Pact intervention in August. (It is hard to judge the importance of nationalism in the events of June 1953 in the GDR, a part of a nation still bleeding after partition by its conquerors. The wish for German reunification was certainly present. Yet the demonstrators were on several occasions explicit that their target was not the Soviet presence, as the guarantor of partition, but their own ruling Socialist Unity Party.)

In Poland, the 'external' nationalist stimulus was always active. But it diminished, rather than increased, between 1956 and 1980. The workers' upsurge of 1956–7 took place against the background of a revolution against Poland's almost colonial subjection to the USSR, and at the height of the crisis the workers' councils in many Warsaw factories were ready to act as centres of armed resistance to Soviet troops. But the three upheavals of 1970, 1976 and 1980 were more exclusively domestic. The level of anti-Russian feeling remained high but more or less stable, even at the moment when invasion was apparently imminent in early December 1980, although it became more visible as political discipline relaxed (the demonstrations on the Katyń anniversary, for example). It was very much part of the style of

1980 to avoid and disown open attacks on the Soviet Union, which not only showed a misunderstanding of where Poland's trouble lay but played the authorities' game of identifying radical change with a threat to the *raison d'état*.

Nationalism directed *inwards*, however, played a larger and larger subjective part in Polish working-class unrest. The movement that began in July 1980, although ostensibly concerned with issues that were mostly economic and social, derived its huge voltage from old-fashioned revolutionary nationalism tinged with Polish Catholic views of patriotism and human rights. Underlying class dynamics were still operating, but in terms of how the rebelling mass understood its own motives, this was the least 'socialist' of all these episodes although – paradoxically – it brought the Polish workers to the point at which they finally recognized their identity as an independent class whose interests were distinct from those of the Party and the ruling bureaucracy. And in a society which had been plagued by xenophobia, real and manipulated, this swivelling-inwards of nationalism brought about a mental liberation. In 1956, ordinary people often accused their old rulers of not being true Poles – of being Russians, or Russian agents, or simply Jews. In 1980, and to some extent in all the revolts of the previous ten years, unpopular leaders and institutions were attacked on the grounds that they were a disgrace to Poland; they were contrasted with some essentially 'Polish' way of doing things – honestly, openly and with mutual respect. In the same way, the 1980 revolt was consciously seen by its participants as a *ralliement* of the nation, a breaking-down of barriers deliberately constructed to keep class from class, the Church from its rightful place in society, truth from the young, rulers from the ruled.

The central charge laid against the Party in 1980 was not that it had offended against human rights, not that it had ruined the economy, not that it had betrayed its trusteeship for the proletariat and not even that it had bound the state too closely to Soviet policies – although all these points and more were made. It was that the Party had divided the nation, and set Pole against Pole.

Workers, Intellectuals and Power

'If all states are instruments for the domination of one class over another, and if in the USSR there are no antagonistic classes and objectively there is no need to suppress other classes, then over whom does the state exercise domination?'[17]

How do we describe the class relationships within a socialist society, and what are their dynamics? Marxists have been inhibited in the search for an answer both by real problems of defining the nature of a ruling group that does not own the means of production and, at a baser level, by political prudery about the admission that fundamental conflicts of a class nature do not necessarily end with the overcoming of capitalism. Non-Marxists have done no better, contributing for the most part descriptive accounts of new élites or question-begging polemic about 'red bourgeoisies'. Similar problems of definition are presented by the élites of the developed West, increasingly opaque to conventional diagnoses of motive and interest.

The question above was posed by Santiago Carrillo, General Secretary of the Spanish Communist Party and the leading exponent of 'Eurocommunism'. In a literal way, it would not be hard to answer. But the problem is not really 'over whom' the state dominates, but 'on behalf of whom'. Is there a ruling class in the USSR, and in other states of the Soviet system, and if there is, what should it be called?

The old definition of Soviet society, worn smooth by use, is that it is composed of two *classes*, the workers and the peasants, and of one *stratum*, the intelligentsia. Although these three groups continue to interact with one another, these interactions are only 'non-antagonistic contradictions': in other words, they do not have the dialectical force of class conflicts in a capitalist or pre-capitalist society. The working class has ceased to be 'an exploited class bereft of means of production', in the words of the standard Soviet account, and now possesses state power. The peasantry has similarly been emancipated from all exploitation, and 'the overwhelming majority of the peasant households ... joined the collective farms, which were based not on private ownership but on collective ownership'.[18]

The intelligentsia of the Soviet Union is for the most part 'an entirely new intelligentsia'. Recruited mostly from worker or peasant families, and also freed from exploitation, the stratum now serves socialism instead of capitalism. It is 'an equal member of the socialist society. Together with the workers and peasants, it [is] building a new, socialist society.' It follows that in such an elysian place where exploitation no longer exists, class struggle in the accepted meaning of the term cannot exist either. As socialism ripens into full Communism, the distinctions between these non-antagonistic groups will fade completely away.

Unconvincing as three wooden dolls with red cheeks and painted smiles, the two classes and one stratum have never been satisfactorily replaced. It has been easier (outside the Soviet Union) to agree that exploitation in both its popular and its Marxist sense does continue in a so-called 'socialist' society. But the search for the exploiter continues, and the hunters are constantly in danger either of falling into theoretical crevasses which the fathers of Marxism did not chart, or of being ambushed by political guerrillas out to perforate anybody who might unwittingly be doing 'imperialism' a service.

For many years, the western far-left has quarrelled over the correct definition of modern Soviet society: a degenerate workers' state, or a form of state capitalism? This argument, nauseating as it has been rendered by endless repetition, does at least identify two main positions among critics of the Soviet system. The older position, shared both by Trotsky and by modern 'Eurocommunists', is that the October Revolution was an irreversible leap forward, and that a post-revolutionary society in which workers and peasants are oppressed by a bureaucratic dictatorship cannot be compared in class terms to the relationships of the capitalist society which preceded it. The transfer of the means of production from private hands to social ownership, even when the subjective liberty and prosperity of the workers are not increased or are even diminished, marks the end of a certain type of exploitation.

This emphasis on a conventional view of what property and means of production are leads to a cautious view of the new ruling groups in the USSR and eastern Europe. Crudely, if they do not own the means of production as their private property, they cannot constitute a social class. Two 'Eurocommunists', Carrillo and Roger Garaudy, late of the French Communist Party, offer strikingly similar accounts. Carrillo objects that 'the bureaucratic stratum cannot be regarded as a capitalist *class*. It does not possess private property, and the part of the profit from Soviet enterprises which goes into its upkeep is certainly less than it costs to maintain the bureaucracy in any capitalist country.' Garaudy in 1969 described a model of a society in which 'social property identifies itself in a permanent way with state property and in which the monopoly of management becomes the specialization, the profession of a particular social group'. But he went on to say, 'This bureaucracy does not constitute a social class for two fundamental reasons: it possesses not the means of production but only its management; and this power of management is not hereditarily transmissible in the manner of property.'[19]

The other position begins with the argument that traditional Marxist categories of property are completely inadequate to describe the societies which arose in the USSR during the 1930s and in eastern Europe after the Second World War. Although Carrillo and Garaudy, for example, are outspoken critics of the Soviet system, their use of obsolete definitions of class amounts to a defensive manoeuvre, a reluctance to take an attitude of total opposition. The truth, according to this more radical view, is that the Russian Revolution did not succeed and that the Stalinist régime which eventually replaced the Tsardom should not be dignified by the term 'workers' state' even when qualified as 'degenerate'. The Soviet Union is a system of state monopoly capitalism which is blatantly converging with the late-capitalist structures of the industrial West, and it is as much a potential subject of class struggle and a site of exploitation as the United States. To bring out this convergence, the notion of property needs to be broadened to cover bureaucratic privilege and, for example, the notion that access to information may in such societies become a precious and heritable form of property.

The Polish intellectuals Kuroń and Modzelewski, in their 1965 'Open Letter to the Party,' wasted no time on the question of exploitation. It was patent. The worker was obliged to sell his labour, he did not own the means of production, he was deprived of the surplus product of his labour. 'To whom does the worker in our country sell his labour? To those who have at their disposal the means of production, in other words, to the *central political bureaucracy.*' These two dissidents, who wrote most of the 'Open Letter' in prison, went on boldly to deal with the problem of who was doing the exploitation: 'The central political bureaucracy is the ruling class; it has at its exclusive command the basic means of production; it buys the labour of the working class; it takes away from the working class by force and economic coercion the surplus product and uses it for purposes that are alien and hostile to the worker in order to strengthen and expand its rule over production and society.'[20]

They brushed away objections that there could be no exploiting 'class' without private property. The bureaucracy had 'the collective property of an élite which identifies itself with the state'. This central political bureaucracy, like a capitalist, used only a tiny fraction of the surplus product on its own personal consumption but spent the rest – in this case, the revenues of the state – to fortify the system of exploitation which guaranteed that consumption.

Kuroń and Modzelewski were drawing a very sharp distinction between the tiny central group – those who directly commanded the state and the economy – and the colossal army of assorted officials, experts and policemen which maintained them in power and was rewarded, in many cases, with privileged levels of consumption. The technocracy was one of those cases of privilege. But the technocrats were by themselves only a 'stratum', not a class, and they were embroiled in conflicts. On one side, they were supervising the exploitation of the workers. On the other, they were coming into open opposition to the central political bureaucracy. The technocrats wanted a decentralized, managerial reform of the socialist economy: 'power to the experts'. They were challenging the existing monopoly of the power of decision at the top.

It was this group, the technocrats or 'technical intelligentsia', that most interested the West. Already familiar with the opposition of creative intellectuals, which had been evident at least since the mid-1950s, western sovietologists believed that the rebellion of the 'qualified' and the experts was the most fundamental challenge to any Communist system. This group had an interest in free competition, in the reduction of censorship, in the substitution of market forces for the power monopoly of the Party. If 'liberals' and technocrats could replace the old governing élite selected for political loyalty rather than professional excellence, effective Soviet control over the individual states of eastern Europe would rapidly dissolve. Any tensions between the new managerial élites and the workers would evaporate as the introduction of 'socialist market economies' raised the general standard of living.

This was certainly not the view of Kuroń and Modzelewski. In the first place, they did not at that time believe in gradual change in eastern Europe. The whole system must be overthrown: 'revolution is a necessity for development'. Secondly, they regarded the antagonism between their 'central political bureaucracy' and the technocrats as a relatively minor stress. The workers and the central political bureaucracy were the two basic classes in society, and they would fight it out. 'The revolution that will overthrow the bureaucratic system will be a proletarian revolution.'

But it was two Hungarians who produced the most unsettling and original approach to the rise of the qualified intelligentsia in socialist societies. 'Intellectuals on the Road to Class Power' was written in 1974 by György Konrád and Ivan Szelényi. Konrád was a novelist who had been a social worker, Szelényi a sociologist who had edited a professional magazine and been sacked for attempting to publish a genuine account of factory life.[21]

Konrád and Szelényi thought they knew the name of the exploiting class. It was the intelligentsia itself. The conflict between the old post-Stalinist political élites and the stratum that had kept them in power had been won by the intellectuals in a very real way. They had become the Party.

Property relations were not a 'supra-historical absolute', the two Hungarians repeated. The right to control redistribution of wealth could matter more. Under capitalism, it had been the possession of capital which gave the title to undertake redistribution. Socialism, however, was a system of '*rational* redistribution', which conferred this power upon a corps of planners and savants. Konrád and Szelényi insisted that there were many forms of ownership which did not involve private property, and accordingly many ruling classes in history which had not been proprietors. They raised the shaky definition of the 'Asian Mode of Production', a phrase used by Marx with cheerful inconsequence to describe societies which he supposed (wrongly, as it turned out) to have supported ruling classes without the institution of private property. The implication of the 'Asian Mode' was that class conflict could exist even when private property did not. This of course directly contradicted the Soviet dogma of the non-antagonistic nature of contradictions under socialism. Konrád and Szelényi observed that a remarkable number of Soviet students of early Chinese economics had been shot.

'Intellectuals on the Road' suggested that a class could perfectly well form around ownership based on life tenancy rather than property. A local Party secretary took a disproportionate share of the social product by virtue of his rank, not as a property-owner. In effect, the authors were describing a society much like that of Kuroń and Modzelewski, in which the workers were exploited by a ruling class that controlled the collective property, with the difference that the composition of this ruling class had changed.

The idea of some irreconcilable contradiction between Communism and the intelligentsia was quite wrong, the two Hungarians went on. Bolshevism had been set up by intellectuals for intellectuals, as Lenin's decision to go for a small, highly trained vanguard party of professional revolutionaries rather than a mass membership revealed. 'The Bolshevik programme relieves the intellectuals of the need to represent the working class, and shows the most direct road to power.' In fact, 'the ruling Communist Parties have a dual class base. They are at the same time mass parties of the intellectual class and cadre parties of the working class.'[22]

These summaries give an idea of the debate about the sociology of modern eastern Europe, a debate which has been in progress ever since Trotsky's first fiery attacks on 'Thermidorian bureaucracies' less than twenty years after the October Revolution, and which shows no signs of reaching a conclusion. How do such ideas apply to developments in Poland?

At first sight, Poland seems to derogate from each model in turn. With 85 per cent of its agriculture in private hands, the antagonism between state and peasantry is real enough. All the promising challenges to the political bureaucracy flung down by the 'experts' or the 'technocrats' or whatever they are named have come to nothing, and it should be added that the size of the Party apparatus has steadily declined over the years since 1956 rather than increased.* The proportion of people with higher education in the apparatus has climbed steeply, but nobody in Poland – after the display of economic illiteracy in the late 1970s – could possibly claim that the intellectuals were acceding to class power.

Kuroń and Modzelewski, who were writing from their own national experience, were broadly right when they predicted that change would come from the rebellion of the workers against the central bureaucracy. Yet the attitude of the Polish workers in 1980–81 has not been remarkably revolutionary. For one thing, the 'self-limiting revolution' has not overthrown the central political bureaucracy and its system, but has agreed on certain conditions to keep it in place. For another, although the working class finally understood itself as an independent class in 1980, it at once put its strength at the service of other social groups, of 'the nation' as a whole.

This moderation did not arise from any great changes in the composition of the Polish working class. Much has been said about the dissolution of the 'classic proletariat' and the rise of a highly qualified, white-coated and perhaps even white-collared labour force. But anybody looking at the thousands of shipyard workers on strike at Gdańsk, with their worn clothes, their bad teeth, their monumental solidarity and patience, could only recognize a 'classic proletariat' of a kind increasingly rare in western Europe. And this, it was necessary to remember, was among the best-rewarded and most privileged work-forces in Poland.

The Polish workers won their chance of seizing class power and declined it in favour of a less oppressive, more responsive system of exploitation. That is one way of looking at what happened at Gdańsk. But did they therefore usher another group, perhaps the intellectuals, through the door of power in front of them? It is a view shared by Polish ultra-leftists and foreign sceptics. Six years before, Konrád and Szelényi had suggested that the intellectuals would need the backing of the workers to make it to the top, just as the bourgeoisie had been obliged to rely upon the plebs to overthrow feudalism: 'The intellectual class will only be able to ... acquire class power if it permits some of the marginal intellectuals to articulate the interests of the working class ... Strategically, the interests of the working class and the technocracy lead in different directions, but in their contest with the élite, they are in tactical alliance.'[23] Were the K OR militants, after all, only just such a group of 'marginal intellectuals' mobilizing the workers in order to use them as cannon-fodder on behalf of their own class?

* The ratio of Party members to Party officials rose from about 100:1 in 1956 to 270:1 in 1970. Gierek's reorganization of local government in 1975 still further reduced the apparatus. See Jane Cave, in *Soviet Studies* (Glasgow), Vol. 33, January 1981.

These are uneasy thoughts. They were certainly not the thoughts of the Polish intellectuals in 1980, who joyfully accepted the leadership of the workers in this latest rebellion against the ruling élite. And that acceptance, a resignation – however temporary – from the idea that it is the educated minority which leads the revolutionary march, was the Polish expression of a loss of political confidence which had afflicted intellectuals in both halves of Europe during the past twelve years. The year of 1968 was a grand caesura not only in the experience of Polish students or Czech writers. Its failures in their own countries affected also the left, especially the young in the universities, in France, West Germany, Italy and Britain.

For all of them, the ideas of 1968 had been in a sense the last expression of 'vanguardism'. At the international level, especially in the West, it had been believed that the liberation struggles of oppressed millions throughout the world could be won by the insurrection of committed intellectuals in the *métropoles*, the imperialist heartlands. In the national focus, there was a trust that the fight begun by the capture of universities could lead by a 'long march through the institutions' to the defeat of late-capitalism and the emancipation of the anaesthetized masses. This was an ancient view of revolution, reaching back to the experiences of nineteenth-century France and beyond. It was a view that Lenin had only adopted to describe how an aware intellectual nucleus could break through the 'trade union consciousness' of the workers.

After 1968, the intellectuals of the European left suffered a deep and lasting loss of self-confidence, accompanied by a returning respect for that power of organized labour they had once dismissed as 'integrated'. In Britain, the 1970s became a decade of trade union militancy unknown for forty years; in France, the veterans of 1968 took their scars into the Communist Party; in Poland, the workers' revolt of December 1970 changed all perspectives. The appearance of KOR in 1976 institutionalized the opposition intellectuals' new humility which was in turn expressed in action in 1980. The workers now carry the banner; wherever they lead, we shall follow and assist.

Perhaps. At the time of writing, there are small signs that the initiative is beginning to pass out of the hands of the working class again. The workers' decision to limit their revolution was a decision to put patriotism, the national interest, above class interest. They did not wish to provoke Soviet intervention and their instinct was to rally and unite Polish society rather than to split it further by taking power as a class.

The workers thus created a vacuum of power, but they did not fill it. Inevitably, some other section of society will do so and the probability that this will be the intelligentsia, the 'qualified', is very high indeed. If the Polish experiment is left to develop, the Party will probably reduce its size and scope to that of a re-politicized force detached from government, administration and economic management which expresses its 'leading role' through guidance and persuasion. The door to power for the non-Party intelligentsia will then swing wide open. Whether as a class or as a stratum, it is impossible to suppose that the intelligentsia will not pass through it.

Chapter Eight

Into Unexplored Territory

Truces and Crises: The First Six Months of 1981

The ceremony under the crosses at Gdańsk in December 1980 was not, after all, the inauguration of a new epoch of partnership between the state and Solidarity. A year after the first strikes of 1980, nobody could yet be certain when or where the Polish lava-flow would come to rest, or what structures could be built upon it with any chance of survival, and the strains and contradictions apparent in late 1980 were continuing to work themselves out. All institutions and relationships, all claims to authority, were tested and weighed. This had diverse results. The spirit of 'renewal' soaked deeper into the public consciousness, but the crime rate rose sensationally. Economic dislocation and shortages grew steadily worse, but many Poles found that neighbours and workmates became more accommodating, less competitive.

The broad rhythm of political events that had been established in 1980 carried through into 1981. Twice more, in February and at the end of March, Poland reached the outskirts of a civil battlefield between the government and the new unions, and the second of these crises brought back the threat of Soviet military intervention. Twice more, conflict was called off at the last moment rather than resolved, and was followed by periods of calm, self-restraint and optimism. But then, gradually, the pressures would again accumulate until they were discharged by a provocative act on the part of the authorities or by some intemperate move undertaken by a local Solidarity branch.

By late May, although there was no sign that this rhythm was coming to an end, the music began to change key. The government began, if not to win these battles, at least not to lose all of them. The negotiators for Solidarity and other protesting groups frequently left the table with much less than they had asked for, sometimes because they had voluntarily brought down their price, sometimes because they had been out-manoeuvred. Several of the important political provisions of the Gdańsk Agreement had still not been fulfilled by the time the emergency Ninth Congress of the PUWP met in July; there was no law guaranteeing independent trade unions and the right to strike, and no law to control censorship. A handful of political offenders, mostly from the Confederation of Independent Poland (KPN), were released and then detained once more as their trial dragged on with many long adjournments.

In December 1980, the régime had been reassured by the atmosphere of the ceremonies along the Baltic coast and by the 'reasonable' new attitude of Wałęsa and his Catholic advisers; it saw no reason to hurry over the fulfilment of the Gdańsk Agreement. In consequence, January produced a sudden rush of conflicts, all arising from grievances that might have been defused if they had been handled in time. Peasants at Rzeszów, in the south-east, began a sit-in to press for recognition of Rural Solidarity. Students at Łódź began their own occupation strike at the university. But the most serious dispute followed the government's announcement that the economic crisis made it impossible to fulfil the understanding in the Gdańsk text that all Saturdays would be work-free. Brief strikes took place in many Polish towns, and there were signs that the Solidarity leaders were not in complete control. On 27 January, when the entire Bielsko-Biała region embarked on an indefinite general strike to secure the dismissal of local officials, Wałęsa was unable to persuade the factories to return to work.

Solidarity took the free-Saturdays question to within a few days of a one-hour general strike throughout the country, but on 31 January a compromise was reached which obliged the Poles to work for only one Saturday in each month. A few days later, the local government team at Bielsko-Biała resigned and the strikers resumed work. Another dangerous strike at Jelenia Góra also demanded local government changes of personnel, and – in a protest against official privileges which was copied all over Poland – insisted on the transfer of a police hospital to the public health service. In both cases, the government tried to hold the position with threats. It talked of declaring a state of emergency at Bielsko-Biała, and warned the strikers at Jelenia Góra that there would be no strike pay for those who joined unauthorized or wildcat protests. Kania accused Solidarity of behaving like a political party, and on 8 February it was announced that an investigation into KOR's 'anti-state activities' was under way. Such gestures only inflamed the situation, and their failure accelerated the régime's loss of control.

A new course, or a new man, had to be found. On 9 February, the Eighth Plenum met and agreed that General Wojciech Jaruzelski, minister of defence, should at once replace Pińkowski as prime minister. The Poles were startled and impressed. The uniform and the medals still carried heavy patriotic authority, faintly recalling the mighty aura of the *Wódz* (Leader) that had surrounded Marshal Piłsudski. Moreover, Jaruzelski was well liked. It was known that he had refused to use Polish armed forces against the strikers in the summer. It was also known, though to fewer, that he had been deported into the Soviet interior as a forced labourer in 1939. He was a national Communist if ever there was one. But his appointment had the air of a final chance (as Wałęsa himself put it). Jaruzelski looked like the last stop before the abyss.

A grand relaxation gradually set in. Jaruzelski called for a ninety-day truce from strikes, and Solidarity gave him a cautiously encouraging answer. He brought in Mieczysław Rakowski, the editor who had argued so desperately that the Party should lead and not oppose the workers' movement, and put him in the hottest of all seats: deputy prime minister in charge of relations with the trade unions. The Jelenia Góra strike was settled; the student protest – which after smouldering at Łódź for a month suddenly flared across the whole nation – was ended on a fairly equal compromise. On 19 February, the government even managed to end the peasants' sit-in at Rzeszów without actually promising them a trade union of their own.

But the problem of Rural Solidarity remained. The régime, probably under Soviet pressure, was resolved not to register the union. Solidarity, and multiplying thousands of private farmers, were equally resolved that the union must be legalized. Most serious of all, the peasant stalemate brought a change in the attitude of the Church.

Until mid-February, the episcopate under Cardinal Wyszyński had worked hard to mediate in these conflicts and even to moderate – partly through the Primate's influence on Wałęsa – the positions that Solidarity was adopting. It was Bishop Dąbrowski, secretary of the Episcopal Conference (and a member of the 'Gang of Four'), who negotiated the settlement at Bielsko-Biała.

In industrial disputes, the Church could perform a role of buffer which was invaluable to the government. But the Church expected in return that the régime would accept the demands of the private peasants, the class to which above all the Catholic hierarchy felt bound. The Rzeszów occupation, a much more pious affair than Gdańsk, had an altar in the hall and was equipped with priests and confessional boxes. Catholic support for the occupation reached a new climax on 6 February when Cardinal Wyszyński assured a Rural Solidarity delegation that he fully supported their campaign for registration. When, four days later, the Supreme Court rejected the union's appeal, the episcopate issued an angry statement affirming the right of private farmers to professional associations. Regarding the court decision as a stroke of bad faith, the Church now refused to pull any more of the government's chestnuts out of the fire and left Jaruzelski to face the workers on his own.

Jaruzelski's appointment marked a sharp and original swerve in strategy by the régime. There had always been talk about separating Party and government. Kania now tried to bring this about – but with an unexpected content. He recognized that the crisis could be mastered only if the government, which had to deal with the unions, won back some public sympathy. It might be possible to achieve this if the Party reserved for itself the unpopular duty of challenging and opposing Solidarity, while the government was seen to pursue its own, more liberal policies. The government would be able to negotiate with the unions uncompromised by responsibility for the much tougher attitudes struck by the Party.*

In this spirit, Barcikowski told one group of Party members that they should not be afraid of using 'polarizing methods', while Żabiński suggested that the Party should no longer worry about its popularity. In the sense that this policy implied a much more politicized and militant Party, it had an appeal to the hard-line elements grouped around Stefan Olszowski. But in a wider way, it began to retreat from the Party's direct leading role in central and local government and in the economy which Olszowski could not approve of. Moreover, the vigorously democratic movement developing at the PUWP grass-roots during the preparations for the emergency Ninth Congress suggested that the Party might not remain committed to 'unpopular' attitudes for much longer.

It was in any case not long before disputes broke out again. As at Jelenia Góra, the special hospitals reserved for the police and employees of the Ministry of the Interior continued to be a focus of resentment. A protest at Łódź against the firing of several Solidarity workers from one of these clinics ended with a one-hour general strike in the whole city on 10 March. The transfer to public use of police hospitals was one of a long list of demands raised two days later at Radom, where the workers also insisted on the removal of officials responsible for the brutal repressions there after the 1976 strikes. A rally was held in Warsaw to commemorate the student protest of March 1968 (an obvious challenge to General Moczar, now back in the Politburo) while the Party set out on its 'unpopular' course by attempting to bring charges of political sedition against Jacek Kuroń and Adam Michnik. The coal miners of Wałbrzych retorted with a threat to strike if the two KOR members were arrested, and Michnik announced that he was ignoring a summons to present himself at the public prosecutor's office.

---

*I have borrowed many ideas here from the paper 'Auto-Limiting Revolution', delivered by Jadwiga Staniszkis to the British Association of Soviet and East European Studies at Cambridge in March 1981.

One of the drawbacks of the 'unpopularity' strategy was that almost nobody knew it existed. An essential point was that the security police were supposed to be seen as under the command of the Party, so that their activities were not blamed on the government. Unfortunately, Kania was reluctant to spell this out in public. Thus when on a Tuesday the prime minister assured Lech Wałęsa that no further measures against KOR were in view, and on Thursday Michnik was taken to the prosecutor's office, told that he was only at provisional liberty and forbidden to leave Warsaw, the result was damage to General Jaruzelski's credibility.

On 19 March, a force of two hundred police burst into the prefecture at Bydgoszcz and used their clubs to drive out a group of Rural Solidarity members who had begun a sit-in a few days before. In the corridor and court-yard, the police apparently played their old game of making prisoners 'run the gauntlet', and twenty-seven union members were injured. Three were taken to hospital, including a member of Solidarity's national committee.

The police action at Bydgoszcz was an act of provocative lunacy. Whether it was a deliberate provocation engineered from above cannot yet be known. The situation in the prefecture was that the occupiers had been holding discussions with the regional council, in the presence of deputy premier Stanisław Mach. The council then broke off the meeting, over the protests of the Rural Solidarity demonstrators, and the deputy prefect then appears to have sent for the police to clear the building.

Posters showing pictures of bleeding Solidarity members now appeared all over Poland. Solidarity issued a national strike alert and demanded the punishment of those guilty for the police action, which it described as a 'blatant provocation aimed at the government of General Jaruzelski'. Wałęsa cancelled a visit to France and rushed down to Bydgoszcz, now swarming with motorized riot police.

There followed a week of desperate tension, in which Wałęsa and moderate elements in the régime like Rakowski struggled to find a settlement which both the union militants and the disciplinarians in the Politburo could accept. Meanwhile the 'Soyuz 81' manoeuvres of the Warsaw Pact, taking place in Poland, the GDR, Czechoslovakia and the Soviet Union, were prolonged beyond their term.

Western fears of a military intervention at once revived. The EEC heads of government, who were meeting at Maastricht, warned that Poland should be allowed to solve its own difficulties. On 26 March, the White House spoke of 'indications that the Polish authorities may be preparing to use force ... We are similarly concerned that the Soviet Union may intend to undertake repressive action in Poland.'

With the greatest difficulty, Kania and Jaruzelski headed off a predictable attempt by Olszowski and his Politburo allies to call a state of emergency. But in spite of a meeting between the prime minister and Cardinal Wyszyński, negotiations broke down on 26 March. The following day, there was a four-hour general strike throughout Poland, the biggest industrial disruption in Poland since the Second World War, and Solidarity went ahead with plans to begin an unlimited general strike on Tuesday, 31 March.

For the second time in four months, the statesmen of the entire world were now huddled over the latest bulletins from Poland. Pope John Paul II appealed for compromise in the spirit of Gdańsk. President Reagan proclaimed that any attack on Polish liberties, whether it came from within or without, would have disastrous results for East–West relations. Even the *People's Daily* in Peking advised the Polish workers to be prudent. The Soviet Union had remained remarkably silent until this point, but on Sunday 29 March *Tass* published a terrifying 'account' of how Solidarity was launching a putsch by blocking highways, occupying telephone exchanges, and seizing a television transmitter.

The PUWP Central Committee met the same day. For the first time, new members were able to voice the opinions of the rank-and-file movement now spreading through the Party base; the result was that this Ninth Plenum, a moment of great danger for Kania and the renewal programme, turned into his overwhelming victory. After a barrage of protests against their hard-line position, Olszowski, Grabski and Roman Ney all tendered their resignations from the Politburo. These were refused, and the existing Politburo was given a new vote of confidence, but the Ninth Plenum weakened Kania's rivals at a critical moment. He could now afford to seek another compromise settlement with Solidarity.

Rakowski and Wałęsa had already roughed out a formula. Seven more hours of talks on 30 March produced a provisional agreement. The government would investigate the Bydgoszcz incident and punish those responsible for a police action which, it conceded, had been ill-judged. More important, the government declared that Rural Solidarity could now act as if it were legal, pending a final decision on registration.

The general strike was called off, and the crisis subsided. But these compromise terms provoked the most violent backlash within Solidarity that Wałęsa had yet had to face. The union's branches had understood this as the decisive contest; at Bydgoszcz, the government had shown unmistakably that Solidarity would be crushed if it did not at last use all the huge industrial strength at its command. The preparations for the general strike had been elaborate – and almost elated; this was the battlefield on which the forces in the Party leadership which still resisted the application of Gdańsk would be beaten for good. Now Wałęsa and his experts – they took much of the blame – were accused of selling out. The government had not been firmly nailed to anything. The punishment of those guilty at Bydgoszcz, the registration of Rural Solidarity, the liberation of all remaining political prisoners – all remained in the category of requests to be merely re-examined.

But the storm slowly blew itself out. Karol Modzelewski resigned as Solidarity's spokesman. The victims of Bydgoszcz protested from their hospital beds that 'Wałęsa has bungled. We can compromise on supplies of onions, but not over spilt blood.' Most poignant of all, the Lenin Shipyard dismissed Anna Walentynowicz from her post as delegate to Solidarity's national committee because she had opposed Wałęsa and pleaded that the strike should take place. Both Wałęsa and Andrzej Gwiazda offered their resignations at moments in this bitter post-mortem but were persuaded to withdraw them.

It gradually became apparent that the Ninth Plenum had been more important than the 30 March agreement. Kania felt secure enough to take further controversial decisions. The talks about Rural Solidarity turned out to be in earnest, and the union was finally registered on 12 May. Solidarity began to publish its own weekly journal in early April, and on 6 May the government provisionally accepted Solidarity's right to a ration of radio and television time. In the familiar way, a crisis was followed by calm, conciliatory weeks.

The attitude of the Soviet leaders, though hard to construe, made Kania's life no more difficult over this period. Apart from the outburst by *Tass* at the height of the Bydgoszcz tension, Moscow had not interfered. At the 26th Congress of the Communist Party of the Soviet Union, which opened in late February, the Russians had used customary clichés to pledge their support to the Polish comrades in their struggle against difficult economic and political problems. A meeting between Kania, Jaruzelski and the Soviet leaders at the end of the Congress gave rise, through a mistranslation, to the idea that the USSR had asked the Poles to 'reverse the course of events', but in reality Brezhnev had only expressed the hope that they could 'master' that course. Western anxiety remained acute, however, until Brezhnev visited the Congress of the Czechoslovak Communist Party and in a speech on 7 May observed that 'the Polish Communists will, one must assume, be able to preserve the cause of socialism'. Whatever one made of this, it was not in itself a threat of intervention. The same evening, the end of the Soyuz 81 manoeuvres was announced.

Solidarity was no longer the aspect of change in Poland which concerned the Soviet leaders most. As the preparations for the Polish emergency Party Congress, now set to open on 12 July, went ahead, the rank-and-file movement within the Party was evolving into a major political force. Some twenty 'horizontal structures' had now established themselves and on 15 April they held a conference at the movement's birthplace of Toruń. The rank-and-file movement was already a force both in the Party commission preparing the congress and, as the Ninth Plenum had shown, in the Central Committee, and the leadership felt obliged to send Zdzisław Kurowski, a senior secretary, as their representative to the Toruń meeting.

The rank-and-file movement proposed a Second Front in the whole Polish revolution. At this point, it was pursuing a democratic Party structure and a complete renewal of the apparatus. But its long-term political significance was far wider. In the first place, the Ninth Congress would be invited to transform the PUWP into a Communist Party of a new type, in which the leading apparatus was directly controlled by the base. Even more important, the movement wanted horizontal organization to be accepted as a permanent feature. This did not merely imply breaking the vertical chain of command. It meant that 'tendencies' would be permitted, ideological factions. The real reason for the appearance of a horizontal formation was that its members disagreed with the majority 'party line' worked out by the official instances of the Party. A Communist Party which not only tolerated but actually institutionalized minority opposition would – if it were allowed to evolve – be something entirely new in the Warsaw Pact systems. Even Dubček had never ventured so far.

The second significance of the movement was that it would, if successful, at last give an essentially political process a political form. In the long run, a genuinely democratic Communist Party would take over from the independent trade unions the creation and execution of a national programme of renewal and reform. Solidarity would then be released from the impossible tension set up by its attempt to load political change on to the vehicle of a trade union.

The Toruń meeting of 'horizontal' Party delegations from all over Poland deeply perturbed the Soviet Politburo and brought to an end the temporary restraint of the Soviet media. Until April, there had been signs that the Soviet leadership had been trying to rationalize its own reluctance to take action, suggesting for example that the Polish working class was historically backward, a 'semi-proletariat' still influenced by the idle, anarchic life-style of the peasantry from which it had sprung. A surgical slash had been enough to rescue the 'healthy' mass of the Czechoslovak working class from a small clique of counter-revolutionaries, but a problem of history, the under-development of a whole class, could hardly be solved in the same way.[1]

This eccentric but promising line of thought was not helpful with the rank-and-file problem in the PUWP. Mikhail Suslov, the elderly custodian of ideological propriety in Moscow, visited Warsaw on 23 April for urgent discussions with Kania and his colleagues. The day after his return, *Tass* published a sharp attack on 'revisionist elements' within the Polish Party who were trying to undermine its leading role. For a moment, the limits of Soviet tolerance appeared with unusual clarity. Some loosening of Party structure and practice would have to take place, but if the entire Central Committee were replaced at the congress by unknown militants and if 'horizontalism' was not strictly controlled, the Soviet leadership would withdraw its confidence from Stanisław Kania's ruling group.

In the early months of the Polish crisis, the Soviet press had made the error of praising 'positive elements' in Poland: loyal workers who stayed in the CRZZ unions, 'healthy' meetings of war veterans, and so on. Later, Soviet journalists displayed more tact. But a nucleus of 'healthy forces' did form. A club for 'Marxist intellectuals' was set up on 16 December under the name Warsaw 80. This group soon spawned another outfit known as the 'Grunwald Patriotic Union',* which seemed a pure throwback to the anti-Semitic and ultra-nationalist line of 1967–8. Grunwald reserved its special detestation for students and for KOR; on several occasions it denounced KOR as a 'Zionist' body and demanded trade unions 'for Poles only'. Although Grunwald was furiously attacked by Party reformers, including the regenerate Moczar, it continued to agitate during the early summer of 1981 against the whole renewal process and the 'liberal Mafia' in the Party. In May, Grunwald claimed implausibly to have 100,000 supporters. Other centres of conservative opposition to Kania included the Ministry of Defence daily paper *Żolnierz Wolności* (*Soldier of Freedom*), which had also been a propaganda instrument for the national-authoritarian line in 1968.

A much more dangerous 'healthy force' appeared on 28 May, when the Katowice Forum, a group of conservative Party members in Upper Silesia, issued a long declaration condemning the Kania leadership for tolerating 'revisionism' and 'counter-revolution'. Similar Forums soon appeared in other cities. A connection with Stefan Olszowski was suspected, but could not be demonstrated; the declaration was given wide publicity, possibly at Kania's suggestion, and provoked a wave of loyal counter-declarations

---

* At the Battle of Grunwald in 1410, the Poles defeated the Teutonic Knights and finally broke their power.

from Party branches. But the Katowice document, grimly orthodox and avoiding the anti-Semitic excesses of its predecessors, left a residue of fear behind it. On the day of its publication, Cardinal Wyszyński died in Warsaw. Poland had lost the man who had protected the nation for over thirty years. His funeral was vast and impassioned, but the crowds in the pouring rain felt bitterly alone in a country where the enemy within was growing stronger.

No link could be proved, although many were suspected, between the Soviet Union and these opposition centres, and the identity of the vandals who began to deface Soviet war memorials throughout Poland also remained obscure. But the USSR forbore to apply pressure on Poland's weakest point: the economy. Essential supplies of Soviet iron ore and petroleum products (still cheaper than oil at world prices) were maintained, apparently without fresh political conditions. Although consumer goods in the Soviet Union were very short, deliveries of food increased and credits were lengthened (the Polish government simply passed most of this hard currency to the West, to pay interest on short-term debts). But the Polish economy continued to run down, and in spite of the introduction of rationing, acute shortages of meat, fats, oil, sugar, chocolate and many other goods condemned Polish shoppers to stand in line for as long as four hours a day.

No coherent plan for economic reform or recovery had emerged, let alone been adopted. Solidarity and the government agreed in general terms about what should be done: enterprises should be more independent and to some degree under workers' self-management, prices would have to be totally reformed with some food costs increasing by over 100 per cent (to be cushioned by income supplements for the lower-paid), and there must be even more generous terms for private farmers. As firms rationalized their costs, there would inevitably be widespread unemployment, but Solidarity economists suggested that industry might be required to retain most of the employees for a transition period and pass on the cost in higher prices. But the government was unable to decide upon any action before the Ninth Congress in July, and many factories, now effectively controlled by Solidarity committees, began to make their own arrangements with clients and suppliers and to ignore the paralysed state economic bureaucracy. Solidarity radicals launched a movement to establish workers' self-government without waiting for the régime to make up its mind. Poland's financial position stabilized slightly on 27 April, when representatives of fifteen creditor governments agreed in Paris to re-schedule Polish debts, allowing an eight-year repayment delay on debts amounting to some $2·5 billion which were falling due in 1981. But private bankers, owed some $2·4 billions in the short term, met strong American opposition to a postponement. Poland's total hard-currency indebtedness now stood at about $25 billion.

In June, the PUWP began the final preparations for the congress. In free and secret elections, district conferences elected new local Party committees and delegates to the congress. There was a general massacre of the ruling apparatus, but – to the surprise of Polish observers – the 'horizontalist' radicals were not very successful either. The conferences voted against both extremes, and also against the towns and factories which had traditionally dominated Party machines. The result was an inrush of unknown and inexperienced men and women, committed to wholesale reform of the Party and a purge of its leading cadres, but without clear links to any faction or programme. Another result, equally unexpected, was that remarkably few workers were elected; in many industrial districts, the new committee and the list of congress delegates had a majority of representatives from the countryside. (Much the same was happening in Solidarity, now electing its own permanent district authorities: the workers, who had led the whole movement in August, were reluctant to stand for election and preferred to vote for administrators, office workers and intellectuals.)

Soviet anxiety about what was happening to the Party could no longer be restrained. On 5 June, a long, imploring letter arrived in Warsaw from the Central Committee in Moscow, hinting that the congress should be postponed and that Kania and Jaruzelski – both named in the letter – had proved incapable of leading Poland out of the crisis. The result, however, was to rally the PUWP around Kania. An emergency Eleventh Plenum opened in Warsaw on 9 June, at which Tadeusz Grabski proposed that Kania and the Politburo should resign. But although a majority of the Central Committee could expect nothing but elimination from power if the congress went ahead, a surge of angry patriotism and Kania's own skilful manoeuvring beat off Grabski's attack and confirmed the existing leadership.

The Soviet letter, in the short term, seemed to have failed in its objects. But although Kania survived and the Ninth Congress was not put off, the shock of the letter – one of the angriest messages ever sent by Moscow to a fraternal Party – instantly sobered the behaviour of the PUWP. The 'horizontal' movement lost its cohesion. Kania, who toured the country addressing conference after conference, was able to achieve something which seemed impossible before the letter: the election of all but two members of the existing Politburo as delegates to the congress. He understood the irrational importance of continuity – familiar faces at the top – to Brezhnev and his elderly colleagues in the Kremlin, and he used all the fresh authority he had won at the Eleventh Plenum to give them this reassurance.

The last weeks of June were again tense. Although there were no more military manoeuvres of a threatening kind,* and no further Soviet political intervention beyond a brief visit by Andrei Gromyko, the foreign minister, on 26 June, everybody in Poland was aware that the invasion of Czechoslovakia in 1968 had been timed to prevent the meeting of the Fourteenth Congress of the Czechoslovak Communist Party which – like the Ninth Congress of the PUWP – was to carry out irreversible democratic reforms within the Party. But on 14 July, the congress delegations gathered as planned at Warsaw, in the windowless white hall which lies under Stalin's gift to the Polish people, the Palace of Culture. What they did there was without precedent in the history of the ruling Communist Parties of the Warsaw Pact. The delegates voted by free and secret ballot; they upset the agenda and made a new one; they attacked some of their leaders and quarrelled over others; they refused Kania's request that they should begin the congress by voting directly on his candidature for the post of First Secretary; finally, they broke with the past in the most expressive way they knew by throwing out almost the whole apparatus and central representation of the PUWP. Seven out of every eight members of the old Central Committee were not re-elected to the new Committee which emerged from the Ninth Congress; among the casualties were seven out of the eleven members of the Politburo and – so great was the distrust of the provincial apparatus – forty out of forty-nine district secretaries. The new Party statutes, approved in outline, limited the time a Party official could occupy Party or government office to ten years, guaranteed free nomination and secret ballot in all Party elections, stated the right of Party minorities to express dissenting views (although their actions must support majority decisions) and gave the congress delegates a mandate until the next congress – in other words, the right to recall the elected leadership if the delegates thought fit at any time in the next four years.

The new Central Committee was in some ways a random choice. Everyone in Poland (including Solidarity) was now using an ultra-democratic voting system which required a successful candidate to win 50 per cent plus one of the total vote. When factions are competing, the result – as the district Party conferences had shown – tends to be the defeat of the

---

* American estimates in June 1981 were that the Warsaw Pact exercises in previous months had already allowed the Soviet forces to set up a communication network in Poland sufficient for an army of 300,000 men.

best-known figures on each extreme. Among the victims of the Ninth Congress on the hard-line side were Grabski, Żabiński, Stanisław Kociołek (the Warsaw secretary), and Lucjan Czubiński, the chief prosecutor, but there also fell on the reforming wing Tadeusz Fiszbach, Józef Klasa (who had been Party spokesman), Roman Ney, the old warrior and intriguer Mieczysław Moczar, and even Mieczysław Jagielski, the negotiator of the Gdańsk Agreement. Kania stood for the post of First Secretary against Kazimierz Barcikowski (such an open contest had been unknown in ruling Communist Parties since Lenin's time) and won comfortably.

The new Politburo numbered fifteen. Only four – Kania, Jaruzelski, Olszowski and Barcikowski – were old hands. But out of unknown newcomers and cabinet ministers, the Central Committee managed to put together a Politburo which seemed to be evenly balanced between conservatives and reformers. One of the newcomers, Zofia Grzyb, was a Solidarity member, and so was about one in five of the Central Committee. And yet, for all this spectacular change of people and style, the congress failed to re-animate the Party. The new Central Committee proved passive, apparently unable to take decisive action for a *rapprochement* with Solidarity or to devise a coherent programme for economic recovery. The leadership turned out to be as divided and irresolute as its predecessor, and by late 1981 the vacuum of political power in Poland was gaping more widely than ever.

As the crisis deepened, Solidarity began to abandon some of the basic assumptions underlying the Gdańsk Agreement of 1980. Then, the workers and their advisers had insisted that they were forming a trade union without political ambitions and had refused to accept co-responsibility for the economy – offered to them by the régime in the guise of workers' self-management. In this view, the existing Party and government would retain the political initiative and the formal monopoly of political power, while Solidarity guarded the achievements of Gdańsk and the interests of the working class. But by the summer of 1981, after a year of confrontations and economic decline, it was obvious that this loose dualism would not work. The Ninth Congress had failed to resolve the paralysis of the régime, and Solidarity decided that it must use its own strength to bring about economic reform by establishing radical workers' self-management at factory and office level (after bitter official resistance, a compromise Self-Management Law was passed by the Sejm in September 1981). At the same time, Solidarity's own first congress, held at Gdańsk in September and October, laid down a programme for the union with plainly political elements, like the call for free elections at local and Sejm level. This reluctant move to fill the political vacuum reflected calls from all sections of Polish society for some new form of authority and leadership, often projected as a 'government of national salvation' which would include elements of Solidarity, the Church and the existing government.

Hindsights

It will be hard to pull down the monument at Gdańsk. For a stranger, that is the only certainty about Poland's future. But Polish intellectuals, in their steely way, are also certain that there will never be a retreat back down the path travelled since August 1980. The new perceptions about the nature of a free Poland are a priceless and permanent gain, even if they cannot be used for a generation. If the Russians come, they will have come too late.

Somewhere along that path, the Poles passed the skull of the Prague Spring. They paid it little attention – too little. To say that the two cases are unrelated because one reform was distributed from above and the other was carried upwards in the arms of a whole people is facile. There is much for the Poles to learn from that defeat in Czechoslovakia. It is nearer the truth to say that the Poles were determined not to let the possibility of a Soviet veto occupy more than the corner of their eye. They were strongly disinclined to see their experiment as one in a series of rebellions against the political models of the Warsaw Pact states. Such a view opened upon discouraging prospects. They preferred to raise a fence of nationalism between themselves and the recent history of their neighbours. This was a Polish matter, they said, answering to their own experience alone.

It was also the culmination of a long failure. Polish Communism, after thirty-five years, had not worn a real foothold into the nation. It had never, except for rare and brief intervals, been generally regarded as an authentic or normal force of government. For much longer periods it had been accepted as a problem which could be greatly mitigated but not removed, like a drought. Never the object of affection, the Party steadily lost its power to instil fear and to command respect. In the mid-1950s and again in the late 1970s, the character of the Party's rule had become so grossly contradictory to the development of Polish society that it became a positive danger to the stability of the nation. From being a drought, it had turned into an affliction like foot-and-mouth disease which required instant and dramatic action.

The conventional explanation for this historic failure was that success could never have been expected. How should an intensely Catholic and nationalist people with a long-lasting dislike of Russian power reconcile itself

274 The Polish August

to the rule of an extremely small Communist minority installed, in the last analysis, by Russian soldiers? But this was much too easy a dismissal. Although the obstacles were huge, there were also factors that should have helped the Polish Communist to dispel the cloud under which their power was born. The mood in Poland after the war was certainly revolutionary. Many Polish Socialists (PPS), who were 'authentic' enough, were ready to co-operate and even to fuse with the Communists on the basis of Gomułka's programme. His 'Polish Road' to socialism was at least winning respect by the time he was deposed in 1948.

There is much to be said for the argument that October 1956 was the great missed chance for Polish Communism. Gomułka had come back from prison and broken through the most formidable of all barriers to legitimation; by successfully defying Khrushchev's threats, he had acquired the full credentials of a patriot. He could have gone on to build the most heretical and libertarian kind of socialist régime compatible with a one-party state without fearing Soviet intervention. But he did not. Gomułka would not give the Party the chance to acquire and share the popular confidence he had won for himself. He did not even take the Party back to its spare, more responsive style of 1944–8. The dogmatic over-centralization of all decisions, a Stalinist pattern, was allowed to survive both in government and in the PUWP itself.

But why did successive administrations in Poland commit such political and economic blunders? Why did governments surrounded by such intelligent advisers, and Party committees containing so many good men and women appalled at the waste of their country's resources, address great problems with such dilettantism? Old Cardinal Wyszyński used to speak in his cleric's Latin about the need for *'prudentia gubernativa'*. The imprudence of Poland's civil governors was phenomenal.

One of the arguments of this book is that incompleteness has been a curse of post-war Poland. There is, of course, a strong case for incompleteness in times when the logical consequence of policy is torture and the firing-squad, and Polish politics, however wild in rhetoric, have always been rather merciful by European standards in practice. Public adversaries maintain private contact, and there has been only one major political assassination in the last sixty years; as Czesław Miłosz has remarked, 'some sort of filter mitigates extremes in Poland'. None the less, mildness has its price. Stalinism in Poland was incomplete, bequeathing a gigantic bureaucratic apparatus which had never been terrified into obedience. The reform of 1956 was incomplete, and those who brought it about were neutralized and then persecuted in a compulsive process which did not end until 1968. The Gierek régime promised the usual political détente and new economic model, but gave both projects up when they presented their first difficulties. The collectivization of agriculture was little more than a sham, and yet the régime could never bring itself after 1956 to accept and draw the consequences from the existence of a peasantry farming privately owned land.

The list could go on. Perhaps only two enterprises were carried through to a proper finish. One was the training and equipment of the armed forces during the 1970s. The other was Gomułka's fourteen-year *Westpolitik* designed to secure West German recognition of the Oder–Neisse frontier, which ended in success a few days before he fell.

But the most serious incompleteness of all was that of protest. The 'natural' impetus of 1956, 1970 and indeed of 1980 was to carry on until the régime had been overthrown. Whether the next régime would have been a socialist one is not important for the argument. What mattered was that Poland's 'geopolitical situation', or *'raison d'état'* – in short, the military power of the Soviet Union – created a consensus that these rebellions must be artificially slowed up before they had run their course.

European constitutional tradition, of which Poland is very much aware, distinguishes between a crisis which changes a government and a crisis which ends a whole political era and brings about a new republic. The history of Poland after the war was that of three *Staatskrisen* masquerading as *Regierungskrisen*. Gomułka, Gierek and Kania were all allowed to behave as if the forces which brought them to power had only wished to change a government, a ruling group, rather than the system itself.

From these incompletenesses, and especially from the central aspect of frustrated revolution, intolerable tensions arose. The sociologist Stefan Nowak has described the high incidence of authoritarian and punitive attitudes in Polish society, sure sign of intense collective repression, and observed what he politely describes as 'a great deal of mutual interpersonal aggression' in social dealings.[2] These tensions were accentuated by the thick fog of euphemism, double-talk and sheer illusion generated to conceal such incompletenesses.

The gap between description and reality – the 'sham' nature of everything, so well recorded by that contributor to the DiP report in 1978 – became particularly hard to bear as Poland's enormous post-war expansion of public education began to produce generations of increasingly well-informed and reflective men and women. It should be said, all the same, that there has always been a propensity to cognitive dissonance in Poland, whether it was the illusion of the petty nobility in the sixteenth century who believed themselves the equals of other nobles who possessed a thousand times as much land, or the post-war paranoia about a Jewish population that no longer existed. Even Solidarity, conceived in a rebellion against double lives and evasions, could be perverse in its refusal to recognize its own political nature. This total confusion over what was real and what was not determined the type of opposition which arose in the 1970s and finally brought Poland to a halt in 1980. A socialist revolution, for example, does at least require some basic certainties – about what socialism is, about the attitudes of all social classes, about the strength of the exploiters and their gendarmes – in order to proceed. No such certainties were available in Poland, a society in which by the late 1970s it was not even clear where real power lay.

In this thick darkness, the instinct of most people was simply to grope backwards to the last solid object they could remember touching. In most cases, this was the Church.* Close to it, and reassuringly firm, were the simple monuments of traditional Polish nationalism. It was here, like fugitives feeling their way out of a smoke-filled building, that Poles came together, sensed their collective strength, and re-grouped.

The ground of this *ralliement* was to some extent imaginary, as all such grounds are. The real history of Polish national risings was they had almost all become at the same time desperate internal class struggles between Pole and Pole. The Catholic hierarchy had not always led the nation from among the ranks of working people; it was Cardinal Wyszyński, above all, who had ensured that the Church would never again become identified with a ruling oligarchy. Above all, a national insurrection which – by compact with its opponents – entirely avoided bloodshed and almost entirely choked back hostile words about Russia was without any precedent. The Polish August of 1980 had many aspects of neo-nationalism. But rather than seek more illusions of chauvinist psychedelia, this movement returned to the nation as a place which could be reached by the cold light of common-sense. When the landscape around could be clearly seen, for the first time in more than thirty years, a way forward from nationalism might perhaps be planned.

The most penetrating of all the ideas generated in the opposition of the 1970s was the call to 'self-organization', Kuroń's proposal for a Poland of 'social movements'. It is not always understood that this was not merely a tactic against an authoritarian state or an aspect of Utopian democracy, but a profoundly traditional idea as well. Poland's history since the late

---

* I once asked a Polish friend why he so diligently attended Mass. He answered, 'Where else in Warsaw can you still get pre-war quality?'

eighteenth century had been one of occupation and resistance, under institutions which were sponsored and sometimes staffed by foreigners. A real, authentic, non-illusory Poland only existed where a group of citizens met and took their own decisions.

The most spectacular 'self-organizations' were of course the national conspiracies themselves. Their importance was not just that they collected pikes and muskets, or barricaded the streets of Warsaw. Their mere existence as genuine Polish centres of debate and decision was revolutionary too. The Poles were alert to this distinction between function and structure, and saw the proliferation of 'unofficial' opposition groups and publications as 'self-organizations' in this dual sense. Where such a band of people gathered together, a small space appeared which in this nationalist perspective could reasonably be named 'Poland'.

In 1979, the mass emotions aroused by the Pope's visit were less important politically than the fact that the Catholic population took over from the state the organization and control of all his meetings and processions. The police stayed away; the government provided helicopters and other logistic supports. But it was young people in white-and-yellow armbands who lined streets and held back crowds. The entire nation saw this on television with a pride and excitement difficult to convey to a western society.

The space this time had become infinitely larger. It lasted for only the two weeks of the pilgrimage, but a spontaneous 'social movement' had covered the whole country for the first time. A year later, the men and women of the Baltic cities organized themselves behind the shipyard gates. Presently these new spaces named Poland ran together, and spread out to enclose every town, village and smallholding between the sea and the southern mountains. Those who made this space, and they numbered many millions, intended that this time it would remain open for ever.

Postscript: December 1981

The 'national tragedy', which so many Poles had contrived to ban from their imaginations, took place in the snowy darkness of Sunday, 13 December 1981. General Wojciech Jaruzelski, who had been named first secretary of the P U W P on 18 October, launched a military coup on a scale and with an efficiency and ferocity that nobody had anticipated. Almost the entire leadership of Solidarity was arrested within hours at Gdańsk, where the union's executive had been meeting, and thousands of union militants, intellectuals, journalists, and individuals suspected of liberal views followed them into prison and into detention camps. All trade unions were 'suspended', Solidarity offices throughout Poland were occupied by security forces, and the union's property and files were confiscated.

Before dawn on the same day, General Jaruzelski proclaimed the formation of a Military Council of National Salvation and the existence of a 'state of war' (the Polish constitution does not provide for a state of emergency). All civil liberties were suspended, and certain services, including public transport, were 'conscripted'; disobedience was defined as mutiny, and offenders against martial law faced punishment by military courts empowered to apply the death penalty.

General Jaruzelski also announced the arrest of Edward Gierek and almost all his senior political colleagues from the Party leadership before August 1980. But he asserted in a speech on 13 December that there would be no return to the methods practised before August 1980, and claimed that when order and discipline had been restored, the processes of 'renewal' and economic reform would be continued. His central appeal was to the working-class membership of Solidarity, which he invited to have faith in him and in the proposition that the union was merely being purged of a small group of extremists who were misusing Solidarity for political ends.

The Military Council stated that they had acted to forestall a plot to overthrow Poland's socialist state. But within a few days, as the initial shock of the coup began to wear off, it became apparent that Jaruzelski faced desperate and widespread opposition from the workers, who occupied factories, shipyards, and coal mines and were supported in their opposition by students, who attempted to hold strikes in universities and colleges. Although all communications between Poland and the outside world were temporarily severed, news soon came of fighting in many cities between workers and military-police commandos sent to storm the occupied places of work. On 17 December, Warsaw Radio, controlled by the new régime, admitted that seven miners had been shot and killed at the

Wujek colliery near Katowice. In the days that followed, travellers emerging from Poland brought news suggesting that the fighting – and the killing – had been very much more severe than the régime was conceding. Although the immediate response of Archbishop Glemp and the Pope was to call on both sides to avoid violence, the Episcopate drew up a communiqué on 15 December demanding the release of detainees and the restoration of free trade unions; the communiqué closely followed the demands being made by Solidarity activists who had escaped arrest.

At the end of the first stage of the 'state of war', Jaruzelski had failed to achieve several conditions crucial to its success. The Church had not accepted the need for the coup nor even counselled submission. The workers in many of the big factories and plants, where Solidarity's strength lay, had refused to abandon the union and were putting up a suicidal resistance. Lech Wałęsa – held in custody near Warsaw – was refusing to negotiate with the new régime. Worst of all, Poles had shed Polish blood again for the first time since December 1970.

This December coup brought to a terrible end the new phase of political struggle that had opened in the late summer of 1981, when the Solidarity congress had at last recognized that Party and state could not control the disintegration of their authority. A political vacuum existed; until it was filled, there was no chance that any programme of democratic reform and economic recovery could be applied. Solidarity accordingly adopted a radical reform programme of its own, including free elections.* The government retorted by accusing Solidarity of breaching its own statutes as a trade union and grasping at political power.

In this fresh crisis, the idea of some political coalition between the main social forces in Poland had taken definite form. On 4 November, Wałęsa met the Primate and General Jaruzelski. Two weeks later, Solidarity and the government began talks on the formation of a Front of National Unity. But mutual distrust was too great. Both sides took up tough opening positions. The government – in effect, the Party – was concerned to reassure its terrified and dwindling following that there would be no real sharing of executive power. Solidarity, now shaken by internal quarrels over tactics and by competing ambitions within its leadership, dared not give its members the impression that it was selling the union's independence for unreliable promises. The government finally produced drafts for new laws on economic reform, on trade unions, and on democratic rights for universities, but in versions that Solidarity refused to endorse. Meanwhile, membership in the Confederation for an Independent Poland

* See page 272.

(KPN), still without any programme beyond extreme nationalism and hatred of Russia, suddenly began to swell – a sinister omen that the young of Poland were increasingly impatient about Solidarity's failure to make further political progress.

It was then, as hopes for a Front of National Understanding faded, that talk of military government began to spread. Jaruzelski already held a conglomeration of powers unique in eastern Europe. He had introduced several generals into the cabinet, and in November teams of soldiers were despatched into the Polish countryside to monitor and revitalize local government; in retrospect, this can be seen as a preparation for their duties after the coup. But even in Solidarity there were some who thought that military government, by-passing Party rule, might be the only way to build a genuine coalition, a 'military shield' behind which at least economic reforms could be applied. The instinct to believe in the armed forces as a genuinely independent institution, with the interests of the nation at heart, was still strong.

In late November, the government suddenly moved into provocative action. A meeting called by Jacek Kuroń to launch a chain of Clubs for a Self-Governing Republic was raided by the police. At the next Plenum, on 27–28 November, central committee members openly demanded that Jaruzelski assume emergency powers, and the General announced that the Sejm would be asked to grant him the right to declare a state of emergency, banning strikes, when he thought fit. Although industrial strikes had almost ceased, following appeals from Wałęsa and Archbishop Glemp, Rural Solidarity and the students were still engaged in a series of occupation protests. On 2 December, police in Warsaw stormed the fire services academy and evicted its occupiers. It was the first time that force had been used since the provocation at Bydgoszcz in March. The message that the régime was now abandoning the Front project and heading deliberately for confrontation could no longer be ignored.

Solidarity called a strike alert, and its leaders met in emergency session next day at Radom. Wałęsa, in despair at the government's betrayal of his personal efforts to restrain the union, admitted that confrontation was now inevitable: what mattered was to win it, and the Solidarity leaders agreed provisionally to call a general strike if emergency powers were applied. Their debate was a wild one, and the Party press was able to publish edited extracts that suggested Solidarity was now preparing to overthrow the socialist state.

In a last effort to avoid disaster, Archbishop Glemp appealed to the Sejm to reject the emergency-powers bill, and he vainly asked Wałęsa and Jaruzelski to another meeting. But the provocations had done their work:

in many factories, Solidarity militants were now trying to evict Party cells from their offices, and the Warsaw branch of the union called for a 'day of national protest' on 17 December, the following Thursday, which was the anniversary of the 1970 tragedy.

Marshal Kulikov, the Soviet commander of Warsaw Pact forces, arrived secretly in Warsaw on Friday, 11 December. Solidarity's executive met in Gdańsk that evening. Wałęsa told journalists that he still hoped for national concord, but the radicals dominated the debates next day. The meeting ended late on Saturday night with resolutions that endorsed the general-strike proposal from Radom, demanded genuine power-sharing with the government, and announced a referendum to test public confidence in the régime and support for free elections to the Sejm. The telephones to Gdańsk had already been cut before the meeting closed. As the delegates dispersed, armoured convoys of troops were already moving out onto roads all over Poland.

The military coup had obviously been planned for many months, but Jaruzelski's real motives for launching it may never be known. At the time, he may have felt that it was the only way to make Soviet intervention unnecessary. Perhaps threats from the hard-line wing of the Party to unseat him also forced his hand. The sudden hardening of government actions, designed to drive Solidarity into making extreme moves and statements, suggests that the final decision was taken in late November.

That there was direct Soviet instigation of the coup remains unproved. What is clear is that this crisis of late 1981 in Poland overcame the very limited resources for mediation or compromise that were available in the Polish system – even the resources of the Church. It is here that ultimate Soviet responsibility for the catastrophe lies. In blindly refusing to permit the PUWP to share power and attempt a quite new interpretation of its leading role, Leonid Brezhnev and his colleagues cut off the Party's retreat and made collision inevitable.

As for the Poles themselves, another generation now entered the darkness that had fallen upon their fathers, their grandfathers, and all their ancestors since the nation was first partitioned nearly two hundred years ago. Before the internment camps of 1981 came Auschwitz, and Piłsudski's concentration camps, and the Russian citadel at Warsaw, and the convoys of men and women making for Siberia in chains. All that was certain was that this generation knew how to hold itself now that its turn had come, that it would invoke those ancestral spirits to retain its courage, that the Poles – in the words of their anthem – would never believe that Poland was lost while some of them remained alive.

The Twenty-Second Demand

Give over telling us you're sorry,
What guilt for past mistakes you carry;
Look in our faces, weary slaves,
Grey and exhausted, like our lives.

Give over calling us to order;
To discipline and honest labour;
Try self-examination when
You call us 'Our Dear Countrymen ...'

Give over classing us as crazy,
Anarchic, inexperienced, lazy;
Stop choking us with poster-glue;
The place to start reforms is – you!

Give over calling us the foe
Of all society, of our brother;
Just count our numbers, and you'll know
How strongly we can help each other.

Give over making us eat lies
With lowered heads and tight-shut eyes,
And for our culture, wait before
One vast, monopolistic store.

Stop prising us apart with wedges
Of conduct marks and privileges,
Suppressing facts that do not fit
And stewing history down to shit.

Put back our words to what they mean,
Words which grew empty and obscene,
So we can live with dignity
And work in solidarity.

Give over telling us you're sorry,
What guilt for past mistakes you carry.
Look at our mothers and our wives,
Grey and exhausted – like our lives.

(Anonymous verses circulating in the main hall of the strike at Gdańsk, in August 1980. From: 'Przestańcie Stale Nam Przepraszac', Wydawnictwo im. Konstytucji 3 maja, Warsaw, 1980, a collection of some of the strikers' poems issued by an 'unofficial' publisher)

The Gdańsk and Szczecin Agreements

Szczecin Protocol

Text of 'Protocol on decisions on the proposals and postulates of the inter-factory strike committee signed with the Government Commission in Szczecin'.

As a result of the discussions and of the examination of the submitted proposals and postulates, the following decisions were adopted:

Self-governing trade unions, which will be socialist in character, in keeping with the Constitution of the Polish People's Republic, will be set up on the basis of the opinions of experts and in accordance with the following principles:

As soon as the strike is over the strike committees will become workers' committees, which will organize – as necessary – general, direct and secret elections to the ruling bodies of trade union organizations. Work will continue to prepare the law, the statutes and other enactments provided for by Article Three of [ILO] Convention 87. A suitable work schedule will be devised for this purpose.

The Government will work out a specific programme to supply the market with foodstuffs and will publish this programme nationally by 31 December 1980.

It was explained that a gradual increase in the wages of all the employees' groups – primarily the lowest wages – will be effected. The principle was accepted that wages will be increased in the individual enterprises and branch groups. The increases will be affected in keeping with the specific conditions of trades and branches and will raise earnings by a single pay step or by suitably increasing other elements of earnings and wage groups. Factory office workers will have their earnings raised by a single step increase in their groups of wages.

The level of the so-called social minimum will be determined and announced to the public by 31 December 1980. After analysis of the state's budget potential, the lowest pensions and annuities will be raised to the necessary level as from 1 January 1981.

The principle was accepted that employees who have lost their health through their work in enterprises will receive [in other jobs] wages not lower than those previously received. In keeping with the agreed principle, by 30 September 1980 the Government will present the Sejm with proposals on new Articles 217 and 218 of the Labour Code.

An analysis of the state's ability to grant a monthly allowance to women on three-year maternity leave will be carried out by 31 December 1980. The level of that allowance will also be fixed by that date. Also by 31 December 1980, the Government will submit to the Sejm draft proposals to modify Article 186 of the Labour Code concerning the above problem.

Family allowances will be the same for all trade groups as they are for military and militia employees. The levelling off of these allowances should be completed in three equal annual instalments, the first instalment being due on 1 January 1981.

It was explained that the 'Human Rights Convention' and the 'Helsinki Final Act' had been published in print by the publishing agencies of the Polish People's Republic and that they will again be published in the form of brochures.

The employees on strike, especially the elected representatives of the work-forces, will not suffer any repression and will not be victimized in any other way for any of their strike activities, except for common criminal offences.

It was asserted that political activists will not be subjected to repression if their activities do not strike in a criminal manner at the socialist system and basic interests of the Polish People's Republic and if they do not commit common crimes.

The establishment of organizations may be effected in accordance with the laws of the Polish People's Republic.

It was noted that the dialogue between the Roman Catholic Church and the state is developing favourably. More extensive access to the mass media will be made possible.

A tablet will be fixed in the vicinity of the main gates [of the Szczecin ship-yards] to commemorate the victims of the events in December 1970. The shape of the tablet and the inscription will be agreed with the shipyard management, the Szczecin architect and a mixed commission appointed by the Government of the Polish People's Republic.

The deadline of completion is 17 December 1980

It was agreed that further improvements are necessary in medical care in Poland, especially in the supply of medicines and in standardizing payments for medicines for the insured people.

Free medicines for the disabled, pensioners, railwaymen and the military will be continued.

It is necessary to stop increases in the prices of staple goods by greater control checks in the state and private sectors and, in particular, by putting an end to so-called stealthy price rises.

The principle was accepted that sales of foodstuffs in the shops run by enterprises and institutions will be based on the same principles.

Improvements in meat supplies for the population will be effected by 31 December 1980.

Also by 31 December 1980 a programme will be presented for improving meat supplies for the population and for eventual rationing of meat through a coupons system.

The PEWEX shops will not sell staple goods of domestic production that are in short supply.

Necessary measures will be taken to explain the reasons for the present situation. The necessary proposals in that regard will be publicized country-wide and the future response to existing irregularities will be prompt and effective.

It is very important to improve the supplies of materials to all work establishments (state and co-operative establishments).

Workers dismissed for strikes between 1970 and 1980 will be reinstated as individual applications are individually considered by managements and trade unions.

The method of curtailing the activities of the censorship in the Polish People's Republic will be presented by 30 November 1980.

The principle was accepted that employees who are failures in leading paid work-free Saturdays or to fix a shortened working time in some other way will be worked out and presented by 30 November 1980.

The Government will present a programme to solve the housing problem and guarantee that the period of waiting [for apartments] is not longer than five years.

The principle was accepted that employees who are failures in leading jobs should be transferred to lower and not to equal jobs.

Travel allowances will be increased as from 1 January 1981. Proposals in this regard will be presented by the Government by 30 September 1980.

Only employees who are distinguished in their jobs and only those who are compelled to change their jobs for health reasons should be sent to schools for outstanding workers and vocational courses at the cost of their factories. In consultation with the factory managements, the trade unions will select workers for such schools and courses.

The state authorities will draw up by 31 December 1980 a new charter for shipyard workers which will include the solutions of social problems and other solutions listed in the charter concerning all workers employed within the shipyards.

During the strike the workforces on strike may be given advance payments amounting to 40 per cent of their individual actual wages. When work is resumed, workers will receive, for the period of the strike, 100 per cent of their individual actual wages.

The agreement concluded will be fully publicized by the mass media (the press, radio and television) and will be transmitted in its entirety to PAP for publication in the information services.

Final Decisions

As a result of the work done by the Government Commission and the interfactory strike committee in Szczecin, an agreement has been drawn up and signed.

The Chairman of the Council of Ministers will appoint a mixed commission composed of representatives of the Government, workers and provincial authorities (five persons each). The commission will be chaired by a representative of the Government. One deputy chairman will be a representative of the workers and the other will be a representative of the provincial authorities. The three will constitute the commission's presidium.

The task of the commission will be to supervise the implementation of the agreement and to inform the workforces of the commission's work and of the implementation of the agreement.

In the event of questions being disputed, the sides must consult one another in the presidium or in the full commission before they take any action whatever.

The interfactory strike committee appeals to all the workforces in factories to make every effort to make good as soon as possible the losses suffered by the economy through work stoppages.

For the interfactory strike committee: (1) Marian Jurczyk, chairman of the interfactory strike committee; (2) Kazimierz Fischbein, deputy chairman of the interfactory strike committee; and (3) Marian Juszczuk, delegate of the interfactory strike committee.

For the Government Commission: (1) Deputy Premier Kazimierz Barcikowski; (2) Andrzej Zabiński, PUWP Politburo candidate member and Central Committee Secretary; and (3) Janusz Brych, First Secretary of the PUWP District Committee in Szczecin.

The Gdańsk Protocol

Text of protocol of agreement between the Government commission and the interfactory strike committee concluded on 31 August 1980 at the Gdańsk shipyards:

Having examined the 21 demands submitted by the striking work forces, the Government commission and the interfactory strike committee adopted the following decisions:

With regard to point one which states: To accept free trade unions independent from the Party and employers as provided for by ILO Convention 87, which was ratified by the Polish People's Republic and which concerns trade union freedom, it was agreed:

1 The performance of trade unions in the Polish People's Republic does not fulfil the hopes and expectations of employees. It is considered expedient to establish new self-governing trade unions that would genuinely represent the working class. No one will have his right to remain in the present trade unions questioned and it is possible that the two trade unions will establish co-operation in the future.

2 In view of the establishment of new, independent and self-governing trade unions the interfactory strike committee declares that they will observe the principles laid down in the Constitution of the Polish People's Republic. The new trade unions will defend the social and material interests of employees and do not intend to play the role of a political party. They approve of the principle that production means are social property – a principle that is the foundation of the socialist system in Poland. Recognizing that the PUWP plays the leading role in the state and without undermining the actual system of international alliances, they seek to ensure

for the working people suitable means of control, of expressing their opinions and of defending their interests.

The Government commission declares that the Government will guarantee and ensure complete respect for the independence and self-governing of the new trade unions both as regards their organizational structure and their performance at all levels of activity. The Government will ensure for the new trade unions all opportunities for fulfilling their basic functions in defending the interests of employees and implementing their material, social and cultural needs. At the same time, the Government guarantees that the new trade unions will not be subjected to any discrimination.

3 The establishment and activity of the independent, self-governing trade unions are consistent with ILO Convention 87 which concerns trade union freedoms and the defence of trade union rights, and ILO Convention 96 which concerns the right to associate and the right to collective negotiations. Both Conventions have been ratified in Poland. The diversity of trade union and employee representations will entail suitable legislative amendments; in connection with this the Government pledges itself to making legislative proposals particularly concerning the law on trade unions, the law on workers' self-government and the labour code.

4 The established strike committees can, if they wish, transform themselves into factory employee representation bodies such as workers' committees, employees' committees, workers' councils or the founding committees of the new self-governing trade unions. As the founding committee of those trade unions, the interfactory strike committee is free to choose the form of a single union of association within the coastal region. The founding committees will function until new authorities are elected in accordance with the statutes. The Government pledges itself to create the conditions for the registration of the new trade unions outside the register of the Central Trade Union Council.

5 The new trade unions should enjoy genuine opportunities for publicly evaluating the new decisions that determine working people's conditions: the principles of dividing the national income into consumption and accumulation, the distribution of the social consumption fund for various purposes – health, education, culture – the basic principles of remuneration and the lines of wage policy – particularly the principle of an automatic adjustment of wages under conditions of inflation, long-term economic plans, investment policy and changes in prices. The Government pledges itself to ensure conditions for the exercise of these functions.

6 The interfactory committee establishes a centre for social and labour studies, whose task will be to analyse objectively the employees' situation,

working people's living conditions and ways of representing employees' interests. The centre will also prepare specialist opinions on the wage and price indices and will propose forms of compensation; it also will publish the results of its research. The new trade unions will also have their own publications.

7 The Government will ensure that the provisions of Article 1 Paragraph 1 of the 1949 Trade Union Act, which stipulates that workers and employees are guaranteed the right to voluntary association in trade unions are observed in Poland. The new trade unions will not join the association represented by the Central Trade Union Council. It is agreed that the new law will preserve this principle. At the same time, representatives of the inter-factory strike committee or of the committees that will found the self-governing trade unions and representatives of other workers' bodies will be ensured participation in formulating this law.

With regard to point 2, which states: To guarantee the right to strike and to guarantee security for strikers and for persons helping them, it was decided:

The right to strike will be guaranteed in the trade union law now under preparation. The law should define the conditions under which a strike is proclaimed and organized, the methods of settling disputed issues and responsibility for violating the law. Articles 52, 64 and 65 of the Labour Code cannot be applied with regard to the participants in a strike. Also, the Government guarantees strikers and persons helping them personal security and the maintenance of their present working conditions until the law is passed.

With regard to point 3, which states: To observe freedom of speech and the printed word, that is, not to repress independent publications and to make the mass media available to representatives of all religions, it was decided:

1 Within three months the Government will introduce in the Sejm a draft law on control of the press, publications and entertainment – based on the following principles. Censorship should protect the interests of the state. This means the protection of state and economic secrets, the extent of which will be more closely defined by legal enactments, and the protection of the state's security matters and important international interests. This also means protecting religious beliefs and, at the same time, the feelings of non-believers and banning texts harming public morals. This draft law would also provide the right to appeal to the Supreme Administrative Court against the decisions of the organs responsible for control of the press, publications and entertainment. This law will be enacted through modifications to the Administrative Procedure Code.

2 The issue of the use of the mass media by religious associations with regard to their religious activities will be effected through agreement between state bodies and the interested religious associations on substantive and organizational problems. The Government will ensure that the radio will transmit a Sunday mass under a detailed accord with the Episcopate.

3 Radio, television, the press and publications should be used to express a plurality of ideas, views and opinions. This use should be subject to social control.

4 Like the citizens and their organizations, the press should be able to have access to public documents (Acts), especially administrative documents, socio-economic plans and so on, issued by the Government and its administrative bodies. The exceptions to the principle of the openness of the Administration's activities will be defined in the law as stipulated in point 1.

With regard to point 4, which states: (i) To restore the former rights of people dismissed from their jobs for the strikes in 1970 and 1976 – [and] the students banned from higher schools for their convictions; (ii) To free all political prisoners (including Edmund Zadrożyński, Jan Kozłowski and Marek Kozłowski); and (iii) end the persecution of people for their convictions; it was decided:

(a) To examine immediately the correctness of the job dismissals over the strikes in 1970 and 1976. In all cases raised, if irregularities are ascertained, immediately to restore the people concerned to their jobs, provided they want to return, and to take into account the qualifications they have acquired in the meantime.

A corresponding procedure will be used in the case of the students expelled from higher education.

(b) To refer the cases of the persons mentioned in point (b) to the Minister of Justice who will examine them and will within two weeks institute the necessary proceedings: in the cases in which the listed persons have been deprived of freedom, their punishment will be interrupted until the proceedings have been completed;

(c) To examine whether there is any justification for detention and to release the persons mentioned in the supplement;

(d) To observe fully the individual's freedom to express his convictions in public and professional life.

With regard to point 5, which states: To publish in the mass media information about the establishment of the interfactory strike committee and to publish its demands, it was decided:

This demand will be fulfilled by publishing this protocol in the national mass media.

With regard to point 6, which states: To take genuine action to extricate the country from its state of crisis through (i) fully informing the public about the socio-economic situation, and (ii) enabling all social communities and sections to participate in the discussion about the reform programme, it was decided:

We deem it necessary to accelerate greatly the work on economic reform. The authorities will outline and publish the basic tenets of this reform within the next few months. It is necessary to ensure that public discussion of this reform is extensive. In particular, the trade unions should participate in formulating the laws on socialist economic organizations and on workers' self-government. The economic reform should be based on radically increased independence of enterprises and on genuine participation in management by the workers' self-government groups. The necessary enactments should guarantee the fulfilment by the trade unions of the functions defined in point one of this agreement.

Only a nation that is aware of its problems and that has a good awareness of reality can sponsor and implement a programme for streamlining the economy. The Government will radically expand the range of socio-economic information available to the nation, the trade unions and economic and social organizations.

In addition, the interfactory committee demands that: lasting prospects be created for developing peasant family farms, which are the foundation of Polish agriculture; all sectors be ensured equal access to all means of production, including land; and conditions be created for the rebirth of rural self-government groups.

With regard to point 7, which states: To pay from Central Trade Union Council funds all employees who are on strike wages for the duration of the strike and for annual leave, it was decided:

Employees in the striking work forces will receive for the period of the strike an advance payment of 40 per cent of their [normal] remuneration, and, after they have resumed work, they will receive up to 100 per cent of the outstanding difference of their remuneration, calculated as for a period of annual leave based on an eight-hour day. The interfactory strike committee appeals to the work forces associated within it that – after the strike has ended and in co-operation with the managements of factories, work enterprises and other institutions – they should take action to increase productivity, economize on materials and energy and enhance conscientiousness in every job.

With regard to point 8, which states: To increase the basic wages of each employee by Z 2,000 a month in compensation for the present price rises, it was decided:

Gradual increases in the wages of all groups of employees, above all in the lowest wage groups, will be effected. It was agreed in principle that wages will be increased in individual factories and in groups of branches. These increases are being implemented and will be implemented in keeping with the specific characteristics of trade, professions and branches, and will seek to upgrade remuneration by a single pay grade or by suitably increasing other elements of remuneration or of the wage group. As for office workers in enterprises, their remuneration will be raised by a single pay grade in their personal wages. Pay rises now under discussion will be completed by the end of September this year in accordance with branch accords.

Having analysed all branches, the Government, in co-operation with the trade unions, will present by 31 October this year a programme for increasing, as of 1 January 1981, the wages of the lowest paid, giving special consideration to families with many children.

With regard to point 9, which states: To guarantee an automatic increase in wages parallel to increase in prices and deterioration in the value of money, it was decided:

Increases in the prices of staple goods must be checked by increasing control over socialized and private sectors, in particular by stopping the so-called creeping price rises.

In keeping with the Government's decision, research will be conducted into the development of living costs. This research will also be conducted by the trade unions and scientific institutes. By the end of 1980 the Government will work out the principles of compensation for increases in the cost of living. These principles will be subjected to a public discussion and, when agreed upon, will be implemented. They should take into account the issue of the social minimum [minimum subsistence level].

With regard to point 10, which states: To ensure complete supplies of food for the domestic market and to export only and exclusively surpluses; and to point 11, which states: To abolish commercial prices and sales for hard currencies under the scheme of so-called internal export; and to point 13, which states: To introduce all meat rationing – food coupons – (until the market situation is mastered), it was decided:

Meat supplies to the public will be improved by 31 December this year by various measures, including: increased profitability of farm production, restricting meat exports to the necessary minimum and additional meat imports. Within the same period a programme will be presented for improving meat supplies to the public and for eventual meat rationing through coupons.

It was agreed that the Pewex shops [selling for hard currencies] will not sell the staple consumer goods produced in Poland that are in short supply. The nation will be informed by the end of the year about the decisions and measures concerning supplies to the market.

The interfactory strike committee has asked for the ending of commercial shops and for the streamlining and standardization of meat prices at an average level.

With regard to point 12 which states: To introduce the principle by which leading and managing cadres are selected by virtue of their qualifications not their party affiliation, and to abolish the privileges of the citizens' militia, the security service and the Party apparatus by equalizing family allowances, ending special sales and so on, it was decided:

The demand is accepted that leading and managing cadres should be consistently selected on the basis of the principle of qualifications and abilities from members of the Party, from the [other political] parties and from non-Party people. The programme for equalizing family allowances for all trade groups will be presented by the Government by 31 December 1980. The Government commission states that only employees' restaurants and canteens, such as those in other work establishments and offices, are operated.

With regard to point 14 which states: To lower the retirement age of women to 50 and of men to 55 or 30 years worked in the Polish People's Republic by women and 35 years by men regardless of their ages, it was decided:

The Government commission regards this demand as impossible to fulfil now in view of the country's present economic and demographic situation. The issue can be discussed in the future. The interfactory strike committee has asked that this issue be examined by 31 December 1980, and to consider the possibility of allowing employees doing strenuous jobs to retire five years earlier (30 years for women and 35 years for men), and in the case of particularly strenuous jobs [to advance retirement age] by at least 15 years. This should take place only at the request of the employee.

With regard to point 15 which states: To equalize the pensions and annuities of the so-called old scheme so that they are equal to the pensions and annuities of the present scheme, it was decided:

The Government commission declares that the lowest pensions and annuities will be increased annually, consistent with the country's economic potential, and will take into account increases in the lowest wages. The Government will present an implementation programme by 31 December

1980. The Government will propose that the lowest pensions and annuities be raised to the level of the so-called social minimum determined by research carried out by the appropriate institutes, presented to the public and controlled by the trade unions. The interfactory strike committee stresses the extreme urgency of this issue and maintains its demand that the pensions and annuities of the old and new schemes should be at the same level and that increases in the costs of living should be taken into account.

With regard to point 16 which states: To improve the working conditions of the health services so as to ensure complete medical care for working people, it was decided:

It is considered necessary to increase immediately the investment capacities of the health services, to improve the supply of medicines through additional imports of raw materials, to increase the wages of all health service workers (to change the wage structure for nurses) and to draw up urgently Government and departmental programmes for improving the state of the nation's health. Other measures in this field are listed in the supplement to point 16:

1 To implement the Charter of Health Service Employee's Rights.

2 To ensure suitable quantities of cotton protective clothing for sale.

3 To pay from the material costs fund an amount equal to the cost of work clothing.

4 To secure such a wage fund as to make it possible to award the necessary extra payments to all people who distinguish themselves in their work – to award them in keeping with theoretically valid considerations.

5 To set increasing additional payments for completion of 25 and 30 years work.

6 To set additional payment for work under conditions that are a strain or harmful to health, and to introduce additional payment for shift work for non-medical employees.

7 To bring back additional payment for work with patients with infectious ailments and for work with infectious biological materials, and to raise the wages for overnight nursing.

8 To recognize spinal ailments as an occupational disease of dental surgeons.

9 To ensure supplies of good-quality fuels for hospitals and creches.

10 To equalize service benefits for nurses without full secondary education with benefits for nurses with diplomas.

11 To introduce a seven-hour working day for all specialist employees.

12 To introduce free Saturdays without the need to work them off later.

13 To pay double rates for Sunday and holiday work.

14 To provide free medicines for health service employees.

15 To make possible a partial repayment of housing loans from social funds.

16 To increase the size of apartments for health service workers.

17 To enable single nurses to obtain apartments.

18 To convert the bonus fund into a 13-month wage.

19 To grant six weeks' leave to health service workers after 20 years of service, and to make it possible for them to obtain paid annual leave to improve their health, as is the case for teachers.

20 To ensure paid leave of four weeks for those studying for a doctor's degree and of two weeks for those specializing.

21 To ensure the right to a day off after a tour of duty as a physician.

22 A five-hour working day for employees in creches and kindergartens, and free food.

23 Cars for employees of the basic health services and kilometre allowances or lump payments for official trips.

24 Nurses with higher education should be treated and paid as are other personnel with higher education.

25 To set up specialized repair teams in the factory trade union organization in order to protect health service installations against further depreciation.

26 To raise the norms of medicine for patients in hospitals from Z1,138 to Z2,700, since this is what it costs for treatment; to raise the food allowance.

27 To issue food coupons for the bedridden.

28 To double available medical transportation because this is needed immediately.

29 To ensure the cleanliness of air, soil and water, especially of the coastal waters.

30 Parallel with the completion of new housing settlements, to complete facilities such as out-patient clinics, chemists and creches.

With regard to point 17 which states: To ensure the necessary vacancies in creches and kindergartens for working women's children, it was decided: The Government commission fully agrees with the importance of this demand. The provincial authorities will present the necessary programme by 30th November 1980.

With regard to point 18 which states: To grant maternity leave for three years in order to raise a baby, it was decided: By 31 December 1980 an analysis will be carried out – in co-operation with the trade unions – of the national economy's potential and the length of leave and the amount of monthly payment to be determined for women on maternity leave (now unpaid) to take care of their babies. The interfactory strike committee demands that such an analysis should consider a payment equivalent to the full wages in the first year after the baby is born and that 50 per cent of these wages be paid in the second year, but that these should amount to not less than Z2,000 a month. This demand should be met gradually, beginning with the first six months of 1981.

With regard to point 19 which states: To cut the period of waiting for apartments, it was decided: By 31 December 1980 the provincial authorities will present a programme for improving the housing situation in order to cut the waiting time for apartments. This programme will be extensively discussed by the people of the district who will consult with the appropriate organizations: the Association of Polish Town Planners – TUP; the Association of the Architects of the Polish Republic – SARP; the chief technical organization – NOT; and others. The programme should also consider the present utilization of the existing plants manufacturing housing components and the further development of the construction trades' production base. The same measures will be taken nationwide.

With regard to point 20 which states: To increase travelling allowances from Z40 to Z100 and [to increase] the family separation allowance, it was decided: As of 1 January 1981 travel allowances and the separation allowance will be increased. Proposals regarding these will be presented by the Government by 31 October 1980.

With regard to point 21 which states: To make all Saturdays work-free, and the employees working on shifts and under the four-brigade system to be compensated for Saturdays by an increased annual leave allowance or by other paid days off, it was decided: We will work out and present by 31 December 1980 principles and methods of implementing the programme for paid work-free Saturdays as well as other methods of regulating a shorter working period. This programme will provide for a larger number of paid work-free Saturdays by as early as 1981. Other measures in this regard are contained in the supplement listing the demands of the interfactory strike committee.

Having made the aforementioned decisions, the following agreement was reached: The Government pledges itself: To ensure personal security and honour the present working conditions of the participants in the present strike and of the persons helping them; to examine on the ministerial level the specific problems of the branches as submitted by the workforces of all the striking factories that are associated with the interfactory strike committee; to publicize immediately the full extent of the protocol of this agreement in the national mass media – the press, radio and television.

The interfactory strike committee pledges itself to end the strike at 1700 hours [local] on 31 August 1980.

[Signed] The Presidium of the interfactory strike committee: Chairman Lech Wałęsa; Vice Chairman Andrzej Kołodziej, Vice Chairman Bogdan Lis; members: Lech Bądkowski, Wojciech Gruszewski, Andrzej Gwiazda, Stefan Izdebski, Jerzy Kwiecik, Zdzisław Kobyliński, Henryka Krzywonos, Stefan Lewandowski, Alina Pieńkowska, Józef Przybylski, Jerzy Sikorski, Lech Sobieszek, Tadeusz Stanny, Anna Walentynowicz, and Florian Wiśniewski.

The Government commission: Chairman Mieczysław Jagielski, Vice Chairman of the Council of Ministers of the Polish People's Republic; members: Zbigniew Zieliński, member of the PUWP Central Committee Secretariat; Tadeusz Fiszbach, Chairman of the district People's Council in Gdańsk; Jerzy Kołodziejski, prefect of Gdańsk.

Supplement to point 21:

1 To change the decree issued by the Council of Ministers on the methods of calculating payments for annual leave and sickness benefits for workers working the four-brigade system; the present method is to use an average of 30 days (whereas the workers work 22 days). This method of calculation reduces the average working day when workers are on short sick leaves and lowers the equivalent for the annual leave.

2 We demand that a single enactment – by the Council of Ministers – should streamline the method by which payments are calculated in individual cases for a given period of absence from work. The vagueness of the present regulations is used against the employees.

3 Workers working the four-brigade work system should be compensated by an additional leave allowance for their work on Saturdays. The fact that these workers are given more days off than others on different work systems does not mean that they can enjoy real days off. Their present days off are just an opportunity to take a rest after very strenuous work. The arguments submitted by the administration maintaining that real days off should be granted only after the amount of hours worked under the two work systems is the same, are not correct.

4 We want every Saturday in a month work-free as is the case in other socialist countries.

5 We want Article 147 of the Labour Code to be abolished. This Article allows for extending the average work norm by nine hours a week when additional days off are due. We also want Article 148 to be abolished; our work norms are among the longest in Europe.

6 To increase the importance of the agreed decisions concerning payments through changes in the labour code, namely: that not only a change in a worker's own wage grade or in other elements of remuneration, but also changes in the methods of payments (piece work) must be declared by the employer. It is necessary to introduce the principle that the wage grade of a worker be related to all the tasks which he performs. At the same time, it is necessary to sort out the issue of employing young workers in keeping with their qualifications so the aforementioned decision does not become an obstacle in professional advancement.

7 To introduce in the shift system an increase of 50 per cent in the allowance for night work in the day system and to increase by 30 per cent the actual earnings under the piece work system. We also want an allowance for work during the afternoon shift (as is the case in the chemical industry). We want the Government to examine these demands by 30 November 1980.

Bibliography

Arendt, Hannah, *On Revolution*, Faber & Faber (London), 1963.

Baring, Arnulf, *Uprising in East Germany*, Cornell, 1972.

Bethell, Nicholas, *Gomulka: His Poland and his Communism*, Penguin Books, Harmondsworth, 1972.

Bieńkowski, Władysław, *Motory i Hamulcy Socjalizmu*, Instytut Literacki (Paris), 1969.

Błażyński, George, *Flashpoint Poland*, Pergamon Policy Studies (Oxford), 1980.

Byrnes, James, *Speaking Frankly*, Harper (New York), 1947.

Carrillo, Santiago, *Eurocommunism and the State*, Lawrence & Wishart (London), 1977.

Checinski, Michael, *A Comparison of the Polish and Soviet Armaments Decision-Making Process*, Rand Corporation report, January 1981.

Ciechanowski, Jan, *The Warsaw Rising of 1944*, Cambridge University Press, 1974.

Dawisha and Hanson (eds.), *Soviet and East European Dilemmas*, Royal Institute of International Affairs (London), 1981.

Deutscher, Isaac, *Soviet Trade Unions*, Royal Institute of International Affairs (London), 1950.

Deutscher, Isaac, *Stalin: A Political Biography*, Oxford University Press, 1949.

Dissent in Poland. Reports and Documents December 1975–July 1977. Association of Polish Students in Exile (London), 1977.

Dross, Armin (ed.), *Polen – Freie Gewerkschaften in Kommunismus?*, rororo aktuell (Hamburg), 1980.

Fišera, Vladimir (ed.), *Workers' Councils in Czechoslovakia: Documents and Essays*, Allison & Busby (London), 1978.

Garaudy, Roger, *Le Grand Tournant du Socialisme*, Gallimard (Paris), 1969.

Hiscocks, C. R., *Poland – Bridge for the Abyss?*, Oxford University Press, 1963.

History of the Communist Party of the Soviet Union/Bolsheviks ('Short Course'), Foreign Languages Publishing House (Moscow), 1951.

Johnson, R., Dean, R., and Alexiev, A., *East European Military Establish-*

ments: The Northern Tier, Rand Corporation study, December 1980.

Karol, K. S., *Visa for Poland*, MacGibbon & Kee (London), 1959.

Konrád, G., and Szeleńyi, Ivan, *The Intellectuals on the Road to Class Power*, Harvest Press (UK), 1979.

Kuncewicz, Maria (ed.), *The Modern Polish Mind*, Secker & Warburg (London), 1963.

Kuroń, J., and Modzelewski, K., *An Open Letter to the Party*, International Socialist Publications (London), 1969.

Kusin, Vladimir, *Political Groupings in the Czechoslovak Reform Movement*, Columbia University Press, 1972.

Leslie, R. F. (ed.), *The History of Poland Since 1863*, Cambridge University Press, 1980.

Lewis, Flora, *The Polish Volcano*, Secker & Warburg (London), 1959.

Lomax, Bill (ed.), *Eyewitness in Hungary*, Spokesman (Nottingham), 1980.

MacShane, Denis, *Solidarity, Poland's Independent Trade Union*, Spokesman (Nottingham), 1981.

Miłosz, Czesław, *The Captive Mind*, Vintage Books (New York), 1953.

Mlynář, Zdeněk, *Night Frost in Prague*, Hurst, 1980.

Osme Plenum KC PZPR 6–7 luty 1971r, Nowe Drogi (Warsaw), numer specjalny, May 1971.

Oxley, A., Pravda, A., and Ritchie, A. (eds.), *Czechoslovakia*, Allen Lane, 1973.

Pelikán, Jiři (ed.), *The Czechoslovak Political Trials*, Macdonald (London), 1971.

Pologne: une société en dissidence, La, (anon.), Maspéro (Paris), 1978.

Ruch Oporu (ed. anon.), Instytut Literacki (Paris), 1977.

Stehle, Hansjakob, *Nachbar Polen*, Fischer Verlag (Frankfurt/Main), 1963.

Strikes in Poland, The, Radio Free Europe Research (Munich), 1980.

Survey (London), Vol. 24/4, Vol. 25/1.

Szczepaniak, M. (ed.), *Polityczna Organizacja Społeczeństwa w Polsce*, Wydawnictwo Poznańskie, 1977.

'Tomalek Pavel' (pseudonym), *Czechoslovakia 1968–70: The Worker–Student Alliance*, Center for International Studies, Massachusetts Institute of Technology (Boston), 1971.

Vierheller, Viktoria, *Polen und die Deutschlandfrage*, Verlag Wissenschaft und Politik (Cologne), 1970.

Wacowska, Ewa (ed.), *Rewolta Szczecińska i jej Znaczenie*, Instytut Literacki (Paris), 1971.

Notes

1. Władysław Bieńkowski, *Motory i Hamulcy Socjalismu* (Paris: Instytut Literacki, 1969).
2. See Hansjakob Stehle, *Nachbar Polen* (Frankfurt am Main: Fischer, 1963), p. 311.
3. R. F. Leslie (ed.), *The History of Poland Since 1863* (Cambridge University Press, 1980).
4. K. S. Karol, *Visa for Poland* (London: MacGibbon & Kee, 1959), p. 101.
5. Leslie, op. cit. See, for example, the account by Jan Ciechanowski in *The Warsaw Rising of 1944* (Cambridge University Press, 1974).
6. Quoted in Nicholas Bethell, *Gomułka: His Poland and His Communism* (Harmondsworth: Penguin Books, 1972), p. 120.
7. ibid., p. 121.
8. See Leslie, op. cit., p. 264.
9. ibid., p. 289, for these figures.
10. Leslie, quoting a pre-war study, gives the surplus rural population in the 1930s, counting those only partly employed, as perhaps 4·5 million.
11. Isaac Deutscher, *Stalin: A Political Biography* (Oxford: Oxford University Press, 1949), p. 536.
12. ibid., p. 554.
13. James Byrnes, *Speaking Frankly* (New York: Harper, 1947), pp. 188–192.
14. See Viktoria Vierheller, *Polen und die Deutschlandfrage* (Cologne: Verlag Wissenschaft und Politik, 1970), p. 132, notes 528 and 529.
15. Leslie, op. cit., p. 306.
16. Figures and quotations from Ross Johnson, Robert Dean and Alexander Alexiev, *East European Military Establishments: The Northern Tier* (Rand Corporation Study, December 1980), pp. 21–2.
17. For an excellent study of the Plan and its effects, see Z. A. Pełczyński, in Leslie, op. cit., pp. 311–23.

18. See accounts of contemporary practice in the Czechoslovak Communist Party in Zdeněk Mlynář, *Night Frost in Prague* (Hurst, 1980).

19. See Antony Polonsky, writing in Leslie, op. cit., p. 143.

20. Czesław Miłosz, *The Captive Mind* (New York: Vintage Books, 1953), p. 10.

21. Quoted in Maria Kuncewicz (ed.), *The Modern Polish Mind* (Secker & Warburg, 1963), p. 326.

22. George Blażyński, *Flashpoint Poland* (Pergamon Policy Studies, 1980), p. xvi.

23. See David Irving, *Uprising* (Hodder & Stoughton, 1981), an account of the Hungarian Revolution of 1956 that has been carefully slanted in this way

Chapter 3: Years of Disillusion

1. Pełczyński in Leslie, op. cit., p. 369.
2. loc. cit.
3. Karol, *Visa for Poland*, p. 198
4. *Zapis*, No. 13, published by *Index on Censorship* (London), 1980, p. 36
5. Błażyński, op. cit., p. 5.
6. *Życie Literackie*, 21 February 1971.

Chapter 4: Gierek and the Third Cycle

1. Leslie, op. cit., p. 420.
2. loc. cit.
3. ibid., p. 434.
4. Blażyński, op. cit., p. 38.
5. Leslie, op. cit., p. 440.
6. ibid., p. 441.
7. See Summary of the report in *Survey* (London), Vol. XXV, No. 1, Winter 1980.
8. Figures quoted by Pełczyński in Leslie, op. cit., p. 451.
9. J. Kane and I. Shapiro, *Inflation and Industrial Militancy: Britain and Poland in the World System* (unpublished paper, 1979), p. 69.
10. *Survey* (London), Vol. XXIV, No. 4, Autumn 1979, p. 8.

Chapter 5: Solidarity

1. I owe much of this detail to Bolesław Sulik and his researches for Granada Television (UK).
2. Quoted by Michael Dobbs in the *Guardian*, 18 August 1980.
3. Jadwiga Staniszkis in *Soviet Studies* (Glasgow), Vol. XXXIII, No. 2, p. 213.
4. ibid., p. 213.
5. Material furnished by Oliver MacDonald.
6. Personal interview with A. Kijowski.
7. See *Dziennik Bałtycki* and *Głos Wybrzeża* for 13 September 1980.

Chapter 6: Towards a National Tragedy

1. *The Times*, London, 5 April 1981.
2. See: *Report of International Metalworkers' Federation Mission to Poland*, Geneva, 1981.
3. *Życie Warszawy*, 6 December 1980.

Chapter 7: Antecedents and Analyses

1. Jiři Pelikán (ed.), *The Czechoslovak Political Trials* (Macdonald, 1971), p. 56.
2. C. R. Hiscocks, *Poland: Bridge for the Abyss?* (Oxford: Oxford University Press, 1963), p. 245.
3. Hannah Arendt, On Revolution (Faber & Faber, 1963), p. 277.
4. Miklós Krassó, in Bill Lomax (ed.), *Eyewitness in Hungary* (Spokesman, 1980), p. 158.
5. V. Kusin, *Political Groupings in the Czechoslovak Reform Movement* (New York: Columbia University Press, 1972), p. 158.
6. A. Oxley, A. Pravda and A. Ritchie (eds.), *Czechoslovakia* (Allen Lane, 1973), p. 158.
7. V. Fišera (ed.), *Workers' Councils in Czechoslovakia* (Allison & Busby, 1978), p. 33.
8. 'Pavel Tomalik' (pseudonym), *Czechoslovakia 1968–70: The Worker–*

Student Alliance (Cambridge, Mass.: Massachusetts Institute of Technology, 1971), pp. 18–19.

9. Jan Walc, in *Zapis*, No. 12, p. 127.

10. B. Sulik, in *La Pologne: Une Société en Dissidence* (Paris: Maspéro, 1978), p. 61.

11. Quoted in Armin Dross (ed.), *Polen: Freie Gewerkschaften in Kommunismus?* (Hamburg: rororo aktuell, 1980), p. 199.

12. See *Labour Focus on Eastern Europe* (London), Vol. I, No. 5 (November–December 1977), and Vol. III, No. 2 (May–June 1979).

13. Hiscocks, op. cit., p. 247.

14. *Ruch Oporu* (Paris: Instytut Literacki, 1977), p. 227.

15. M. Szczepaniak (ed.), *Polityczna Organizacja Spoleczeństwa w Polsce* (Poznań: Wydawnictwo Poznańskie, 1977), p. 111.

16. Isaac Deutscher, *Soviet Trade Unions* (Royal Institute of Foreign Affairs, 1950), p. 27.

17. Santiago Carrillo, *Eurocommunism and the State* (Lawrence & Wishart, 1977), p. 157.

18. *History of the Communist Party of the Soviet Union/Bolsheviks* ('Short Course') (Moscow: Foreign Languages Publishing House, 1951), p. 524.

19. Roger Garaudy, *Le Grand Tournant du Socialisme* (Paris: Gallimard, 1969), pp. 174–5.

20. Jacek Kuroń and Karol Modzelewski, *An Open Letter to the Party* ('A Revolutionary Socialist Manifesto written in a Polish Prison') (International Socialist Publications, 1969), p. 15.

21. This account was by Miklós Haraszti, subsequently published as *A Worker in a Workers' State* (Harmondsworth: Penguin Books, 1977).

22. G. Konrád and I. Szelényi, *The Intellectuals on the Road to Class Power* (Harvester Press, 1979), p. 179.

23. ibid., pp. 220, 230.

Chapter 8: Into Unexplored Territory

1. See, for example, Mark Frankland in the *Observer*, 18 January 1981.

2. Stefan Nowak, 'A Polish Self-Portrait', *Polish Perspectives* (Warsaw, 1981), No. 2.

Index

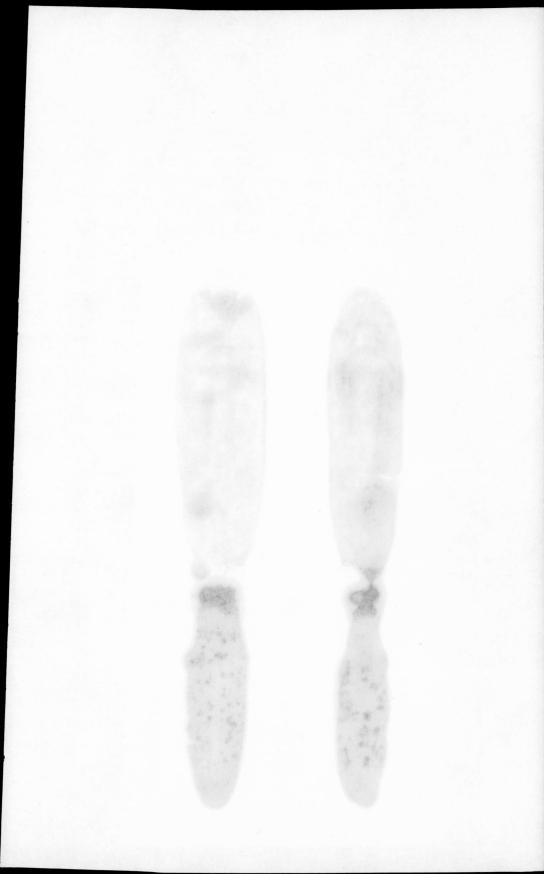